PRAISE FOR

"Peter Kwasniewski is a sane and learned voice crying out from within a Catholic Church which – in its earthly, visible aspect – seems to have lost its mind. I have no doubt that in any future attempt to salvage what is left of the Church, the analyses of Kwasniewski will be invaluable, as this new collection of outstanding essays demonstrates. What we have in this exceptional philosopher and theologian is a faithful son of the Church who conjoins every one of his devastating attacks on current abuses to a case for why Catholics should, despite everything, stay in the Church and be faithful to Jesus Christ, their Lord." – **SEBASTIAN MORELLO**, Senior Editor, *The European Conservative*

"This thoroughly researched and cogently argued book could not have been published at a better time. As the papal tyranny continues to tighten its persecution of faithful Catholics, sound principles are a necessity. Dr. Kwasniewski skillfully avoids the Scylla of rebellious rejection of legitimate authority and the Charybdis of subservient pandering to illegitimate despotism." – **BRIAN M. MCCALL**, Orpha and Maurice Merrill Professor of Law at the University of Oklahoma and author of *The Architecture of Law: Rebuilding Law in the Classical Tradition*

"Peter Kwasniewski's new book both summarizes his recent thought and serves as a guide and resource for beleaguered faithful. Starting from a thorough historical and theological discussion of the nature of Catholic Tradition, papal authority, obedience, and the common good, the author offers insights and advice on practical issues ranging from tactics for preserving the Latin Mass at the parish level to the status of the Society of St. Pius X. At once theoretically challenging and eminently useful, *Bound by Truth* should find a place on the bookshelf of every traditionalist." – **STUART CHESSMAN**, author of *Faith of Our Fathers: A Brief History of Catholic Traditionalism in the United States*

"The life of the Bride of Christ and her children is inextricably bound to the fullness of the truth taught by Jesus Christ and the grace that comes from membership in His Body. Sophistic defenders of a 'spirit of the times' always sacrifice Catholic tradition (the bond uniting us to Christ and all our forebears) to one or another form of the golden calf: an idolatry of the present. In *Bound by Truth*, Kwasniewski critiques the latest (and historically worst) abandonment of our grip on the cord that ties us, through tradition, to the Word Incarnate – and indicates the paths along which health and sanity will be recovered." – **JOHN C. RAO**, author of *Catholic Christendom versus Revolutionary Disorder*

"As in the times of the Protestant Reformation, the crisis in the Church today revolves around the issue of obedience. Unlike a sixteenth century fraught with illegitimate disobedience, however, our crisis lies at the opposite extreme: a false notion of obedience that grants almost limitless powers to Church leaders. This misunderstanding – tragically foundational to the priestly abuse scandals – has led many Catholics to see the pope, not as a guardian of tradition, but as an inventor of novelty. In *Bound by Truth*, Kwasniewski examines the difficult topics of authority and obedience with forthrightness and a willingness to engage even the most controversial debates. Whether one agrees with all of the author's proposals or not, this book is a timely guide to how Catholics might respond when truth and tradition are under attack by those who should be their foremost defenders." – **ERIC SAMMONS**, Editor of *Crisis Magazine*

"Peter Kwasniewski's book *Bound by Truth* comes at a very difficult time in the life of the Church and of the world. Explicitly throughout Western political life, and implicitly in the Church since the last Council, the age-old idea that authority is set among men by God for the purpose of helping them pursue a common good – a good that either conduces to or constitutes man's last end – has been set aside. Authority in the new dispensation (albeit for differing reasons in Church and State), so far from being a divine gift ordained to guide man to his end, becomes a mere tool by which those 'in power' may abuse or oppress their subjects as they choose – whether it be locking them up during COVID for the civil masters, or abusing the orthodox and tradition-minded for the ecclesiastical. Kwasniewski's analysis here, offered with his usual mixture of scholarship and wit, is primarily and accurately applied to the situation in the Church, but the principles he explores in this book also admit of far wider application." – **CHARLES A. COULOMBE**, author of *Vicars of Christ: A History of the Popes* and *Blessed Charles of Austria: A Holy Emperor and His Legacy*

"Written with Peter Kwasniewski's characteristic wit and unmatched turn of phrase, *Bound by Truth* provides invaluable insights into papal authority, details practical ways of resisting 'papal overreach,' and demonstrates the futility of attempting to suppress the Church's ancient liturgical heritage. Animated by true charity for his coreligionists, he identifies true obedience as the mean between rebellion and 'self-destructive submissiveness.' As with his earlier books, so here, Kwasniewski emerges as an apostle of tradition and a paladin of the ancient Roman rite. A book to be treasured." – **MICHAEL SIRILLA**, author of *The Ideal Bishop: Aquinas's Commentaries on the Pastoral Epistles*

BOUND BY TRUTH

Bound by Truth

AUTHORITY, OBEDIENCE, TRADITION, AND THE COMMON GOOD

✠ ✠ ✠

PETER A. KWASNIEWSKI

Angelico Press

First published in the USA
by Angelico Press 2023
Copyright © Peter A. Kwasniewski 2023

For information, address:
Angelico Press, Ltd.
169 Monitor St.
Brooklyn, NY 11222
www.angelicopress.com

ppr 978-1-62138-962-0
cloth 978-1-62138-963-7
ebook 978-1-62138-964-4

Book and cover design
by Michael Schrauzer

For all priests who have sacrificed
comfort, security, ambition, or reputation
to remain true to Catholic Tradition
and to keep it alive for Christ's faithful

The Lord is your inheritance
and the Church will one day
sing your praises

Love is not blind; that is the last thing that it is.
Love is bound; and the more it is bound the less it is blind.

G. K. Chesterton

CONTENTS

PREFACE

ONE DOES NOT HAVE TO BE PAYING PARTIC-ularly close attention to the Catholic Church to see that it is laden with difficulties and riven with disputes. Thanks above all to the erratic and contradictory receptions of Vatican II and the tumultuous pontificate of Pope Francis, authority and obedience are among the topics most hotly debated, together with their context and defining elements: the common good, truth, revelation, tradition, justice, charity, the complex network of duties and rights within a hierarchically structured society. In close association are numerous questions about the office of the papacy and how it relates to the episcopacy, the lower clergy, religious communities, and the laity. In our times we see the rise and spread of problems for which one can find few, if any, precedents in Church history; and even matters that might have seemed thoroughly settled by theologians and spiritual writers in past centuries now take on a very different look in the enormous crisis of faith and pastoral life through which we are passing.

In 2021, I published *True Obedience in the Church: A Guide to Discernment in Challenging Times*, a little book that has turned out to be extremely popular, especially with clergy. To date, editions have appeared in Spanish, Italian, Portuguese, French, German, and Polish, and reviews have been published in newspapers, magazines, and journals.[1] Its worldwide reception proved, if any proof were needed, just how relevant and urgent this topic is for everyone in the modern Church as well as in the modern secular world;

---

1 See, for example, Maike Hickson, "Liturgical expert shows how Catholics needn't obey papal decrees that attack common good of the Church," *LifeSite-News*, March 14, 2022; John Paul Sonnen, "Book Review: True Obedience in the Church," *Liturgical Arts Journal*, April 6, 2022; Joseph Shaw, "Obedience, Disobedience, and Rash Obedience: A Virtue in a Time of Crisis," *OnePeterFive*, May 12, 2022; Michael Charlier, "Obedience in Crisis," *Rorate Caeli*, May 14, 2022; Matt Gaspers, "Kwasniewski's *True Obedience* Provides Critically Important Insights," *Catholic Family News*, June 22, 2022; John R. T. Lamont, "Dominican Theologian Attacks Catholic Tradition" [a response to Fr Henry Donneaud, OP's critique of *True Obedience*], *Rorate Caeli*, September 13, 15, 17, and 19, 2023, available as a PDF at https://rb.gy/fsp1t. I particularly commend this Lamont essay to the reader's attention, as it provides extensive support for the claims I make not only in *True Obedience* but also in this book.

indeed, an unprecedented "shutdown synergy" between Church and State during the Coronavirus pandemic alerted everyone to the dangers of authority run amok and obedience gone awry. Still more alarming has been Pope Francis's ongoing frontal attack on Catholic tradition and lovers of tradition, codified in the motu proprio *Traditionis Custodes* of July 16, 2021. This costly campaign, aimed at some of the most faithful Catholics in the Church, has brought worldwide attention to the "liturgy wars" and reaffirmed the need for a sound, thorough, and honest presentation of the multiple issues at stake, which certainly go far beyond the liturgical sphere (even if that will always be of capital importance).[2]

Although *True Obedience* made a good start, there was more work to be done. That is my motive for publishing the present book. As one can see from glancing at the titles of the chapters, there is no "beating around the bush" here. Part I, "Papacy, Patrimony, and Piety," addresses the teaching of Vatican I on the pope's universal jurisdiction; the limits of his authority, in light of other authoritative principles such as liturgical tradition; the properly Catholic way to interpret and follow the Magisterium; and the virtue of intelligent, God-fearing, and communally perfective obedience versus its vicious distortions: willful rebelliousness on the one hand, and a blind, thoughtless, self-destructive submissiveness on the other. Part II, "Faithful Resistance," looks at several examples of prelates who legitimately pushed back against papal overreach; discusses how clergy should navigate unjust episcopal decrees on private Masses, the use of the *Rituale Romanum*, concelebration, the manner of distributing Communion, church closures, and so forth; shares advice and strategies for laity who seek to promote and defend tradition in their dioceses, including the construction of home oratories and the restoration of shuttered buildings; and draws inspiration from persecuted religious sisters, whether their tormentors were Soviet Communists or apparatchiks of the postconciliar ecclesiastical bureaucracy.

---

2   On the papacy in general and Pope Francis in particular, see the two anthologies I edited—*From Benedict's Peace to Francis's War: Catholics Respond to the Motu Proprio* Traditionis Custodes *on the Latin Mass* (Brooklyn, NY: Angelico Press, 2021) and *Ultramontanism and Tradition: The Role of Church Authority in the Catholic Faith* (Lincoln, NE: Os Justi Press, 2024)—and my two-volume set *The Road from Hyperpapalism to Catholicism: Rethinking the Papacy in a Time of Ecclesial Disintegration* (Waterloo, ON: Arouca Press, 2022).

The book concludes with the text of a 1976 letter—though it might as well have been written in 2023, with a slight shift in addressee—sent by the great Michael Davies to the Most Reverend Hugh A. Donohoe, bishop of Fresno, California. Since the motto of our current leadership seems to be "Back to the '70s!," readers will find the candor of this Welsh convert and Latin Mass apologist a refreshing tonic. Essentially, our struggle has remained the same; but, whereas in 1976 the "new and improved" religion had just gotten under way and enjoyed unequivocal institutional support, today it looks dated and dull, and sparks no enthusiasm beyond aging Vatican II hippies, a gaggle of negligible specialists, and a coterie of official cheerleaders. In spite of our present hardships, the future looks far brighter than it would have looked to Michael Davies at the end of his career (and, of course, he is one of many to be thanked for the progress tradition has made, if one may use a paradoxical turn of phrase).

One general point deserves emphasis. The following pages speak predominantly about the traditional Latin Mass (which will, occasionally, be abbreviated "TLM"), and no wonder: the Holy Sacrifice of the Mass is the font and apex of the Christian life, the highest and most solemn act of prayer offered to the Most Holy Trinity by the Catholic Church and by each individual believer in union with Christ our Eternal High Priest; moreover, Catholics practice their religion above all at the Sunday Mass, the axis of the week, the little Easter, the *Dies Domini*. For that reason, negligent or malicious church governance is nowhere more keenly felt than in the inconvenient, inconsistent, or non-existent provision of the traditional Mass on Sundays and holy days of obligation. [3] That is why the traditionalist movement is found to be speaking so often of the Mass. Yet we are concerned about far more than this central act of divine worship. The same great goods are at stake with regard to *all* of the traditional liturgical rites of the Church—baptism, confirmation, marriage, holy orders, penance, extreme unction, the Divine Office, blessings, exorcisms, the dedication of a church, the consecration of virgins, and so forth. The arguments presented here on behalf of the continuation of the classical Roman Mass apply analogously to every part of our Roman Catholic birthright. Tradition is an inheritance whole and entire; it is to be handed down and received whole and entire.

---

3   See chapter 21.

Although Pope Francis is discussed a good deal throughout, the issues with which we are grappling go far beyond his pontificate and his peculiar way of exercising the papacy. The arguments and advice presented here would have been true (if less urgent) prior to 2013, and they will certainly remain true and relevant long after the Argentinian Jesuit has vacated the chair of Peter and new bishops occupy it. The crisis we are living through stretches back many decades and, sadly, is likely to last several more. Indeed, there may be more evils yet to come, more abuses of papal or episcopal power; but this book, by going to the roots of authority, obedience, tradition, and the common good, equips the reader with the perennial principles needed to evaluate them.

The chapters herein started out as lectures and articles. I thank the editors of *Crisis Magazine* (chapters 2 and 15), *The European Conservative* (chapter 6), *LifeSiteNews* (chapters 23 and 24), *New Liturgical Movement* (chapters 16, 19, and 25), and *OnePeterFive* (chapters 1, 3–5, 11, 13–14, 17–18, 22, 26–27) for permission to include material that first appeared at their sites. I thank also those who invited me to lecture in Columbia, SC and in Chicago (chapter 7); in Charlotte, NC (chapter 8); in Rome at the Paix Liturgique Conference, October 28, 2022 (chapter 9); in Bozeman, MT (chapter 10), and in Arlington, VA (chapter 12). Chapters 20 and 21 were first published at my Substack, Tradition & Sanity. The writing has been revised, updated, and synthesized in various ways, so this book should be considered the definitive version of all that it contains.

To avoid needless clutter in the notes, hyperlinks for online sources have generally been avoided; instead, the author, title, site, and date are listed, which are more useful than a lengthy URL. All internet citations were verified as of November 2023.

Lastly, early in 2024, my publishing company Os Justi Press will release an anthology entitled *Ultramontanism and Tradition: The Role of Church Authority in the Catholic Faith*, with contributions by Cardinal Raymond Leo Burke, Bishop Athanasius Schneider, Thomas Pink, Edward Feser, Joseph Shaw, Sebastian Morello, John Lamont, Charles Coulombe, Eric Sammons, James Baresel, José Antonio Ureta, Stuart Chessman, Roberto de Mattei, and others. Since it delves into many of the same issues as the present book does, it will surely be of interest to the same readers.

PART I

1

The Three Pillars
of Christianity

ISTORICALLY AND THEOLOGICALLY, THERE
are three "pillars" of Catholicism: Scripture, Tradition,
and Magisterium. Each is necessary; all are mutually
implicated; and none of them is absolute, in the sense that it can
be taken as greater *in every respect* than the others. Each is first
in a different way. There is an almost Trinitarian *perichoresis* or
circumincessio among them.

Protestants exalt Scripture to the extent of denying or mini-
mizing the other two. As a result, even Scripture is eventually
corrupted in them. Eastern Orthodox, on the other hand, exalt
Tradition, to the extent of denying a universal Magisterium and
teaching authority in the Church, and even to the extent of denying
some premises of Sacred Scripture (e.g., the teaching on marriage
and divorce). But what does their devotion to Tradition mean, if
some of their most respected theologians can accept universalism,
contraception, and homosexual "marriage" (as apparently Kallistos
Ware did)? A disordered devotion to "Tradition" can result, ironically, in its cancellation.

But the third group is the most interesting: I shall call them
Reductive Catholics (although one could also say Magisterialist
Catholics or Hyperpapalist Catholics, etc.). *These* exalt Magisterium — and, practically speaking, the papal office — above Scripture
and Tradition, so that it becomes the sole principle by which we
know truth. It becomes, in a sense, *all* truth, so that it would never
be possible to challenge assertions of the Magisterium (e.g., *Amoris
Laetitia* chapter 8 or the death penalty change to the *Catechism*) on
the basis of Scripture and Tradition. As with the behavior of the
other two groups, so with this one too: the exaggerated exaltation of the Magisterium ends up canceling out the Magisterium of
preceding popes and councils. It turns into a "Magisterium of the

moment," much as Protestant preachers effectively privatize the Bible, or the Orthodox selectively appropriate Tradition.

The Roman Catholic, at least ideally, is one who holds *all three pillars* to be essential, irreplaceable, and non-fungible. Each supports the other; none can stand without its companions. Each of them is what it is only in and through the others. This means there may be times of confusion and disputation when it seems that claims based on one conflict with claims based on another. This is part of the "engine" of doctrinal development, but it is also a "check and balance" to ensure that none of the three becomes hypertrophic. For it is certainly unhealthy, and leads to distortions of doctrine and Church life, whenever one of these elements is allowed to atrophy.

Now someone might say: "But isn't the Magisterium the final court of appeal, the one that tells us what Scripture and Tradition mean or contain?" Yes, that's true; but with some important caveats. Scripture is the inerrant and inspired Word of God. The Magisterium is not this, so it is inferior to it and at the service of it.[1] The universal ordinary Magisterium and the extraordinary Magisterium are infallible guides to and declarers of truth.

The problem arises in areas in which the Magisterium *could* be in error, and when people, in those circumstances, say something like: "I don't care what Scripture says about ABC; Pope Francis says XYZ, and that's what we have to follow." Or "It sure seems like Scripture says ABC, but Francis says it means XYZ, so that's what it must mean." Or: "It doesn't matter if the Church has uninterruptedly believed or done ABC; Francis has issued a motu proprio that says we should believe or do the opposite, and that's the end of the matter." *Roma locuta, causa finita* cannot mean "Rome has spoken; the Bible and the Church's witness are irrelevant."[2]

As I said above, each has a certain primacy with respect to the others. That is why no one should ever give up *lectio divina* (prayerful reading of Scripture) in favor of a "*lectio ecclesiastica*" where the sole reading material would be papal documents. Nor should anyone ever given up a traditional *lex orandi* in favor of a newly constructed one, based on the latest model of the *lex credendi* according to a

---

1   As *Dei Verbum* itself states in no. 10.

2   See Boniface [Phillip Campbell], "The Last Gasp of Our Akhenaten," *Unam Sanctam Catholicam*, November 5, 2023.

Vatican chief. This is why the documents of the Magisterium themselves have been careful – certainly in past times – to draw heavily upon Scripture and other traditional sources in order to show that the official teaching *derives from* the witnesses on which the Faith is based. And it explains why Christianity will always be corrupted if there is *only* Scripture and Tradition, without a final authority that can resolve difficult questions or questions that may not be difficult in themselves (e.g., the immorality of contraception) but are difficult for some people due to bad intellectual habits or disordered concupiscence. Without a teaching authority, a Magisterium, the voices of Scripture and Tradition can be garbled or suffocated.

Let us examine next how, if any one of the three "pillars" is taken as an absolute, it becomes hollow, contentless.

ABSOLUTISMS: TEMPTATIONS AND REALITIES

Some forms of Protestantism hold to the principle *sola scriptura*, "by Scripture alone." If this principle were applied rigorously, the result would be the loss of Scripture itself – and not only because of the commonly adduced fact that the very content of the canon is known only by Tradition. The situation is actually worse: absent any tradition, that is, acceptance of the previous generations' work, each generation would be required to start the long journey of understanding all over again, and no generation would get further than one generation's walk down the path. Even that one generation's energies would be wasted, dissipated in many directions, because no one among them would have authority to cut off fruitless lines of inquiry.

Of course, the *reality* is that communities that say they hold to Scripture exclusively always develop some form of tradition over time (though they would doubtless avoid calling it by that Catholic-sounding name) together with at least a *de facto* substitute for a magisterium. Only extremists within the Protestant world actually try to live out *sola scriptura* in all its purity. Such congregations generally number about as many believers as can be persuaded to sit inside a single building listening to a single self-appointed pastor. We could call this not the "on-the-ground reality" of Protestantism but its besetting temptation.

Conversely, some tendencies within Eastern Orthodoxy could be called *sola traditione*, "by Tradition alone." If tradition is taken as an absolute, the handing-down of antiquity takes precedence over every other consideration. In this mindset, revival means returning to past ages – not a return to Jesus Christ as a present reality, but a return to the received icons of Christ, to the received texts of His words, to the received teachings on His nature, all as past realities. Tradition taken as an absolute becomes a complacency with things as they are, a practice of "churchliness" rather than Christian discipleship (the term "churchliness" is from Orthodox scholar Fr Alexander Schmemann).[3] To look at any one of the received treasures for a moment as living and active – Scripture, for example – would be to wake up and acknowledge another source besides tradition. Taken as an absolute, tradition contradicts itself, denying access to the very riches it claims to provide.

Of course, many Orthodox Christians, although in principle denying any universal living Magisterium, nonetheless *do* turn to Scripture and to magisterial texts with attention to what God has to say *now*.[4] Only in Orthodoxy's worst tendencies do we see a *sola traditione* mindset at work. Again, we could call this not Orthodoxy as practiced on the ground, but Orthodoxy's besetting temptation. It tends to be the default position in apologetics or polemics.

The third absolutism, *solo Magisterio*, has been the strange preserve of Roman Catholicism – strange because it is inherently less plausible than the other two. When the Magisterium's authority is taken as an absolute, it trumps not only all Scripture and all Tradition but also all previous acts of the Magisterium. Only what the *current* papal monarch says carries weight. Those living under such a mindset have to embrace today's papal statements wholeheartedly, but they have to drop them just as wholeheartedly if the next pope says something different or new. Anything else would deny the current pope's absolute authority. Consequently, on this view there is no content definitive of Catholicism.[5]

---

3   See John A. Jillions, "'Thicket of Idols': Alexander Schmemann's Critique of Orthodoxy," *Wheel Journal* online, www.wheeljournal.com/blog/2018/7/24/john-jillions-alexander-schmemann.

4   I have heard it said that Orthodox theologians for decades have quietly consulted Vatican documents on bioethics for authoritative guidance, since they have nothing superior to the good work that has been done in this area under John Paul II and Benedict XVI (alas, not so much under Francis, who has been systematically dismantling the legacy of his predecessors).

5   For further thoughts along these lines, see Eduardo Echeverria, *"Solum*

Of course, as we have seen among the Protestants and the Orthodox with their besetting temptations, most Roman Catholics who practice their faith do not in fact think that the Magisterium has absolute power over Scripture and Tradition; but there are extremists who think that way, as can be seen from perusing some of the hyperpapalist apologetics. Perhaps this, then, is the besetting temptation of Roman Catholicism.

"A THREEFOLD CORD IS NOT EASILY BROKEN" (ECCLES 4:12)

While many Protestants reject in principle any authority but Scripture, and Orthodox Christians, taking refuge in Tradition, reject in principle any living universal Magisterium, Roman Catholics in principle accept *all three*. While it may be unclear sometimes how to reconcile what comes from different sources, holding all three together is the key to holding *any one* of them. How so?

Only with Tradition and the Magisterium can we accept and take in the whole of Scripture rather than wandering away into private, idiosyncratic interpretations that may even remove parts of Scripture deemed faulty or superseded (Marcionism being an extreme example).[6] Only with Scripture and the Magisterium can we accept and take in the whole of Tradition rather than wandering into idiosyncratic, ethno-nationalistic embodiments of tradition (as in Orthodoxy). And—crucially—only with Scripture and Tradition can we accept and take in all that the Magisterium has said, *both* yesterday *and* today, rather than yielding to a "Magisterium of the moment" dependent on the personality and preferences of the reigning Roman pontiff. Each of the three "pillars" is built into the nature of the others.

To shift metaphors, these three elements are like three parts of an organic body that requires all three to function. When

---

Magisterium?," Crisis Magazine, September 15, 2023; Eric Sammons, "The Hyperinflation of the Papacy," *Crisis Magazine*, November 8, 2023.

6 Pope Francis holds this view, having declared that "biblical texts (such as Exodus 21:20-21) [and] certain considerations in the New Testament regarding women (1 Corinthians 11:3-10; 1 Timothy 2:11-14) and other texts of Scripture and testimonies of Tradition . . . cannot be materially repeated today," because they express "cultural conditioning" that is not part of the "perennial substance" of divine revelation ("Pope Francis responds to dubia submitted by five cardinals," *Vatican News*, October 2, 2023). For analysis, see John Lamont, "Pope Francis as Public Heretic: The Evidence Leaves No Doubt," *Rorate Caeli*, November 24, 2023.

one or two of the elements is shorn away, the body that remains tries to grow back what it has lost. The new parts are stunted and unsightly, but they serve in a clumsy way to substitute for what is missing.

For example, when Protestants are polemicizing, they talk as if Scripture alone is their guide; but if you watch closely how they think, speak, and live among themselves as social animals, it's obvious that they look *not only* to Scripture *but also* to the traditions of whatever denomination or group they belong to; and it's no less evident that they have some kind of authority who can decide what is and is not acceptable within the community (even Protestants have their hierarchies and excommunications).[7]

Similarly, when the Eastern Orthodox polemicize, they talk as if the consensus of the Fathers reflected in an unchanging Divine Liturgy determines all that they believe and do; but if you watch how they think, speak, and live among themselves, the reality is much more complex, and certainly involves an interplay of all three elements, even if the magisterial one suffers from hypoplasia.

In like manner, when Catholics are polemicizing, they can talk as if the Magisterium alone is their guide; but if you watch how they think, speak, and live among themselves, they draw from Scripture and from Tradition in ways that do not (or need not) look to the Magisterium and can even occasionally be in tension with its lower levels.[8]

We see here two important facts. First, polemics tend to make each of these groups fall into its besetting temptation in an exaggerated way. Second, whenever one of the three elements is downplayed or denied, sooner or later something *like* it is developed to substitute for it.

---

7 Indeed, the need for authority arises as soon as there is a community – such is life for social animals, and such is the will of God. See Leo XIII, Encyclical Letter *Diuturnum Illud*, in *A Reader in Catholic Social Teaching from* Syllabus Errorum to Deus Caritas Est (Tacoma, WA: Cluny Media, 2017), 20–31.

8 I heard a hyperpapalist Catholic say that Catholics should not read Scripture on their own because all that they need to know is what is taught by the official documents of the Church or by the Bible in the liturgy, and that it is dangerous – even Protestant – to read the Bible unless the Magisterium has stated what a given passage means. That such a view, which would have the effect of canceling out (for example) the entire tradition of monastic *lectio divina*, could even have arisen in anyone's mind is symptomatic of the problem of what has been called "the spirit of Vatican I" (see chapter 3).

Most basically, we can know that "Magisteriumitis" is a sickness because the Magisterium *receives* the matter on which it speaks – it does not *generate* the matter about which it speaks (or if it did, that would be a sign of a pseudo-magisterium). It is, rather, a court of appeals that hands down judgments, which requires that there be *something prior* about which a judgment can be made. Catholics, after all, believe the Faith and talk about it using what has been handed down in writing and orally and using their power of reason, and the Magisterium intervenes when necessary to offer correction or clarification. It presupposes something on which to work.[9]

FIDEISM UNDER THREE DISGUISES

Each of these extremes turns out to be a form of fideism.

The Protestant fideist believes something "just because the Word of God says it," without realizing that we cannot understand this Word without the operation of our reason, the witness of Tradition, and the guidance of the Holy Spirit working in the hierarchy of the Church.

The Orthodox fideist believes something "because we have always said or done it this way," without realizing that this judgment presupposes a prior and more authoritative source for what is always to be said and done. After all, there are some things that were said or done for a time, or in a certain area, that have either ceased to be said and done or were never said and done by everyone; and there are beliefs and practices that arose long after antiquity.

The Catholic fideist believes something "because the Magisterium says so," without recognizing that the Magisterium is a servant of that which is prior and more authoritative to it, namely, the written and unwritten Word of God, and the sum total of ecclesiastical tradition that mediates and expresses this Word.

All forms of fideism have a grain of truth – that is why they can gain traction – but also lead to manifest distortions and, in their extreme form, to an irrational and arbitrary construct that has lost any bearings outside of itself.

Now, someone might object that the traditionalist movement within the Catholic Church is a "*sola traditione*" group because

---

9   On this point, see Sammons, "Hyperinflation of the Papacy."

(according to the objector) it denies the authority of the pope to do things the traditionalists happen to dislike.

But there is a different and better way to think about the origin of this moniker "traditionalist." As many theologians maintain, Tradition, in its root meaning, is the *sum total of that which God has handed down to us in divine revelation.* The portion of it that was written down is called Scripture, and the rest is called unwritten or oral Tradition. Within this handed-down content is the power to interpret revelation, or the teaching authority of the Church, the Magisterium. That is, Scripture and the Magisterium are *pre-contained in Tradition.* The traditionalist, therefore, is the one who emphasizes the unbreakable unity of the three pillars in their fundamental source, and who therefore rejects any hypertrophic exaltation of Scripture (as per the Protestant temptation), Tradition in a reductive sense (as per the Orthodox temptation), or Magisterium (as per the temptation of "conservative" or "magisterial" Catholics).

For example, Pope Francis's teaching that capital punishment is *"per se* contrary to the Gospel," "inadmissible" and "immoral," and "abases human dignity," stands against the triple witness of Scripture, Tradition, and Magisterium, and therefore cannot be accepted by a Catholic. If such a "development" were possible, no reversal in Catholic teaching would be impossible, because any change whatsoever could be justified by the same kind of evolutionary dialectic invoked for the death penalty change.[10]

In this sense, then, the Catholic traditionalist of today is simply a Catholic who is free from the mental disease of Magisteriumitis and who strives—in his faith, his life, his thought—to hold together the three pillars of original Tradition, namely: written Tradition, unwritten Tradition, and the guardianship of Tradition.

---

10   See "What Good is a Changing Catechism? Revisiting the Purpose and Limits of a Book," in Kwasniewski, *Hyperpapalism to Catholicism,* 2:137–55; cf. Thomas Heinrich Stark, "The Historicity of Truth: On the Premises and Foundations of Walter Kasper's Theology," in Kevin L. Flannery, SJ, ed., *The Faith Once for All Delivered: Doctrinal Authority in Catholic Theology* (Steubenville, OH: Emmaus Academic, 2023), 69–100. Evidence of the way the progressives think may be found in Michael Haynes, "Cardinal Schönborn cites death penalty revision when asked about changing Catechism on LGBT issues," *LifeSiteNews,* October 23, 2023. For an extensive recent treatment, see Edward Feser, "Fastiggi on Capital Punishment and the Change to the Catechism," in two parts, August 26 and August 30, 2023, at https://edwardfeser.blogspot.com/.

2

Conundrums about Interpretation

C ASEY CHALK'S ARTICLE "THE PROTESTANT Doctrine That Gave Us Pro-Trans Churches"[1] details the impossible tangle that results from *sola scriptura* and offers a fine summary of the classic Catholic case for why there must be a God-appointed interpreter of the Bible, since it is not self-interpreting.

As a Roman Catholic traditionalist, I have often pondered certain epistemological dilemmas that confront us today, which bear a likeness to the *sola scriptura* tangle. These dilemmas have always been there, but they've usually taken milder forms and concerned only specialists. Today, they take on an acute and undeniable form, and, thanks to social media, everyone who is following Church news with any seriousness is aware of them. One of these dilemmas runs as follows.

No text interprets itself; every text requires an authoritative interpreter. However, the authoritative interpreter's interpretation is usually transmitted as a text. This text does not interpret itself, but requires an authoritative interpretation; and that text requires another. Thus is created the specter of an infinite regress, in which no one can ever be certain that he possesses the correct meaning of a text.

"Surely that's an exaggeration?," one might object. "The Magisterium speaks very clearly about all sorts of things: Nicaea on the divinity of Christ, for example. Or Trent on the transubstantiation of the bread and wine at Mass. Or Pius IX on the Immaculate Conception and Pius XII on the Assumption. Or the dogma of papal infallibility at Vatican I." In a way, that's all quite true: these

---

1 Published at *Crisis Magazine* on March 23, 2023. For a full treatment, see Chalk's book *The Obscurity of Scripture: Disputing* Sola Scriptura *and the Protestant Notion of Biblical Perspicuity* (Steubenville, OH: Emmaus Road Publishing, 2023).

dogmas are transmitted to us with considerable clarity and some have found liturgical expression.

But the waters can be muddied at times. Let's take Vatican I. The meaning of the dogma of papal infallibility is notoriously controversial,[2] and nowadays one can find extremely different, even incompatible interpretations of it, let alone of all its implications and corollaries – and one can find support for different views in papal documents and actions of the past 150 years. The views of Leo XIII or Pius X are not necessarily those of John Paul II or Benedict XVI. Compatible, perhaps; in continuity, arguably; but diverse.

Then there is the problem (the scandal, to speak more accurately) of hierarchs, from Pope Francis down the line of his creations – Cupich, McElroy, Roche, Fernández, et al. – who selectively quote magisterial documents against what most people would call their "natural meaning," or who openly contradict such documents. Cardinal Cupich cherry-picks the Council of Trent and the encyclical *Mediator Dei* in support of the Novus Ordo and against the traditional Latin Mass.[3] Absurd, yes; but he's trying to build magisterial scaffolding to hold up his own point of view. *Amoris Laetitia* was another case where an instrument of the Magisterium was used as a blunt weapon to cancel out former magisterial teaching of a quite clear nature – clear, at least, on the level of a natural or unforced reading of texts.

So, it seems like the embarrassing Protestant pluralism to which Catholic apologetics triumphantly points as evidence of the inadequacy of *sola scriptura* and of the need for a divinely-appointed guide comes back to haunt us in the form of *magisterial pluralism* – or better said, a mixture of Magisterium formally speaking (at all its varying levels) and of the pervasive "official theology" that Thomas Pink has done us a great service in describing.[4]

2   For the best recent overview, see John P. Joy, *Disputed Questions on Papal Infallibility* (Lincoln, NE: Os Justi Press, 2022).

3   See Cardinal Blase Cupich, "A Eucharistic Revival that Renews the Church," Parts I and II, March 12 and 22, 2023, at www.eucharisticrevival.org/.

4   See Thomas Pink's groundbreaking study "Vatican II and Crisis in the Theology of Baptism," one of the most important pieces I have read on the shift from pre-Vatican II to post-Vatican II theologies. It may be found in *Integralism and the Common Good: Selected Essays from* The Josias, Volume 2: *The Two Powers*, ed. P. Edmund Waldstein, O. Cist. (Brooklyn, NY: Angelico Press, 2021), 290–334. Here Pink defines "official theology" as "prevailing theological opinion in official circles," and continues: "Official theology is the Church's theological account

There are plenty of times when Catholics, in order to know what the truth is and not be misled by error, must point to a Church document and say, perhaps to the head of the John Paul II Institute in Rome, or to prominent figures in the Synod on Synodality, or to Cardinal Roche: "Look, it is *really clear* from this *evident* text of *Veritatis Splendor* that you cannot say XYZ"; or "Look, Pius XII in this passage of *Mediator Dei* condemns the false antiquarianism that the Consilium relied on," or "*Mediator Dei* proves that the laity do truly offer the Holy Sacrifice of the Mass with the priest, but in an essentially different way than the priest offers it." Examples of that sort can be easily multiplied.

In such cases, people are relying on what we might call "the doctrine of *magisterial perspicuity*," ranged against deviant "official theology," arbitrary manipulations of ecclesiastical documents, or even errors in the non-infallible ordinary magisterium (a thing the Church tells us is indeed possible, since the opposite of infallible is fallible). [5]

In premodern times, the common folk learned a simple catechism modeled on creed and commandments; worshiped at a nearby church in a rite handed down since time immemorial; paid their tithes; and died with a crucifix or a rosary in their hands. We would like to think that such a childlike faith is still possible; one catches a glimpse of it in communities where tradition thrives. In a traditional parish of today, one can sense the strength of the eternal truths that pulse through the old catechisms, the self-evident goodness of the Latin Mass, the generosity of believers who orient

---

of herself and her mission where the provision of this account is official – it involves official bodies or persons – but does not of itself impose any obligation on our belief as Catholics. Official theology may convey magisterial teaching, or it may go beyond magisterial teaching. It may even, unfortunately, obscure or even contradict magisterial teaching. But official theology is not itself a further case of magisterial teaching. The Church constantly produces official theology. It is an ever present and essential element in the Church's life. . . . Official theology is communicated in the training of clergy, through seminary manuals and lectures. It can be found in what passes as usual in sermons, homilies, and ecclesially provided devotional literature. It can be found in all manner of official explanations of liturgy or pastoral practice. It can be found especially in what is not said. Official theology can reveal itself in silence – in what is not treated as of significance or comment in the Church's life, as well as what is" (292–93). See the same author's "Papal Authority and the Limits of Official Theology," *The Lamp* online, December 2, 2022.

5   See Joy, *Disputed Questions on Papal Infallibility*, 8–18.

their lives to God, the common yearning to die in His grace and live with Him forever.

This life of simple faith is still real, as real as the Real Presence that calls it forth and sustains it. But it is under grave threat from factions in the Church – not the Church herself, the immaculate Bride of Christ, but churchmen who dare to speak on her behalf[6]– who despise the simple faith of "the little ones,"[7] who vilify love of tradition as "backwardism," adherence to dogma as "fundamentalism," insistence on sound morality as "moralism," and desire for coherence as "integralism." These factionalists do not want to leave the Catholic shires in peace;[8] they make a lot of noise about "needs of modern man" and "development of doctrine" and "irreversible reform." They practically force upon us, whether we're interested or not, the necessity of discerning between authentic and inauthentic Catholic teaching. You may not be interested in the revolution, but the revolution is very interested in *you*.

Thus, Catholics who have the blessing of the Catholic Church as divinely-appointed teacher will *still* need a principle or a set of principles for receiving, interpreting, and harmonizing what Church authorities say, or even for distinguishing between authentic and inauthentic, licit and illicit uses of authority. And this brings us back to the intelligence and conscience of the believer. There will always be a hermeneutical "filter" when I receive Church teaching; that's unavoidable. I will at least implicitly ask myself: "Does this make sense given what I have *already received* from the Church? Does this contradict something that is more fundamental, or something I know with greater certitude?"

To hold, as some attempt to do, that one must simply fall in line with whatever the current pope says, regardless of whether it seems to clash openly with what the Church has taught in the past, is to

---

6   See Jacques Maritain's important discussion of the distinction between "the person of the Church," supremely holy, unblemished, and full of truth, and the "personnel of the Church," who are neither indefectibly holy nor always inerrant: *On the Church of Christ*, trans. Joseph W. Evans (Notre Dame: University of Notre Dame Press, 1973), 135-51; one may also profitably consult the ecclesiological writings of Charles Journet.
7   See Bishop Athanasius Schneider, in conversation with Diane Montagna, *Christus Vincit: Christ's Triumph over the Darkness of the Age* (Brooklyn, NY: Angelico Press, 2019), 113-14, 154-55, 168, 307.
8   See Julian Kwasniewski, "The Universal Call to Hobbitness," *Crisis Magazine*, December 19, 2022.

my mind a complete nonstarter. For one thing, such hyperpapalism denies the first principle of all thought, which is the principle of non-contradiction (if the death penalty, in Scripture and throughout Christian history, is an expression of the moral virtue of justice, it will not do to say that it is "contrary to the Gospel and to human dignity"). For another, authoritarianism offends the dignity of the person, a free and rational individual who should be treated as such — who is owed an account of the Faith that "holds water" and doesn't make him a water-carrier for a political ideology or a partisan agenda.

Finally, the hyperpapalist gravely harms the Church's evangelizing mission by making her look, to outsiders, like a sect whose members change their minds depending on what their leader says is the latest message from above (or, in terms more familiar to us from the past decade, the latest intervention of the "God of surprises" as conveyed by his mouthpiece, the "pope of surprises").

The grave harm done to the Church's image *ad extra* by *Traditionis Custodes*, for example, is undeniable. How can it possibly make sense to non-Catholics, let alone to Catholics, that communities known for their high rate of practice, fidelity, and generosity would be shut down simply because they find it more fruitful to worship the way Catholics had done for most of their religion's history? It's the purest possible example of scandal, about which Our Lord spoke some very precise words (cf. Mt 18:6-9).

The moral character of the hierarch propounding a teaching is also relevant to how that teaching should be received, and this can be said without lapsing into some version of Donatism that equates Church membership or ruling authority with moral righteousness. If, for example, we have reasonably formed an opinion, by the usual ways in which we form opinions, that a particular pope or bishop is a liar, manipulator, hypocrite, gaslighter, abuser, protector of abusers, etc., then we will take what he teaches *cum grano salis*, and reasonably so; we will at least have a certain hesitation or suspension of judgment, since the immoral character of the propounder calls into question the motives and the content of what is being propounded.

While none of this lands us in an inescapable subjectivism or relativism, it nevertheless demands of us a rigorous honesty in making the apologetic argument against Protestant subjectivism or relativism. We need to have the humility to admit that we ourselves have an analogous challenge *within* Catholicism that rests on the same basic law of hermeneutics, namely, that no text interprets itself — at least, not perfectly so, such that everyone will necessarily agree about its meaning, even presupposing the best of intentions.

So far from casting us onto a desolate beach of a remote island of skepticism from which there is no escape, this fact is among the strongest supports of Catholic traditionalism (by which I mean simply Catholicism — but we give it a special name owing to a peculiar circumstance of our age, namely, that modernism or progressivism has largely replaced Catholicism in many institutions and individuals).[9] The root principle of traditionalism is this: we should hold fast, as much as we can, to the Catholic Faith as taught, described, depicted, and especially enacted in worship over the centuries and millennia.

The longer a practice has endured (think: the Rosary), the longer a formulation has remained (think: the Nicene Creed or the Eucharistic doctrine of St Thomas Aquinas and the Council of Trent), the longer a liturgy has been prayed (think: the unbroken continuous development of the Roman Rite of Mass until the mid-twentieth century),[10] the more reliable it is to lean on it, to take it as true, good, holy, right, divinely approved. So much so that if a pope were, God forbid, to attempt to ban the Rosary, we would ignore that ban and continue praying the Rosary as before.

There is a way out of the infinite regress. As Catholics, our default is to fall back on the cumulative and converging inheritance of tradition — yes, as mediated through the Magisterium, but not as reduced or reducible to "the Magisterium of the moment." This Magisterium includes the universal ordinary Magisterium of all the bishops as reflected in traditional catechisms[11] and liturgical rites,

---

9   See my article "Can We Call Ourselves 'Traditional Catholics'?," *OnePeterFive*, April 12, 2023.
10   See my book *The Once and Future Roman Rite: Returning to the Latin Liturgical Tradition after Seventy Years of Exile* (Gastonia, NC: TAN Books, 2022), 34–67, 197–215, et passim.
11   The TradiVox project has been republishing dozens of classic old catechisms across a period of many centuries and incorporating their texts into a digital database. In doing so, the consistency of Catholic teaching can be dramatically demonstrated, against which the sharp deviations of recent decades stand out with utter clarity.

as well as the extraordinary Magisterium of popes and councils, which cannot be in error.

Again, the philosophical problem I am focusing on is not "how do we know that Catholicism is true," but "how do we know that we know, with a reasonable certitude, *what Catholicism is*," at a time when there are many competing "Catholicisms" on offer, and some of the most outlandish candidates are being pushed by high-ranking ecclesiastical authorities. Our certainty about the Faith is based on having a *sensus Catholicus*, a *sensus ecclesiae*, a *sensus fidelium* nourished upon proven sources known collectively to be sound and reliable in transmitting the dogmas and practices of the Faith.

In my opinion, this area of "intra-ecclesial apologetics" is a greater challenge for today's apologists than refuting the Protestants, who, in spite of good will, are rather blithering and bumbling opponents, already refuted countless times from the era of Cajetan, Bellarmine, and Francis de Sales through the *Radio Replies* of Frs. Rumble and Carty[12] down to Thomas Howard,[13] Scott Hahn, and the innumerable apologists whose works populate our bookstores. We've driven a stake through the heart of the "five solas" so many times that it's a wonder they still squirm and kick. Meanwhile, the need for *intra*-ecclesial apologetics seems to be unacknowledged or, worse, brushed off with an airy (and lazy) hyperpapalism or with its Siamese twin, a brazen (and equally lazy) sedevacantism.

Such thought-stopping tactics do not solve anything. Instead, they occasion a crisis of conscience and temptations to apostasy among Catholics who cannot square what they have learned from any standard catechism or any historic liturgy with what they are seeing and hearing from the mouthpieces of the Church today. Either we must intelligently vindicate the rights of tradition and the light of reason, or we must surrender to fideism, authoritarianism, positivism, and evolutionism. This intra-ecclesial terrain — a distinctively Catholic terrain — is where the great apologetic battles are yet to be fought.

---

12   All of them helpfully online at www.radioreplies.info/.
13   See *Evangelical Is Not Enough: Worship of God in Liturgy and Sacrament* (San Francisco: Ignatius Press, 1988).

3

The "Spirit of Vatican I" as a Post-Revolutionary Political Problem

N HIS FASCINATING BOOK *VATICAN I: THE Council and the Making of the Ultramontane Church*,[1] John W. O'Malley details the movements, ideas, personalities, and events that coalesced in the First Vatican Council of 1869–1870. My intention here is not to furnish a complete summary, much less to offer tidy theological "solutions," but rather to highlight points from O'Malley's intricate narration that we should bear in mind as we continue to discuss the problem of "hyperpapalism."

THE OLD PARADIGM AND THE INFLUENCE OF DE MAISTRE

In O'Malley's telling, what was broadly called "Gallicanism" points not so much to something peculiarly French as to a common set of beliefs throughout historic Latin Christendom. No one accepted or taught a papacy with completely arbitrary and totally unchecked power. Rather than Tradition finding its origin in the papacy and radiating out from there, it was understood that Tradition existed throughout the Church and found its convergent central focus in the papacy. From thence the Tradition could be sent out, but only having been already received. It was a two-way street: the Tradition flows *into* Rome just as the Tradition flowed *out from* Rome.

The revolutionary spirit propelled a dramatic change away from that historic understanding of the papacy. The new concern was: How can secular forces and revolutionary powers be checked? The answer: by the pope! The pope was an indomitable

---

1   Cambridge, MA: Belknap Press of Harvard University Press, 2018.

force standing against the rise of injurious secular forces that sought the Church's extinction.[2]

Enter Joseph de Maistre, author of *Du Pape* (1819), an important text that influenced the Ultramontane movement. Broadly speaking, de Maistre was a faithful Catholic counter-revolutionary and leader against the hubris of Liberalism in Europe.[3] However, he had become disillusioned by Liberalism's insistence on "checks and balances." All power – secular, and therefore also religious – needs to be reduced to one man, who must be empowered to do anything he judges necessary for the good of his subjects, and no one can question him at all. Eventually de Maistre's ideas caught on owing to practical need. What de Maistre did not account for was what happens when his unchecked singular power itself becomes the problem. For him, there's no recourse.

THE PARTIES AT VATICAN I

In the mid-nineteenth century, those opposed to an *isolated* papal infallibility fell into two basic camps.

There were the so-called Gallicans, who represented the old paradigm that, while one must hold the bishop of Rome in the highest possible regard, he should not be viewed as a divine oracle. They saw the pope as a centering point of unity with a unique primacy and teaching authority; but they also saw in local variety something of divine origin, something *also* constitutive of the nature of the Church. The Church does not reduce to the bishop of Rome, as if the latter could say *"L'Église c'est moi."*

Then there were the so-called Liberal Catholics, on board with the Enlightenment and the new ideas of a Liberalism the tenets

---

2   One can hardly fail to notice how we are facing exactly the opposite situation: a pope who plays the marionette to leftist, anti-religion secular powers. If yesterday the concern was how might the pope be a check to wayward secular power, today our question is: What power is capable of checking a wayward pope?

3   I will capitalize Liberal/Liberalism in this chapter to make it clear that I am referring to the original meaning, which we often expand to "classical liberalism" in the United States (where it is confused with "conservatism," which it most definitely is not). See Louis Cardinal Billot, SJ, *Liberalism: A Critique of Its Basic Principles and Various Forms*, trans. George Barry O'Toole and Thomas Storck (Waterloo, ON: Arouca Press, 2019), esp. the Introduction by Storck; cf. Thomas Storck, "Liberalism's Three Assaults," in *From Christendom to Americanism and Beyond: The Long, Jagged Trail to a Postmodern Void* (Kettering, OH: Angelico Press, 2015), 22–33.

of which read like a synopsis of American civics: religious liberty, freedom of speech and of the press, republicanism contra monarchy, separation of Church and State. Their agenda was to advance this in the Catholic Church, and they saw the papacy as a roadblock.

Both of these parties opposed, for different reasons, the Ultramontanes — determined anti-Liberals[4] who were pushing for a new conception of papal infallibility.

Here we must distinguish explicitly between Gallicanism as a kind of general mindset, according to which there are limits to papal authority, and Gallicanism as a definite *theory* about what those limits are, as expressed in the Gallican articles of 1682. The former has much to commend it; the latter has been excluded as heretical. We might say that the Gallicans were correct in a broad way although wrong on several definite points, whereas the majority at Vatican I was correct about the several definite points defined in *Pastor Aeternus* but wrong in the broader sense about how to combat Liberalism effectively. The traditional Catholic position is then a combination of the definite articles of Ultramontanism (that is, primacy and infallibility) within the general framework represented by the older view, which was also held by those definitely *not* Gallican in the strict sense, such as John Henry Newman.

In any case, the way things turned out was quite a surprise. The papal infallibility party got their definition, and therein thought their defense against Liberalism was secure. As it happened, the Liberal party captured the papacy and used that ultimate power to force Liberalism on the entire Church.

The self-contradictions are manifest. Our current pope, in the name of the ideals of Liberalism or progressivism, suppresses any and all he regards as standing in the way of his agenda. It is analogous to the way Communists function. They say they are "for the people" or even that they speak on their behalf, but enforce their own ideas on the people with absolute power;[5] they install and benefit their own inner circle of cronies,

---

4 A point well insisted on by Roberto de Mattei and José Antonio Ureta in their writing on ultramontanism.
5 The parallels with the propaganda on "synodalism" are striking. As Umberto Eco pointed out in his celebrated essay "Ur-Fascism": "The People is conceived as a quality, a monolithic entity expressing the Common Will. Since no large quantity of human beings can have a common will, the Leader pretends to be

placing personal loyalty as the only thing that really matters. So too, the neo-liberal or neo-modernist party in our day now *celebrates* the virtues of absolute papal power. It was once their enemy, but now that they have captured it, they rather enjoy having and exercising that power for their own ends. The neo-liberals – both civil and ecclesiastical – greatly value the ability to have and exercise absolute power. They advocate for suppressing free speech and the press. They wish to use power to suppress all their "right-wing" opposition. They do not require kissing the papal foot literally, but they have found other substitutes that suit them. They wish to reconnect Church and State, but in reverse order, allowing the *State* to dictate terms to the Church, with the Church functioning as the State's chaplain, giving a ceremonial wink and nod to socialist agendas, open borders, abortion, and the sex and gender agendas (to name a few relevant issues). In our modern epoch, the leftists and revisionists are totalitarians: they capture centralized power in order to enforce centralized planning and the destruction of tradition.

If there is to be any effective opposition to the centralized authority, we must devote our efforts to building small local communities where tradition may live and thrive, usually far from the reach of the higher echelons. Today's traditionalists are akin to the old traditional European party: valuing the papacy as a servant of Tradition, not as an all-powerful divine oracle free to impose arbitrary personal whims and fancies. We see the papacy as having elements of a "constitutional monarchy," where power is set within a texture of principles, precedents, protocols, and promises.

Paradoxically, the pope is both an absolute and a constitutional monarch, which no one else can be. He is absolute inasmuch as he is a monarch limited only by divine and natural law; yet that divine law includes within itself a constitution for the society that the pope governs, in a way that the same divine law does *not* include a constitution for societies governed by a secular monarch.

---

their interpreter. Having lost their power of delegation, citizens do not act; they are only called on to play the role of the People. Thus the People is only a theatrical fiction. . . . [T]he emotional response of a selected group of citizens can be presented and accepted as the Voice of the People." *New York Review of Books*, June 22, 1995, reproduced at https://theanarchistlibrary.org/library/umberto-eco-ur-fascism.

THE DEBATE OVER THE DEFINITION

There had been a preparatory document on ecclesiology that covered far more material than what was eventually approved.[6] Near the end of the schema was the treatment of papal primacy and infallibility, followed by denunciations of religious liberty, separation of Church and State, freedom of the press and speech, and so forth.

Now, the non-Liberal bishops had in common a desire to emphasize those doctrines that Liberalism challenged and to anathematize the contrary errors. This numerical majority seemed to think the best "silver bullet" defense against this hydra-like evil was simply to declare papal infallibility, for, after all, the pope could be trusted to condemn Liberalism: *Roma locuta, causa finita.* Apparently it did not occur to them that someone might come along and use the papacy itself as an advocate for Liberalism. So the Ultramontane enthusiasts campaigned to lift papal primacy and infallibility out of the long document and to address them alone; Pius IX concurred.[7] O'Malley notes that this effort was against the rules of the Council, causing critics to call it a "coup" (similar to what happened when the "European Alliance" circumvented the rules at Vatican II to take control of that Council).

Unlike Vatican I's first document *Dei Filius* on reason, faith, and the knowability of God, which had enjoyed either unanimous consent or nearly so, the primacy and infallibility document *Pastor Aeternus* met with fierce opposition. The so-called "minority" bishops who were opposed to the definition of papal infallibility numbered among them some of the most prestigious and learned bishops at that time.

O'Malley points out that much of the debate over the definition—other than the Liberal opposition and concerns over the "opportuneness" of its timing—focused on the problem that this infallibility would be viewed as being: (1) personal, (2) absolute, and (3) separate. Even among the bishops who supported infallibility, there was immense concern to clarify that the definition did *not* mean

---

6   Many bishops simply wanted to take the *Syllabus of Errors* and adapt it into definitions and canons. Imagine if that had happened!

7   O'Malley points out that had this not happened—and it very nearly didn't—the taking of Rome would have paused indefinitely the council's proceedings long before papal primacy and infallibility could have been discussed, much less voted on.

this charism was personal, absolute, and separate simply speaking. Bishop Karl Josef von Hefele (1809–1893) – an ecclesiastical historian – pointed out that even the *Tome of Leo* was examined and considered by the Council Fathers at Chalcedon before they approved it. That is, the Council Fathers did not, as a matter of first principle, hold that *if* they heard from Leo, *then* the matter was settled. Rather, they heard *what* Leo had to say, weighed it, and then hailed it as Catholic dogma.

In his *relatio*, Bishop Gasser explicitly addresses the three issues of personal, absolute, and separate.[8] He says that infallibility is personal in the sense that it attaches to each individual pontiff and not merely to the Roman See in general – rejecting the Gallican distinction between *sedes* and *sedens*. But it does not attach to all of his actions. It is not in any way absolute – that would be true only of God. Rather, it is limited in three crucial ways: by the subject, by the object, and by the act.[9] And it is not separate in the sense that the pope is isolated from the Church in defining, although his definitions are infallible *ex sese*, that is "of themselves."

Note how different this is from the boundless enthusiasm of the contemporary "apologists" of hyperpapalism, who brand themselves as critics of traditionalist Catholics and write them off as akin to Protestants or perhaps to the Eastern Orthodox. Seen historically, we can regard them as de Maistre-style papalists, insisting that the individual pope's authority is personal, absolute, and separate. Any concession that the pope's acts of teaching or governance are or could be flawed would constitute (for them) a falsification event for Catholicism. Obviously this is untrue.

DOES THE FORMULA OF HORMISDAS SUPPORT HYPERPAPALISM?

The so-called Formula of Hormisdas (which, when it was accepted by the Eastern bishops in 519, ended the first East-West "Acacian schism"), so far from lending support to these apologists as they

---

8 A *relatio* is an official explanation given at a council to clarify questions about a document before the final vote and promulgation take place. As such, the *relatio* represents the official and authoritative explanation of a conciliar document.
9 See *The Gift of Infallibility: The Official* Relatio *on Infallibility of Bishop Vincent Gasser at Vatican Council I*, trans. with commentary by Rev. James T. O'Connor (Boston, MA: St. Paul Editions, 1986), 45–46.

sometimes suppose,[10] in fact supports the stance of Bishop Hefele. The Formula runs thus:

> The first condition of salvation is to keep the norm of the true faith and in no way to deviate from the established doctrine of the Fathers. For it is impossible that the words of Our Lord Jesus Christ who said, "Thou art Peter and upon this rock I will build my Church" (Matt. 16:18), should not be verified. And their truth has been proven by the course of history, for in the apostolic see [Rome] the Catholic religion has always been kept unsullied.[11]

Let's examine this language. The condition of salvation is the "doctrine of the Fathers." Why not the doctrine "*of Peter*," if that's what they meant? The standard is that of the *Fathers*, not Peter as personal, absolute, and separate. If anything, this Formula teaches that the pope — as a condition for his own salvation (!) — must hold the doctrine of the Fathers. That is, the pope is not bound to keep his own personal doctrine as a condition for his personal salvation — which is what de Maistre would have us believe. How strange that this Formula could be held to mean that the pope defines *for himself* the condition for his own salvation, not to mention the condition for the salvation of all mankind! The Formula states, as a matter of first principle, that it is the "doctrine of the Fathers" — that's "Fathers" with an "S" at the end, not the "Holy Father" as personal, absolute, and separate — that is the condition for salvation. This Formula binds the See of Peter by the doctrine of the Fathers.

A parallel to the Formula can be found in the Sixth Ecumenical Council, which concluded that the letters between Patriarch Sergius and Pope Honorius "are entirely alien to the *apostolic teachings* and to the *decisions of the holy councils* and to *all the eminent holy Fathers* but instead follow the false teachings of the heretics," and in Pope Leo II, who repeated the condemnation of Pope Honorius as one who strayed from "the immaculate rule of the apostolic tradition."[12]

---

10 See, e.g., Michael Lofton, "That Time the Eastern Churches Accepted Papal Infallibility," *Catholic Answers*, June 6, 2022.

11 Robert B. Eno, *The Rise of the Papacy* (Eugene, OR: Wipf and Stock, 2008), 131.

12 See the excellent essay by Claudio Pierantoni, "The Need for Consistency between Magisterium and Tradition: Examples from History," in *Defending the Faith against Present Heresies*, ed. John R. T. Lamont and Claudio Pierantoni (Waterloo, ON: Arouca Press, 2020), 235–51.

What, then, of Peter? The Formula makes an historical observation. As of that time, the See of Peter had kept the doctrine of the Fathers, and this was testimony to the truth of the Petrine logion of Matthew 16:18. The Formula certainly states that the See of Peter is the See upon which the Church has been built. However, the Formula does not explicitly state that the See of Peter cannot err *in any way*, period. The Formula does *not* teach papal infallibility; what it *does* teach, explicitly, is that the pope himself must "keep" the "norm of the true faith" and the "established doctrine of the Fathers," even on pain of losing his own salvation.[13]

In its historical context, this document forced the Eastern bishops to "pledge their loyalty" to the See of Rome as the final arbiter and *not* the Emperor and his chosen bishop, the Patriarch of Constantinople, who had perpetrated the Acacian schism. In short, this document was designed to settle a debate about ecclesiastical power between the pope and the Eastern emperor. Eastern bishops were brought back into communion when they (1) confessed the Apostolic faith *of the Fathers* and (2) submitted to Roman primacy *contra* "imperial primacy" in matters of faith and morals.

INFLATING THE PAPAL PERSON

In the view of de Maistre-inspired enthusiasts, bishops do not receive their office from Christ, *only Peter does* — and Peter, in turn, grants the office to the bishops on his own authority. Thus the episcopal office is a grant of authority from the pope. In other words, the office of bishop itself is not of direct divine institution, having its own authority or power, but rather is an appendage of Petrine authority. Such a view in effect makes Peter *to be* the Church — personal, absolute, separate — and then the rest of the Church becomes

---

13   For clarity: the pope's obligation to teach only what has been handed down in the tradition is not an additional criterion for infallibility. While tempting, that would reduce the actual dogma to a triviality: we are all infallible anytime we faithfully pass on to others what we have received through the Tradition of the Church. There is, in any case, a positive moral obligation on the pope to teach only what he has received; and then there is a negative guarantee that God will intervene to prevent an erring pope from teaching his errors in a binding way. It has been argued by some theologians that if a pope were to attempt to enforce heresy, he would be self-deposed in the very act of doing so, falling away from the papacy. This point is discussed thoroughly in Arnaldo Xavier da Silveira, *Two Timely Issues: The New Mass and the Possibility of a Heretical Pope* (Spring Grove, PA: The Foundation for a Christian Civilization, 2022), 155-247.

an extension of him, almost as the Mystical Body emanates from Christ.[14] Simply to formulate this view, which was in fact propounded by Louis Veuillot (1813–1883), is to expose its absurdity.

For example, Veuillot adapted the text of the *Veni Sancte Spiritus* thus: "To Pius IX, Pontiff King, Father of the poor, Giver of gifts, Light of hearts, Send forth thy beam of heavenly light!" On October 8, 1869, he wrote in a newspaper column: "Just as the Father begets the Son and from them comes forth the Holy Spirit, so does the pope beget the bishops and likewise from them comes the Holy Spirit [in the church]."[15] Like de Maistre, Veuillot was a faithful counter-revolutionary on other matters.[16] But here, he clearly succumbed to exaggeration, with unfortunate consequences.

During Vatican I, a Dominican cardinal in a speech to the bishops said that the definition should include language saying that the pope, before defining a dogma, would consult the bishops, as was the custom—that is, the pope would deign to *learn* something before declaring a dogma infallibly. Pius IX was furious with him; he even made it a personal issue, calling the cardinal into his office and excoriating him, accusing him of taking the side of heretics and enemies of the Church. Pius reminded him: "You were *nothing* before me; I made you a cardinal." It was like a meeting with the Godfather! Loyalty is what matters.[17] The humiliated cardinal said he had spoken honestly according to his conscience and the Tradition he had received. Pius IX shouted at him: "I, *I* am the Tradition! I, *I* am the Church!" According to O'Malley, historians have examined the event and agree that it happened as recounted.[18]

---

14   On this view, the ancient axiom *ubi Petrus, ibi ecclesia* comes to be taken not in the modest sense in which it was originally meant—a statement of the unity of the bishops around their head, all equally successors of the Apostles, and all holding in common the Faith of the Fathers that is entrusted in a special way to Peter's safekeeping—but rather as a simple conflation of the terms: *Petrus est ecclesia*. To this error, Cardinal Cajetan replies ahead of time: "As for the axiom 'where the Pope is, there is the Church,' it holds when the Pope comports himself as Pope and chief of the Church; otherwise, the Church is not in him, nor is he in the Church" (Charles Journet, citing Cajetan, II-II, Q. 39, art. 1, no. 6; in Silveira, *Two Timely Issues*, 238–39).
15   O'Malley, *Vatican I*, 87.
16   See John C. Rao, "Louis Veuillot and Catholic 'Intransigence,'" in idem, *Catholic Christendom versus Revolutionary Disorder* (Waterloo, ON: Arouca Press, 2023), 26–53.
17   See Matthew Schmitz, "Pope Francis has followed a similar path to Pius IX," *Catholic Herald*, January 24, 2019.
18   See O'Malley, *Vatican I*, 212–13.

From this story and others, we can see that the "minority bishops" were hesitant or skeptical for good reason. In fairness, it should be noted that the same pope accepted the German bishops' letter to Bismarck giving a minimalist reading of the definition and insisting that the bishops are not "vicars of the pope" – language that would be taken up almost a hundred years later in *Lumen Gentium* 27, and subsequently undermined in practice by Pope Francis.[19] We may note here, too, that Blessed Pius IX, an incorrupt saint, may have been misinformed about the intentions of the cardinal, or perhaps he sinned in anger in this moment, as many saints have done on the arduous climb to sanctity. And, supported by the aforementioned Counter-Revolutionary Catholics, the Pontiff himself was the leader of the "Ninth Crusade."[20]

MAXIMALIST AND MINIMALIST READINGS

What, then, was the episcopal vote on the actual definition of papal infallibility?

It pleases: 451

It pleases, but with reservations: 62

It does not please: 88

Of 601 voting bishops, about 75% voted that it pleased *simpliciter*. But that also means about 25% did *not*. About 15% said the definition was seriously on the wrong track. About 10% said it was basically on the right track, but some serious clarifications and modifications needed to be made. Not exactly a clear affirmation of something supposedly handed down from the Apostles to the bishops as a dogma of the Fathers! Pius IX had claimed ten or fewer would dare to vote that it did *not* please. It is fair to say this vote, with 150 who did not accept the text as formulated, "triggered" him and many other enthusiasts. From then on, they completely shut

---

19 See chapters 4 and 14; cf. "Is the Pope the Vicar of Christ or CEO of Vatican, Inc.?," in Kwasniewski, *Hyperpapalism to Catholicism*, 2:266–71.

20 The "Ninth Crusade" was an army of international Catholic volunteers who defended the Papal States from the unjust invasion of revolutionary Italian forces (see Roberto de Mattei, "The 'Ninth Crusade' of the Papal Zouaves," *The Remnant*, April 1, 2020). John C. Rao notes how Bl. Pius IX seems to have had a weakness about his personal prestige that allowed him to be manipulated by the Liberals; for certain, like the Ultramontanes themselves, he had a blind spot in not anticipating undesirable effects of the Ultramontane definition. For a sympathetic portrait, see Roberto de Mattei, *Blessed Pius IX*, trans. John Laughland (Leominster: Gracewing, 2004).

out the minority bishops from having any further input on the final version. It would not substantively change thereafter.

The final language of the definition suggested a maximalist interpretation but was patient of a minimalist interpretation as well. The latter was given official sanction by the pope, inasmuch as Hefele, one of the last "holdouts," said he assented to it as interpreted by Austrian Bishop Joseph Fessler in *The True and False Infallibility of the Popes*. Since this proviso was accepted, the Hefele-Fessler "minimalist" interpretation at least remains on the table.[21] The definition still allows bishops to find fault with a pope who might dare to claim that (or to act as if) Tradition reduces to his cogitations and volitions.[22]

In the end, Vatican I left an opening for a conservative or traditional view of the pope. The pope speaks with the *Church*'s infallibility — not his own, as if it were a private possession.[23] He must use his office as dictated in the Word of God for the purpose of bringing souls to the knowledge of the truth and to salvation. If the pope is not doing that, he's not an agent or bearer of the Church's infallibility.

VATICAN I ESTABLISHES THE LIMITS OF THE PAPAL OFFICE

In its Dogmatic Constitution on the Catholic Faith (*Dei Filius*), Vatican I itself provides the best means for interpreting the same council's definition of papal primacy and infallibility. For here we learn that truth is objective, not subject to human volition; that truth is knowable by a person not primarily (much less exclusively) because the pope teaches it, but because man himself is capable of knowledge as a gift given him from God; that men can know many truths by

---

21   The 1875 English version of Fessler's work, with an excerpt from Pius IX's Brief of Approbation, is available at https://en.wikisource.org/wiki/The_True_and_the_False_Infallibility_of_the_Popes.

22   Fessler argues that the pope has the gift of infallibility only as "supreme teacher of truth revealed by God," and that in his role as "supreme legislator in ecclesiastical matters" he does not enjoy this gift. That is, the disciplinary laws he imposes need not be seen as infallibly true or good; rather, they would be guaranteed not to contradict revealed truth, and that is all.

23   Gasser argued that the charism of indefectibility lies in the body of the episcopacy, which includes the pope; moreover, he notes that a definition by council will always be more solemn than one by the pope alone, as if to suggest that the apostolic office is more evident here. The Oath against Modernism speaks of the charism of infallibility in the episcopacy, without mentioning the papacy separately.

the use of reason, even without divine revelation – including the twin truths that God exists and is knowable to us. We learn that Scripture itself is true, not because the pope says so but because it is true by its very nature, a divinely revealed gift from God so that men may know God. One may deduce, of necessity, that if such is true of Scripture, it is likewise true of the Word of God more broadly, written and unwritten, as well as of all truths necessary for salvation. Truth is truth of its very nature, not because the pope speaks it and thereby makes it true. Rather, the pope must *learn* truth in order to *give* truth, and he, like any man, cannot give what he does not have. While God certainly has the power to give the pope knowledge of anything, God has called the pope to learn by ordinary human means what has been handed on and what the pope is to hand on.

In *Dei Filius*, the ordinary use of faith and reason is dogmatized, so that the faithful, in their ordinary life as Catholics, need not have recourse to the pope in order to know the Faith.

By supplying us with definite teaching on the nature of divine revelation, truth, and human knowledge, on what development of doctrine is *and is not*,[24] and so forth, Vatican I establishes the foundations of the traditionalist view. It assures us that we have the tools to recognize and to deal with the present crisis; we are not helpless victims if a pope turns out to be an errant monarch. We do not need to defend papal errors and abuses, nor should we try. We can choose to fall silent, and sometimes this is the best way; but in accord with our ability and calling we can also throw lifelines to those who are being desperately and ruinously scandalized.

Paradoxically – or providentially – the First Vatican Council shows us how to deal with hyperpapalism, establishing clear delimitations for the exercise of the papacy. How much worse would our situation be if, believing in papal primacy and infallibility as all good Catholics have always done (with greater or lesser explicitness), we did not know that there were conditions for their exercise, or did not know of the several paths to certainty established for us by God? As it is, thanks to Vatican I, we can dismiss Pope Francis's errors quickly and easily with a clear conscience, because they have nothing to do with the papal office as set forth in the First Vatican Council.

---

24   See Serafino M. Lanzetta, *"Super Hanc Petram": The Pope and the Church at a Dramatic Moment in History* (Lincoln, NE: Os Justi Press, 2023), 93–105; 169–80.

4

Objections and Replies on *Pastor Aeternus*

T THE TERM "HYPERPAPALISM" REFERS TO AN extreme or exaggerated ultramontanism in the Church.[1] Naturally, critiques of this deviation are bound to precipitate objections. Here are two common ones, given in the very words of the individuals who sent them to me.

OBJECTION 1

Pastor Aeternus declares in no. 2:

> Both clergy and faithful, of whatever rite and dignity, both singly and collectively, are bound to submit to this [papal] power by the duty of hierarchical subordination and true obedience, and this not only in matters concerning faith and morals, but also in those which regard the discipline and government of the Church throughout the world.

I once believed that the qualifying "true" in the phrase "true obedience" excused my lack of obedience when I relied on tradition against papal orders, but I now believe that was a misreading. It is simply an emphatic adjective, to show that the obedience must be real and not dissimulated. This follows from paragraph 7, where we read:

> This gift of truth and never-failing faith was therefore divinely conferred on Peter and his successors in this See so that they might discharge their exalted office for the salvation of all, and so that the whole flock of Christ might be kept away by them from the poisonous food of error and be nourished with the sustenance of heavenly

---

1 For more background, see "My Journey from Ultramontanism to Catholicism," in Kwasniewski, *Hyperpapalism to Catholicism*, 1:1–27, and the anthology *Ultramontanism and Tradition: The Role of Church Authority in the Catholic Faith*, ed. Peter A. Kwasniewski (Lincoln, NE: Os Justi Press, 2024).

doctrine. Thus the tendency to schism is removed and the whole Church is preserved in unity, and, resting on its foundation, can stand firm against the gates of hell.

My Reply to Objection 1

The difficulty here is that paragraph 7 does not interpret itself. It does not say, for example, that a pope's personal opinions, or even his non-infallible magisterial acts, will always and necessarily redound to the good of the Church or better preserve its unity. This is one of the dubia of Vatican I.[2] I stand with John Henry Newman on this point: we should never say that a dogma requires *more* of us than the strictest interpretation of it requires. This is a principle of epistemic humility and realism.

Paragraph 7 is, on the face of it, a rather generic description of the way the office of Peter will be discharged if and when it is being discharged in the manner in which *Pastor Aeternus* describes – that is, in obedience to apostolic tradition, and in accord with natural law. Indeed, this is so obvious a condition that it is usually not even necessary to say it. It would be like saying "The pope is always to be obeyed (except when he commands something that must not be obeyed)." Examples come to mind: Francis on the death penalty or chapter 8 of *Amoris Laetitia*. In these cases, it is clear that Peter as this particular man, as this individual Christian, has departed from the Faith, and the protection of God consists here in preventing him from defining error or mandating sin. That's what I mean by a minimalist interpretation of infallibility and primacy. In subsequent chapters, I will cover many more examples, including liturgical ones.

I do not claim to have "the whole picture" in which all tensions and difficulties are resolved (does any one of us have such a picture?), but I do intend to keep in view the truths I *know* by faith and by reason, lest I sin against the light. Whatever understanding we have of the papacy, it cannot be one that compels us to reject what we know to be true by reason or by faith, or even to call it into question. We may question the adequacy of our own understanding, but we may not embrace contradiction or surrender the obvious meaning of the Church's dogmatic and moral teachings.

---

2   See Timothy Flanders, "The Dubia of Vatican One," *OnePeterFive*, September 15, 2022.

Pastor Aeternus gave us the limits of papal *infallibility*. It will be Francis – and also, to some degree, John XXIII, Paul VI, John Paul II, and Benedict XVI – who will provide the material for assessing the limits of papal *fallibility*.

OBJECTION 2

Recognizing the problems with our modern hyper-ultramontane papacy, I was not surprised to see your critical view of a maximalist reading of *Pastor Aeternus*. I was, however, surprised to see what looks like a certain enthusiasm for Gallicanism, since down that road went the fellow travelers of Ignaz von Döllinger into the schism of the Union of Utrecht and the disastrously modernist "Old Catholic" churches.

Given the tragedy of what happened to those who rejected the definition of the First Vatican Council, I see a likely outcome for any similar return to a more Gallican understanding of the papacy. Wouldn't this simply result in a further dissipation of the unity of the Faith by today's modernist bishops waging a diocese-by-diocese war on Tradition? How could such a view of papal primacy do anything other than aid the heresies of something like the German Synodal Way, cloaking itself in the guise of "local needs"?

I would be grateful if you could share your views on how to push back on the maximalist reading of *Pastor Aeternus* without dissolving the Latin church into division and schism, as occurred in 1870.

My Reply to Objection 2

From our limited human vantage, it's not at all clear how we shall pass safely through the torrent of evils that inundate us, or rather, what manner of deliverance Divine Providence has arranged in due season. I am convinced that Our Lord is trying to teach us three significant lessons, too easily forgotten: that we must (1) hold fast to what is certainly true as opposed to what is in any way dubious, and do so using the faith and reason He gave us; (2) throw all our cares on Him and put all our trust in Him as the ultimate Head of the Church, and (3) be able to live with difficulty, obscurity, and uncertainty – "to walk by faith, not by sight" as it were. We do not have to have a ready-made, implementable, neoscholastically approved solution in order to be able to see the problems themselves and to name them for what they are.

The enthusiasm for the Gallican mentality that you thought you saw in my overview of Vatican I was solely and simply for the Gallicans' traditional understanding of the rootedness of the Church in episcopacy and Tradition, as opposed to seeing Tradition and episcopacy as somehow radiating from Rome. The Old Catholics committed ecclesial suicide by refusing to accept the dogmatic definition when it was finally made. That is why, it seems to me, the minimalist interpretation is important: it shows that Vatican I does not *equal* hyperpapalism, *even if* the popes themselves, in their ordinary (fallible) magisterium and *obiter dicta*, have strongly encouraged this way of thinking.

The papal primacy is necessary for the unity of the Church. Therefore, with Roberto de Mattei, I fully believe that God will grant us a good pope someday, who will flex the muscles of his primacy to put an end both to the lavender mafia by deposing them from their offices and to the modernists by anathematizing their errors into oblivion. In so doing, he will, in fact, be doing what a pope is traditionally supposed to do: feed the flock and repel the wolves. Although this kind of intervention may look autocratic or heavy-handed, it is manifestly designed to rid the local churches of impediments to their own flourishing in episcopal integrity and liturgical tradition. In fact, every bishop has the divinely-given authority to do this sort of thing *right now in his own diocese.*[3]

LIGHT FROM GERMANY

As a "coda" to the preceding replies, I would like to discuss two documents that are far too little known.

The German Chancellor Bismarck, a bitter opponent of the Church, published a forceful denunciation of *Pastor Aeternus* in December 1874. (Who can blame him? His understanding was that the pope was now being said to be a God on earth... you know... the way Catholics have commonly treated popes since the writing of *Pastor Aeternus*. So his obtuseness is helpful, and moreso as time passes.) In January and February of 1875, the Catholic bishops of Germany composed a reply, which all of them signed:

---

3   See Timothy Flanders, "Every Bishop Must ACT NOW," *OnePeterFive*, March 10, 2023; cf. chapters 14 and 15.

Responses to the Circular Letter of Chancellor Bismarck on the Interpretation of the Constitution "Pastor Aeternus" of the First Vatican Council.

Why is this document not plastered all over the internet, given that its content was endorsed by Pius IX himself? As far as I can tell, only the tiniest snippets of it exist online. The full text is printed in Denzinger, 43rd ed., nos. 3112-16. Let's have a look at what the German bishops — back then, apparently a good lot — say in their *Responses*. First, they summarized the false doctrines that Bismarck (echoed by today's hyperpapalists) derived from his false reading of *Pastor Aeternus*:

> In virtue of these decisions, the pope has appropriated to himself the rights of the bishop in every diocese, and he has replaced the territorial power of the bishop with his own papal power. Episcopal jurisdiction has been absorbed by papal jurisdiction. The pope no longer exercises, as he did in the past, certain definite rights reserved to him alone, but now all the rights of the local bishops have passed into his hands. As a matter of principle, he has taken the place of each bishop, and it depends on him alone at any time with regard to practical matters to take the place of the bishop in negotiations with the civil government. Now the bishops are only his instruments, his functionaries without personal responsibility; regarding the civil government, they have become officials of a foreign sovereign; indeed, of a sovereign who, because of his infallibility, enjoys absolute authority, more than any absolute monarch in the world.

The bishops refute Bismarck's misconceptions with admirable clarity:

> All of these assertions are bereft of any foundation, and they contradict the wording and the meaning of the decisions of the Vatican Council, a meaning clearly and repeatedly expressed by the pope, by the bishops, and by the experts in Catholic studies.
>
> To be sure, according to these decisions the ecclesiastical jurisdiction of the pope is a *potestas suprema, ordinaria, et immediata* (supreme, ordinary, and immediate power) that was conferred on the pope by Jesus Christ, the Son of God, in the person of St Peter; this supreme authority

is exercised over the whole Church and therefore over every diocese and every individual believer. . . . [Yet] the decisions of the Vatican Council offer no basis for the assertion that the pope, because of them, has become an absolute master. . . .

First of all, the area covered by the ecclesiastical authority of the pope is essentially different from that over which the earthly power of a sovereign monarch extends, and Catholics do not challenge in any way the sovereignty of kings and princes over civil matters. But prescinding from that, the application of the term "absolute monarch" to the pope in reference to ecclesiastical affairs is not correct because he is subject to divine laws and is bound by the directives given by Christ for his Church. The pope cannot change the constitution given to the Church by her divine founder, as an earthly ruler can change the constitution of a State. In all essential points the constitution of the Church is based on divine directives, and therefore it is not subject to human arbitrariness.

Just as the papacy is of divine institution, so also is the episcopacy. The latter has its own rights and duties in virtue of having been instituted by God, and the pope has neither the right nor the power to change them. Therefore, a complete misunderstanding of the Vatican decisions is involved if one concludes from them that "episcopal jurisdiction has been absorbed by papal jurisdiction," that the pope, "as a matter of principle, has taken the place of each bishop," that the bishops are only "his instruments, his functionaries without personal responsibility". . . . With regard to the [last] assertion in particular, we must reject it categorically; it is certainly not the Catholic Church that has embraced the immoral and despotic principle that the command of a superior frees one unconditionally from all personal responsibility.

Finally, the opinion according to which the pope is "an absolute sovereign because of his infallibility" is based on a completely false understanding of the dogma of papal infallibility. As the Vatican Council has expressed the idea in clear and precise words and as the nature of the matter requires, infallibility is a characteristic of the papacy that refers exclusively to the supreme [i.e., extraordinary] Magisterium of the pope; it is coextensive with the area of the infallible Magisterium of the Church in general, and it is restricted to the contents of Holy Scripture and tradition and also to the dogmas previously defined by the teaching authority of the Church. Consequently, the teaching on infallibility has not changed in any way the popes' administrative actions.

Pope Pius IX—not just any pope, but, at the cost of belaboring the obvious, the very one who supported and promulgated *Pastor Aeternus*—addressed an Apostolic Letter *Mirabilis Illa Constantia* to the Bishops of Germany, dated March 4, 1875, in which he forthrightly endorsed their entire interpretation:

> You have increased the glory of the Church, venerable Brothers, because you have taken upon yourselves the task of reestablishing the true sense of the definitions of the Vatican Council that had been distorted by a widely distributed and deceptive circular letter. [You wrote in order that the aforesaid letter of Bismarck] might not deceive the faithful and, subverted by envy, provide a pretext for intrigue against the freedom of the election of a new pope. The clarity and solidity of your declaration is truly of such a nature that, since it leaves nothing more to desire, it can only give rise to Our deepest congratulations, unless the cunning voice of certain newspapers should require from Us an even stronger testimony. For, in order to put some power back into the letter that you rightly rejected, they tried to attack the credibility of your document by claiming that the doctrine of the conciliar definitions was toned down by you and therefore in no way corresponds to the intention of this Holy See. We therefore reject this cunning and calumnious insinuation and suggestion; for your declaration presents the truly Catholic understanding, which is that of the Holy Council and of this Holy See; you defended the teaching so skillfully and brilliantly with convincing and irrefutable arguments that it is obvious to any honest person that there is absolutely nothing in the attacked definitions that is new....[4]

---

4 Heinrich Denzinger, *Enchiridion symbolorum definitionum et declarationum de rebus fidei et morum*, 43rd edition, ed. Peter Hünermann, Robert Fastiggi, and Anne Englund Nash (San Francisco: Ignatius Press, 2012), no. 3117.

Many theological discussions when left to theologians (or would-be theologians on YouTube) tend in two opposite directions: either the esoterically complex, or the clumsily oversimplified. It is when a teaching "hits the streets," so to speak, that Catholics are forced to explain themselves in common language that harmonizes well, in the sight of the common man, with the preceding teaching of the Church. In this case, when the dogma of papal infallibility "hit the streets" in Europe, Chancellor Bismarck was shocked and confused by what he was hearing (no doubt from triumphalistic Ultramontanes). We see in the German bishops' *Responses* an explanation of the dogma in plain language that any man can understand, and we see in Pius IX's endorsement of it a conviction that this dogma represents nothing "new" (*novus*).

Obviously, not everyone who has studied papal history and ecclesiology would agree, without demur, that this definition of 1870 contained nothing new. That is a point on which one will have to consult a specialist on papal history and documentation.[5] Germane to our present situation, however, is the *limited* understanding of papal monarchy reflected in the above documents and the reaffirmation of the rights and duties of the *episcopacy* — matters of the most urgent relevance under the tyrannical regime of Pope Francis, which has violated in numerous ways the divinely-ordained constitution of the Church as regards relations between the pope and the bishops. A large number of bishops who, replying to a CDF survey to say they were quite content with how the policies of *Summorum Pontificum* were working out in their dioceses, were stymied. Bishops have been removed without cause or process.[6] Many bishops have been coerced into harming members of their presbyterate and their flocks who are customarily and virtuously attached to the traditional rites of the Church. Wicked men have been appointed as bishops or created cardinals, while virtuous men have been passed over. In every way, we are looking at another *saeculum obscurum* (the third such period in the history of the Church[7]) in which the papacy is blackened by its own misdeeds.

---

5 See, e.g., Erick Ybarra, *The Papacy: Revisiting the Debate Between Catholics and Orthodox* (Steubenville, OH: Emmaus Road, 2022).
6 See "Is the Pope the Vicar of Christ or CEO of Vatican, Inc.?," in Kwasniewski, *Hyperpapalism to Catholicism*, 2:266–71; cf. chapter 14 below.
7 See Timothy Flanders, "The Third Pornocracy: What We Are Living Through," *OnePeterFive*, December 16, 2021.

The solution is not to abandon the papacy or embrace neo-Gallicanism. The solution is to hold fast to the traditional Faith and to pray daily to the Lord for the spiritual, moral, cultural, and intellectual regeneration of the hierarchy of the Church and for the deliverance of His people by His strong right arm.

5

Custom and the Force of Law

S OMETHING MISSED BY CATHOLICS ENAM-
ored of the postconciliar mentality—that dangerous blend
of innovation and centralization—is that, in the past, *custom
was as good as law*. St Augustine could not have been clearer on this:
"The customs of God's people and the institutions of our ancestors
are to be considered as laws. And those who throw contempt on the
customs of the Church ought to be punished as those who disobey
the law of God."[1]

St Thomas Aquinas concurred: "When a law is changed, the
binding power of the law is diminished, in so far as custom is
abolished."[2] Cardinal Newman, in a sermon cited in Dom Alcuin
Reid's *The Organic Development of the Liturgy*, harks back even
to the apostolic age wherein Jewish custom was maintained in
many respects in order to ensure the Church's continuity with the
divinely-fostered devotion of Israel; indeed, a simple rejection of
ancestral worship would have been inconceivable. Even St Paul,
who opposed St Peter to his face over the integration of the Gentiles
into the Church, shaved his head in fulfillment of a vow of the kind
Jews would make, and he had St Timothy circumcised (Acts 18:18;
Acts 16:3). Referring to the role of ritual customs, Newman beautifully remarks: "Precious doctrines are strung, like jewels, upon
slender threads."[3]

These slender threads have been acknowledged and conserved
throughout the liturgical history of the Church. In places here
and there where some have tried to sever them, piety stood strong
against their destruction. History shows us clear precedents for bad
liturgical reforms corrected by subsequent authorities.

1. Cardinal Quiñones's radically new breviary – commissioned
by Clement VII in 1529, first released in 1535, and imprudently

---

1   *Ep. ad Casulan.* 36.
2   *Summa theologiae* I-II, Q. 97, art. 2.
3   The sermon in question is "Ceremonies of the Church," *Parochial and Plain
Sermons*, vol. 2, no. 7.

promulgated by Pope Paul III for private recitation in 1536 – was halted in its publication by Paul IV in 1558 and banned outright by St Pius V in 1568, over thirty years after its introduction.[4]

2. Urban VIII's 1631 meddling with the breviary in order to satisfy humanist admirers of classical Latin (among whom Urban himself could be counted) was never accepted by the monastic orders and was, after a very long time, quietly scuttled by (of all people) Paul VI, whose *Liturgia Horarum*, in one of its few positive moves, restored certain ancient hymn texts.[5]

3. The liturgical innovations promoted by the Synod of Pistoia in 1786, inspired in part by the liturgical innovations of the French church, were resisted – in a way akin to the way traditionalists today resist the reforms of the twentieth century – by Pope Pius VI in his bull *Auctorem Fidei*.[6] It is scandalous, to say the least, that church authorities of our time, so far from reiterating such pastorally helpful censures, have sided with the Pistoians against inherited tradition.

4. The "Bea psalter," named after Cardinal Augustin Bea, SJ, was a new and supposedly more "elegant" Latin version of the psalms that Pius XII introduced with the intention of having it displace the age-old translation by St Jerome that had been prayed by innumerable monks, nuns, and clerics. Critics said: "adauget latinitatem, minuit pietatem" (it increases Latinity but diminishes piety).[7] In spite of the immense worldwide admiration for Pius XII, this version of the psalter never caught on, and was dropped into oblivion by his successor John XXIII – who also, incidentally, celebrated the pre-55 Good Friday ceremonies instead of following Pius XII's "Solemn Afternoon Liturgical Action."

5. In the radical revision of Holy Week approved by Pius XII, the Easter Vigil prophecies were cut down from their ancient number of twelve to only four. By the time the scissors-and-paste committees of the Consilium were meeting in the mid-60s, it was a

---

4 See Pierre Batiffol, *History of the Roman Breviary*, trans. Atwell M. Y. Baylay (New York: Longmans, Green and Co., 1912), 181–203.

5 See Batiffol, 221–22; for further discussion, Kwasniewski, *Once and Future Roman Rite*, 201–3.

6 For a refutation of the frequent hyperpapalist abuse of this document, see Kwasniewski, *Hyperpapalism to Catholicism*, 1:84–90.

7 On the Bea psalter, see Yves Chiron, *Annibale Bugnini: Reformer of the Liturgy*, trans. John Pepino (Brooklyn, NY: Angelico Press, 2018), 37–39.

foregone conclusion that something like the ancient number of readings should be restored. Although the restoration was very imperfect, this was a candid admission that what a pope had approved about a decade before was untenable.[8]

Custom is an irreplaceable element of social life and has usually been respected as such by the entire hierarchy, including the popes. However, we have seen the development in the West of a bizarre "two-track" theory of liturgical law: while acknowledging the traditional view of custom, Catholics also appear to accept that the pope possesses a nearly unlimited authority to legislate on liturgical matters – even, it would seem, to abolish the most ancient or long-standing customs, if he so desires. How this is compatible with a healthy philosophical, theological, psychological, sociological, or legal understanding of the nature and role of custom is entirely beyond the purview of human reason.

Papal authority should be recognized and obeyed until and unless it despises, or acts contrary to, the objective liturgical tradition of the Church, in which case it may be ignored or disfavored due to its lack of prudence in undermining the strength of custom. Roman centralization, albeit not initially detrimental to the liturgical integrity of the Church – quite the opposite, it functioned as a conservative safeguard against its ruin, as we see with St Pius V – has inflated Rome's sense of control over the liturgical piety of her subjects and, most grievously, has decoupled papal authority from any sense of loyalty to other sources of law and the law-abiding spirit. Papal positivism may not be necessitated by ultramontanism, but undoubtedly it is enabled and encouraged by it.

Fr Louis Bouyer related the following in 1959: "After all (said an Englishman in a recent article), the supreme authority of the Church is not bound by anything and could freely give us an entirely new liturgy, answering to today's needs, without any further concern for the past."[9] If this is true, then we can clearly see the fuzzy thinking that paved the way for the Bugnini-Montini dyarchy. Fr Bouyer himself found the idea frankly preposterous.

---

8   See Gregory DiPippo, "A Few Notes on the Reform of the Readings of the Easter Vigil," *New Liturgical Movement*, May 15, 2020.
9   "The Word of God Lives in the Liturgy," in *The Liturgy and the Word of God* (Collegeville: Liturgical Press, 1959), 65.

Although Pope Benedict XVI assured us that the old Roman rite (but let us be honest: the only authentic Roman rite) had never been abrogated, advocates of absolute papal monarchy believe that it *could* be abrogated. The embedded irony of Paul VI's 1969 Apostolic Constitution *Missale Romanum* is that, in positivistically promulgating a liturgical book dissevered from organic development and driven by hypothetical pastoral expediency and speculative opinions, it thereby prevented any actual *liturgy* from being constituted, since, if anything is obvious from history, it is the fact that liturgy was never a mere *posited entity* and was never yoked to a momentary vision of temporal utility or academic theory.

(Mr. Praytell LaCroix is shifting and muttering over in the corner: "How silly of you to speak so favorably about the crusty old liturgy of the Tridentine church, for, as we all know, it was a terribly corrupted liturgy... God had taken His hands off the ecclesial wheel for those Dark Ages – for over a thousand years – before reasserting His Holy Spirit in the 1960s. And he did it through His Vicar on earth, the mouthpiece of the same Spirit – even as Francis is today! Henceforth, we can rest assured that God won't take his hands off the wheel again, or withdraw His Spirit as He did for most of Church history...")

In all seriousness, what a tremendous insult it is to the Holy Ghost – however sophistically the view may be argued by "liturgists" – to maintain that the Roman rite as constituted, lived, and transmitted over so many centuries by the piety of our ancestors could be rife with defects, errors, clericalism, inadequate ecclesiology, and could become an impediment to the Church's mission or the faithful's sanctification! That is the ultimate insult that can be aimed at Christ and His Church. Have we forgotten that these deadly ideas were dealt with by a dogmatic council of the Church, where, instead of masquerading as "pastoral expediency," they were simply known as "Protestantism"?

Beyond merely acknowledging the impiety of these ultramontane-positivist ventures of modern popes – whether Pius X's abandonment of the traditional Roman *cursus psalmorum*, Pius XII's revamping of Holy Week, Paul VI's library of new liturgical books, or nearly the sum-total of Francis's pontificate – are we able to say that these ventures are anything other than absurd? For as long as these acts of violent rupture are considered legitimate or licit, where does this leave the simultaneous reality and legal normativity of liturgical tradition? Does custom survive as anything more than an attenuated shadow of its former self?

Sacramental validity is the "low bar" demanded by the Church's indefectibility; and this indefectibility does not, strictly speaking, require anything more than that.[10] When traditionalists insist that the products of last century's Montinian tyranny are *valid*, we show more charity to our detractors than they do to us—and, incidentally, we show more faith in the Church—since *they* reject most of the Church's once-normative traditional practice and seek to prohibit us from continuing it, whereas *we* accept both it and the validity (but not the legitimacy) of the attempted supplantation. The pope's supreme legislative authority exists to protect the Church's dogma and liturgy, not to obfuscate, dilute, or shatter it. Manifestly, the Church's common good may be wounded by the reckless imprudence of specific exercises of papal prerogatives. While the Pauline Missal is not evil *per se*, that is, nothing actually false or blasphemous is stated in it or required by it, it is nevertheless abhorrent in how it wounds the Church peripherally and accidentally, through its discontinuities, ambiguities, omissions, and rubrical inadequacies. That is why a traditionalist cannot accept its legitimacy and will find its licitness to be at least questionable.[11]

While we acknowledge the primacy of organic *development*, what should we make of institutional *initiatives*, which may look like "seismic shifts," and how should these initiatives be evaluated? After all, there was a point when Christian Latin was sufficiently refined that the popes of the fourth century could successfully accomplish a transition from Greek to Latin—not to "adopt the vernacular" in a twentieth-century sense but to establish the new faith more firmly in the aristocratic and literary world of the evolving Christian Roman Empire.[12]

---

10   Here I take seriously Newman's principle that one should interpret ecclesial claims or demands in a minimal way, not a maximal way.
11   See chapter 21.
12   See my essay "Was Liturgical Latin Introduced As—and Because It Was—the Vernacular?," in *Illusions of Reform: Responses to Cavadini, Healy, and Weinandy in Defense of the Traditional Mass and the Faithful Who Attend It*, ed. Peter Kwasniewski (Lincoln, NE: Os Justi Press, 2023), 114–22.

Liturgical innovators will point to such precedents as evidence that "seismic shifts" may and should take place throughout Church history, but this view relies on a Newtonian notion of absolute space and time, in which all temporal periods of the Church are to be taken as equivalent to each other: there is no essential difference between the first, the fifth, the thirteenth, or the twentieth century as regards the right relationship between tradition and development, inheritance and innovation. That is why they can accuse the centuries between Trent and Vatican II of "immobilism": there *should* have been changes, they maintain, as occurred in earlier times, and the lack of those changes indicates that something had gone wrong.

As I have refuted this view at length in my book *The Once and Future Roman Rite*, I will make only a few remarks here. From her potent apostolic origins, the Church ascended like a rocket up to the summits of the Roman Empire, and grafted this Empire into Christ's Mystical Body. The early Church was graced with a special charism of effectiveness in preaching and miracle-working precisely to overcome the disadvantage of its small size and as-yet undeveloped culture. One of the young Church's charisms was the power to develop Christian liturgical rites, which experienced prodigious growth early on, and tapered off as the first millennium wore on, as they achieved their fullness of form. This, indeed, was in God's Providence: that later generations, in their admiration of earlier ones populated with saints, would humbly take what they received from them. Fixity of form is a natural outgrowth of the divine guidance of the Church.[13]

Much later on, the Church could have no possible need to radically alter those fixed forms; in that way, later centuries are *not* equivalent to earlier ones, and it is only under the influence of a dechristianized modern philosophy that one might believe them to be of the same status, or even believe that modern times will be in a position superior to ancient or medieval times when it comes to designing liturgical rites. In truth, the lowlier position of modernity together with the momentous *decline* the Church is suffering—an inversion of the ascent of antiquity—is a double

---

13   See my article "From Extemporaneity to Fixity of Form: The Grace of Liturgical Stability," *New Liturgical Movement*, October 11, 2021.

reason why modern Catholics have no business concocting new rites to insert haphazardly into our liturgical patrimony.

If we had not already lost the privilege of introducing new rites owing to the providential differentiation of times and seasons, we would have lost it thanks to the betrayal of Christendom by its own representatives.[14] Christendom's decadence, manifested above all in two World Wars and in the nearly universal triumph of the culture of death, so far from endowing churchmen with a right to "make their own contribution" to the liturgical treasury, deprives them of any moral authority to do so – particularly if their contribution consists in burying some of the treasure out of sight, pawning off the rest, and adding costume jewelry. Providence says to them, as it were: "Don't flatter yourself. You don't deserve to reform that which you are unwilling to venerate and unworthy to celebrate." The question of authentic institutional initiatives is immaterial for us today. How can we possibly develop the liturgy – much less initiate it! – when we are simultaneously all too busy repudiating the patrimony that gave it meaning?

The Liturgical Movement originally sought to replenish a Catholic spirit in attendees of the liturgy, in the hopes that a new-found appreciation of our traditional worship would remedy the no-doubt widespread situation of the Mass of the Ages appearing (because of countless sins, offenses, and negligences) as an empty routine, a box to check off. *It was not the liturgy that needed correction, but souls.*[15]

With this in mind, the positivism of Paul VI appears all the more sinister. At a time when decisive confrontation with widely welcomed modern errors and reaffirmation of the perennial value

---

14   By "new rites" I am referring to rites at the level of the Roman or the Byzantine, not minor additions like a "new rite of blessing" for an automobile when such a machine is new. See Kwasniewski, *From Benedict's Peace to Francis's War*, 224n3, concerning Pius XII's statement in *Mediator Dei* that "The Sovereign Pontiff alone enjoys the right . . . to introduce and approve new rites." It should also be noted that Pius V's *Quo Primum* nowhere uses the phrase "new rite," which, unfortunately, a poor but much-cited internet translation introduced when it split a long Latin sentence into shorter English sentences.

15   On the virtues and vices of the Liturgical Movement, see Peter Kwasniewski, *Noble Beauty, Transcendent Holiness: Why the Modern Age Needs the Mass of Ages* (Kettering, OH: Angelico Press, 2017), 89–133; *Reclaiming Our Roman Catholic Birthright: The Genius and Timeliness of the Traditional Latin Mass* (Brooklyn: Angelico Press, 2020), 48–53.

of tradition was most needed, the liturgical reform took the path of accommodation to the norms of a liberalized, decadent Christendom, already pickled in the brine of false modern philosophies. Is the Church and her sacramental life indefectible? Yes. But has much been omitted from the new rites that would serve as a tonic, a remedy, an antidote? Are vast swaths of the faithful being denied armor and weapons with which to combat the Evil One? Most regrettably so. If this were a price one would be willing to pay in order to shore up the pope's standing as an absolute monarch whose will is law, who can identify, shape, and break liturgical tradition as he pleases, it would be too high a price to pay for any reason whatsoever—too high, that is, for anyone still in possession of the twin powers of faith and reason. Such papolatry, being irrational and destructive, could not be of God.

Never can we despair. Christianity, in its cruciform beauty, contains always the promise of triumph over death. All the same, suffering and dying, however triumphant their issue, cannot but be painful. God, in His Providence, is permitting His Church to be crucified. Such torture the Church has endured many times, and from the concentration of faith engendered in those chaotic periods came her fiercest glories. Sacred Tradition asserts itself most of all in moments when the Mystical Body is under attack, either from without or from within. How satisfying to come out on the other end with the invincible Tradition of the Church fresh in hand, like a sword that was just waiting to be sharpened and wielded anew! It is not for us to know the times or the seasons which the Father hath put in His own power (Acts 1:7). It is our privilege to remain faithful to the deposit of faith and the treasury of Tradition we have inherited from the Church of all ages—from the saints, from the popes in their totality—and to defend it against anyone who pretends to be its lord and master.

6

Escaping Papal Absolutism[1]

MARTIN R. CEJKA: *One of your most recent books is the two-volume treatise* The Road from Hyperpapalism to Catholicism: Rethinking the Papacy in a Time of Ecclesial Disintegration. *Judging from the title, one could confuse it with a work by a liberal theologian or indeed a synodal reflection by Pope Francis himself. Yet your view reflects a different position entirely.*

PETER KWASNIEWSKI: Indeed, there is a superficial resemblance between those who today question a hypertrophism of the papacy and the liberals or progressives who try to find ways to get around uncomfortable, countercultural teachings, like those we find in *Humanae Vitae*.

But at a deeper level my concerns are exactly the opposite of theirs. As any Catholic ought to do, I gladly embrace *Humanae Vitae* because it is an authoritative judgment that reaffirms what the Catholic Church has always taught on the subject of the procreative finality of the nuptial act and the intrinsic evil of contraception. The pope here perfectly fulfills his role as the *remora* (in Newman's term), the "barrier" against harmful novelty or deviation from the deposit of the Faith. The liberals, on the other hand, wish to be freed from traditional teachings they no longer agree with. They are dissenters from Catholic tradition. Today's traditionalists are not dissenters, but rather, upholders of the perennial magisterium and practice of the Church, which is now under attack from the pope himself.

This is why I compare our situation to an autoimmune disease: the body is attacking itself. The head is attacking the members and, indeed, attacking the eternal head, Jesus Christ, as well as the entire line of vicars who have served in the capacity of head of the

---

1   This interview, conducted by Czech writer and journalist Martin R. Cejka, originally appeared in Czech on December 13 in *Hodie*, the online news service of the Prague-based magazine *Te Deum*, as well as in issue number 5 of the magazine of that title. The English version was published online at *The European Conservative* on January 15, 2023.

Church over the past 2,000 years. And that's why I also speak of "ecclesial disintegration." The Church will not actually disintegrate, in the sense of ceasing to exist; but there are centrifugal forces tearing apart the Church on earth. It is truly a dramatic time.

What exactly do you mean by "hyperpapalism"? Does it differ in any way from the already established term "papolatry," where a pope is perceived like a guru?

The trouble with the term "papolatry" is that, to some ears, it sounds excessively pejorative. After all, who really *worships* the pope? He isn't being put on a pedestal before which his courtiers kneel and burn incense. The term "hyperpapalism" strikes a different note – that of an exaggeration, a distortion, too much of a good thing. Papal authority is required for the coherence and continuity of the Church, for her visible unity, for her doctrinal safety; and yet it is currently being abused in a direction quite the contrary of its purpose. Healthy Catholics who know their Faith and live it, confronted with such a scandal, would simply criticize the abusive pope – respectfully, yes, and with prayers for him, but without "guilting" themselves into silence or, worse, thinking they ought to let themselves be abused. But "hyperpapalist" Catholics think (or pretend to think) that we must all simply change our minds with each new pope and move in whatever direction he says, without leaning on any other support for knowing the content of the Faith or the right way to live.

In connection with "hyperpapalism," you sometimes mention "ultramontanism," which has contributed to this distorted view of the papacy. But shouldn't we make a distinction between "ultramontanism" as a faithful defense of the papacy and "ultramontanism" as a view of the authority of the pope? In the latter case there are indeed writers who essentially see the pope as the embodiment of God's will. But I probably wouldn't attribute it to all ultramontanists.

I've been criticized by some people for using the term "ultramontanism" negatively. Well, let us not dispute too much about language. Looking over the mountains to what the pope of Rome is saying or doing can be a helpful shortcut in a period of revolutionary upheaval when everyone is confused and in need of a clear path forward, but it doesn't seem to be a good *normal* policy for Catholics always to be looking over their shoulder to find out what the pope is saying or doing – as if they had no access to the content or practice of the Faith otherwise.

For most people through most of Church history, the pope was a distant figure one never saw and about whom one heard little. He was there to do what only he could do, but most affairs were taken care of locally. This kind of subsidiarity and non-centralization is indeed a feature of a well-functioning social body. It seems to me that the increasing magnitude of the papacy in modern times, particularly from the middle of the nineteenth century onward, has caused a corresponding weakening in the episcopal body's pastoral care and doctrinal alertness, since it seemed the pope would "take care of" whatever needed to be done or said. The universal encyclical, a letter from the pope to all bishops or even to all mankind, replaced diocesan pastoral letters, interventions, and initiatives.

Notoriously, on account of increasing centralization, the relationship of the faithful and the clergy to the sacred liturgy was at risk of becoming external and superficial; there was a temptation to think of the liturgy as simply whatever the pope or the curia legislates: in other words, a pure legal positivism. Yet throughout Church history the faithful and the clergy were, on the contrary, deeply knowledgeable of and devoted to their traditional liturgical rites. The rites were as much a part of their lives as every other aspect of culture, woven into their family customs, arts and crafts, music and poetry, town celebrations of feasts and fasts. The rites of worship were their "daily bread," their profound source of identity, their main occupation. Seen from that angle, "ultramontanism" could have the appearance of a great *weakening* of Catholic identity, like a body in which the limbs are paralyzed but the head retains its functionality.

Postconciliar times have revived discussions not only about the authority of the pope, but also about the extent of his infallibility. These questions used to be asked by people associated with the Catholic traditionalist movement but more and more voices from the so-called conservatives are joining the debate under Pope Francis. But does this debate have any meaning? Is it any good?

It is urgently necessary to have these discussions now, for the simple reason that papal infallibility *does* have clearly defined limits. Vatican I by no means taught that the pope was an absolute monarch whose will is law. When the German bishops wrote a clarification for Bismarck saying that bishops remain true authorities and that the pope is bound by divine law and natural law, etc., Pope Pius IX himself endorsed their letter![2]

The tradition and history of the Church show that popes can err on points of doctrine (the condemnation of Honorius and the resistance to John XXII are notable in this respect, but there are other examples too); that they can commit the worst imprudences; that the discipline they establish may be dubious and worthy of criticism. It is insane to think that the papacy automatically wraps a mantle of inerrancy and impeccability around papal acts. His word is not the Word of God, and his acts are not simply equatable with the acts of Christ. Rather, he is given the grace of office to teach true doctrine and to promote the common good of the Church – but he must *cooperate* with this grace and collaborate well with others. He is no automaton, like an AI system that cranks out answers and policies. A papal saint is one who cooperates to a heroic degree with God's grace, and a bad pope is one who limps along on his own.

Currently we have one of the worst popes ever to have reigned in the series of 266 popes of the Catholic Church. His pontificate has been an unending series of clerical and financial scandals, doctrinal chaos, globalist-environmentalist collusion, ecumenical-interreligious error, and ecclesiological rupture in the area of liturgy. I truly believe that the Bergoglian pontificate will go down in history as a low-water mark of the Catholic Church. That is what volume 2 of my work *The Road from Hyperpapalism to Catholicism* documents in painful but necessary detail. Volume 1, on the contrary, lays the groundwork for a genuinely Catholic appreciation of the papacy: what it is, what it is for, what its limits are, and how we are to respond, spiritually and theologically, to times of tempest.

How is it possible that theologians are still asking questions concerning papal infallibility? Wasn't the problem sufficiently resolved by the First Vatican Council?

---

2   See chapter 4.

The difficulty is not so much with Vatican I as it is with the "spirit of Vatican I," that is, the popular conception of what was taught on infallibility, which does not match the more careful articulation of the doctrine at the council, in Gasser's *relatio*, in the German bishops' letter, and in subsequent theological discussion. On this point, I would highly recommend the work of Dr John P. Joy, whose book *Disputed Questions on Papal Infallibility* is a succinct but profound and penetrating treatment of the subject. He brings more clarity to it than anyone else I have ever read. After reading Joy, one can experience a tremendous peace of soul, knowing that the Church's teaching, though it transcends reason, does not contradict reason – and even better, does not contradict the "supernatural common sense" known as the *sensus fidei fidelium*.

Do you see any dangers on the "road from hyperpapalism to Catholicism"? Isn't there a danger that the papacy might come to be seen by its downsizers as just a kind of honorary office, or that such Catholics might slide into Eastern Orthodoxy or even Protestantism? How should we avoid these pitfalls?

One challenge we are facing today, I would say, is a relative lack of awareness that the Catholic Faith is handed down through many channels and in many forms. It is not the pope's personal possession; it is the common heritage of the Church and therefore of every baptized man, woman, and child.

For example, hundreds of catechisms over the centuries bear witness to the universal ordinary magisterium, which is infallible. Sacred Scripture, though subject to magisterial interpretation, is the inspired and inerrant Word of God, and in many cases its plain meaning – e.g., its condemnation of adultery and homosexuality – establishes the unchanging and unchangeable Faith of the Church. The consensus of the Church Fathers, where it exists, is also considered a safe sign of true doctrine. The twenty ecumenical councils prior to Vatican I offer us *de fide* dogmas and solemn anathemas. The popes themselves have left us with precious, lucid, repeated teaching on many important matters. All these things *determine* what a given pope may do or teach, and what he may *not* do or teach. This is not Protestantism (*sola scriptura*) or Orthodoxy (*sola traditione*); it is instantly recognizable as the symphonic and self-consistent vision of Catholicism.[3]

There is, of course, the danger that Catholics will become so impatient with a bad pope or bad bishops that they will be tempted to "break free" from the institution and try, somehow, to set up a "safe place" far away from this corrupt hierarchy. But that is quite impossible to do. We can be zealous critics of what has gone wrong, but we must remain in union with the pope and the bishops, at least to the extent of accepting what they do and teach that is in harmony with the Faith or not obviously in disharmony with it. It's like being a member of a family in which one has to keep a certain distance from some relatives, without, as it were, disowning them. Not an easy situation, and one sometimes feels these days as if one is walking on a tightrope. But that is our challenge, given to us by Divine Providence, and we cannot either contradict our reason or abandon our love for Holy Mother Church. We have to keep living the Catholic life of prayer, sacraments, and good works, even when we are legitimately at odds with or scandalized by the hierarchy.

In saying this, I do not mean to say that there would not be some situations where a certain underground existence may be practically necessary, but this is a last resort and a temporary expedient. We are always praying and working for a normal, above-ground solution in every case. Traditionalism does not seek a new Church — that would be Protestantism — but a cleansing and renewal, on earth, of the one and only Catholic Church there is.[4] We are interested in restoring what has crumbled and faded, not in bulldozing the structure or whitewashing it, as the revolutionaries of (and after) Vatican II sought to do. We can see the deadly results of their theological and liturgical iconoclasm everywhere, and we oppose it categorically and ceaselessly.

Finally, let me ask you for a few words of advice for our readers.

In my view, sincere and earnest Catholics must above all hold fast to the Faith as it was always taught and lived prior to the time of great confusion that descended on the Church during and after

---

3   See chapters 1 and 2.
4   See my article "Are Traditionalists Guilty of 'Private Judgment' Over the Popes?," *OnePeterFive*, December 22, 2021.

the last ecumenical council. Nothing in our Faith tells us that we cannot have a wicked pope, and we know that the pope's non-infallible teaching is, by definition, fallible – that is, capable of being in error. If the constant teaching and practice of the Church *prior* to the Council – the cumulative witness of so many liturgical rites, councils, popes, catechisms, and saints – was wrong, then the claims of the Church herself are destroyed. That conclusion is unacceptable. Tradition always takes precedence over the present and the future; it is and has always been the guiding light for Catholics. In times of confusion, we take refuge in what is stable, established, approved, certain, and known to be good. This is the essence of the traditionalist position; it is no more than supernatural common sense.

It is a privilege to be alive at this time, carrying the torch of tradition through the darkness. Those who are seeking the light will see it, rejoice in it, and follow it. They will be the remnant God uses to reestablish His kingdom, if indeed He wishes it to flourish again before the Parousia.

7

The Common Good as the Basis of Authority and Obedience

ᛗOST CONVERSATIONS AMONG CATHOLICS about church affairs come around, sooner or later, to the question of "who's in charge" and "who must obey." We have inherited an impoverished framework of discussion, one in which the only poles are power and submission. This is rather like trying to evaluate great paintings with only black and white photos, or trying to understand the art of sculpture on the basis of two-dimensional images. In fact, it's worse: it is a totally inadequate approach that makes a caricature of both godly power and righteous submission.

We cannot understand a hierarchical structure unless we apprehend clearly the relationship between authority and the common good, and how this relationship, in turn, illuminates the virtue of obedience. Although I have written about these matters in *True Obedience in the Church: A Guide to Discernment in Challenging Times*, I will develop the ideas further in this chapter.[1] A note on terminology: the word "authority" is typically used in two related senses, and I shall use it in both: (1) someone who exercises authority, as in "this law was issued by the authority in charge of the territory," and (2) the basis on which, or the title by which, he exercises it: "By what authority do you issue that law?"

WHAT IS A COMMON GOOD?

Authority exists whenever there is a society of persons who together share goods that need to be fostered and protected. We call such shared goods "common." This requires a bit of explanation.

---

1 I also recommend P. Edmund Waldstein's lecture "The Primacy of the Common Good," published on June 19, 2023 at *The Josias* website.

When we think of good things, we tend first to think about good *stuff*, like food and drink, that are obviously good for us (as long as it's at the right time, in the right manner, in the right amount, etc.). Material or sensible things that suit us as animals are truly good things. But they are not the best kind of good things. Far better are goods that relate people to one another, being good for many people at the same time without being diminished or divided. That's what we call a *common* good.

Private goods—all material goods can be called by this name— get used up or removed from circulation when they are possessed. When a cake is divided up into pieces, each of us may get a piece (if we're lucky), but only I can eat my piece and you yours. When I am wearing a certain piece of clothing, no one else can wear it simultaneously. Private property, though it can be put to a hospitable and charitable use, is limited in this way: by right and in practice, it is not equally everybody's to use, and it is diminished or worn out by use. Anything private, in other words, is limited in its reach, and may suffer loss from use.

A truly common good, on the other hand, can be shared simultaneously by many, perfecting them all. The peace of a family and the just ordering of a society are goods like this, since the more such a good exists, the more we all share in it, without its diminishment. Truth is a common good: if two people know the Pythagorean theorem, each of them possesses it completely and their intellects are perfected by it; now they can discuss it and make further discoveries from it.

We could also say that the beauty of great works of music, such as a Mass setting by Palestrina or a symphony by Beethoven, although it has to be brought into existence at a particular moment by a live performance or by the playing of a recording, is nevertheless something that many can share in simultaneously, delighting together in its loveliness, and possessing it in their souls: one and the same good, not only *not* diminished by the sharing, but better understood and appreciated as more and more enjoy it and ponder it.

For these reasons, the common good is *better* than the private good—that is to say, it is better even for the individual than any merely individual good that is consumed, limited, or worn out by use. This is an important point because it means that it will always be unreasonable to choose the merely individual good to the detriment of the common good. As animals, we need food and drink more than we need truth or beauty; but as rational animals, we are made for truth and beauty, and we will suffer a far worse kind of malnourishment and starvation if we neglect them, or if we were to put food and drink habitually ahead of them.

When the two come into conflict – if we are forced to choose between a private good and a common good – normally we should choose the common good, as being better for us, better for everyone, and, in fact, as Aristotle says, "more divine," more like God who is the Good itself, infinitely knowable, shareable, and enjoyable.[2]

LITURGICAL WORSHIP AS A COMMON GOOD

In heaven, all of the blessed angels and saints participate in the happiness of God, but He is certainly not diminished by that, as a pie is diminished by being shared; on the contrary, His glory is augmented, multiplied by as many spirits or souls as enjoy Him. God is "glorified in His saints," as Scripture teaches (2 Thess 1:10); the joy of each is enhanced by the mutual knowledge that this joy is possessed by many simultaneously. We know this already from our everyday experience: a really successful party is one in which all the individuals not only are enjoying themselves, but also know that the others are enjoying themselves too!

Worshiping Almighty God in church is another example of a common good, because, unlike with that apple pie or chocolate cake, which dwindles and eventually disappears as more people have a go at it, the worship of God is not diminished by an increasing number of worshipers; on the contrary, the more numerous are the faithful engaged in adoration, the more God is glorified and souls are sanctified. It follows that the better a liturgy disposes the faithful to adoration, the more it contributes to the common good of the Church. Indeed, the very fact that liturgy is inherently a public or social activity indicates that it is not, by nature, a private good. It is, to be precise, the action of Jesus Christ the High Priest,

---

2   "To secure and preserve the good of the city appears to be something greater and more complete [than to do so for an individual]: the good of the individual by himself is certainly desirable enough, but that of a nation and of cities is nobler and more divine." Aristotle, *Nicomachean Ethics*, Bk. 1, ch. 2, 1094b8-11, trans. Robert C. Bartlett and Susan D. Collins (Chicago: University of Chicago Press, 2011), 3.

who, as God, is the common good of the Church simply speaking.[3]

Liturgical worship is directly concerned with God, who is the greatest of all common goods; it is founded upon revealed truth, which is also inherently a common good; and it distributes grace, which, while it is an individual good as partitioned to you or to me, has a single infinite source and no upper limit. The best imaginable situation would be one in which *all* of mankind is worshiping God: in this case the good that He is would be most widely shared, and we would all benefit from that sharing. For these reasons, reducing or limiting or abolishing a form of divine worship legitimate in itself and fruitful to souls can *never* be a rightful exercise of ecclesiastical authority.[4] I will come back to this point later in the chapter.

AUTHORITY'S STRICT RELATIONSHIP WITH THE COMMON GOOD

Having explained what a common good is, we now need to turn to what authority is. If, per impossibile, there were only one person existing in the world, there could be no authority. Sure, you could say that such a man is "king over himself," but this is a metaphorical way of speaking, inasmuch as there's a certain plurality even in an individual: reason should rule over passion, the soul over the body. But properly speaking, ruling and being ruled presuppose multiplicity of persons, one of whom (or a few of whom) are rulers while the rest are subjects.

The ruler doesn't exist for his own sake, as if he's simply *there* without any justification for being there and for commanding obedience. The ruler exists *in order to* foster and protect the common good of the society over which he is placed. The common good, in other words, not only gives the rationale for any authority's existence, but also, and for the same reason, places limits on what he may or may not do.

If a ruler is there to promote the good of his people – their peace, their economic justice, their virtuous social life, their access to

---

3 St Thomas Aquinas says more: the common good of the entire universe is found in Christ. See *Super I ad Cor.*, cap. 12, lect. 3.

4 As Joseph Shaw writes: "Any liturgical form that enjoys a place in the life of the Church is justified in terms of how it contributes to the Church's mission of saving souls and glorifying God. If it brings people to faith, and strengthens and sustains those already there, then there can be no objection to it" (*Sacred and Great: A Brief Introduction to the Traditional Latin Mass* [Lincoln, NE: Os Justi Press, 2023], 67).

natural and divine truth – then to the extent that he wars against the good of his people, his rulership lacks authority, or, to put it more simply, to that extent or in that regard, he isn't a ruler but a tyrant, an *abuser* of authority. That doesn't (necessarily) mean he ceases to be a ruler altogether, but it does mean that he is acting "*ultra vires*," beyond his powers, at odds with the nature of his office. He is like a teacher who teaches errors rather than truth; such a person is not a teacher, properly speaking, but a corrupter of minds. Or like a policeman who beats up citizens rather than protecting them; such a one isn't a law-enforcement officer but a lawbreaking rebel whose badge testifies against him.

Another way of seeing this truth is to remember why we say that a ruler has or occupies or exercises an "office." The word *office* comes from the Latin *officium*, which means duty, responsibility, obligation, service. Having an office means exercising a duty or a responsibility. And what is that duty or responsibility? Quite simply, to foster and defend the common good.

I hammer on this point because it is the only correct way to understand authority. If you bracket the question of the good of the society or more specifically the good of its members, you will end up with an absolutist or positivistic conception of authority, where it seems to exist "for its own sake," barking out commands and imposing burdens. That is a caricature of authority and in fact tends to tarnish its reputation and multiply resentments. The worst enemies of authority are the ones who refuse to be tethered to the good or goods their authority is meant to serve, who hide behind the noble shield of office in order to promote private agendas contrary to it.

What I am arguing here is by no means the esoteric brainchild of traditionalists. John Paul II's *Catechism of the Catholic Church* teaches exactly this doctrine: "Authority is exercised legitimately only when it seeks the common good of the group concerned and if it employs morally licit means to attain it."[5] Pope Benedict XVI stated in one of his homilies: "The exercise of authority, at every level, must be lived as a service to justice and charity, in the constant search for the common good."[6]

---

5 CCC 1903.
6 Benedict XVI, General Audience on St. Elizabeth of Hungary, St. Peter's Square, October 20, 2010. Compare what he says in the encyclical *Caritas in Veritate* (no. 3): "The more we strive to secure a common good corresponding to the real needs of our neighbors, the more effectively we love them. Every Christian

HOW OBEDIENCE IS DETERMINED
BY THE COMMON GOOD

Now that we have this fundamental principle down – namely, that authority exists to foster and defend the common good of the society over which it is placed – we can turn to the virtue of obedience. For, as St Thomas Aquinas explains, every subject has an obligation to obey his ruler, his superior, in precisely those matters to which the superior's authority extends. In other words, the subject should obey for the same reason the ruler should rule: the common good.

Giving my obedience is the way in which I cooperate with the ruler in pursuing that common good. Since this good will not automatically take care of itself if everyone goes his merry own way, and since the good is vulnerable to internal and external enemies, the ruler must act on its behalf and the subject must obey, also on its behalf. In short, the common good is not only the reason why authority exists, but also the reason why *obedience* exists: it makes obedience obligatory and virtuous, while placing limits on who should be obeyed and under what circumstances.

The sphere of an authority's power is the common good of the society over which he is placed. Thus, the sphere of a subject's obedience is the same common good, looked at this time from the side of one who is enjoying the benefit of it, and who is beholden to the authority for its defense and promotion. The sphere of obedience, in other words, is limited, just as authority is limited, and for the same reason: it is virtuous to obey when we are obeying for the sake of the good of our society.

Normally we do not need to think about this very much. Most of the time, authorities are dealing with minor matters or matters that do not seriously inconvenience law-abiding subjects, and we should, and usually do, give legitimate authorities the benefit of the doubt by assuming they are well-intentioned and sincerely working for the common good. However, if and when it becomes apparent that an authority is grievously failing to serve the common good, or even attacking it outright, then we must be on our guard and

---

[that includes the pope! – PK] is called to practice this charity, in a manner corresponding to his vocation. . . . This is the institutional path – we might also call it the political path – of charity."

be prepared to withhold obedience. After all, we too have an obligation toward the common good, and – depending on our position and our opportunities for action – if we allow it to be assaulted or undermined, we may become guilty of sins of complicity, negligence, cowardice, injustice, and disordered charity.

Let us not forget, too, that any and every authority belongs to a hierarchy of authority culminating in the supreme ruler and universal common good, God Himself. This is why any ruler who sets himself against God or the law of God is, to that extent, detaching his subjects from obedience to him.

EXAMPLES OF "DISOBEDIENCE" FOR THE SAKE OF OBEDIENCE

Let me offer some examples for clarity.

If the father of a family regularly came home in a drunken rage and threatened the lives of his children, the wife, even though she acknowledges his God-given authority as head of the family, would need to take steps to protect herself and her children from him. She would take such steps for the sake of the very good of the family that the father has a solemn obligation to foster. In removing herself and her family from harm's way, she is in fact honoring the office of the father and the good entrusted to him.

Another example: If the president of a country ordered the military to open fire on citizens because they would not support his hare-brained ideas, the citizens should resist him, because he is turning against the citizens he is empowered to serve.

A third example: If an abbot of a monastery canceled the Divine Office in order to free up time for playing golf, the monks should respectfully refuse to go along with this policy because it is directly opposed to the reason why he is the abbot and why they are there, which is to offer God the sacrifice of praise: "Let nothing be preferred to the work of God," as St Benedict says in his *Rule*.

In such cases, although one *might* say that the wife, the citizen, the monk is "disobeying" his superior, it would be more accurate to say that they are refusing to be obedient to a ruler who has forfeited the right to be obeyed in this matter. Materially it *looks like* disobedience, but it is actually obedience to a higher law that governs both ruler and ruled.

60

A UNIVERSAL ACCOUNT

The foregoing account is true of *all* authority – including that of the bishops of the Catholic Church. The episcopacy does not exist in an alternate universe governed by a different divine law and a different natural law. It, too, does not exist for its own sake, as a self-perpetuating bureaucracy. It exists for the common good of the Church – that is its *raison d'être*. That is also why bishops can be judged to be unfaithful and wicked servants: when (and to the extent that) they act contrary to their office, to that extent they are not ruling in Christ's name but in their own (or, perhaps, in that of a secular lord or even an infernal lord).

We sometimes allow ourselves to be dazzled by ecclesiastical splendors, but any and every structure of authority works essentially the same way. Only God's authority is absolutely incapable of swerving from justice and therefore absolutely immune to any legitimate protest or resistance on the part of the creature. No human authority, however exalted – even the locus of supreme authority in the Church on earth, the papacy – could be incapable and immune in this way.

THE POPE AND THE CHURCH'S COMMON GOOD

Is it possible for a pope to act against the common good of the Church? Has a pope ever abused his authority and has he ever been resisted for that reason? The answer to these questions is yes, as Roberto de Mattei demonstrates in his book *Love for the Papacy and Filial Resistance to the Pope in the History of the Church*. There, he talks about popes who caused harm to the Church in one way or another, such as Liberius (352–366), Vigilius (537–555), Honorius I (625–638), Stephen VII (896–897), John XII (955–964), Benedict IX (1032–1044, 1045, 1047–1048), Paschal II (1099–1118), John XXII (1316–1334), Innocent VIII (1484–1492), Alexander VI (1492–1503), Clement VII (1523–34), Paul III (1534–1549), Urban VIII (1623–1644), and Pius VII (1800–1823). That list includes popes from the fourth, sixth, seventh, ninth, tenth, eleventh, twelfth, fourteenth, fifteenth, sixteenth, and seventeenth centuries. Other candidates could be considered for inclusion, and it would be like shooting fish in a barrel to add examples of abuses of authority from the past hundred years – and that's not even touching the past ten years, which have quintupled the bimillennial registry.

In a stunning document read at the Diet of Nuremberg in 1523, Pope Adrian VI admitted that a corrupt papacy and priesthood were largely responsible for the rotten state of the Church at that time. He wrote:

> We know well that for many years things deserving of abhorrence have gathered round the Holy See; sacred things have been misused, ordinances transgressed, so that in everything there has been change for the worse. Thus it is not surprising that the malady has crept down from the head to the members, from the popes to the hierarchy. . . . Therefore . . . we shall use all diligence to reform before all things the Roman Curia, whence, perhaps, all these evils have had their origin; thus healing will begin at the source of sickness. We deem this to be all the more our duty, as the whole world is longing for such reform. . . . We desire to wield our power not as seeking dominion or means for enriching our kindred, but in order to restore to Christ's bride, the Church, her former beauty, to give help to the oppressed, to uplift men of virtue and learning, above all, to do all that beseems a good shepherd and a successor of the blessed Peter. Yet let no man wonder if we do not remove all abuses at one blow; for the malady is deeply rooted and takes many forms.[7]

What an outstanding example of honesty and humility in a Roman Pontiff unafraid to admit the source and magnitude of the evils threatening the Church's common good in that Renaissance era!

UNFORGETTING FORGOTTEN ADVISORIES AND EXAMPLES

Many great theologians and canonists have given serious attention to the possibility of papal misgovernance and have clearly articulated how the faithful may or should respond. The great Dominican Sylvester Prierias (1456–1523) reasoned as follows:

> He [the pope] does not have the power to destroy; therefore, if there is evidence that he is doing it, it is licit to resist him. . . . If the pope destroys the Church by his orders and acts, he can be resisted and the execution of

---

7 Roberto de Mattei, *Love for the Papacy and Filial Resistance to the Pope in the History of the Church* (Brooklyn, NY: Angelico Press, 2019), 57–58.

his mandate prevented. The right of open resistance to prelates' abuse of authority stems also from natural law.[8]

In a similar way, Thomas Cardinal Cajetan (1469–1534) writes: "You must resist, to his face, a pope who is openly tearing the Church apart." Francisco de Vitoria (1483–1546) agrees: "If the pope by his orders and his acts destroys the Church, one can resist him and impede the execution of his commands." St Robert Bellarmine (1542–1621) elaborates: "As it is lawful to resist the pope, if he assaulted a man's person, so it is lawful to resist him, if he assaulted souls, or troubled the state, and much more if he strove to destroy the Church. It is lawful, I say, to resist him, by not doing what he commands, and hindering the execution of his will." Fellow Jesuit Francisco Suárez (1548–1617) takes this view even further: "If the pope lays down an order contrary to right customs one does not have to obey him; if he tries to do something manifestly opposed to justice and to the common good, it would be licit to resist him."

The saintly English prelate Robert Grosseteste (1175–1253), bishop of Lincoln and "one of the most learned men of the Middle Ages,"[9] had the courage to put this constant teaching into practice. The pope at the time, Innocent IV, had, with a perfectly legal instrument, appointed his Italian nephew to a vacant canonry at Lincoln cathedral—in short, the pope wanted to siphon off money for the pockets of his relative. A classic case of nepotism. Grosseteste would have none of it, writing to the pope:

> No faithful subject of the Holy See . . . can submit to mandates, precepts, or any other demonstrations of this kind, no, not even if the authors were the most high body of angels. He must needs repudiate them and rebel against them with all his strength. Because of the obedience by which I am bound, and of my love of my union with the Holy See in the Body of Christ, as an obedient son I disobey, I contradict, I rebel. . . . [T]he Apostolic See in its holiness cannot destroy, it can only build. This is what the plenitude of power means; it can do all things to edification. But these so-called provisions do not build up, they destroy.

---

8   This and the following quotations are from Paul Casey, "Can a Catholic Ever Disobey a Pope?," *OnePeterFive*, July 17, 2020.
9   Ibid.

The historian W. A. Pantin explains the significance of Grosse-teste's argument:

> Since the *plenitudo potestatis* [the pope's plenary jurisdic-tional power] exists for the purpose of edification and not of destruction, any act which tends to the destruction or the ruin of souls cannot be a genuine exercise of the *plen-itudo potestatis*. . . . If the pope, or anyone else, should command anything contrary to the Divine Law, then it will be wrong to obey, and in the last resort, while pro-testing one's loyalty, one must refuse to obey.[10]

Regarding the principle enunciated in 2 Corinthians 10:8, Ludwig Ott writes: "As the supreme *lawgiver* of the Church, the pope is not legally bound by ecclesiastical decisions and usages, but by divine law alone. This demands that the papal power, in consonance with its purpose, should be employed for the building-up of the Mysti-cal Body of Christ, not for its destruction (2 Cor 10:8). The divine law, therefore, is an efficacious brake on arbitrariness."[11] The key principle is that papal authority was bestowed *for a purpose*, and it must be used in consonance with that purpose. Using papal power to damage the Church rather than to build it up—for example, by damaging the customary worship-life of the faithful or the ecclesias-tical monuments on which they rely as aids—is a perversion of why the papacy exists to begin with. It could be called a "performative contradiction," like using speech to tell lies, or using the generative faculties in a way contrary to generation. With justice we could call such a use of papal authority mendacious and contraceptive.

---

10 William Abel Pantin, "Grosseteste's Relations with the Papacy and the Crown," in *Robert Grosseteste, Scholar and Bishop*, ed. D. A. Callus, OP (Oxford: Clarendon Press, 1955), 183. Although Pope Innocent IV was furious, he was prevailed upon by his cardinals to take no retaliatory action, on account of the immense honor in which Grosseteste was held by all.

11 Ludwig Ott, *Fundamentals of Catholic Dogma*, trans. Patrick Lynch, ed. James Canon Bastile, rev. Robert Fastiggi (London: Baronius Press, 2018), 307. This passage should be read carefully: the pope may not be legally bound, but he is morally bound, since these decisions and usages pertain to the Church's common good and, in some cases, to the *status ecclesiae*. Thomas Pink argues against *Traditionis Custodes* in exactly this way: not inasmuch as it is legislation, but inasmuch as it is gravely prejudicial to the life of the Church, to which law is supposed to minister. See his essay "Is *Traditionis Custodes* Lawful?," *The Lamp*, Issue 18 (Assumption 2023); cf. his "Papal Authority and the Limits of Official Theology." Fr Réginald-Marie Rivoire, FSVF, reaches a similarly negative judg-ment by way of a rather different argumentation: see *Does "Traditionis Custodes" Pass the Juridical Rationality Test?* (Lincoln, NE: Os Justi Press, 2022).

POPE FRANCIS'S CAMPAIGN AGAINST
THE CHURCH'S COMMON GOOD

Exactly this situation confronts us today under Pope Francis, who wages war almost daily against the common good of the people of God.[12] Here, I will focus on his campaign against the traditional Roman Rite. Although I will speak mainly of the Mass, I do not mean to limit myself to the Mass, because the motu proprio *Traditionis Custodes* concerns or affects the Church's entire liturgy: all of the sacramental rites, pontifical ceremonies, blessings and exorcisms, and the Divine Office.

We have spoken much about the Church's common good; but can we be more specific in defining this good? I would argue that this common good is nothing other than the divine life of Jesus Christ, her sovereign Head – the superabundant grace of His divinized soul, shared with His members through the illumination of the intellect by revelation and the inflaming of the heart by the supernatural charity of His Heart – and the divinization of souls by the sacramental life and prayer (chiefly the solemn, formal, public worship we call the sacred liturgy). To this common good belongs the treasury of all the goods that God has revealed to us, all the goods Christ has obtained for us by His Most Precious Blood, and all the goods that the Father and the Son together have poured forth upon the Church by the descent of the Holy Spirit not only at the moment of Pentecost but, beginning then, over her entire history until the Second Coming.[13]

Please note that it is not liturgy in the abstract, or just any sort of worship, that is pleasing and acceptable to God, but precisely those "received and approved rites" of which the Council of Trent and various papal oaths down through the centuries speak.[14] The

---

12   For an abundance of documentation on the ways Francis has acted against the good of the Church, see Lamont and Pierantoni, *Defending the Faith*; Kwasniewski, *Hyperpapalism to Catholicism*, vol. 2; and Lanzetta, *"Super Hanc Petram."* In fact, a number of books have been devoted to this theme – among them Marcantonio Colonna [Henry Sire]'s *The Dictator Pope*, George Neumayr's *The Political Pope*, Phil Lawler's *Lost Shepherd*, and Ross Douthat's *To Change the Church*.
13   This paragraph and the next borrow some formulations from my book *True Obedience in the Church: A Guide to Discernment in Challenging Times* (Manchester, NH: Crisis Publications, 2021), 22–23, 28–29.
14   See Matt Gaspers, "Can the Pope Abolish the Traditional Latin Mass?," *Catholic Family News* online, March 3, 2023; Peter Kwasniewski, "The Pope's Boundedness to Tradition as a Legislative Limit," in *From Benedict's Peace to Francis's War*, 222–47.

traditional rites of the Church, Eastern and Western, are not merely human works but works conjointly of God and men – of the Church moved by the Holy Spirit who inhabits her. The traditional liturgical worship of the Church, her *lex orandi* or law of prayer, is a fundamental and normative expression of her *lex credendi* or law of belief – one that cannot be contradicted or abolished or heavily rewritten without rejecting the Spirit-led continuity of the Catholic Church as a whole. This imposes a direct obligation or responsibility on the pastors of the Church, at all levels, to receive, preserve, defend, and promote exactly this inheritance. Their motto is, or should be, the words of St Paul: *Tradidi quod et accepi*, "I have passed on that which I have received." Pope St Gelasius I confirms this, saying: "It is settled that the faithful submit their hearts to all the priests in general *who pass on divine things rightly*."[15]

THE TRADITIONAL MASS IS A GOOD THAT ATTRACTS AND NOURISHES

It is impossible to deny a well-documented fact: the old Latin Mass attracts young people and burgeoning families. Obviously there is something attractive *in* the TLM that draws them to it and brings them back again and again – something they were *not* finding, or not finding to the same degree, at the Novus Ordo, and even at the "unicorn" Novus Ordo that some of them may have attended previously, which they might later on regard as a stepping-stone to what is better (as it was for me).[16]

One thing we can appreciate about the online world, which has so many downsides, is that it enables us to "take the pulse," so to speak, of fervent young Catholics who describe what made them convert or what keeps them in the Church at a time when it is definitely not "cool" to be Catholic, as far as the secular world's wokus-pocus pseudo-religion is concerned. Such Catholics almost always circle around, sooner or later (usually sooner), to the attractive

---

15   In context, the pope is setting up a comparison, but the force of the comparison rests entirely on the first premise of the hypothetical: "If it is settled that the faithful submit their hearts to all the priests in general who pass on divine things rightly, how much more must they submit to the prelate of that See, whom the highest Divinity willed also to be preëminent above all priests, and which the piety of the universal Church subsequently celebrated?" (*Famuli vestrae pietatis*, §2).
16   See the "Thoughts of a Young Modern Traditionalist Catholic" that I posted at *New Liturgical Movement* on July 3, 2023.

power of tradition. A young man left this comment on social media, speaking not only for himself but for his circle of friends:

> All forward-looking Catholics, especially the young ones, see the necessity of embracing the continuity of tradition. Francis wants to lead us into the past of 1970, into a fabricated liturgy which has no roots because a plastic tree cannot take root. The Church's DNA is tradition, so healthy cells will not stop growing to replace the ones he destroys, as long as there is life and breath in Her.

In an article in the *San Diego Union-Tribune* published on April 7, Luke Heintschel, a father of three small children, writes:

> That ancient liturgy has a sort of beauty to it that is otherworldly. Life is saturated with all that is new, relevant and flashy, but this form of worship seems set apart from the rest of life. My family has come to appreciate this silent order as a retreat from a chaotic world of sensory overload. . . . Catholics who are attracted to this form of worship are not worshiping ashes. We hope to preserve the fire of our living tradition. Many parents have a desire to hand on a Christian way of life that seems to be disappearing from today's society. That is what tradition is: handing on. The rituals and forms of worship of our forebears are important in that handing on.[17]

A priest described a solemn traditional Latin Mass held for the feast of the Assumption in the cathedral-basilica of Philadelphia as follows:

> There are still many daunting challenges for those who love the Traditional Rites of the Church but we have come such a long way and we must never stop moving forward. Love for the Traditional Mass and Rites is a youth movement. Those involved are on fire with the Catholic Faith. One thousand people spent two hours and fifteen minutes, in church, on a beautiful Friday evening in August. They could have gone to a seashore resort, to a baseball game, to a night club or to any diversion; instead they immersed themselves in prayer, relished the Sacred Liturgy, honored Our Lady, and praised God; and they

---

17 Luke Heintschel, "Opinion: I'm a Catholic who prefers Latin Mass. For my family, it's about handing on tradition," *The San Diego Union-Tribune*, April 7, 2023.

went out into the world filled with grace and joy. What a blessed event![18]

A young lady of my acquaintance wrote to me these stirring words:

> Coming to appreciate this continuity with our Catholic past was hugely important in my liturgical "conversion." When I was on the Novus Ordo side of things, I felt a lot of angst and embarrassment about the difference between the modern liturgies in which I assisted and the Latin Masses I saw in old movies or heard described by elderly people. I knew that the traditional liturgy was that of virtually all of the saints, and I had an uneasy sense that the saints – my towering models and my interceding friends – would not be pleased with what we had done to the Mass. But when I came home to the traditional Mass, I felt no angst or embarrassment. Grafting myself onto the worship of the earliest centuries was quite literally like being a little tiny branch that suddenly experiences the benefits of being attached to a wide and towering tree.

A German monk who had converted to the Faith as a young man and then discovered the traditional Latin Mass at the age of twenty-one shared with me this account of his experience:

> At the age of 18 I converted from Protestantism to the Catholic Church. The reason: to come home. But I was not really satisfied, because the liturgy was just too "flat" for me. With the "Lutherans" everything was rather conservative. At that time I had never heard of Vatican II. Then there was a good hint. In a magazine I read something about the Abbaye du Barroux in Provence [which follows the old Latin rite]. In that very year, it was September, I took the big trip to the south. A real adventure. After many hours by train, then by bus, I finally arrived in Le Barroux. With my small backpack, I walked up the small road, up a hill, till someone picked me up and gave me a ride the rest of the way. I spent two weeks in this monastery. It was all new to me, but at the same time so familiar... After the solemn ceremony, I went out of the church with a feeling of being filled to the brim. I could

---

18   Fr Robert Pasley, "Mater Ecclesiae's Assumption Mass," *New Liturgical Movement*, August 17, 2014. The same grand Mass for the Assumption has been offered each year since then in the same basilica, always with overflow crowds.

not stop my tears. Finally I knew that God had touched the earth and that I was infinitely loved by Him.

Another gentleman explained in an interview on EWTN that the final push in his decision to convert to Catholicism was attending a solemn Latin Mass. He describes his reaction as follows:

> And I wept like a baby . . . that was the moment in my life when I said "This has to be it! . . . I don't know why this has to be it, but this has to be it," because Christ revealed Himself to me in this liturgy. . . . I knew intellectually that the Church was it, but I didn't trust Her yet, because I didn't actually see Her *living*, and for me, it was the traditional Latin Mass which really made me first say "I *need* to become a Roman Catholic."[19]

These are powerful testimonials! In the early years of the *Summorum Pontificum* era, I tried to keep a collection of all such testimonials I came across, because I figured it would be helpful for my writing on the subject. It *was* helpful,[20] but eventually I had to give up collecting them in any systematic way because the sheer volume of such statements became overwhelming.

The same trend continues in the era of *Traditionis Custodes.* For example, the United States Conference of Catholics Bishops asked young Catholics back in 2019 via Twitter: "If you are a young Catholic who is still Catholic, what has made you stay?" An avalanche of replies from young men and women sang the praises of the old Mass and its captivating effects on them, and testified to their hunger for orthodox doctrine and clear moral teaching. The bishops weren't expecting this at all, and to their credit, allowed the comments to stand. Let me share just one of these:

> I converted to the Catholic faith at 25 years old – because Catholicism is TRUE. I found the Latin Mass and immersed myself in the works of the Saints and traditional catechetical materials. Young people don't need a watered down, easy faith – we need the support of our Bishops![21]

---

19 Gregory DiPippo, "You Are Evangelizing Through Beauty!," *New Liturgical Movement*, June 9, 2020.
20 See, for example, the testimonials quoted in my books *Noble Beauty, Transcendent Holiness*, 7–9, 96; *Reclaiming Our Roman Catholic Birthright*, 39, 53, 84, 109, 237–38, 241, 276–77, 279–80, 299–300; *Once and Future Roman Rite*, 22–24.
21 Lisa Bourne, "Will bishops look at why millennials are fleeing the church? The

A similar thing happened in worldwide "synodal listening sessions," where the topic of Catholics feeling persecuted for loving tradition and for seeking unrestricted access to it came up again and again. Participants at World Youth Day in Lisbon, when asked by the organizers to contribute prayer intentions "for the Synod and for the Church," submitted many intentions like the following: "Do not forbid the Tridentine Mass," "A return to orthodoxy and tradition," "Priests dedicated to their vocation," "That Catholics who find spiritual fulfilment in the TLM may be accepted and allowed to attend the Mass of their choice." The Vatican Synod Twitter account, notable for its outrageous progressivism, to everyone's surprise shared photos of these tradition-friendly intentions. Perhaps the reason is simply that, as one observer noted, they had little choice: "90% of the Post-It notes in São Domingos had this sort of message on it."[22]

WHY DISSUADE ATTENDANCE AT THE TRADITIONAL LATIN MASS?

On the assumption that it is self-evidently *good* for Catholics to assist at Mass and *good* for them to desire fervently to do so, there can be two and only two reasons for anyone in authority to attempt to dissuade them or even forbid them from doing so because the particular Mass they wish to assist at is the venerable preconciliar Mass of the Roman Rite. First, a doctrinal reason: the new Mass contains a different expression or presentation of the Faith that is truer or better than the old Mass's (this is what some people, such as Cardinal Roche and Cardinal Cantalamessa, explicitly say). Second, an ecclesial-disciplinary reason: the new Mass is what recent popes ordered, and everyone must conform to what they ordered—must, indeed, enjoy it *more*!

Now, it is very difficult to see how it is possible to argue that the new Mass is theologically superior to the old Mass. Different, yes; complementary, perhaps; but not superior, unless one wishes to consign to inadequacy nearly the entire history of worship in the Latin-rite Church, which is not a defensible position for a Catholic to take (it's the sort of position a Protestant or a modernist might

---

answer is closer than they think," *LifeSiteNews*, June 21, 2019. This happened less than a month before *Traditionis Custodes* was released. The juxtaposition is telling.
22 See "Synod Forced to Acknowledge What Young People Really Want: An End to TLM Restrictions," *Rorate Caeli*, September 8, 2023.

take).[23] Nor is it any easier to see how it might be possible to argue that a council or a pope will necessarily be correct in ascertaining the spiritual needs of the people of God and in adopting a specific course of action intended to meet those needs. A council or a pope, in short, can't command people to like X, Y, or Z, to find it better for prayer, more suited to their needs, more fruitful or more enticing. Authorities can try something out, but what actually happens in the minds and hearts of the faithful is in *God's* hands, not theirs. And if it turns out that a sizeable number of the faithful newly fall in love with the unreformed rites and find that this ancient worship "speaks to them" more powerfully, no one can say they should not or must not feel that way, nor can anyone make them feel differently. A good thing attracts, and not even God can make it so that a good thing does not attract; on the contrary, He gave the Church her liturgical tradition as something good, so that it *would* attract. Even if "appeal" is not the only aspect to be taken into consideration, it remains a significant one in any case. Dom Alcuin Reid nicely expresses this common-sense perspective:

> *Summorum Pontificum* was a wise recognition of "what the spirit is saying to the churches" (Rev. 3:22). Pope Benedict could see clearly that many, including large numbers of the young, were experiencing in the older rites of the Church that full, conscious, and real participation in the liturgical rites for which the Second Vatican Council called (cf. *Sacrosanctum Concilium*, 14). Whilst this was utterly unexpected (everyone assumed that the ritual reforms were *essential* to the participation desired by the Council), it was and is a living, fruitful reality in the Church of the twenty-first century: one which must be not only acknowledged, but one which, for the good of the Church and the salvation of souls, must live and grow unfettered by the numerous potentates whose ecclesiastical careers more than incarnate the boast...: "And I never thought of thinking for myself at all"![24]

---

23 See Kwasniewski, *Once and Future Roman Rite*, 197–215.
24 Alcuin Reid, "Benoît XVI: liturgiquement inclassable" (accompanied by English translation), *Esprit de la Liturgie*, January 17, 2023. At the ellipsis in this quotation, Dom Alcuin refers to the "Modern Major-General" of *The Pirates of Penzance*, which is a mistake; the unthinking Gilbertian potentate is Sir Joseph Porter KCB of *H. M. S. Pinafore*.

The papacy exists not to dictate whatever laws the pope may please, but to support the life in Christ of all the faithful, the life that the Holy Spirit causes to well up among them and within them. What sustains this life is *ipso facto* worthy of the pope's support and protection; whatever damages it cannot be included within the ambit of his office. He cannot determine, all by himself, what will prove fruitful to the Mystical Body on earth; wishing won't make it so. Either the Novus Ordo succeeds according to its stated purpose or it does not; either the traditional Latin Mass attracts, converts, and nourishes souls, or it does not; a pope cannot change objective facts, no matter how much he flexes his pontifical muscle. If the ancient Mass succeeds *better* at the same set of goods for which divine worship exists, the pope cannot make it to be otherwise, no matter what he wishes were true. He cannot make a success out of a failure, or a failure out of a success; he cannot cancel out the manifest good caused by the Holy Spirit working through the tradition the Spirit Himself inspired, as Pius XII tells us in *Mediator Dei*.[25] In short, the pope cannot control, and may not abolish, the Holy Spirit's work.

If Catholics of all ages, races, cultures, languages, incomes, backgrounds, young people and the elderly, families with children, are eagerly frequenting the Holy Mass and the sacraments of the Church in their traditional form and finding in this encounter joy and peace as well as grace for living the Christian life, it would take an exceedingly hard heart, an impenetrable spiritual blindness, a demonic cruelty of mind, to seek to restrict the faithful's access to it, shut down what they love, or compel them (if it were possible) to think and feel differently – in short, to drive them away from the springs of salvation to which God in His Providence has led them, the same springs to which He led His Church for so many centuries.

AN IDEOLOGICAL FIXATION AGAINST
TRADITION CANNOT BE LAWFUL

One of my contacts was telling me about friends of his who, having planned a traditional Nuptial Mass to which they were greatly looking forward, were told only days before that it would not be allowed. He wrote to me:

---

25 See Kwasniewski, *Once and Future Roman Rite*, 33–77; *Reclaiming Our Roman Catholic Birthright*, 149–60.

In a period of egregious offenses against the Catholic religion—especially the indiscriminate reception of Communion by pro-abortion politicians and those who vote for them, and the Vatican-encouraged "mercy" towards divorced-and-remarried as well as towards homosexuals—how absolutely bizarre that a bishop would try to punish traditionally-minded members of his flock, sticking it to them on their wedding day. . . . Such is the wolfish behavior to which Pope Francis has habituated his hirelings. The seething lack of charity is scandalous, the hypocrisy of the sloganeers of inclusivity who act exactly contrary to it, the invention of enemies where they do not exist and the betrayal of friends of Christ and of the Church where they do exist. Historians will look back to this age and marvel at the shortsightedness, the meanness, the almost Stalinist contempt for the living, breathing faithful whom Christ redeemed with His precious Blood.

At the end of the day, it really doesn't matter that Vatican II said, in 1963, that the liturgy needed to be reformed according to a laundry list of mid-twentieth-century desiderata. If the primary purpose of the reform was to lead Catholics to frequent the Mass and the sacraments with greater fervor and to participate in them more deeply, and if this is happening unexpectedly in the old forms, then bless the Lord and let it flourish! Such good fruits are obviously from God and equally obviously belong to the Church's common good that her shepherds are obliged to support. John Lamont rightly points out the *supernaturality* of the traditionalist movement:

> The decree [*Summorum Pontificum*] produced or expanded traditionalist communities all over the world, whose congregations were characterized by large families, low average age, and doctrinal orthodoxy. Traditionalist communities also produced vocations to the priesthood and religious life out of all proportion to their numbers. This was an extraordinary result. . . . The traditional communities that sprung into being after [Benedict XVI's] restoration were almost entirely composed of Catholics to whom the heritage of Latin literature, culture and history were unknown. In Europe and North America, the culture, if it can be called that, in which these communities were born was a complete negation of the cultural basis of the Latin

Mass. The success of these communities has few parallels in religious history. Africans and Native Americans had adopted the Latin liturgy with enthusiasm when exposed to it by missionaries in the 16th to the 19th centuries, but this adoption could be seen as benefiting from the prestige and power of the European states from which the missionaries had come. There is now no prestige attached to the Latin Mass, which is still often celebrated in school gyms and the chapels attached to funeral homes. Its growth can only be reasonably explained by a purely religious power inherent in the traditional liturgy.[26]

If there are problems here and there in the traditionalist movement, then let them be dealt with here and there, on a local level, by personal intervention, which is the only effective way problems are dealt with. The idea of "collective guilt"—for example, that all the Jews are responsible for the death of Christ, or that all traditionalists deny the validity of Vatican II—was abandoned, ironically, *at* Vatican II, which taught that groups should not be blamed for the sins of individuals. This is both the plainest common sense and the supernatural perspective of true Christians. To buy into the campaign against the traditional Latin liturgy is already to reveal that one is in the grip of an ideological passion or fixation that has nothing to do with the Gospel, the Commandments, or the Beatitudes.

What happens when canon law is unmoored from its first principles and obedience is twisted against its nature? That is what we must examine next.

ATTACHMENT TO TRADITION IS NORMAL AND GOOD, THE OPPOSITE IS ABNORMAL AND BAD

Sometimes our opponents say to us: "Why do you trads make such a big fuss over the TLM? Surely you could just go to *any* valid liturgy, it shouldn't make a difference. You're making an *idol* out of your preferred form of Mass!"

This objection makes about as much sense as saying to a man: "What's the big deal with your wife? You could take any woman, it shouldn't make a difference." Or to a parent: "Why are you so

---

26   John Lamont, "The Significance of Pope Francis for the Church," *The Society of St. Hugh of Cluny*, March 21, 2023.

attached to your kids? There are lots of kids around. The state could supply you with more. Kids are kids." Or to a friend: "Why are you so attached to your best friend? He's just a guy, there are plenty of guys you can get to know!" Deep attachment, familiarity, association, companionship, intimacy – you can't just throw these things off like a blanket or a jacket. The liturgy in all its concreteness, its *givenness*, forms and shapes us, as it is supposed to do; and it becomes a part of us deep down, a favored instrument and a mighty conduit for the work of Almighty God, who paints His masterpiece on the canvas of our souls with the brushes and paints of tradition – the chants and ceremonies, antiphons, readings, and prayers, feasts and fasts, symbols and silences.

Whereas knowledge is of universals, love is of (and towards) the good as it really exists, as it comes to us here and now, as we encounter it in the particular, in the flesh, "in person." Ideology elevates theories over realities, ideas over persons, cerebral abstractions over the fleshy tablets of the heart. It fails to see, or closes its eyes to, the ways God manifests Himself in history, in time, in the world, in our neighbors. It denies the "scandal of the particular" in favor of the imposition of the false universal.

We find all of these traits combined in the enemies of the old Roman rite – particularly, I would say, the denial of the incarnational scandal of the particular. They are at war with not just 400 years' worth or a millennium's worth of tradition, but, taking into full account all the Hebrew and early Christian antecedents and developments, 3,000 years' worth of liturgy lived and loved, pondered and prayed. They are at war with revealed religion and its highest expression, the liturgy, where revelation is at home, where it is actualized and perpetuated in our midst.

CRIMES ARE COMING TO LIGHT, SCALES FALLING FROM EYES

Consider a pair of absurd statements. "I love humanity but I hate my next-door neighbor. I love liturgy but I hate the historic Roman rite." The only basis for hating someone or something is if he or it is evil, an evil to be overcome for the sake of the good. That is exactly the mentality of the enemies of the classical Roman Rite: to them, it is bad, wrong, harmful, and must be limited and eliminated.

This, of course, cannot be and could never be the attitude or mentality of a believing Catholic; it could only be the attitude or mentality of a heretic, a schismatic, or an apostate. It would be *possible* for a Catholic to believe, albeit naively, that a simplified rite would be or is better for some people at some particular time; but this, of course, is compatible with the standing obligation to maintain religious respect for existing rites and to let them flourish wherever they can and will.

Imagine, on the other hand, not caring whether or not there is substantial continuity in our divine worship, our most solemn expression of faith in God and homage to Him. Imagine not caring whether or not people hold on, with grateful admiration, to the riches accumulated (for our benefit!) over many centuries of prayerful immersion in the mysteries of Christ. Imagine not caring if we have a quintessentially modern arrogance toward tradition, judging all of it as if we were superior to it, and willfully tossing aside things that were said or done for hundreds, even thousands of years, by innumerable ancestors, with impressive ranks of the greatest saints among them.

Actually, no need to imagine, since we have concrete examples of such attitudes all around us. The liturgical reformers of the twentieth century did not care. Their legacy is the huge number of Catholics who do not care, indeed, who do not even know there is anything to care about, and who drift away, generation by generation, from a Church that seems to care so little for them and for their nourishment. The suppression and severance has been nearly complete.

Except that there *are* those who know and who care: the traditionalists. And they are not going away. On the contrary, their number is growing. A crime of the magnitude of the liturgical reform cannot remain hidden forever; Divine Providence will expose it, and call forth fruits of repentance and restoration. Think about the millions who have watched *Mass of the Ages* Episode 2, and have been pierced in heart and convicted in mind by watching the sequence where a scrolling missal is deconstructed and defaced at the hands of barbarians.

Consequently, for those who love the classical Roman Rite to allow it to be taken away from them or canceled out—this applies as much to the laity as to the clergy—would be to act against the Church's common good; against the Father's Providence, Christ's Headship of the Church, and the Holy Spirit as Lord and giver of life; against the saints and angels in whose heavenly worship we participate; and even against the pope and the bishops, by allowing them to commit grievous sins, inflicting lasting harm on the Church.

DIOCESAN PRIESTS: DO NOT GIVE UP!

Here I wish to make a special appeal to diocesan priests. I know that you are often "between a rock and a hard place" and that you are torn in conscience about how to respond to the restrictions or cancellations occasioned by *Traditionis Custodes*. Here is it important to remember that the promise (not vow) of obedience you made to your bishop cannot take precedence in an absolute sense over the goods it exists to foster.

Let's recall the examples of authority gone awry. A bishop who shuts down the traditional Latin Mass or in any way molests the community of the faithful that God has raised up around it is like that abusive husband, or the unhinged president warring against his citizens, or the golf-crazy abbot. In that situation, you priests— like the wife, the citizen, and the monk in my earlier examples—are not required to obey; indeed, you should *not* obey. In this way you *protect* the very good that the episcopacy exists to serve—you best serve your bishop by refusing to consent to his abuse of office. All it takes is a moral certainty that grave pastoral harm is being done in order for you to have a legitimate reason to withhold obedience in that regard and to continue serving the people of God, upon whose generosity you can rely, as I have seen time and again.

In a very basic sense, dear priests, you were ordained to serve *them*, the faithful, not to serve the bishop; for Christ our Lord said: "I came not to be served, but to serve," and a bishop who acts as if the whole point is to serve *him* by blind obedience is departing from the way of Christ. The building up of the Church in charity and holiness is the goal; the bishop is one of several means established to ensure that goal.

Nowadays certain people have exaggerated the good of obedience to such an extent that they have surreptitiously substituted it for the very purpose of the Church. Instead of holding that *salus animarum suprema lex* – the salvation of souls is the highest law – they effectively maintain that *obedientia est suprema lex* – obedience is the highest law. It is *not* the highest law, for the reasons already given; and you, diocesan priests, who are on the front lines of the spiritual battle, who were called by God to give the riches of Christ to His people and not to withhold them by the arbitrary dictates of your bishop, have an *officium*, a duty, to stand by your flocks, holding fast to the sacred and great tradition of the Church and upholding the common good.

This is what your intellect, your conscience, your heart tell you when you peel away the layers of fear of reprisal, fear of canonical casuistry, or fear of the future. As Joseph Ratzinger memorably said in 1986, speaking of the Church: "For her, concern for the faith of the little ones must be more important than fearing the opposition of the powerful."[27] The same is true for the Church's ministers.

GROUNDED IN OBJECTIVE TRUTH,
NOT SUBJECTIVE FEELINGS

Those of us who have grown to love the ancient rite of Mass reach a point where we know, with more certainty and conviction than that with which we know anything except our very existence, that we could not turn away from, much less turn against, the traditional liturgy without sinning against the light God has given us, the truth He has opened to us, the faith He has nourished in us in precisely *this* way, the love He has kindled by it. We would have to deny not only our inmost identity and convictions, but the witness of all who have found the same graces in the traditional liturgy – both today and in every past century. We would have to deny the Face of Christ as it has been revealed to us through *these rites*, permeated with His Presence, saturated with His symbols – a highly articulate expression of His love and His beauty. We cannot deny the fruits of the renewal of tradition without denying our senses and even our reason. We cannot deny the natural and supernatural good that we see, superabounding in the garden of the classical Roman Rite and

---

27 The original speech in Italian is heavily quoted in the post "Cardinale Ratzinger Lectio su teologia e Chiesa," *Cooperatores Veritatis*, April 9, 2018. The relevant passage is: "Per lei la preoccupazione per la fede dei piccoli deve essere più importante del timore dell'opposizione dei potenti."

all that goes with it. To deny these things would be to deny Christ, to spit on His face, to step on His image, to spurn His gifts.

This is not just a "feeling," like some Protestant saying: "I feel that the Holy Spirit is speaking to me" or "I am saved now and always!" These are subjective claims, deceptive and untenable. The traditional Catholic liturgy is something we *know* has been sacred and great across the ages of the Church. We *know* that the saints themselves prayed with it, contributed to it, praised it, defended it — even, at times, shed their blood for it. Our attachment to the liturgy is not just a matter of feelings, of whims. We adhere to it not for subjective reasons but for objective reasons. It itself is good and holy and beautiful and great. We know it to be so with certainty because it is the uninterrupted and continuous use of the Church of God. It is solemnly *received and approved* by the Church and therefore by God Himself, who does not contradict Himself, who does not change.

The ones who have to justify their preferences or attachments are the ones who use a liturgy ridden with novelties and deformities, options and adaptations, wide-open rules and clumsy rubrics, cut off from the entire Western liturgical tradition as the laboratory brainchild of modern-day scholars weary of the virtues, study, and discipline required by the great tradition. It is not possible to study the liturgical reform and not to see that it was revolutionary and seemed to call into question much of the Church's theology (to this extent, Cardinal Roche's admissions show him to be simply a product of the system).[28] The presence of the traditional Latin Mass is a powerful witness to Catholic continuity: that is one among many reasons we not only adhere to it but have an *obligation* to adhere to it.

No, this "attachment" of ours is not about feelings, it is about facts, truths, reasons — objective, defensible, stable, received and approved. The traditional Catholic stands on firm ground, on solid rock. Our opponents stand on shifting ground, the sand of their theories and opinions, preferences and dreams, which have led to

---

28   See James Baresel, "Archbishop Roche: 'The Traditional Mass Must Go,'" *Inside the Vatican*, https://insidethevatican.com/magazine/archbishop-roche-the-traditional-mass-must-go/; Peter Kwasniewski, "Cardinal Roche (Unwittingly?) Utters the Most Ironic Statement Since the Council," *Rorate Caeli*, August 30, 2022; José Antonio Ureta, "Cardinals Roche and Cantalamessa: The Mass of Paul VI Corresponds to a New Theology," *Rorate Caeli*, April 11, 2023.

anarchy, out-of-control do-it-yourself pluralism, a wasteland of heterodoxy and a wilderness of unbelief that nothing can rein in and no one can fix. There is one and only one coherent solution to the mess of the modern Latin-rite Church, and that is a principled, resolute, consistent, humble, and zealous restoration of the fullness of our tradition in its bimillennial plenitude, before the "I know betters" of the twentieth century began to tweak it, tinker with it, and finally hack it to pieces. Full restoration is the way forward; there is no other right way of rescuing the liturgy from its enemies.

CANON LAW IS FOR THE GOOD OF SOULS

"Hold on a minute" (the objection will come, fast and furious). "Are not the pope and his allies following canon law and doing everything legally—and so, we must obey them?" My analysis up until now provides the key to the answer, which, as it happens, is nicely summarized by Dr Joseph Shaw:

> In the Church, canon law does not simply impose itself on meaningless facts, but has to find a foundation in reality for the good of souls, if it is to work as law. For human law is an attempt to order reality for the common good, and can either succeed in this or fail. Law that has failed [to do this], however, is ultimately not law; it imposes no obligation. This . . . may seem of no practical consequence: it *looks* like law and we can expect it to be treated like law for practical purposes. It does, however, make a difference to how we should view it, as a matter of conscience.
>
> Some people have said, in response to these documents, that we are living through a post-law period of the history of the Church. This, however, is impossible: the Church is a community governed by law, based on the law of God. If ecclesiastical legislation fails to be real law, then our response to it needs to take that into account. In the end, as the final canon in the Code of Canon Law reminds us, *salus animarum est suprema lex*: the good of souls is the supreme law in the Church, because that corresponds to the very nature of the Church. A law which prevents the Church from fulfilling the mission entrusted to her by God is not a law binding on the Church.[29]

---

29   *Gregorius Magnus* 15 (Summer 2023): 38.

Many in the Church today are genuinely struggling with the complexities of papal authority. Many recognize that it is at least morally wrong for a pope to act against the patrimony of the Church and against the spiritual good of Catholics. Such people, be they old-school liberals or "JP2 conservatives," are willing to make common cause with us against *Traditionis Custodes*.

On the other hand, the proponents of hyperpapalism seem to be suffering from a deep insecurity that demands an authoritarian ruler who brooks no opposition, who has no objective duties to tradition or to the faithful legitimately attached to the Church's traditional rites of worship. In the hyperpapalist worldview, the whole of ecclesial life is fundamentally altered: the Church becomes a hostile, chilling place, where, ultimately, the faithful have no rights, and there is no common good except what the ruler defines it to be: in short, a religion whose God is the unholy trinity of nominalism, voluntarism, and positivism. The entire normative structure of reason, law, and faith is corrupted by such a view. That is why it can be called a form of dogmatism or ideology: there is nothing that could disprove it, nothing that could shake its hold. The hyperpapalist's Bible is paper-thin, comprising a single verse: "The Lord Pope giveth, the Lord Pope taketh away; blessed be the Name of the Lord Pope."

Catholics who are grounded in reality, in history, in philosophy and theology, in common sense, in neighborly charity, know that this is false. There is no authority on earth that is absolute. Only God's authority is absolute. Only He is always right and always to be obeyed. Any mortal ruler can sin against his office, against his people, against the common good of the society over which he has been placed. It is possible for us to know when this is happening. And when it happens, that tyrant must be resisted, justly and firmly.

8

The Primacy of Tradition and Obedience to the Truth

HATEVER LIMITATIONS THERE MAY BE IN his analysis of the liturgical question, and however much we bitterly deplore his decision to abandon the papal throne, Joseph Ratzinger gave consummate expression to key principles of the traditional movement, and his clarity of insight in this regard remains unsurpassed.

In an address on October 24, 1998 to pilgrims who had come to Rome for the tenth anniversary of John Paul II's apostolic letter *Ecclesia Dei*, Cardinal Ratzinger said:

> It is good to recall here what Cardinal Newman observed, that the Church, throughout her history, has never abolished or forbidden orthodox liturgical forms, which would be quite alien to the spirit of the Church. An orthodox liturgy, that is to say, one which expresses the true faith, is never a compilation made according to the pragmatic criteria of different ceremonies, handled in a positivist and arbitrary way – one way today and another way tomorrow. The orthodox forms of a rite are living realities, born out of the dialogue of love between the Church and her Lord. They are expressions of the life of the Church, in which are distilled the faith, the prayer, and the very life of whole generations, and which make incarnate in specific forms both the action of God and the response of man.[1]

The reference to St John Henry Newman is likely to his sermon "Ceremonies of the Church," in which he writes (still as a High Church Anglican but certainly well on his way to the Roman Church, where his opinion remained the same):

---

1   Translated by Fr Ignatius Harrison, O. Cong., published at *Southern Orders*, March 11, 2010. If the Church has always treasured its tradition as a rule, then we know with certainty that an attack on tradition cannot be from the Church. Those who speak on behalf of the Church are not mechanically and automatically to be taken as her mouthpieces or the Lord's.

The services and ordinances of the Church are the outward form in which religion has been for ages represented to the world, and has ever been known to us. . . . [T]hese [liturgical] things, viewed as a whole, are sacred relatively to us, even if they were not, as they are, divinely sanctioned. Rites which the Church has appointed, and with reason, – for the Church's authority is from Christ, – being long used, cannot be disused without harm to our souls.[2]

It seems to me that this double truth – that it would be alien to the spirit of the Church to abolish or prohibit orthodox forms, and that doing so is inherently harmful to souls – led to the famous doctrinal formulation that serves as the central premise of *Summorum Pontificum*:

What earlier generations held as sacred, remains sacred and great for us too, and it cannot be all of a sudden entirely forbidden or even considered harmful. It behooves all of us to preserve the riches which have developed in the Church's faith and prayer, and to give them their proper place.

As many have pointed out, Pope Benedict here speaks in a manner that is decidedly not prudential or disciplinary; rather, he is making a universal truth-claim as pastor of the universal Church.[3] He uses absolute, unequivocal language about what must be so and what cannot be so, and he draws moral imperatives from it.[4] He formulated the same judgment on a number of occasions. In 1996 he said, in the interview published under the title *Salt of the Earth*:

I am of the opinion, to be sure, that the old rite should be granted much more generously to all those who desire it. It's impossible to see what could be dangerous or unacceptable about that. A community is calling its very being into question when it suddenly declares that

---

2   Peter Kwasniewski, ed., *Newman on Worship, Reverence, and Ritual* (N.p.: Os Justi Press, 2019), 79.

3   I do not claim infallibility for his statement, but neither does it require a special status, for it enunciates a principle that can be false only if Vatican II introduced a rupture in Catholicism so profound that it necessitates the abolition of orthodox forms and their total substitution by new forms.

4   Hence, John Lamont argues that this assertion in *Summorum Pontificum* constitutes a dogmatic fact: see "Dominican Theologian Attacks Catholic Tradition (Part 3): Getting Our Dogmatic Facts Straight," *Rorate Caeli*, September 18, 2023.

what until now was its holiest and highest possession is strictly forbidden and when it makes the longing for it seem downright indecent. Can it be trusted any more about anything else? Won't it proscribe again tomorrow what it prescribes today?[5]

In the interview published in the Jubilee Year 2000 under the title *God and the World*, he said:

> For fostering a true consciousness in liturgical matters, it is also important that the proscription against the form of liturgy in valid use up to 1970 should be lifted. Anyone who nowadays advocates the continuing existence of this [older] liturgy or takes part in it is treated like a leper; all tolerance ends here. There has never been anything like this in history; in doing this we are despising and proscribing the Church's whole past. How can one trust her at present if things are that way?[6]

In such statements, which attain a crystalline form in *Summorum Pontificum* and the accompanying letter to the bishops, we have a judgment at once theological, moral, historical, and canonical.

Now, is this just Benedict XVI's personal opinion or feeling, no more authoritative than a fondness for Bavaria and beer? Certainly not. We can see throughout the history of the Church the strongest testimonies to the pope's *boundedness to tradition*. Let me offer a few choice examples. The early medieval "Papal Oath" contained in the *Liber Diurnus Romanorum Pontificum*, a handbook of formularies used by the pontifical chancellery, some of which date back as far as St Gregory the Great, states:

> I, *N.*, by the mercy of God deacon, elect and future bishop, by the grace of God, of this Apostolic See, swear to you, blessed Peter, prince of the Apostles . . . and to your Holy Church, which today I have taken up to rule under your protection, that I shall guard with all my strength, even unto giving up the ghost or shedding my blood, the right and true faith . . . I shall keep inviolate the discipline

---

5 *Salt of the Earth*, trans. Adrian Walker (San Francisco: Ignatius Press, 1997), 176-77.
6 *God and the World*, trans. Henry Taylor (San Francisco: Ignatius Press, 2002), 416. For additional relevant texts, see "Best Quotes on the Liturgy by Joseph Ratzinger/Benedict XVI," *New Liturgical Movement*, January 2, 2023.

and ritual of the Church just as I found and received it
handed down by my predecessors . . . nor shall I admit
any novelty, but shall fervently keep and venerate with
all my strength all that I find handed down as verily my
predecessors' disciple and follower . . .[7]

Similarly, the fifteenth-century Council of Constance (1414 - 1418),
in the thirty-ninth session, which was ratified by Pope Martin V
and Pope Eugene IV,[8] states: "Since the Roman Pontiff exercises
such great power among mortals, it is right that he be *bound all the
more* by the incontrovertible bonds of the faith and by the rites that
are to be observed regarding the Church's Sacraments." According
to Constance, the newly elected pope was to make an oath of faith
that included this passage:

> I, N., elected pope, with both heart and mouth confess
> and profess to almighty God, whose Church I undertake
> with his assistance to govern, and to blessed Peter, prince
> of the apostles, that as long as I am in this fragile life I will
> firmly believe and hold the Catholic Faith . . . and likewise
> I will follow and observe in every way the handed-down
> rite of the ecclesiastical sacraments of the Catholic Church.

The Profession of Faith established at the Council of Trent recognizes,
as essential to Catholicity, adherence to "received and approved ceremonies of the Catholic Church in the solemn administration of all
the sacraments." The phrase "received and approved ceremonies"
obviously refers to the traditional rites. In fact, this is simply the
Catholic *forma mentis* or frame of mind – what it means to think and
love as a Catholic (and not, say, as a Protestant or a Jew or an atheist).

Given this attitude, we should hardly be surprised to find
eminent canonists and theologians maintaining that a pope
guilty of injuring either tradition or the Christian people who
rely on it deserves to be resisted. Juan de Torquemada states
that if a pope fails to observe "the universal rite of ecclesiastical

---

7   Translated by Gerhard Eger and Zachary Thomas, from the Vatican MS text as
edited by Hans Foerster in his critical edition *Liber Diurnus Romanorum Pontificum*
(Bern: Francke Verlag, 1958), 145 - 48. For the full Latin text and additional notes,
see "'I Shall Keep Inviolate the Discipline and Ritual of the Church': The Early
Mediæval Papal Oath," *Canticum Salomonis*, July 31, 2021.
8   This and the quotation following it were papally ratified "absque tamen
præjudicio juris dignitatis et præeminentiæ Sedis Apostolicæ" (in the words of
Eugene IV), that is, without prejudice to the rights, dignity, and preeminence
of the Apostolic See.

worship,"[9] he is neither to be obeyed nor "put up with."[10] Cajetan counsels: "You must resist, to his face, a pope who is openly tearing the Church apart."[11] Francisco Suárez declares:

> If the pope lays down an order contrary to right customs, one does not have to obey him; if he tries to do something manifestly opposed to justice and to the common good, it would be licit to resist him; if he attacks by force, he could be repelled by force, with the moderation characteristic of a good defense.[12]

Suárez moreover claims that the pope could be schismatic "if he wanted to overturn all the ecclesiastical ceremonies resting on apostolic tradition."[13] (Note he says "resting on," *apostolica traditione firmatas*: he's talking about the whole structure that has been raised upon apostolic origins. That would mean something like the 1570 *Missale Romanum*.) Sylvester Prierias explains that the pope "does not have the power to destroy; therefore, if there is evidence that he is doing it, it is licit to resist him. The result of all this is that if the pope destroys the Church by his orders and acts, he can be resisted and the execution of his mandate prevented."[14]

All of these theologians assume that Catholics are *capable of recognizing* when the pope is failing to adhere to the Church's received and approved rites, assaulting souls, undermining the common good, or destroying the Church. In other words, we are not passive blobs who are waiting to be *told* that the pope is saying something false or doing something wrong that deserves to be rebuked and resisted; there is some role for our informed reason and faith to play in evaluating his words and actions (and those of any other bishop, for that matter).

---

9 He has in mind just such "received and approved ceremonies" as Trent did later on.

10 *Summa de ecclesia*, lib. IV, pars Ia, cap. xi, § Secundo sic (fol. 196v of the 1489 Roman edition, p. 552 of the 1560 Salamanca edition, and p. 369v of the 1561 Venice edition). For the full text, see my lecture "Beyond *Summorum Pontificum*: The Work of Retrieving the Tridentine Heritage," *Rorate Caeli*, July 14, 2021, n13.

11 Thomas Cardinal Cajetan, *De comparatione auctoritatis papae et concilii*. This and the next several references are from Casey, "Can a Catholic Ever Disobey a Pope?"

12 Francisco Suárez, *De Fide*, disp. X, sect. VI, no. 16.

13 Suárez, *De Caritate*, disp. XII, sect. 1.

14 Prierias, *Dialogus de potestate papae*, cited by Francisco de Vitoria, *Obras*, pp. 486-87. For further discussion, see Kwasniewski, *From Benedict's Peace to Francis's War* and *True Obedience in the Church*.

Popes are subject to a great temptation – perhaps in accord with Lord Acton's not entirely false axiom "power tends to corrupt and absolute power corrupts absolutely": a temptation to identify themselves as the source and measure of Catholicism, when they are rather its recipients, stewards, and defenders. The low-water mark of this deviation is illustrated by Pius IX's remark to a Dominican cardinal who dared to disagree with the formulation of papal infallibility at Vatican I. The pope shouted at him: "*Io, io sono la tradizione! Io, io sono la chiesa!*" [I, *I* am the tradition! I, *I* am the Church!].[15] This is the ecclesiastical equivalent of Louis XIV saying: "*L'État, c'est moi,*" as if a pope were to say, "*L'Église, c'est moi.*" A correct understanding of papal authority – even according to the actual teaching of Vatican I, taken together with all other pertinent doctrine – shows it to be not absolute and unbounded, but relative and limited in a number of ways, justifying Gregory the Great's famous description of the pope as "the servant of the servants of God."

This is why *Traditionis Custodes* is absolutely null and utterly void from its first letter to its last punctuation mark. It is premised on an impossibility, an incoherence, a contradiction.[16] It attacks the Church's self-identity in her godly and God-approved worship. It attacks her *lex credendi*. It attacks the common good of *all* the faithful – both those that make use of the Roman liturgy and those that make use of other Western rites and Eastern rites, whose position has been radically destabilized. It attacks in a bewildering variety of ways the rights of bishops, priests, deacons, religious, and laity,[17] as many commentators have pointed out. And that is

---

15 See O'Malley, *Vatican I*, 212, and the discussion above in chapter 3.
16 Put more simply: either Benedict XVI is right in his universal statement, or Francis is right to (implicitly) deny it – they cannot both be right. A sign that the enemies of the traditional liturgy are aware of this Achilles' heel in their position is their tireless propaganda effort to reinterpret *Summorum Pontificum* as an olive branch to the SSPX or as a temporary concession for disgruntled nostalgics. Yet it is obvious from the gradual and accelerating rehabilitation of the *usus antiquior* that such propaganda is false: Paul VI in a limited way (the indult for England and Wales), John Paul II in a much less limited way (the worldwide indult), and Benedict XVI in a nearly unlimited way (the opening to all Latin-rite clergy without a need for permission) supported the ongoing use of the traditional Roman Rite, which obviously included its spread: a living Church at prayer is a Church that grows. One would sin by seeking to suppress supernatural growth.
17 One may note that even the 2004 Instruction *Redemptionis Sacramentum* of the Congregation for Divine Worship and the Discipline of the Sacraments recognizes (rather incongruously in the context of the Novus Ordo) a right to tradition: "arbitrary actions are not conducive to true renewal, but are detrimental

why it is not only *not* necessary to follow *Traditionis Custodes* or any further legislation or policy based on it, it is rather necessary *not* to follow it. We do not have merely a freedom of protest; we have an obligation of non-recognition and non-compliance. While this refusal to follow vacuous legislation can take more open and more hidden forms, depending on prudential evaluation of the circumstances, nevertheless one must be careful to avoid giving the impression that one accepts that legislation. As St Meletius of Antioch (r. 360–381) wrote in circumstances as harrowing as our own: "Do not show obedience to bishops who exhort you to do and to say and to believe in things which are not to your benefit. What pious man would hold his tongue? Who would remain completely calm? In fact, silence equates to consent."[18]

The fundamental principle of the traditionalist movement is that the liturgy of the Church in her immemorial, venerable, universal, approved and received rites is at the core of what it means to be Catholic, to believe as a Catholic, and to live as a Catholic. The *lex orandi* (the rule of prayer, how and what we pray) is a permanent witness to and embodiment of the *lex credendi* (the rule of belief, what we believe) and the *lex vivendi* (the rule of living, how we live). The liturgy is not an optional add-on but the daily axis and center of our lives, the heart of our encounter with God. It follows as a corollary that no one, not even the pope, has the authority to deprive Catholics of their traditional liturgy, to suppress the rites with which the Church has prayed for centuries, or to radically modify these rites past recognition and thereby introduce an undeniable rupture with the content and patterns of divine worship.

The traditionalist movement is therefore founded in a primordial act of material disobedience for the sake of a higher obedience.[19]

---

to the right of Christ's faithful to a liturgical celebration that is an expression of the Church's life in accordance with her tradition and discipline" (no. 11). Such a right is not the effect of positive law but the expression of what is perennially true. See note 28 on page 140.

18 Andrei Psarev, *The Limits of Non-conformity in the Byzantine Church (861-1300): A Study of Canon 15 of the First and Second Council in Constantinople (861)*, 13, available at www.rocorstudies.org/wp-content/uploads/2011/06/psarev_canon15_1n2council.pdf.

19 "Material disobedience" in the sense that certain Catholics did not do what they were told to do, and did what they were told not to do—disobedience as to the matter at hand—which did not constitute formal disobedience because they were in the right, obedient to a higher law.

From the first moment of the reform that began with the creation of the Consilium in 1964, Paul VI demanded that everyone follow his initiatives and eventually adopt his new books and cease to use the old books, practically without exception.[20] A commission of nine cardinals summoned by John Paul II in the summer of 1986 – Cardinals Ratzinger, Mayer, Oddi, Stickler, Casaroli, Gantin, Innocenti, Palazzini, and Tomko – concluded that Paul VI had never suppressed the old rite. This was the basis of Benedict XVI's statement that it had not been abrogated, with the implication that it *could* not be abrogated, for the reasons already given.[21] So, Paul VI did not abrogate the old rite (this indeed is beyond any pope's authority), but he made it absolutely clear that he intended for it to be definitively set aside, and ordered that it no longer be used and that his modern rite be used exclusively instead.

The traditionalists simply refused to do this. Even when papal apologists of that time threw at them (as the descendants of those apologists throw at us today) quotation after quotation from papal documents saying, essentially, "you must obey every jot and tittle of what the pope tells you to do," the traditionalists did not and would not acknowledge Paul VI's authority to suppress tradition and to command novelty. Neither did they hold the seemingly respectful but ultimately incoherent position of Karl Rahner that the pope has the hierarchical authority to do such a thing but not the "moral" authority – in other words, that a pope *could* legitimately abolish a traditional liturgical rite but *should not* do it, that his will has the force of law, even if he would sin by enacting his will.

That position could never make sense. As Leo XIII teaches, God gives power only for that to which power can legitimately extend.[22]

---

20   There was a sliver of an exception made for the old and infirm clergy unable to read the new missal, as long as they would celebrate Mass without a congregation. That, and the Heenan (or "Agatha Christie") indult for England and Wales in 1971, were the only official openings until 1984.

21   See "The 'Norms' of 1986," https://lms.org.uk/the-norms-of-1986. For more details, see Peter Kwasniewski, "Minutes from the Commission of Cardinals That Advised John Paul II to Lift Restrictions on the Old Missal," *New Liturgical Movement*, January 9, 2023.

22   Among the encyclicals of Leo XIII, see *Diuturnum Illud*, *Libertas Praestantissimum*, and *Immortale Dei*, and my commentary in "The Kingship of Christ and the Anti-Kingdom of Modernity," *OnePeterFive*, February 8, 2018. British philosopher Stephen R. L. Clark says: "Whenever a clear innocent is condemned, especially to death, by the powers and principalities of this world, it is those

A president, for example, who supports abortion is not making an unfortunate use of his legitimate power, he is *abusing* citizens by doing violence to them *against* his legitimate power. Traditionalists hold the same about the papacy and the tradition of the Church—not only in liturgy but also in doctrine and morals. As Cardinal Alfons Maria Stickler, one of the nine commission members of 1986, stated: "This attachment to tradition in the case of fundamental things which have conclusively influenced the Church in the course of time certainly belongs to this fixed, unchanging status [the *status ecclesiae*], over which even the pope has no right of disposal."[23]

That is why, again, the first traditionalists[24] refused to "submit" to what neither their minds nor their hearts could accept as compatible with the essence of the Catholic Faith, just as today, for the same reason, we reject Francis's errors—for example, that the death penalty is immoral; that adulterers may receive Communion; that faith alone (*sola fide*) is necessary for receiving the Eucharist; that

---

powers and principalities which are themselves condemned, and lose the moral authority they abused. We owe, or feel we owe, a primary obedience to authority—but that authority is borrowed from a higher source, and can be lost. Those who observe the event can feel themselves released, if not from reasonable fear of what the abusers can do, at least from any sense that the abusers have a right to do it" (*Can We Believe in People?: Human Significance in an Interconnected Cosmos* [Brooklyn, NY: Angelico Press, 2020], 113).

23   See "Recollections of a Vatican II Peritus," *New Liturgical Movement*, June 29, 2022. As Brian Tierney relates: "The Decretists had a clearly formulated idea that the maintenance of the *status ecclesiae* was an overriding consideration in all matters of ecclesiastical policy. . . . In the Decretist writings (as in the Conciliarist works of two centuries later) the necessity to preserve the *status ecclesiae* was always presented as imposing a limit on papal authority rather than as a ground for extending it. . . . For them 'the state of the Church' was not a vague indefinable concept which might be used to justify any extraordinary action of the Church's ruler, but was rather a living reality, closely identified with the rules of ecclesiastical life laid down in the laws of General Councils and confirmed 'by universal consent'" (*Foundations of the Conciliar Theory: The Contribution of the Medieval Canonists from Gratian to the Great Schism* [Cambridge: Cambridge University Press, 1955], 51–52). Phillip Stump points out: "When *status ecclesiae* is used as a criterion for limiting papal power, for example in the teaching that the pope could not grant dispensations against the decrees of the first four Ecumenical Councils, it has the meaning of 'constitution' or 'fundamental structure or nature' of the Church" (*The Reforms of the Council of Constance 1414–1418* [Leiden: E. J. Brill, 1994], 254).

24   Let us recall that the International Una Voce Federation was founded in 1965 to defend the Latin language and the Gregorian chant that were rapidly disappearing from the Roman rite, prior to pivoting to a defense of the old Roman rite as such after 1969. See Joseph Shaw, ed., *The Latin Mass and the Intellectuals: Petitions to Save the Ancient Mass from 1966 to 2007* (Waterloo, ON: Arouca Press, 2023), xxxi, 90, 219, and passim.

God wills the diversity of religions as he wills the diversity of sexes; and so forth, all of which a well-catechized schoolchild could see are incompatible with the Catholic Faith.

In an important interview, Dom Alcuin Reid, prior of the Monastère Saint-Benoît in France and one of the world's outstanding liturgical scholars, explains why he refuses to recognize his "suspension" and his monastery's "suppression":

> Regardless of the decrees issuing from our Chancery, our daily life with its eight hours of the Divine Office and Mass, its manual and intellectual work, the welcoming of guests, etc., continues unabated – with great joy and peace amidst the thorns. We knew that suspensions and suppressions may be on the horizon, but we are the proprietors of our own property, not the diocese, so we cannot be evicted... That [monastic life] is our vocation and our duty to which we are vowed before Almighty God. We must be faithful to that. We can do nothing else without becoming mere hirelings that flee with the onset of the wolves (cf. Jn 10:23).
>
> If we must be canonically independent for a while, so be it. We do not wish this, of course, and shall ensure that we maintain good relations with other monastics and shall invite appropriately experienced monks to make visitations every three years, and so on. If we must be independent, we must not become insular. In time, in God's Providence, the authorities will come to recognize the integrity of our life and grant us the appropriate authorization – as has happened in the not-so-distant past.
>
> The most obvious parallel is that of the first two decades of the history of the Abbey of Le Barroux: its founder, Dom Gérard Calvet, was suspended and expelled from the Benedictine order for having his men ordained without permission (those ordained were suspended also) – only for him to be blessed as an abbot by a cardinal sent by the Vatican some fifteen years later.
>
> Let us not forget the origins of the Fraternity of St Peter or of the Institute of the Good Shepherd: they would not exist today if it were not for the conscientious disobedience of several decades ago that ensured that the Society of St Pius X continued on when it was canonically suppressed in the 1970s.

People who benefit from the good work of these Institutes today, or indeed who admire the Abbey of Le Barroux, should not forget the fact that they exist today because historically their founders took conscientious decisions to ignore parts of canon law and decrees of suppression that would have otherwise brought about their death. Our times, unfortunately, seem to be becoming as extraordinary as were theirs and may well necessitate similar actions.[25]

These are strong words coming from Dom Alcuin, who is known for his habit of understatement and for the utmost respectfulness he has always shown and encouraged toward Church authority.[26] I think he simply recognizes the situation for what it is — and so must we.[27] Tragically, the era of liturgical peace and organic growth inaugurated by Benedict XVI has been canceled out; we have gone (to use the title of an anthology of writings on *Traditionis Custodes*) "from Benedict's peace to Francis's war." We are not in a situation where our enemies are willing to parley amicably with us and arrive at a compromise. They are seeking our marginalization, ostracization, extinction, and annihilation. If what we have in our Catholic tradition is true, good, right, holy, and beautiful, it is worth living for, fighting for, and dying for — no compromises, no pandering, no bowing and scraping, no pussyfooting, no backtracking, no false obedience. It is a time for heroic commitment, not for the wringing of hands, wistful regrets, shrugged shoulders, grudging compliance, or, worst of all, self-accusatory surrender.

It is a simple fact that if our forefathers in the traditional movement had not refused to obey Paul VI on the grounds that he was

---

25 "Interview with Dom Alcuin Reid on his ordination, his community, the diocese of Fréjus-Toulon, and *Desiderio Desideravi*," *Rorate Caeli*, July 15, 2022.
26 See, for example, his lecture "Reflections on Authority in Liturgy Today," *Catholic World Report*, July 14, 2019.
27 As Shawn Tribe has written: "Ultimately the problem [of rupture] wasn't rooted out by the *Summorum* years; what the *Summorum* years did accomplish however was that . . . many people saw into . . . the richness and beauty of the Roman liturgical tradition. The *SP* years were the 'live and let live' years. So here we are, but fortunately the Church has always thrived in response to persecutions and the present persecution of the *usus antiquior* may well be what is finally needed to put the rupturist school to bed permanently in the end. The more obvious the disdain and open the attack upon this patrimony, the more transparent it is that there is a significant ideological problem and it has invited open criticism [of the liturgical revolutionaries] of a sort that we didn't see in the *SP* years" (comment on Facebook).

owed no obedience in this matter since he was acting *ultra vires* or outside of his authority, we would not have, sixty years later, the traditional Mass, any of the old sacramental rites, or the Divine Office in our midst.[28] They would have been buried along with everything else that that haunted man spent his time consigning to the graveyard of *aggiornamento*.[29]

I want to emphasize this point: when tradition is under attack, the only right response of the orthodox Catholic is to defend it, to cleave to it all the more, and to resist those who are attacking it. Obedience can never be morally legitimate to those who are disobedient to what is higher than and prior to themselves. Put positively, we are obliged to disobey materially their commands and prohibitions, in order to obey the higher law of divine truth that is contained in and made manifest by our rites, our beliefs, and our way of life.

Anyone who is not a ferocious reductionist loves the "smells and bells" of the traditional Latin Mass. But a traditionalist's love for it goes deeper, right to its core – to its texts, its ceremonies, its rubrics, its presentation of the Faith, its abundant and manifest adoration of the Most Blessed Trinity and the Most Holy Body and Precious Blood of Christ. We do not love the old Mass just for the smells and bells that we could, theoretically, find elsewhere (some of them, sometimes...). We love it because of *what it is in itself*, just as we love a best friend not so much for what he can do for us, or how he might please us, or how he may dress, but for *who he is* and the place he holds in our lives and affections.

The traditionalist movement has grown somewhat flaccid and self-indulgent in this regard, because we have perhaps allowed ourselves to be persuaded that ours is simply a "preference," rather like chocolate versus vanilla ice cream. If that were the basis for our actions, we would be rightly censured for our stubbornness and

---

28   We do well to bear in mind that the attack on the traditional Mass began in earnest with the Instruction on Implementing Liturgical Norms *Inter Oecumenici* of 1965, which led rapidly to the near-extinction of Latin, the near-disappearance of chant, the turning of the priest *versus populum*, and so forth. Indeed, since very few were aware that the Consilium was hard at work on a new rite, it was quite common for people between 1964 and 1969 to use the term "new Mass" to refer to the Tridentine Mass in its amputated, musically trendy, vernacular, *versus populum* form – thinking that this was going to be what the fulfillment of *Sacrosanctum Concilium* looked like.

29   For a detailed discussion of Paul VI's mentality, see Kwasniewski, *Once and Future Roman Rite*, 109-43 and 381-97.

rightly demanded to comply with whatever directives are given to us.[30] But if we are committed to the authentic Roman Rite because of the most profound theological, moral, and spiritual reasons — as indeed we are, or should be — then we ourselves may rightly censure churchmen for *their* abandonment of tradition and *their* dereliction of duty. We occupy the moral high ground and we have nothing to be ashamed of or to apologize for.

These considerations apply to priests in a special way. A priest must be prepared to be materially disobedient to the revolutionaries who have occupied seats of power if he would be truly obedient to Christ and to His Church as they exist in eternity and as they straddle twenty centuries of human history. Those who would abuse, restrict, or suppress the ecclesiastical monuments of tradition, especially the super-monument of the Mass, are not only *not* worthy of obedience, they are — whether they realize it or not — rivals of Christ, exterminators of the Church, and abusers of the faithful. Insofar as they are such, they must not be allowed to triumph. Nothing could be worse than allowing their false narratives, erroneous claims, progressivist or beige theology, and utter lack of respect for tradition to prevail and to establish itself yet further and deeper, like a cancer that wastes away more and more of the body.

Canon law derives from natural and divine law and ecclesiastical tradition and must remain subordinate to them and interpreted by them. We must not allow hierarchs of the Church to weaponize canon law against the faithful or the clergy by depriving them of powerful spiritual resources, denigrating their legitimate desires, or undermining their adherence to what is good, true, beautiful, holy, and right. As Dom Alcuin said and as many others have reiterated, canon law abused in this manner ceases to have any force since it undermines the basic rationale of all law, namely, that it be for the common good of the people governed by it.

---

30   See Yves Chiron, *Paul VI: The Divided Pope*, trans. James Walther (Brooklyn, NY: Angelico Press, 2022), 285, for Paul's stern command that all must take up his new missal. Many authors have demonstrated that Paul VI did not, in fact, legislate the new missal as obligatory (and therefore as excluding the use of the old missal). For a detailed and conclusive account that draws on all of the relevant primary sources, see John Salza and Robert Siscoe, *True or False Pope? Refuting Sedevacantism and Other Modern Errors* (Winona, MN: STAS Editions, 2015), 493–524. Sadly, this book is out of print and its authors seem to have moved in a different direction.

Let us be clear: either we accept that the pope is *not* the lord and master of the liturgical rites of Christendom, that he is in some definite sense *bound* to receive and respect them, even if he may gently modify them in small ways, and that he has a solemn obligation before God, rooted in his very office, to "pass on that which he has received" (cf. 1 Cor 11:23; 1 Cor 15:3); *or* we must grant that the pope has complete and unlimited authority over liturgical rites in every respect except the bare minimum of words necessary to produce a sacramental effect, and, accordingly, that he *could* legitimately – if stupidly – abolish all the Eastern rites and replace them with the Novus Ordo, or abolish all Western rites and replace them with the Syro-Malabar rite; or could decree that Mass should be celebrated in clown costumes, with plastic tableware, dancing girls, and constant whistling and clapping. (Actually, this already happens in Chicago, but that's another matter.) These are your only two logical possibilities. *Tertium non datur.* To repeat it more simply: *either* the pope is bound by tradition in a very real sense, such that acting notoriously against it would invalidate both his acts and any subsequent acts based on them, *or* he is not bound by tradition and can say with Pius IX: "*I* am the Tradition; *I* am the Church."

Some might think that I'm making up a straw man with this latter viewpoint. I assure you, I am not, although I wish it were so. There are energetic apologists online who, based on a tendentious reading of *Pastor Aeternus* and related documents – which they read in a manner totally devoid of the qualifications afforded by *Dei Filius* and other authoritative teachings, displaced from historical context, and divorced from plain common sense[31] – argue that the pope's universal jurisdictional authority comprises absolute power over all liturgical rites.

It is clear that the *sensus fidei fidelium* of the Church manifestly cannot allow this to be true. It cannot be true without making our religion laughably absurd. The thought that tradition is nothing more than "a toy of popes,"[32] a plaything they can smash at will like spoiled children if they so desire, would be the acid, the solvent, of all piety and devotion. Religion is constituted by rites of worship,

---

31   See chapter 3.
32   In the words of Bishop Rob Mutsaerts: see his article "An Evik Ukase from Pope Francis," in Kwasniewski, *From Benedict's Peace to Francis's War*, 133.

and these rites are necessarily ancient, venerable, inherited, and, as time passes, increasingly treated as untouchable. Until recently, this attitude has characterized every Catholic who has ever lived. It requires no special faculty of perception to see the massive damage that has been caused when popes suddenly make numerous large-scale changes to the rites of religion. By the light of reason, by the truths of psychology, anthropology, and sociology, we can know that such changes will *always* cause a damage disproportionate to any possible gains (this, indeed, is the reason Aquinas gives for why it is foolish to change laws too much or too often).[33] It would be philosophically incoherent and culturally self-destructive to embrace this legacy of damage, or better, self-harm, as if it were somehow a "new tradition" or a "part" of tradition. Such aggression leaves lasting wounds that must be healed by the restoration of the original healthy condition. That is what traditional Catholics believe and fight for.

Writes Fr Zuhlsdorf: "Hardship, deprivation, suffering, challenges are not always only mere evils to be endured. Sometimes they are needed corrections, cures, even coercions allowed or provided by God to help us get to the truth of who we are."[34] I agree with him. I believe that God permitted the evil of *Traditionis Custodes* and all subsequent implementations as a wake-up call addressed to all traditionalists, a kind of shock-therapy to bring us back to our roots, to reorient us to the first principles of our movement, to reanimate the zealous commitment that will be required to get beyond the final and worst flare-up of postconciliar progressivism. I say "final" because the people in power now are the last Vatican II nostalgics, and for them, *everything* is on the line; their entire life's commitment and project—to create a new Church for modern times—is on the line. When they are gone, there will be almost no one who cares about the Council with the same golden-calf devotion they have.

I especially want to highlight the *courage* of the original traditionalists. At a time in the Church, the tempestuous 1960s, when ultramontanism was still riding high—when it had not yet been battered and bruised by decade after decade of disastrous episcopal

---

33   See St Thomas, *Summa theologiae* I-II, Q. 97, art. 2; cf. discussion in chapter 5.
34   "When Life Gives You Manure, Maybe It's Time for Changes," *OnePeterFive*, July 23, 2022.

and cardinalatial appointments, by Assisi interreligious gatherings and Koran kissings, by a failure to discipline all but the most outrageous heretics, and by a dismal record of failing to correct ubiquitous liturgical abuses and clerical sex abuse – I say, at a time when ultramontanism was still a plausible mental attitude, the traditionalists refused to consent to the denigration and dismantling of centuries of liturgical tradition, the banishment of Latin and Gregorian chant, the turning around of the priest to face the people, the placing of the Body of Christ into the hands of standing communicants, the feminist preferment of women into ministerial roles, and so forth (the catalogue of pseudo-antiquarian innovations is long and tedious). These things they refused *as a matter of principle* – both because they rightly loved the tradition and had supernatural conviction and natural confidence in its goodness, and because they quite reasonably inferred and expected many evils to come from its eviction; indeed, they were already starting to witness, even while the Council was in session and certainly in the years immediately after it, a growing rash of experiments and sacrileges that would have been unimaginable in the years before the Council.[35]

Why did the first traditionalists offer this unprecedented degree of resistance to decrees being handed down from Rome, from the Vatican, from the desk of the pope himself? They offered it on the dual basis of reason and faith.

On the side of reason, they looked at what was being proposed, what was being enforced, what was being allowed, and they saw that it was irrational, that it made no sense – it was nonsense. A man could not swallow it and still respect himself as a thinking and thoughtful being, as one who wishes to be consistent, logical, and coherent. One who *knows* with the certainty of immediate and oft-repeated experience the supreme beauty and spiritual power of the chanted Latin High Mass cannot then turn around and say this

---

35 I am not saying there were no egregious abuses prior to the council – Guardini's and Parsch's *versus populum* Masses come to mind as examples. But there was not the same feverish atmosphere, and most of the critics of preconciliar Catholicism were not heretics who wanted to overthrow the whole liturgical tradition, but woefully naïve and misguided zealots. A whole book waits to be written about the ardent reformists who sobered up in the wake of the actual reform and expressed feelings ranging from disappointment to disgust. See, for starters, Kwasniewski (ed.), *Illusions of Reform*, 15–16, 66, 80–81.

is no longer "relevant" to modern man, that it will no longer attract souls to Christ and lead them to the heights of contemplation. To make such a denial would be to betray oneself, one's innermost certainties, and the wisdom of the ages, in the name of a blind obedience that requires the sacrifice of intellect, the faculty that makes man human and capable of divinization.

On the side of faith — or more precisely, the *sensus fidei fidelium*, the "sense possessed by the faithful of that which belongs to and is in harmony with the Faith, and that which is not"[36]— the original traditionalists asked how that which council after council, pope after pope, and century after century of believers had practiced, defended, praised, and promoted could now suddenly be wrong or useless or outmoded. (Recall Ratzinger's observation that the Church would be utterly inconsistent to prohibit today what it venerated yesterday, or to declare harmful that which was its highest and most precious possession.) To say to a man who believes in the Real Presence and has a well-developed Eucharistic piety: "Okay, get up from your knees, dust off your trousers, stick out your hands, and take the host," is to invite a reaction of utter incomprehension and scorn. He would never do that, not if you threatened and tortured him. Or at least, he ought not. It would be a sign of lack of faith and lack of piety — indeed, something worse: a sign of total personal immaturity and human imbecility — to be willing to throw over perennial customs of reverence practiced all of one's life and by centuries of one's predecessors only because "Father knows best" and "the bishop said so" and "the pope decreed it." Can we not see how the entire clerical abuse crisis was facilitated by this infantile mentality of uncritical trust and spineless conformism? The traditionalists, however, knew *and felt* that the Church had been right in what she had been doing time out of mind, and, therefore, that her spokesmen could not but be wrong in trying to cancel it all out, in trying to fundamentally reorient and reconfigure and even refound the Church for modern times.[37]

The liturgical reform was "sold," so to speak, on a mighty promise of the countless wonderful blessings it could not fail to bring

---

36 See Kwasniewski, *True Obedience*, 43–51.
37 I say "refound" because the irresponsible rhetoric of "a new Pentecost" suggests as much. See Kwasniewski, *Once and Future Roman Rite*, 173–77.

to the Church. The Second Vatican Council's Constitution on the Sacred Liturgy, *Sacrosanctum Concilium*, begins with a statement of what the Council hoped to achieve, with the liturgical reform as its poster-child:

> This sacred Council . . . desires to impart an ever-increasing vigor to the Christian life of the faithful; to adapt more suitably to the needs of our own times those institutions which are subject to change; to foster whatever can promote union among all who believe in Christ; to strengthen whatever can help to call the whole of mankind into the household of the Church.

As my colleague Gregory DiPippo, esteemed editor of *New Liturgical Movement*, has pointed out on more than one occasion: "None of this has happened. The Christian life of the faithful has not become more vigorous; its institutions have not become more suitably adapted to the needs of our times; union has not been fostered among all who believe in Christ; the call of the whole of mankind into the household of the Church has not been strengthened."[38]

As I have said, the traditionalists objected to a massive reform as a matter of *principle*, on the twin basis of reason and faith, because they could not see how it would be right to sacrifice the tradition already certainly known and loved for a non-existent future possibility uncertainly known and impossible to love. In 1971, at the time of the first (so-called Agatha Christie) indult, no one had the freedom to argue for keeping the old liturgy on the grounds that it would be "pastoral" to do so, or because of its venerable theology, since, as Joseph Shaw notes, "the whole point of the reform was the [promised] pastoral effectiveness, as yet of course untried, of the reformed missal, and the [hoped-for assimilation of the] theological insights of Vatican II."[39] The only defense that (partially) worked with the ecclesiastical authorities back in 1971 was an artistic and cultural defense.

Today, we are in a vastly different position. We have not only the same principles of faith and reason as our forefathers, we also have behind us a half-century of desolation, desecration, and dramatic

---

38   Gregory DiPippo, "The Revolution Is Over," *New Liturgical Movement*, August 1, 2022.
39   Shaw, *Latin Mass and the Intellectuals*, 209.

decline in church life as a monumental witness of unarguable *fact* against the prophesied success of the liturgical reform. We know now that the prophets of renewal – even if they wore the mitre of a bishop or the fisherman's ring – were false prophets who said "peace, peace, when there was no peace" (Jer 6:14, 8:11), who promised plenty but brought down famine. To defend the superiority of Catholic tradition today, we don't need to have even *half* the insightfulness of the original traditionalists, because we can see that every one of *their* predictions has been proved true to the last degree. They predicted that sudden and massive change would have catastrophic effects, and that the *particular* changes pushed through would undermine Catholic faith and practice. They predicted that where tradition was treasured, the Church would weather the storm and produce good fruits. They have been abundantly vindicated in the event, for it is the very success of the traditionalist renewal against all possible odds that has roused the dragon's ire.

To be a traditionalist today requires no great wisdom, for the good and bad fruits have reached full maturity. We still have the same power of reason and the same *sensus fidei fidelium* that tells us when something is irrational or when it refuses to harmonize with what a sound catechism teaches us. The one thing we need more of, much more of, is courage, fortitude, boldness. The traditionalist movement both benefited from and suffered from the fifteen-year "pax Benedictina," the peaceful space of coexistence put into place by Benedict XVI. We benefited because many more priests learned the old rite and many more faithful grew to love it. So our movement has grown tremendously in *numbers*. But we suffered, too, because in a lot of places things became easier for us, and perhaps we grew soft, as soldiers may do in peace time; suddenly we had friendly (or at least not openly hostile) bishops, we had parishes springing up here and there; it seemed like a gently rising and irresistible tide.

And then came the unexpected *Traditionis Custodes*. This document, whose title can be translated "prison-guards of treachery," threw us suddenly back into a state of open conflict that many – especially, I would say, "cradle traditionalists" and recent "tradverts" – were quite unprepared for. Hence, we really need to step up our game. Everyone who has drifted to the old Latin Mass because they love the Eucharistic reverence, the silence, the music, the community of young families, the orthodox preaching, whatever it might be, or even just because they hated masks and hand sanitizer and the Branch Covidian religion – all of them need to pick up some good books and educate themselves.[40] They need to find out what happened in the 1960s and why traditionalism *as a movement* began.[41] They need, in short, to move from being tourists of tradition to apostles of it, from nomads to homesteaders, from admirers to defenders. We were sold a kind of half-truth, that we could have the tradition if we "preferred" it; and that was a false compromise, because tradition is not something we "prefer," it is something we know and understand, believe and live – it is a treasure without which we cannot live and without which the Church cannot thrive. It is not a preference but a vital necessity, a fundamental identity. When we recover this awareness, this conviction of the *truth* of how things really stand, and act accordingly, then we will deserve to inherit the name and the success of the first traditionalists who fought and suffered so much in the '60s and '70s. A coterie of nostalgic Vatican II hippies now in positions of power has thrust us back into that chthonic world from which we had begun to emerge. Let us strive, by God's grace, to be worthy of standing side by side with those who first led the people of God out of the Egypt of the "reform" into a land flowing with the milk and honey of Catholic tradition. We can do it. God has given us reason, He has given us faith, He has given us models to look to, He has given us intimate personal experience, He has given us the collective wisdom of twenty centuries of Catholicism. The victory is ours if we will hold fast and never lose heart.

---

40 One might start with my books *Reclaiming Our Roman Catholic Birthright* and *Once and Future Roman Rite*, then move on to Michael Fiedrowicz's *The Traditional Mass: History, Form, and Theology of the Classical Roman Rite* (Brooklyn, NY: Angelico Press, 2020).

41 For this, two books are indispensable: Stuart Chessman's *Faith of Our Fathers: A Brief History of Catholic Traditionalism in the United States, from Triumph to Traditionis Custodes* (Brooklyn, NY: Angelico Press, 2022) and Joseph Shaw's *Latin Mass and the Intellectuals.*

9

The Rights of Immemorial Tradition and the Limits of Papal Positivism

WHENEVER TRADITIONALISTS OBJECT TO or reject a particular papal determination on the liturgy – be it the creation of novel liturgical books or the severe limitation of the use of customary rites – our so-called conservative opponents are ready to assail us with a battery of proof-texts drawn from popes like St Pius X or Pius XII, or from Vatican II, or from neoscholastic manuals, to the effect that "the pope has the right to change the liturgy, to institute or abolish this or that rite as he wishes," etc., because, as Vatican I teaches, he has supreme, universal, and immediate jurisdiction over the Church.

There is some truth to such an assertion, but it doesn't prove as much as those who say it think it proves.

First, any statement like this is governed by certain implicit norms. For example, that the pope can institute or alter rites has never been taken to mean he can abolish a rite altogether, e.g., one of the Eastern rites of the Church over which he is technically the supreme head with universal and immediate juridical authority. And if he were to do so, the Byzantine Catholics would be fully within their rights to ignore his action altogether and carry on as if nothing had changed. There are misuses or abuses of authority that cancel out its action, and we are capable of formulating criteria for such cases, as I do in this book.

Second, the pope may arguably have the authority to institute new rites, but these would be supplemental to, and not in contradiction to, traditional rites. Moreover, the only basis on which a pope can justly introduce a new edition of a liturgical book that supplants a former edition is if there is manifest continuity between the old and new books, so that one can truthfully say: "It is the same book, only augmented with new feasts, or edited in minor ways, or purged of typographical errors," etc. That is why we can say that each *editio typica* or official edition of the missal of St Pius V—the 1604 *editio* from Clement VIII, the 1634 from Urban VIII, the 1884 from Leo XIII, and the 1920 from Benedict XV—is still the same missal, containing the same Roman Rite. When, however, we reach Pius XII's severe alterations to Holy Week, which made their way into the 1962 *editio typica* of John XXIII, we are already looking at a seriously problematic situation: it is not possible to claim that the Pacellian Holy Week is essentially in continuity with the cumulative preceding tradition. So, in the 1962 missal there is already a compromising "crack" in the structure, as it were, and this was interpreted by many liturgists at the time as the anticipation of (and invitation to) a total alteration, a substantial change, yet to come. Once we get to the Novus Ordo missal, in which only 13% of the euchological or prayer-text material is identical to that which is found in the 1962 missal, [1] we are manifestly dealing with a *different* missal, having of course some generic resemblances, but certainly not "in the same line" of development—not another individual of the same species. Hence it is a *new rite* of Mass (and the same can be said of the other new sacramental rites, the Liturgy of the Hours, the Book of Blessings, etc.), and so, logically, its introduction does not abrogate or obrogate the old rite of Mass; it simply joins it as a sibling (again, I'm giving here the most positive interpretation possible). In no way, shape, or form could Paul VI's action be construed as a replacement of one Roman Missal with another edition of it. And he himself seems to have recognized this fact quite clearly because he was the first pope since 1570 to exclude Pope Pius V's bull *Quo Primum* from the front matter of his missal, signifying that it no longer belongs to the same family as the Roman Rite canonized (but manifestly not created) by St Pius V. [2] As Alfons Cardinal Stickler said:

> It cannot . . . escape experts of the old liturgy what a great distinction exists between the *corpus traditionum*, which was alive in the old Mass, and the contrived Novus Ordo—to the decided disadvantage of the latter. Shepherds, scholars, and lay faithful have noticed it, of

---

1   See Matthew Hazell, "'All the Elements of the Roman Rite'? Mythbusting, Part II," *New Liturgical Movement*, October 1, 2021.
2   See Shaw, *Latin Mass and the Intellectuals*, 3–17.

course; and the multitude of opposing voices increased with time. . . . It is becoming clearer and clearer that the radicalism of the post-Conciliar reformers did not consist of renewing the Catholic liturgy from its roots [as one might do by applying a well-chosen fertilizer], but in tearing it from its traditional soil. [The reform] did not rework the Roman rite, which it was asked to do by the Liturgy Constitution of Vatican II, but uprooted it.[3]

IGNORING THE ACTUAL HISTORICAL RECORD

Catholics who defend the idea that the pope has a virtually unlimited power to change the liturgy[4] are wrong precisely because of the way they have framed the conversation. To start by placing the liturgy on the operating table like an anaesthetized patient with the pope as the head surgeon is to begin with so fundamental an error that one will not be able to avoid a cascade of absurd conclusions.[5] Since the belief that the liturgy is the "pope's toy" (to use the colorful expression of Bishop Mutsaerts) is out of the question before any discussion begins, there need not be a laborious inquiry into whether he can smash his toy or replace it with a toy he likes better. Indeed, the hyperpapalists never seem to ask themselves a very simple question: If what they maintain were true, why has no pope prior to modern times ever behaved *as if* it were true? Put differently, how does one explain the fact that, of 266 popes, only a handful made significant changes to the liturgical rites, while the vast majority were content to hand on what they received, with a default conservatism? And of those that made the most significant changes, why should it be the case that

---

3   See Stickler, "Recollections of a Vatican II Peritus." An alternative translation of the last sentences reads: "It is becoming more and more evident that the radicalness of the postconciliar reformers has not consisted in renewing the Catholic liturgy from its roots but in uprooting it from its traditional soil. They have not revised the Roman Rite as they were directed to do by the Constitution on the Liturgy of Vatican II. They have eradicated it" (*Precious Blood Banner* 26 [October 1995]).

4   I have in mind the work of popular theologaster Michael Lofton. Some traditionalists, in spite of their candid acknowledgment of the superiority of the traditional rites, maintain that the pope has an absolute power of disposal over anything in the liturgy that does not pertain to the "matter and form" of the sacraments. For a critique of this viewpoint, see Lamont, "Dominican Theologian Attacks Catholic Tradition."

5   As John Monaco has shown: see "Are There Limits to Papal Power?," *Catholic World Report*, October 13, 2021; "Was the Sacred Liturgy Made for the Pope, or the Pope for the Sacred Liturgy?," *Catholic World Report*, July 28, 2021; "The Church of the Papal Fiat," *Crisis Magazine*, January 20, 2022.

most of them are concentrated in the twentieth century, indeed, in the second half of the twentieth century? And can we explain why, if we take *all* the changes of the popes prior to Paul VI and put them together, they would still weigh less in the balance than those that *Paul VI alone* pushed through?

Judging from the actions and words of popes and the general practice of the Church, the impression one gains from Catholic history is that the sacred *rites* — not just the "form and matter" of the sacraments — are a hallowed inheritance to be received and revered with humility. The idea that a pope, especially after a long period of stability, could draw up new rites from scratch to replace old ones was unthinkable. When online apologists dig up forgotten scholastic treatises arguing that the pope can do practically anything he wants with the liturgy, they demonstrate only that they as well as the scholastics, on this point, are, like ivory-tower intellectuals, defending a principle that is *irrelevant* to the actual historical record and life of the Church. If a pope were to change everything but the matter and form of a sacrament, he would deserve condemnation from an ecclesiological, anthropological, spiritual, and every other point of view, regardless of whatever arguments might be made for his supposed "authority" to do so. Nor would the Christian people in healthier times have tolerated any such assault on their inheritance, since their minds had not yet been poisoned by a heartless legal positivism.

Shouldn't we take more seriously the fact that *for fifteen centuries* the Church was able to proceed in her liturgical life *without* the need for a centrally curated, papally promulgated missal? For fifteen centuries, Christendom had tens of thousands of missals scattered on tens of thousands of altars, copied by hand from one generation to the next, without the *nihil obstat* and *imprimatur* (so to speak) of the Roman Pontiff. I do not deny that the Council of Trent's and St Pius V's centralizing moves made sense in the emergency situation then present, but would simply draw out a lesson we can learn from three-fourths of the Church's history: the liturgy was obviously something that belonged to — and was seen to belong to — *the Church as a whole*. It was not anyone's property to dispose of, but everyone's privileged inheritance to receive and hand on. Certainly, the pope can insert himself into this process, but precisely on the condition that he too, as a member of the Church, a recipient of tradition and a guardian of the *status ecclesiae*, does not treat the liturgical rite as his own property to dispose of.[6] This is why some older authors say the pope could become "schismatic" by attacking the rites of the Church.[7] It's not simply a question of bare validity, which is what a materialist, reductionist mentality would find sufficient or perhaps exhaustive; it's about the honorable standing of the rites of divine worship in the sight of God and of the Church, which endows them with a certain priority over *any* member of the Church. It is for this reason that a Catholic, faced with two bad situations, should prefer to have someone like Alexander VI as pope rather than Paul VI or Francis. Alexander may have been a morally bad man, but he did not *dare* to touch the traditional rites of the Church. He celebrated the papal Mass with respect for the rituals and rubrics, as any believing Catholic would do.

What we are dealing with, I suppose, is a typically modern (Enlightenment, liberal, individualist, secularist) failure to understand or even to acknowledge the concept of tradition as such. What room is there for *paradosis* or *traditio* in a worldview of nominalism and voluntarism, where the Roman Rite can be whatever the pope says it is, regardless of continuity or rupture with the past? This worldview seems to deny any positive meaning to Christian history, seeing only the present moment (or worse, the interpretation of the present moment) as having any weight. The reason why popes did not act in accordance with the absolutizing papal theories of Franzelin *et alii* is that the popes had a healthy, inherited, almost instinctive understanding that rites are an expression of the living faith of the Church and of the working of the Holy Spirit across the centuries. To change them substantively would be to reject the gifts of Divine Providence, to undermine the stability of the *lex credendi*, and, in so doing, to unsettle the entire body of the faithful.[8]

---

6   By which I mean: radically alter or abolish. See Hazell, "Mythbusting."
7   Cardinal Juan de Torquemada (1388-1468), for example, states that if a pope fails to observe "the universal rite of ecclesiastical worship" and "divides himself with pertinacity from the observance of the universal church," he is "able to fall into schism" and is neither to be obeyed nor "put up with" (*non est sustinendus*). For this and other examples, see Kwasniewski, "The Pope's Boundedness to Tradition as a Legislative Limit" and Silveira, *Two Timely Issues*.
8   See Kwasniewski, *Once and Future Roman Rite*, 33-77.

QUO PRIMUM AND TRADITIONIS CUSTODES

With this perspective in mind, let us return to the great Pope St Pius V. The *Missale Romanum* he promulgated in 1570 was not a new creation but an act of conservation: a book that definitively embodied and represented the cumulative millennial tradition of Rome as well as the Council of Trent's dogmatic confession, which this missal enshrined for all times and places.[9] That is why the bull that accompanied it, *Quo Primum*, is not "merely disciplinary" in nature: Pius V sought to "canonize" the Roman Rite of Mass because it flawlessly contains and transmits the authentic Catholic Faith, over against the errors of the Protestants (and many other heresies besides, from ancient times onward). In contrast, Vatican II, though a valid council, defined nothing dogmatically and anathematized no errors. It is therefore impossible to see Paul VI's new missal as a *dogmatic* synthesis mandated by a dogmatic Council. Moreover, nearly everyone by now is aware of the huge gap between what the Second Vatican Council asked for and what Paul VI approved, which would mean that, by any objective rational standard, the Mass of Paul VI cannot even be considered "the Mass of Vatican II."[10]

Moreover – and this is the crucial point – if the supposed "Mass of Vatican II" is so different from the "Mass of Trent" (or, in other words, the Mass of the whole of the Latin tradition) that it cannot be celebrated by the same priests and the same faithful on the same altars but must definitively *replace, supplant, and cancel out* the old liturgy, then it must be a *false* liturgy – one that has departed from tradition, from the undeniable witness of the saints, councils, and popes that used it before and confessed the one true Faith through it.

Pope Francis famously claims in *Traditionis Custodes* that we are in possession of liturgical books that constitute "the unique expression of the *lex orandi* of the Roman Rite." Yet this assertion, whatever its author may have imagined, does not have the effect of cancelling out the *old* liturgy; it has the effect, rather, of cancelling out the *new* liturgy, as well as his own authority (at least in regard to this matter). It is a brilliant example of someone sawing off the branch on which he is sitting. One cannot declare the past liturgical

---

9   See Shaw, *Latin Mass and the Intellectuals*, 3–17.
10   For a thorough treatment of this last point, see Kwasniewski (ed.), *Illusions of Reform*.

tradition to be no longer reflective of the theology of the Church without implying that this theology has changed so decisively that it is no longer essentially the same as it was. In short, the Church would have fundamentally altered her *lex credendi*, and that is why a new *lex orandi* was deemed requisite. But if that is true, then the "new theology" and the "new worship" are false and must be rejected. In short, the exercise of papal authority must be logically consistent and theologically coherent or it self-destructs, as it is presently doing.[11]

PAPAL AUTHORITY IN A TIME OF DOCTRINAL CRISIS

Do we say, then, that Francis has no authority? That he is not the pope? If he is pope, surely his documents are magisterial and his determinations – such as a motu proprio on liturgical law – carry force. I reply with Fr John Hunwicke that St John Henry Newman offers us a powerful explanatory principle in speaking of the "suspension" of episcopal authority during the Arian crisis, when most bishops no longer openly professed and passed on the Catholic Faith in the divinity of Christ. In our time, too, the pope's magisterium, analogously to that of the Arian or Semi-Arian or complicit bishops, is in a "state of suspension." In regard to matters on which the pope has gone astray, his teaching and his decrees are without standing or force; they are prevented by intrinsic defects from taking effect. A large number of statements and actions of Pope Francis meet this description. Michael Charlier explains this point well:

> We assume that . . . the papal magisterium is currently in a state of suspension. The pope talks and writes a lot; some of it agrees with the traditional Magisterium of the Church, some of it directly contradicts it, and some of

---

11 Every legitimate rite comes from the same Father (God in His Providence) and the same Mother (Holy Mother Church in her act of *paradosis* or handing on). If a rite is not born in this way, it is alien to the family. Some have tried to argue that there can be multiple *leges orandi* and *leges credendi*, without any of them being incorrect or one superior to another; they might merely differ in points of emphasis. But surely, this is true of the diversity of liturgical rites in general, throughout East and West; and so one must either believe that such diversity is good (and harmless), or one must believe that the pope could abolish all rites except for a single one and impose it on everyone because he happens to prefer its take on the *lex orandi/credendi*. The former view is the one that the Church has generally acted on; the imposition of rites on those to whom they are foreign has frequently been condemned as an abuse.

it eludes immediate classification because of its incoherence. Dealing with this situation is unfamiliar and highly irritating for Catholics, but by no means impossible, and without succumbing to the illusion of a "Magisterium in constant flux" created by Francis.

To put it very briefly, when Francis repeats something that the Church has always taught, we are happy to hear it without recognizing in it a magisterium of the pope's own. It is nothing but unbroken tradition. Where he says something that directly contradicts the traditional Magisterium and Tradition, we take note of it with chagrin as his personal opinion – an opinion, however, that does not bind Catholics in any way. And where he says something that seems incomprehensible or incoherent, we will recognize in it – at best – an impetus for reflection.

In this reflection on papal contradictions, however, we will in no case let ourselves be guided by the ludicrous construct of his Jesuit colleague Spadaro that "in theology" "2 + 2 can also add up to 5." Theology is not mathematics, that is true; but "2 + 2 = 5" is in any case nonsense, it is untruth, and therefore a blasphemy against the divine order. Such a thing cannot become the content of the ecclesiastical Magisterium even if a pope should say it.[12]

In a period of time in which some ecclesial documents no longer have "any connection to the positions held by the Magisterium prior to the Second Vatican Council," the Catholic is faced with a choice, says Fr Chad Ripperger: he must be either a "magisterial positivist" who believes that "whatever the current Magisterium says is always what is 'orthodox,'" or a "traditionalist" who takes "Scripture, intrinsic tradition, extrinsic tradition, and the current Magisterium as the principles of judgment of correct Catholic thinking." The positivist is ready to change his mind – literally to contradict himself or any authoritative source of the past, including dogmatic definitions and immemorial monuments of faith – if an authority says he must do so. The traditionalist, however, receives and abides by *all* authoritative sources according to their inherent weight, seeing them as permanent witnesses to the truth. Fr Ripperger says that each of us must take a stand: Do I believe that "[the newer] is necessarily

---

12   Michael Charlier, "Suspendiertes Lehramt zum Xten," *Motu-proprio: Summorum-Pontificum*, July 4, 2022; translation mine.

better . . . because it is *present* (Hegelianism), because it *comes from us* (immanentism)," or do I "hold to the extrinsic tradition as something good, something which is the product of the wisdom and labor of the saints and the Church throughout history"?[13]

Thus, when someone challenges us: "Do *you* know better than the pope?," our response is simple and serene: "In this matter, yes." Just as, in other matters, St Athanasius of Alexandria (and every layman who supported him) knew better than Pope Liberius; Justinian than Pope Vigilius; St Maximus than Pope Honorius; King Philip VI of Valois than Pope John XXII; the French laity than Leo XIII's policy of *ralliement* that favored an anticlerical Masonic government – so too, the traditionalist laity, clergy, and religious know better than Paul VI's liturgical reform and Francis's assault on the common good of the People of God. We don't even need to be half as intelligent or brave as our forefathers in the movement, who, from the mid-1960s onward, *predicted* the disasters that would befall the Church if the reform continued in the direction Paul VI had set. Today, more than half a century after the infamous promulgation of the *Novus Ordo Missae* and the rest of the novelties, we can verify with our own senses the global catastrophe, the abomination of desolation, that has replaced Catholic divine worship and driven away millions of the baptized. No need to burden the reader with mounds of statistics and a plethora of horror stories with which he is already familiar and which are so easy to find on the internet.

The equivalent of "2 + 2 = 5" in the liturgical domain is the statement that "The liturgical books promulgated by Saint Paul VI and Saint John Paul II, in conformity with the decrees of Vatican Council II, are the unique expression of the *lex orandi* of the Roman Rite." That quotation from *Traditionis Custodes* is perfect nonsense, an untruth, and therefore a blasphemy against the divine order. Even as a habit of lying begins with "white lies" and moves on to more and bigger lies, so too, starting from this primordial falsehood, Pope Francis, Cardinal Roche, and other enemies of the liturgical heritage of the Church gain momentum as they pursue the liquidation of the *usus antiquior*. Yet we know well, as Joseph Ratzinger said

---

13　Fr Chad Ripperger, "Conservative vs. Traditional Catholicism," *Latin Mass,* Spring 2001; also available online at www.latinmassmagazine.com/articles/articles_2001_SP_Ripperger.html.

many different times, that it is contrary to the spirit of the Church to actively abolish or persecute any of her orthodox rites.[14]

The entire framework of *Traditionis Custodes* and the *Responsa ad Dubia* is constructed on the basis of the assumption that the rites of the Church are the pope's toys.[15] All further structures and strictures based on this erroneous notion of papal power are equally unlawful. In dealing with the fallout of these documents, while we are permitted to be "wise as serpents and innocent as doves" (Matt. 10:16) — in other words, to be pragmatic in finding workarounds and making strategic concessions — we must never forget there are *questions of truth* at stake. To compromise the truth for the sake of expediency or comfort is cowardly and unworthy of the One whom we wish to serve, the One whom the office of Compline calls *Deus veritatis*, the God of truth. Gabriel Marcel observes: "Bravery by no means consists in deluding oneself about a given situation. It reaches its zenith, on the contrary, when the situation is most clearly appreciated."[16] Let us clearly appreciate our situation, that we may act bravely.

THE SYSTEMATIC ABUSE OF LAW AND OBEDIENCE

Remember: the bullies in charge use law as a weapon and obedience as an arena for psychological manipulation and intimidation. Motu proprios and the like are, for them, smokescreens for their broader agendas. They do not care about logical consistency. Moreover, they do not care about following the rules that they themselves establish (as we can see when Pope Francis, in arbitrarily removing bishops he doesn't like, refuses to follow due canonical process, violating rules he earlier approved). They do not care about unity or the good of souls. They care about *power*, and they will use that power to advance a modernized "catholicism." As Hilary White pointed out:

> The people who do these things — this pope and his col-
> laborators — have never in their lives been constrained by

---

14   See the quotations from Ratzinger and Newman at the start of the preceding chapter.
15   And when you let the pope make the liturgy his "toy," you end up with a situation in which everything is politicized. The liturgy need not be a political football, but a pope can easily make it such.
16   Gabriel Marcel, *The Mystery of Being*, vol. 2: *Faith & Reality*, trans. René Hague (Chicago: Henry Regnery Co., 1960), 178.

the letter of any laws, neither civil/secular, nor moral nor divine law, nor even any law they themselves have written. These are people of criminal minds with only their own goals and purposes before them.

This is the key we must understand: *they know the law is important to the people they are attacking*, which is why they're using it as a weapon against the remaining faithful. But they themselves don't care about the law, and do not understand it. They have a completely prescriptive, positivist view of the law. The mind of a tyrant is like the mind of a six-year-old child; the law is what is written down and you must obey it. There is no "higher law," no concept that the law serves a higher set of purposes or [has] principles that lead or guide it. Though they will happily mouth such nostrums, not one of them has ever conceived of laws as servants to any greater good. Law = power.[17]

Knowing that rulers in the Church are abusing their authority and deploying canon law like cannon artillery, we should be clear that our principled resistance is not a matter of "being disobedient." Such resistance stems from recognizing with one's faith and reason what is inherently right and then doing it, in the fear and love of God, without begging, wheedling, or apologizing. Obedience, after all, is grounded always in reason and in the *sensus fidei fidelium* or "supernatural common sense," as it might be called. Right obedience will never contradict faith and reason, cancel them out, or trample on them. Our thoughts and actions must be rooted in *true principles*, so that we may avoid or escape the trap of an exaggerated, overly-spiritualized and even fetishized "obedience" that derives from the dubious *"perinde ac cadaver"* ideal cultivated in Jesuit religious life.[18]

---

17 Hilary White, "Don't be afraid of the Big Bad 'Traditiones Custodes,'" *World of Hilarity*, January 15, 2022, emphasis added.
18 That is, "in the manner of a corpse" that is passively carried here or there. In the words of Fr Robert P. Imbelli, "one under obedience should allow himself to be directed 'as if he were a lifeless body'" ("Perinde ac Cadaver," *Commonweal*, February 21, 2008). See John Lamont, "Tyranny and Sexual Abuse in the Catholic Church: A Jesuit Tragedy," *Catholic Family News*, October 27, 2018. We can make our own the truth declared by the Stoic Epictetus: "When presented with valid principles, treat them as if they were the law and it would be sacrilegious to go against them" (*Handbook*, ch. 50, in Kevin Vost, *Memorize the Stoics* [Brooklyn, NY: Angelico Press, 2022], 97).

APPEAL TO PRIESTS

Dear priests of God who offer the old Mass and the old rites of the sacraments, who use the *Rituale Romanum* and pray the *Breviarium Romanum* — you who know what the *usus antiquior* means in itself; what it has come to mean to you personally; what it means to the people to whom you minister — you cannot stand by and comply with this tyranny. Your promise of "obedience to the bishop" must never serve as cover for the modernist takeover of the Church that we are witnessing. It is not "the Church" or "the bishop" that is asking you to renounce what is noble, great, beautiful, holy, true, nourishing to you and to the faithful, and mightily redounding to the honor and glory of God. Neither Jesus Christ who bestowed upon us the bimillennial heritage of the Church nor His immaculate Bride who lovingly received it would ever ask such a suicidal renunciation, nor would any shepherd who walks in the footsteps of the Lord and who loves His Bride.

No, it is the "prison-guards of treachery," *custodes traditionis* — that is, the progressives, liberals, and modernists who have occupied high positions, the lavender mafia who use threats, blackmail, and bribes — who command you now (and who manipulate bishops lower on the roster) to throw away the wisdom of Benedict XVI, to abandon your missals and your flocks, to grovel for a permission they will eagerly deny. These men would rather see a dying Church wedded to a dying modern West than a living Church witnessing to the joy of timeless Truth. To bind yourself to them is to bind yourself to death, and to abandon the wellsprings of spiritual and ecclesial life.

We know that the liberals, progressives, and modernists are wrong in what they are saying and doing precisely because it is uncatholic or anti-Catholic. The traditionalists are the ones who are striving to live and fight for what is and has always been and will always be Catholic. Do not let conservatives get away with claiming there is a logical parallel between, for example, dissenters from *Humanae Vitae* and so-called dissenters from *Traditionis Custodes*. There is no parallel. The situations are, in fact, contraries. We obey *Humanae Vitae* for the same reason we reject *Traditionis Custodes*: that is, we adhere to the constant teaching and practice of the Church, which has ever been against contraception, and ever in favor of liturgical tradition.

There is a mentality of legal positivism that must be overcome if Catholicism is to flourish again. It is a tremendous sickness to reduce the treasury of the Faith to a schoolroom exercise in connecting canonical dots or checking off boxes of compliance. There are higher laws and higher goods at stake. Just as philosophy and reason itself have nearly been asphyxiated by scientific positivism, so theology and faith are being asphyxiated by legal positivism. I say this to all tradition-loving Catholics across the world, who are or may soon be faced with unjust and burdensome restrictions (like those imposed on the faithful in Washington, DC; Arlington, Virginia; Chicago; and Savannah): yes, *pray* for your bishops, *pray* for the pope, *pray* for your enemies and persecutors, fast and pray that the demons may be cast out and peace restored; but do *not* put your own salvation at risk by obeying that which must never be obeyed, by refusing to resist that which must be resisted if you expect to look at yourself in the mirror and not flinch because you have denied what you know to be right and true.

LOOK TO OUR TRADITION-LOVING FOREFATHERS

In many ways, our situation is bleak. Is it time for us to surrender to despair? Of course not. We pray more than ever, especially with the Rosary and the Divine Office. We support more than ever the ancient Roman Rite, the priests who offer it, and the communities and institutes dedicated to it. We give our money only to good causes. We show up for pilgrimages and public protests. We learn from our tradition-loving forefathers in the 1970s. We never give up the fight. We take our inspiration from the clear-thinking and courageous priests of the decades immediately following Vatican II who refused to comply with what they knew was disastrous to the life of the Church: the brilliant Fr Bryan Houghton; the formidable Fr Roger-Thomas Calmel; the monastic founder Fr Gérard Calvet; the forthright Abbé Georges de Nantes; the erudite Fr Gregory Hesse; Fr Gommar dePauw; Fr Yves Normandin; Fr George Kathrein; and many others, including priests who tried to say the new Mass for a while and then gave it up as a lost cause.[19] We owe a huge debt of

---

19   See, *inter alia*, Fr Bryan Houghton, *Unwanted Priest: The Autobiography of a Latin Mass Exile* (Brooklyn, NY: Angelico Press, 2022); Père Jean-Dominique Fabre, *Le père Roger-Thomas Calmel, 1914-1975: un fils de saint Dominique au*

gratitude to all of these priests (and a few bishops, too – above all, the valient and tireless Archbishop Lefebvre) for keeping the flame of tradition burning bright in a dark time, when it almost seemed as if, after all, Hannibal had conquered Rome. Because of them, we are able to say today: The liturgical tradition of the Roman Church has never been totally and irreparably broken; it continues, alive, alongside the inorganic, incoherent Montinian Rite that sought to replace it. It has always been right and just to give thanks to God for the heroes who resisted the rupture with tradition, but now, after July 16, 2021, we should rediscover our origins and acknowledge our debts all the more. I would like to pay homage in a particular way to Michael Davies, who was a tremendous personal inspiration to me in taking up the work I have been doing now for many years. In a 1976 letter to Bishop Hugh Donohoe of Fresno, California, Davies wrote the following words, which have gained a new relevance nearly fifty years later:

> A law can cease to bind without revocation on the part of the legislator when it is clearly harmful, impossible, or irrational. If forbidding faithful Catholics to honor God by worshipping Him in the most venerable and hallowed rite in Christendom does not meet those conditions, it would be hard to imagine anything that did.[20]

Inspired by "so great a cloud of witnesses" (Heb 12:1), we are preparing ourselves for a period like the early 1970s, when lovers of Catholic Tradition – in spite of their own instincts and wishes! – had to set themselves against the institution's leaders in order to carry forward the full inheritance of the saints. And this perseverance, which stalwartly ignored "disciplinary action," is what led eventually to the *Pax Benedictina*, that is, to *Summorum Pontificum*, with its still-burgeoning fruits. In the words, once again, of Michael Charlier:

XXe siècle (Suresnes: Clovis Fideliter, 2012); Yves Chiron, *Dom Gérard Calvet, 1927-2008: tourné vers le Seigneur* (Le Barroux: Éditions Sainte-Madeleine, 2018); Fr Yves Normandin, *Pastor out in the Cold: The Story of Fr Normandin's Fight for the Latin Mass in Canada* (St. Marys, KS: Angelus Press, 2021); Fr Alphonsus Maria Krutsinger, CSsR, *The Story of Fr George Kathrein* (St. Marys, KS: Angelus Press, 2022); *Priest, Where Is Thy Mass? Mass, Where Is Thy Priest?*, expanded ed. (Kansas City, MO: Angelus Press, 2004).
20   The full text may be found in the appendix.

If Francis does attempt to completely displace the authentic Roman rite from the Church of Rome, and if one or more successors should follow him in this, the question will arise sooner rather than later for all who know that this rite cannot and must not be abandoned, as to how they are to accomplish the maintenance of an independent "rite church," even if this should bring great difficulties, distress of conscience, and the slander of being "schismatics." The recognition of such a church of the rite of Pope St Gregory by the pope of Rome will then follow someday. Perhaps a future Gregory XVII is already a seminarian of a faithful community.[21]

This is what it looks like today to rely on Divine Providence: not to throw away the Faith or its highest and noblest expressions because a pope or a bishop tells us to, owing to his own hatred of a glorious heritage that stands in judgment over our modern vices and errors, but rather, to hold fast to all that is true, good, beautiful, and holy, relying on God to deliver us from our enemies, to make straight our paths, to prosper the work of our hands. When we do what is within our hands to do, He will bless our fidelity to Him and raise up in the future the structures of support and recognition we desire and deserve.

PRINCIPLED RESISTANCE:
A BATTLE OVER THE FAITH

The question of what to do in the current crisis is not easy to answer, because we do not know what the future holds, either for diocesan clergy or for the so-called "Ecclesia Dei institutes."[22] It is my considered opinion that the policy of *Traditionis Custodes* will eventually be reversed and that the Ecclesia Dei institutes will endure; but this pope is capable of any irrational and cruel act, and his successor

---

21 Michael Charlier, "The amorphous 'Roman rite' and the authentic Roman Rite," *Rorate Caeli*, July 6, 2022; cf. "Interview with Dom Alcuin Reid."
22 By this phrase I refer to any *usus antiquior*-based community of priests or religious that was canonically established, reconciled, or assisted through the good offices of the Pontifical Commission Ecclesia Dei, which handled such affairs from its foundation in 1988 by John Paul II until its dissolution into Section IV of the then-Congregation for the Doctrine of the Faith 2019 by Francis. With *Traditionis Custodes*, the "extraordinary form" legally disappeared and with it the last breath of *Ecclesia Dei*.

might be cut from the same cloth. Catholicism cannot persist indefinitely without a pope who actually does his job, and at the very least does not actively carry out villainy by attacking the things he is supposed to defend. But it seems to me that such a state of dysfunctionality, a veritable ecclesial autoimmune disorder, is possible for a long period of time. How long? There's no way to know. Yet there are truths—luminous, majestic, imperishable, utterly reliable—that we *can* know; that we have a *duty* to know; and that we have a *right* to embrace, cherish, act upon, and hand down, as we build our lives upon the rock of truth. Holding fast to the ancient liturgy of our forefathers in the Faith is unquestionably part of the "way out" of this unprecedented crisis. In the stirring words of Fr Kevin Cusick:

> The ancient form of the Mass is part and parcel now and always of the Catholic Faith. Because this is so, no man, pope or lay, may alienate the faithful, by any means, from this most sacred ritual. There is no power on this earth which can violate the Divine Will manifest in this or any other form of revelation.
>
> The new Mass, by contrast, has never been accepted by everyone in the Church, beset as it has been from the beginning by controversy, bringing with it rampant abuses, scandal, sacrilege and loss of faith. The only constant by which it can be measured is a continuing decline in attendance. Men may try [to oppose the *usus antiquior*], as they have tried before and failed, but the Mass of all time will never be extirpated from the earth any more than the Faith itself can be erased. All that is necessary is the perseverance of one faithful soul. There is an army of such souls who keep the flame of faith alive throughout the world, now as always.[23]

The opponents of the Western liturgical heritage can thunder and fulminate, call names and wag fingers, ghettoize and demonize, threaten, cancel, suspend, and suppress—they can try all of that, as their mentors did right after the Council, using the same tactics. Yet they will ultimately fail, because those of us who hold on to the traditional Roman liturgy (and with it, the traditional Catholic Faith *in toto*) do so as a matter of *principle*, not as a pragmatic "take it or leave it" affair, and there are more of us all the time—far more than there

---

23   Fr Kevin Cusick, "The Death of a Parish," *Rorate Caeli*, August 4, 2022.

were in the dark days of the 1970s. Moreover, our human enemies are much less guarded about their intentions; they have made no attempt to hide their modernist agenda. They have made it easy for us to see through their specious reasons and disdain their illicit acts. It might have been possible once upon a time for some to imagine that our disputes were only about liturgical fine points, but now we can see that they implicate the integrity and truthfulness of the Catholic Faith, the unity of the Church with herself over time. This is, as it has always been (but never so clearly), a battle over the Faith.

Even as it is said that the devil cannot comprehend any human action springing from humility, the anti-traditionalists too have a fatal blind spot. Owing to intellectual and moral impediments, the Church's enemies within do not understand the precise kind of attachment or adherence we have to the traditional rites of the Church. Because this is the secret strength of our movement, compensating for our minority status and our relative lack of worldly resources, it is worth a closer look.

THE NATURE AND ROLE OF PIETY

The virtue of *pietas*, piety in its deepest meaning, is the love one has for one's country in all its concrete beauty and complexity, the *patria* or fatherland for which one is prepared to suffer and die. *Pietas* is bound up with the love one has for family members to whom one is bound by the most intimate ties of generation, familiarity, longevity, homage, gratitude, and devotion. We have piety toward that which suckles and nourishes us, educates us, and lifts us up. We are links on a living chain going back and going forward. This piety is something so deep that it can barely be accurately described: it is both psychological and ontological, in one's bones as well as in one's soul, a matter of the heart more than of the head (which is not to say that one could not argue for it when hard-pressed; yet words will never do it justice).

Our love for the traditional worship of the Church is a *pietas* for our spiritual fatherland as Catholic Christians. This piety grows over time as we are, so to speak, grafted more and more into the family of the saints and the wisdom of the centuries. It is not some kind of "preference" in a marketplace of merchandise, or a "consolation" we seek for selfish reasons. It is simply *who and what we are* as Catholics worshiping God and loving the beauty of His holiness as we experience it in this awe-inspiring gift of His Providence, the *usus antiquior.* As we put our roots deeper into the tradition, we see ever more clearly that the Novus Ordo is a different rite, a different family and bloodline, even a different world. We would just as soon give up the ancient rites of the Church as we would give up our mothers and fathers, our husbands and wives, our sons and daughters. Because we are dealing with the deepest bond at the core of a person, we can see that the attacks on the traditional Latin liturgy are destined to fail. So far from being a battle over "externals," this war is about what is deepest in the human heart – the place in which faith becomes flesh, and beauty becomes life, and prayer becomes real.

But those who are on the outside, who have not yet tasted this gift, cannot understand us; they will think it's enough (or "should" be enough) to have a command from an authority, and then we'll all fall in line with its dictates. They will think it's enough to add the "smells and bells," as if our interest were so superficial as the merely sensible – as if we are liturgical materialists, so to speak. I do not blame the apologists of new liturgical forms for their misjudgment of their brethren. The new forms are period fabrications, machines for praying, baubles and books changeable at will, imposed in a moment and disposed of in a moment. There can be no deep, abiding, heart-gripping devotion to such things – no *pietas.* They are like pieces of clothing you put on and take off.

Thus, the stalwart adherents of the Novus Ordo *cannot* understand their traditional brethren. That is why, as they try to "help" us or even to "discipline" us, they continue to make the most egregious self-defeating and martyr-creating blunders. The more they rage against the tradition, the more free advertising they give us, leading more souls to raise the essential questions that must be raised and to seek convincing answers, which will be found only in faithfulness to tradition.

UNITY IN WORSHIP IS NECESSARY

In conclusion, Pope Francis and his court say they want "unity" in the worship of the Latin-rite Church. Traditionalists absolutely agree with him! Unity is something we all want and need. But it is *Catholic* unity we seek, and that means:

· *Unity in language:* Holy Mass should be celebrated in Latin in every corner of the Catholic world where the Latin rite exists, so that it is experienced as always the same, always familiar: everywhere we are at home, instead of being lost in a welter of more or less inadequate translations.

· *Unity in ritual:* Holy Mass should be offered with beauty, solemnity, and orderliness, a stable prayer within which one can pray freely and deeply, without chaotic options or trendy inculturations.

· *Unity in clergy.* Holy Mass should be celebrated in a fixed, constant, reliable way, according to strict and detailed rubrics, so that it makes little or no difference which priest is offering it—rather than varying wildly depending on the celebrant's degree of reverence, taste, and theology.

· *Unity in orientation:* Holy Mass should be offered eastward, with priest and people alike facing the same direction, a single body looking in hope for the coming of the Lord—not the other way, as a self-enclosed circle of horizontal humanism.

· *Unity in music.* Holy Mass should be adorned with the same sacred chant that has been sung for centuries, even millennia—not plagued by a cacophony of second-rate imitations of modern styles.

· *Unity in tradition.* Holy Mass should be offered in continuity with the worship known by Western saints and sinners across the ages, our brothers and sisters in the Mystical Body—not in a state of rupture from it.

May Our Lord Jesus Christ, Eternal High Priest, "the author and perfecter of our faith" (Heb 12:2), bless and multiply the efforts of traditional Catholics around the world to help restore to our beloved Catholic Church the visible manifestation of the marks we profess in the Creed—*unam, sanctam, catholicam, et apostolicam*—which are under such assault from the forces of darkness. May Our Lady smile upon us, her children, in this vale of tears.

10

The Corruption of the Best Is the Worst: When Obedience Becomes the Devil's Tool

EVERY CENTURY OF THE CHURCH BRINGS with it something fundamentally new – something that has not been seen before and that has to be dealt with on its own terms. It is not that Catholics ever face a situation for which principles to deal with it are entirely lacking, but rather that the new situation has no *exact parallel* in earlier times, some sort of easy equivalency that would permit a formulaic response. For example, when Arianism arose in the fourth century and spread like wildfire, including among the episcopacy, the Church was facing a new state of emergency and had to respond accordingly. Humanly speaking, it was a close call; as St Jerome famously said, "The whole world groaned, and was astonished to find itself Arian." But equally new was the sudden and violent arrival of Islam, which swept away many of the most ancient, even original, Christian communities in North Africa and Asia Minor. Another unwelcome novelty was the so-called "pornocracy" of the Dark Ages, when the pope's chair in Rome was bought and sold by fornicators. Then there was the Great Western Schism, when at one point three rivals claimed to be pope, and each had the backing of cardinals, bishops, and secular rulers. The Protestant Revolt, too, though it was prepared for by a couple of centuries of rumblings, burst on to the scene as something unprecedented in the severity of its rejection of the Catholic tradition and its rapid multiplication of man-made doctrines. Church history is nothing if not full of surprises, of hair-raising crises, razor-thin escapes, devastating tragedies, and altogether unexpected resurrections.

I maintain that the crisis after the Second Vatican Council is precisely one of these fundamentally new situations: "The whole Church groaned, and was astonished to find itself modernist."

Indeed, this crisis is greater than any that came before, because, to use Pope Pius X's exact phrase, "modernism is the collection of all heresies" (*omnium haereseon conlectum*), and this modernism, in a soft and elegant form, though sometimes also with the jackhammers of iconoclasm, established itself in all the seats of learning and power.[1] The age we are passing through is characterized by an incredibly arrogant rejection of centuries of Church tradition, of historical rites, customs, monuments, laws, even settled dogmas and morals, called into question not by raving wild-eyed reformers at the margins of civilization but by cardinals, bishops, and even popes, with countless sympathizers at every level of the Church.[2] So great is the rupture that occurred in the sixties and seventies, as known to those who experienced it or who have studied it subsequently, that there are still days when one can find it hard to believe that the so-called "liturgical reform" actually happened or could have happened; for it should strike any calm observer as the most freakish betrayal of Catholicism's essence in the entire history of the Church. It's almost too shocking to comprehend. The scale of the disaster beggars the imagination.[3]

This is also why neo-Catholic coping mechanisms like "there's always confusion after a council" or "we've had rough times before" are so weak and unconvincing. We have *not* been here before. We are in *terra incognita*, in the fearful unknown. We can't always interpret what we encounter with reference to ancient paradigms, because it doesn't always align. Sometimes we have to figure things out for the first time. There is a first time for every major error in Christian history, and the error of our day – the rejection of tradition as good, right, normative, trustworthy, and providential – is an error that never existed before in this naked, austere, unmitigated form. As a consequence, our crisis raises questions about authority and

---

1   See my lecture "Pius X to Francis: From Modernism Expelled to Modernism Enthroned," in *Hyperpapalism to Catholicism*, 2:283-306.

2   It is for this reason that applying the truisms of neoscholastic manuals to the present situation after the manner of cookie-cutters applied to dough is bound to produce nonsense – more than that, dangerous nonsense, because its sheer lack of plausibility will incline truth-seekers to turn away from the Catholic Church.

3   As one of the finest historians of the modern Church expresses it: "The story of how the liturgical revolution was put through is one that hampers the historian by its very enormity; he would wish, for his own sake, to have a less unbelievable tale to tell" (H. J. A. Sire, *Phoenix from the Ashes: The Making, Unmaking, and Restoration of Catholic Tradition* [Kettering, OH: Angelico Press, 2015], 251).

obedience, for the simple reason that the revolution that took place and rapidly turned itself into the ecclesiastical establishment was initiated and consolidated by so-called "authorities" who claimed the unquestioning allegiance or obedience of all subordinates.

Just as every earlier major crisis in Church history led to the clarification of certain hitherto ambiguous or underdeveloped concepts, so too our crisis will eventually lead to – and indeed has already begun to produce – a far better, more nuanced, realistic, transfigured understanding of Church authority (especially the nature and limits of the papal office) and the corresponding virtue of obedience. There will come a time when the laity and parochial clergy will no longer be expected to swallow unsatisfying and self-injuring absurdities for breakfast while an abusive clericalism consumes the Church's inheritance and replaces it with nothing of value. The question of the relationship of authority to obedience is central to our present situation and that is why it must be addressed forthrightly.

THE NATURE, CONDITIONS, AND LIMITS OF OBEDIENCE[4]

Let there be no mistake about it: properly understood and lived, obedience is a supreme virtue, modeled by Christ Himself. Our Lord and the saints practiced obedience and so must we; a rebellious mentality is foreign to Christianity (and to natural ethics). However, because tyrants, manipulators, and abusers of all sorts have freely taken advantage of habits of obedience, it has acquired a bad reputation. It is time to rehabilitate the virtue by looking carefully at what it is (and isn't). True obedience is never blind or unconditional: it must be based on *truth* and *charity*, in the sense that we must be commanded to do what is truly good, and for the sake of growing in love for the good. This is why it is not *obedience* that comes first, but *truth* and *charity*. The relationship of superior and subordinate always takes place within the context of God's revealed will as authoritatively taught by the Church. Demands for obedience that flow from falsehood, hatred, envy, or any other evil foundation are destructive and should be resisted in proportion to the damage they are causing or threatening to

---

4 The next few pages summarize the main argument of my book *True Obedience in the Church*.

cause.[5] If one has a serious and well-founded *doubt* about whether a particular human command is compatible with divine, natural, or ecclesiastical law, one should not obey it.

Authority is born to serve and promote the shared good of many, that is, what we call the common good. If a particular wielder of authority deploys his office overtly *against* the common good, then that command lacks moral binding power. The Church's common good is the divine life of Jesus Christ, her Head, and the divinization of souls by the sacramental life and prayer. Crucially, the traditional liturgy is inherent to the Church's common good. Why? Because the traditional rites of the Church are not merely human works but works conjointly of God and men — of the Church moved by the Holy Spirit. The traditional liturgical worship of the Church, what is called her *"lex orandi,"* is a basic, normative, stable expression of her creed or *"lex credendi,"* and cannot be contradicted or abolished or heavily rewritten without rejecting the Spirit-led continuity of the Catholic Church as a whole. Only two groups have ever rejected the traditional *lex orandi*: the Protestants, who did so because they openly dissented from the creed it expressed, and the Modernists, who maintained that, as the meaning of the creed perpetually evolves, so too should the prayer that reflects it. In reality, we know from Pope Pius V's *Quo Primum* that the classical Roman Rite canonized after the Council of Trent contains and transmits the Catholic

---

5   Consider St Thomas's words about envy, a vice that seems, alas, to be a strong element in the reaction of progressive churchmen against the flourishing traditionalist communities that "draw away" (as they see it) parishioners who are bored or scandalized by the typical worship options: "There is a kind of envy which is accounted among the most grievous sins, envy of another's spiritual good, which envy is a sorrow for the increase of God's grace, and not merely for our neighbor's good. Hence it is accounted a sin against the Holy Ghost, because thereby a man envies, as it were, the Holy Ghost Himself, Who is glorified in His works" (*Summa theologiae* II-II, Q. 36, art. 4). Having cited this passage, Reid Turner notes: "The typical traditional church offers parishioners timeless elements of Holy Mass: Latin chant, incense, silence, statues, icons, etc. Confessionals are often open and busy before and during Mass and homilies are usually short exhortations to moral purity. There are many families in attendance that are often large and appropriately dressed. It can only be out of envy that Church authorities are actively trying to suppress [such a community], falsely claiming that it causes spiritual harm when it clearly produces the opposite. . . . It seems as though Church authorities have decided to stamp out tradition once they realized that it was only a matter of time before it won the hearts of a majority of Catholics" ("Papal Polemics and the Disparagement of Grace," *The Five Beasts*, May 17, 2023, https://thefivebeasts. wordpress.com/2023/05/17/papal-polemics-and-the-disparagement-of-grace/).

Faith—as do all venerable Christian rites—and, as such, cannot be abolished or abrogated; rather, it remains a permanent treasure and testimonial, guaranteed to Latin-rite clergy and laity in perpetuity.

We must be absolutely clear about this: any attack on the traditional Mass is an attack on the Providence of God the Father, who guided His Church to develop and exalt this liturgy for the better part of her 2,000-year pilgrimage on earth; a rejection of the work of Christ, the King and Lord of history, who is adored in it; a blasphemy against the fruitfulness of the Holy Ghost in the Church's life of prayer; a stance against the unanimous practice of every age of the Latin Church, of every saint, council, and pope prior to the twentieth century; a rejection of the dogmatic confession of faith contained in this traditional liturgy as it organically developed over two millennia; a rejection of the communion of the Western saints who share a common lineage and patrimony of ecclesiastical worship.

Because of the tight connection between prayer and creed, history and providence, ecclesial communion and dogmatic confession, it follows that abolishing or prohibiting or working against the immemorial Roman Rite is a notorious and damaging attack on the Church's common good. This is why Pope Francis's attempt in *Traditionis Custodes* to restrict and eventually repeal the traditional Roman Rite embodies a profoundly uncatholic, indeed anti-Catholic, point of view. The liturgical reform, its subsequent implementation, and Pope Francis's renewed efforts to extinguish the preceding tradition are unreasonable, unjust, and unholy, and therefore cannot be accepted as legitimate or embraced as the will of God. As a matter of fact, it is *love for the office of the pope and for the pope's immortal soul* that moves us to denounce the abuse of papal authority wielded against the good of the faithful.

Yes, ordinary Catholics are capable of recognizing *when* authorities are acting against the common good. A 2014 document from the International Theological Commission bore witness to the Catholic faithful's instinct for the truth:

> The *sensus fidei fidelis* confers on the believer the capacity to discern whether or not a teaching or practice is coherent with the true faith by which he or she already lives... The *sensus fidei fidelis* also enables individual

believers to perceive any disharmony, incoherence, or contradiction between a teaching or practice and the authentic Christian faith by which they live.... Alerted by their *sensus fidei*, individual believers may deny assent even to the teaching of legitimate pastors if they do not recognize in that teaching the voice of Christ, the Good Shepherd.[6]

Note this language: even our legitimate pastors – pope, bishop, local pastor – fail to speak with the voice of the Good Shepherd when they impose disharmony, incoherence, or contradiction on the faithful. It was none other than St Thomas Aquinas who famously said that unjust laws are "acts of violence rather than laws... Wherefore such laws do not bind in conscience."[7] If we are convinced that something essential, something decisive in the Faith is under attack from the pope or any other pastor, we may and must refuse to do what is being asked or commanded, refuse to give up what is being unjustly taken away or forbidden. Any penalty or punishment meted out by the revolutionaries for "disobedience" to their illicit requests or commands would itself be illicit, having no force. If a punishment is given on false theological or canonical premises, it is null and void.

Ultimately, it is for the *salus animarum* that the entire structure of ecclesiastical law exists; it has no other purpose than to protect and advance the sharing of the life of Christ with mankind. There can be situations of anarchy or breakdown, corruption or apostasy, where the ordinary structures become *impediments* to, not facilitators of, the Church's mission. In these cases, the voice of conscience dictates that one should do what needs to be done, in prudence and charity, for the achievement of the sovereign law. It is a *necessity*, not a luxury, for some priests and religious in the Church to bear witness by their very lives – by their consistent, principled, integral fidelity to tradition – that the Catholic Church must be the same today as ever she was, and that what was sacred and great in the past can never fail to be so in the present and until the end of time. The moment tradition is proscribed, so too is the Church's substantive continuity, and with it, the basis of ecclesiastical authority, since the episcopacy and the papacy are themselves transmitted to us by tradition. No officeholder in either the Church or the State

6   International Theological Commission, "*Sensus Fidei* in the Life of the Church," nos. 61-63.
7   *Summa theologiae* I-II, Q. 96, art. 4.

has the authority, before God, to prohibit Mass or refuse the sacraments to otherwise well-disposed Catholic faithful.

This is the framework. Now we have to drill deeper.

THE SPIRITUAL POWER OF
THE TRADITIONAL LATIN MASS

Consider the sheer spiritual power of the traditional Mass. Over the years, I've heard from or read accounts of many priests whose discovery of the ancient rite has transformed their priesthood and their entire spiritual life, renewing their youth like the eagle's. It's amazing the number who go through this conversion experience. Typically, they start by saying Mass in the *usus antiquior* once in a while, then it moves up to once a week on their day off, then they find a way (or found a way, prior to *Traditionis Custodes*) to get it into the parish schedule, even adding a Sunday Mass. In some cases—more numerous than most people realize—they reach a point where they admit before God: "I wish I could do this all the time," or even: "I can't do the modern rite any more." They have found a pearl of great price and are ready to sell everything to buy the field where it lies buried.[8]

Sometimes this conversion story has a happy ending—for instance, a bishop appoints a priest as a Latin Mass chaplain or puts him in charge of a rural shrine. Sometimes, alas, especially in the current climate, it has a tragic ending: the priest is called on the carpet, stripped of his faculties, hung out to dry—because, don't you know, we have so many *extra clergy* on our hands that we can afford to retire them early if they don't fit the mold.

Here's a million-dollar question: Do you ever hear about a priest starting with the traditional Latin Mass and then "discovering" the greatness of the Novus Ordo and moving over more and more to *it*, until he offers it exclusively? Until he has a longing in his heart and in his hands to offer *just* the Novus Ordo, even to the point of suffering for it, and possibly losing everything? Once in a blue moon, one hears of a traditionalist priest who enters the diocesan presbyterate and alternates between the two rites for pastoral

---

8   See my articles "Discovering Tradition: A Priest's Crisis of Conscience," *OnePeterFive*, March 27, 2019 and "Not Abandoning the Flock—Not Abandoning the Truth," *OnePeterFive*, July 13, 2022.

reasons – but never the spiritually transformative experience that I described. To me, this says more about the realities we are dealing with than a thousand documents from the Vatican could ever tell us. We know, moreover, that it is not only priests and religious, but, in far greater numbers, the lay faithful who find their encounter with the traditional liturgical life of the Church utterly transformative. The testimonials are now impossible to keep track of, there are so many of them online and in print.

Last Christmas Day, as I gazed out from the choir loft at all of the families jammed into pews brimming over with children, and the sanctuary covered with candles, poinsettias, and pine trees, and as I followed the awesome beauty of a solemn High Mass clothed in gold vestments and the otherworldly music of chant, using the same prayers, antiphons, readings, and ceremonies that the Roman Church has used for well over a thousand years – seeing all this, it was brought home to me with renewed force that any attack on this glorious patrimony, and on the faithful who love it, is and cannot be other than Satanic. The sooner and better we grasp this, the sooner we will see that our response must be a total repudiation of not only *Traditionis Custodes* and the follow-up documents based on it, but of the entire liturgical revolution spearheaded by Annibale Bugnini and Giovanni Battista Montini (inter alia) and now revived by its last convicted disciples, newly empowered after a deceptively peaceful interlude of "live and let live."

What we are seeing today is certainly more malicious than the naive attitude of the 1960s, captured in the slogan "Man Has Come of Age, So Should the Mass"; but it is no different *in kind* from the initial rupture with tradition engineered by the Consilium and executed by Paul VI. Perhaps that is the greatest grace of this present moment: to shake us awake from slumber about the issues that are *really at stake*, beneath the surface squalls of so-called "preferences" and "tastes" and "opinions." Let's not mince words: the enemies of tradition would rather see a shortage of priests than to have an abundance of Latin Mass priests; would rather see monasteries and convents go into hospice and shutter their doors than to be revitalized with religious who joyfully embrace tradition; would rather see contracepting families than families with many children reared in the traditional Faith. Isn't that enough, and more than

128

enough, to show that the father of this anti-traditional onslaught is not God but the devil?

Bishops who accept and implement the motu proprio and the Dicastery for Divine Worship's responses align themselves with the father of lies. Priests who willingly accept these irrational, unjust, and harmful restrictions sin against the virtue of obedience to God's law and to the sovereign law of the Church, which is the good of souls; therefore, also against Christ, the model of obedience, and against His Father, who establishes authority and obedience for the advancement of the Church's mission and life, not for their derailment or distortion.[9] If the tradition of the Church is abundantly fruitful in graces and other spiritual goods, then we can see instantly why the Enemy of God and of Human Nature, Satan, would be so keen to see it suppressed, and work sleeplessly (as only angels can do) to move his human instruments to wage war against it. Indeed, we were warned many times that this ecclesiastical autoimmune disorder, in which the Church's own leaders *attack* the Body of Christ, would come to pass in our days. Remember Pope Leo XIII's vision in which he heard the devil ask for time to overthrow the Church? We know that the Church can never be overthrown altogether; but we also know, from the record of Scripture and from subsequent Church history, that Almighty God, for our testing and our purification, at times allows matters to reach the brink of disaster. How striking are the words written by Leo XIII in the little-known *longer* Prayer to St Michael, where,[10] speaking of men whom the "leader of the proud," the "malignant dragon," has induced to take his side, the pope writes:

> Most cunning enemies have filled with bitterness and drenched with gall the Church, the Spouse of the Lamb

---

9 As St Paul says in another context, speaking of the complicity of willing collaboration: "They who do such things are worthy of death – and not only they that do them, but they also that consent to them that do them" (Rom 1:32).
10 The familiar short prayer was not an abbreviation of the longer prayer; they are different (though contemporaneous) texts. The long prayer was included in the *Acta Apostolicae Sedis* of 1890 and the *Rituale Romanum* of 1898. The immediate occasion of the prayers was the loss of the Papal States and ongoing hostility toward the Church at the hands of anti-Catholic forces. When, later on, these relations had improved, the long prayer was considerably pruned, which is the form it took in the twentieth-century editions of the *Raccolta*. Nevertheless, in the original version one cannot help but see further levels of meaning in the words chosen by Leo XIII – a sort of "dual fulfillment" of his text.

without spot, and have lifted impious hands against all
that is most sacred in it. Even in the holy place where
the See of Blessed Peter and the chair of truth was set up
to enlighten the world, they have raised the abominable
throne of their impiety with the iniquitous hope that the
Shepherd may be stricken and the flock scattered abroad.[11]

THE LAW OF PRAYER AS THE NORM OF NORMS

Now, we all know what our opponents always say to us: "Aren't we
Catholics supposed to let ourselves be guided by the pope and the
bishops in regard to liturgical law?" The answer is yes... and no.
Yes in regard to all that concerns the devout, fitting, and edifying
celebration of the "received and approved" traditional rites of the
Church; no, if that "guidance" leads us to turn against that sublime
inheritance, which comes down to us from innumerable saints—a
severance quite beyond the authority of any hierarch of the Church
to effect or enforce. As Alan Fimister explains:

> If the Church's Rites are Patristic Monuments ultimately
> traceable to the Apostolic age then they would quite nat-
> urally be immune to the vicissitudes of ecclesiastical pos-
> itive law. As St Jerome observed in such matters, "each
> province may follow its own inclinations, and the tradi-
> tions which have been handed down should be regarded
> as apostolic laws." Even if each of the particular elements
> of each tradition cannot be traced with certainty or even
> plausibility to the apostles [themselves], the fact remains
> that as monuments to the Church's unwritten tradition
> they cannot be abrogated by ecclesiastical authority,
> just as the authority of St Athanasius, St Augustine, or
> St John Chrysostom cannot be abrogated. The divinely
> instituted matter of many of the sacraments (olive oil,
> wine, bread) is taken from the staple crops of the Med-
> iterranean world and the Rites which transmitted them
> objectively form part of the witness to the deposit of
> faith. The Church cannot repudiate them without repu-
> diating herself and her Lord.[12]

---

11   *The New Raccolta, or Collection of Prayers and Good Works to which the
Sovereign Pontiffs Have Attached Holy Indulgences,* from the 3rd Italian edition
(Philadelphia: Peter F. Cunningham & Son, 1903), 365.
12   Alan Fimister, *Iron Sceptre of the Son of Man:* Romanitas *as a Note of the
Church* (Lincoln, NE: Os Justi Press, 2023), 15.

In other words, it is not just a reductively-understood "form and matter" of the sacraments that constitute the tradition to be upheld, but the entirety of the rites that surround, interpret, and mediate the sacraments to the faithful, forming and informing them with the *lex orandi*'s witness to the Catholic Faith. These handed-down rites are not incidental and indifferent constructs that each generation may judge, rewrite, or discard as it pleases, with the attitude of someone superior to what he evaluates; instead, the generations that follow recognize, with grateful humility, their need to be formed by (and the accompanying indebtedness to and duty towards) the accumulated prayers and practices of their forefathers. That is simply the way Catholics have always acted and will always act.

A church that has no place of unquestioned honor for hallowed tradition but only room for power and submission is not the Church founded by Jesus Christ. The papacy, the hierarchy, all the structures that pertain to the visible society we call the Catholic Church, exist from and for tradition: they themselves are part of what is handed down, together with the dogmatic and moral teaching, the liturgy and sacraments, the ascetical and mystical doctrine, all forming a mutually reinforcing totality. The Church exists to receive, preserve, and hand on this sum total of divine wisdom, in the service of man's union with the Triune God. Any attempt to defraud the faithful of this inheritance, to subvert it, deface it, suppress it, or mingle it with alien ideas and goals (as we see happening with the synodal process epitomized in the Synod on Synodality), counts as a move away from Christ and His Church, regardless of the specious legal forms in which it may be dressed. Such an attempt—and we have seen a record number of attempts during the past decade, but also, cumulatively, in the past sixty years—points to the existence of a parallel body that subsists parasitically on the Catholic Church, a man-made simulacrum or virtual schism masquerading as the Church.[13]

---

13 See Silveira, *Two Timely Issues*, 239–41 et passim. As Fr Linus Clovis formulates it: "Modernism, remaining within the Catholic Church, has metastasized into the anti-Church. It is self-evident that the Catholic Church and the anti-Church currently co-exist in the same sacramental, liturgical, and juridical space. The latter, having grown stronger, is now attempting to pass itself off as the true Church, all the better to induct, or coerce, the faithful into becoming adherents, promoters, and defenders of a secular ideology" ("The Anti-Church Has Come. Why Faithful Catholics Should Not Be Afraid," *LifeSiteNews*, May 18, 2017).

A frontal attack on that which was once central, unquestioned, exalted, jealously guarded, and always handed down in the life of the Church—I refer, of course, to the Roman Rite as restored and canonized by Pius V, in perfect fidelity to the dogmatic teaching of the Council of Trent—is in and of itself a dead giveaway that we are dealing with an outrageous abuse of power that not only may but must be resisted for the good of souls. It is therefore not a burden but a privilege, an honor, for us to be able to refuse our obedience to the designs of a renegade vicar of Christ who contradicts the truth and wounds the common good, and thus to give our unconditional allegiance to Christ our King, the Lord of history, the head and ruler of His Church, who will prepare, in due time, the deliverance and the restoration for which we long and pray.

SATAN'S MASTERSTROKE

How ever did we reach this point? That is a long and complicated story: ideas, practices, assumptions, attitudes emerging in the Protestant Revolt, sharpened in the Enlightenment period, radicalized in the age of Revolutions, and popularized in the secularism of the twentieth century have all played their part in the reshaping of the Catholic Church, sociologically speaking (I am not talking about the Mystical Body and Immaculate Bride of Christ in her interior purity and heavenly glory, but about the visible institution on earth, which, as Our Lord illustrated in His parable of the wheat and the tares, is made up of both true Christians and false ones, so that the body of Christ and the body of the devil, so to speak, are commingled until the end of time).[14] It should come as no surprise that it is entirely possible for the hierarchy of the Church at a given point in history to be occupied more by false Christians than by true ones—that is, to be occupied by those who do not profess the Catholic Faith in its dogmatic, moral, and liturgical fullness, but who are, to a greater or lesser extent, material heretics and material schismatics in regard to it, or, let us say, who carry with them, perhaps not even realizing it, the weight and the harm of the heretical ideas that are so plentiful in modern times, as well as schismatic

---

14   This is a common theme in St Augustine, and taken up also by Joseph Ratzinger.

tendencies drawing them apart from the great communion of the Church of all ages.[15]

Here, I wish to focus on what I will call "Satan's masterstroke." There's an old adage: *corruptio optimi pessima* – the corruption of the best is the worst. A well-known illustration is Aristotle's claim that monarchy (rule by one virtuous man) is the best form of government, but its corruption, tyranny (rule by one vicious man) is the worst form of government.[16] Fr John Saward argues that Lucifer, the most beautiful of the angels, became the ugliest after his fall from heaven.[17] St Thomas Aquinas argues that obedience ranks particularly high among moral virtues because by it we are willing to "slay our own will" for God's sake; since the will is our innermost principle of self-determination, to the degree we give up our will, we sacrifice ourselves (which becomes, for the religious who professes a vow of obedience, a holocaust or whole burnt-offering). What is more, an act of virtue gains in merit when it is done not only because it is good in itself but also because it has been commanded by another to whom we are subject – God, of course, as well as all superiors who stand in His place, such as rulers, fathers,

---

15   Fr Thomas Weinandy – no friend, incidentally, of the TLM – recognizes the peril: "What the Church will end up with, then, is a pope who is the pope of the Catholic Church and, simultaneously, the de facto leader, for all practical purposes, of a schismatic church. Because he is the head of both, the appearance of one church remains, while in fact there are two" ("Pope Francis and Schism," *The Catholic Thing*, October 8, 2019; cf. William Kilpatrick, "Francis, Fatima, and Garabandal," *Crisis Magazine*, September 14, 2023).

16   In the Philosopher's own words: "The best of these [good forms of government] is kingship. . . . The deviation from kingship is tyranny, for while both are monarchical, they differ the most because the tyrant looks to what is advantageous for himself and the king to what is advantageous for the ruled. . . . But tyranny is in this respect the opposite, for the tyrant pursues the good for himself; and it is quite manifest in this case that tyranny is the most inferior regime, since the opposite of the best is the worst" (Aristotle, *Nicomachean Ethics*, Bk. 8, ch. 10, 1160a36–b9; Bartlett and Collins, 178).

17   "The devil's sin was an act of pride, and the motive of someone's pride is his excellence. Now Lucifer had the greatest excellence in which to glory, and he did so glory, in contempt of the God from whom he received everything he had and was. Thus, the best, once corrupted by his pride, became the worst. . . . The corruption of the best is the worst, and the disfiguring of the most beautiful is the ugliest. But the pure spirituality of the angelic nature has a greater likeness to the infinite goodness and beauty of God than does the nature of any bodily creature. The devil is therefore, in his pride and obstinacy, hideous beyond description" (*World Invisible: The Catholic Doctrine of the Angels* [Brooklyn, NY: Angelico Press, 2023], 126–27).

and pastors.[18] But if all this is true, obedience could also become a preeminent vice: *corruptio optimi pessima.*

As far as I can see, the devil uses three main methods for leading Christians away from the path of life. The first is the blunt method of open, bloody persecution. But the blood of martyrs is the seed of Christianity and the Church tends to spread all the more when openly persecuted, so the devil reaches for a second and more subtle method: internal moral corruption in the form of the seven deadly vices. Yet even moral corruption is at times too repulsive and self-sabotaging in its outward manifestations to be successful, and so the devil lays hands on the most subtle strategy of all: the twisting of obedience until it becomes a means of spiritual suicide or bureaucratic euthanasia.

Historically speaking, this last campaign required a long preparation before it could be launched. The devil had to build up a skewed notion of blind obedience over the course of many centuries, because only in *this* way could the overthrow of Catholic liturgy, doctrine, morals, and culture be brought about. That is, the destruction had to come (or at least seem to come) from the pope and the hierarchy so that it could be plausibly presented and accepted as "God's will," imposed on people who would already be conditioned to go along with it. Once this demonic deception is set up, it's hard to overcome it, because any attempt at overcoming it is deemed to be rebellious pride: "Who are *you* to question this or that church leader?" Indeed, since many spiritual writers had equated the essence of holiness with a total and blind obedience equivalent to a "death to self," it followed that the slightest doubt or hesitation about obeying the order of a superior could be seen as selfish or even sinful. Catholics in search of spiritual perfection were trained to choke down their difficulties, stifle their supernatural common sense (the *sensus fidelium*), and silence the voice of their consciences.

Consequently, a supreme inversion was made possible: the reception and transmission of Catholic tradition by those who still believed the Faith got labeled as "rebellion," and then punished as if it were truly such, while blind "obedience" given to ideas or ways

---

18   See *Summa theologiae* II-II, Q. 104, art. 3; cf. II-II, Q. 186, art. 6; *De perfectione spiritualis vitae*, chs. 11–12.

of life *contrary to* our Catholic tradition was lauded and rewarded, even though objectively it imitated the rebellious pride of Satan, who hates tradition. The deception is shrewd: we all need to grow in humility, so what better way than to obediently accept whatever God's own representatives on earth demand, no questions asked? And our response will be even more meritorious if what's asked of us is repulsive – the more repulsive, the more meritorious! You have to admit: this is a masterful ploy for one who wishes to undermine the Church.

Let us contrast how God works with how Satan works. God positively wills the virtues we have; He does not will the evil of our vices. But he can make use of our vices, as occasions for humiliating us and bringing us to conversion. For example, the Lord does not will the drunkenness of the drunkard, but He can make use of the drunkard's down-and-out despair to effect a conversion. In this way, He brings good out of evil, as only God can do. In contrast, the devil positively wills the *vices* we have: lust, gluttony, avarice, pride, these are his stock in trade, and as long as we're acting by them, he's quite content with our performance. But for those who are not in the grip of vices, he has a more subtle strategy: to urge them to misuse their *virtues*. He can urge the humble to a false humility that fails to acknowledge rights and duties, or accepts humiliations that are self-destructive and destructive of those who do the humiliating. He can urge the meek to a refusal to be justly angry, a refusal to fight and resist when that would be the virtuous thing to do. He can tempt those who love the virtue of obedience to practice a *blind* obedience toward teachers who are teaching error or shepherds who are abusing their sheep. In themselves, humility, meekness, obedience, are virtues and are therefore good; but it is in the nature of any created good to be able to be abused, and virtues, too, can be abused when they are misused, misapplied, misdirected. To be humble or meek by letting one's rights be dashed to the ground by another who abuses his office is to make humility or meekness an accomplice of someone else's sin. To be obedient to one who is himself disobedient to God is to become guilty of disobedience. [19] This is the way that the devil, when he cannot tempt

---

19 Conversely, rebelling against rebels is fidelity, as Fr Raymond Dulac, an early and intrepid critic of the liturgical reform, explained all the way back in

someone to obvious vices, tempts them rather by the very virtues they hold dear. In this way, rather than bringing good out of evil, as God does, Satan brings evil out of good, which is his specialty.

We know from Aristotle that there are two kinds of vices relative to every virtue. Thus, courage or fortitude is a mean or middle between the extreme of cowardice, which is a deficiency in facing danger, and the extreme of rashness, which is facing danger excessively or recklessly.[20] However, Aristotle makes the astute observation that one of the extremes is closer to the mean, and resembles it more: thus, recklessness resembles courage more than cowardice does, and similarly, not enjoying food and drink enough is closer to temperance than gluttony is.[21] For Aristotle, too much of a good thing becomes a bad thing, and so it is with obedience: too much obedience paid to earthly figures, an indiscriminate and total adherence to their will, is a vice – and yet it looks more like the virtuous mean than rebelliousness does, and so it tends to be confused with the virtue. That confusion is a key part of the devil's strategy.

INFILTRATION AND INVERSION

A book called *AA-1025: Memoirs of the Communist Infiltration into the Church* gives us the posthumous memoirs of a communist agent who entered the seminary and was ordained a priest, but who all along forwarded the agenda of the communists for whom he worked, with a view to the auto-demolition of the Church. That such infiltrators existed is no longer disputed; the only questions are, how many there were, and how high did they rise. Those who have read Malachi Martin's *Windswept House* and know the reporting about Cardinal Bernardin's involvement in Satanic rituals will have some idea of the kind of things that happened (and,

---

the 1960s: "There is no example in the entire history of the Church of such a 'reform': radical, hasty and contrary to the true wishes of the baptized. This reform is a revolution, but it is also a revolution unlike any other. It is not a revolution from the bottom up, but from the top down. A revolution imposed on the people.... So, this wonderful thing happened: the people [who loved tradition] rebelled against the rebellion" (*In Defence of the Roman Mass*, trans. Pedar Walsh [N.p.: Te Deum Press, 2020], 43-44).

20 See the second book of the *Nicomachean Ethics* for the general account of moral virtue and vice, and Bk. 3, chs. 6-9 for the detailed treatment of courage.

21 *Nicomachean Ethics*, Bk. 2, ch. 8.

in all likelihood, are still happening).[22] The editor of the *AA-1025* manuscript, Marie Carré, writes: "The holy virtue of obedience is today the extremely powerful weapon that our enemies, who pretend to be our friends, make use of against what we *were*, to put up in its stead what they have decided to have us become." Carré's assertion implies that there is an ersatz Catholicism—some call it "neo-Catholicism"[23]—that our enemies seek to impose on us. Dr Thaddeus Kozinski has well explained what this substitute is, and how it functions:

> The intimate encounter with God immunizes us to nothing worship, the robust encounter with real being is the prerequisite for divine encounter, and authentic tradition enables the intelligible encounter with reality. The devil knows all this, being an expert logician, and so he desires above all the annihilation of authentic tradition. His main target, of course, is Catholic Tradition, for it provides the surest means to an intimate encounter with both natural and supernatural reality. . . . Realizing that any authentic tradition, even a barely-breathing one, is a receiver and transmitter of the divine, his stroke of genius was to inspire the construction and establishment of an abstract anti-tradition that would receive and transmit nothing. Although similar in its unreality to the abstractions of communism, fascism, and Nazism, it would bear such a striking resemblance to the Christian tradition that it would escape detection. *Implemented surreptitiously* and *cloaking itself in the form of its host*, it would serve as *the tradition to end all tradition*. Not only would there be no counterattack this time, men of good will would have no idea what hit them – or even that they had been hit.[24]

What Ryan Topping says about the "vocabulary reassignment surgery" of modern times applies above all to words like "obedience," "tradition," and even "Church":

---

22   See "Bernardin: Homosexual Predator Satanist," *Church Militant*, June 26, 2019.
23   For a complete definition of this term and a defense of its appropriateness, see Christopher A. Ferrara and Thomas E. Woods, Jr., *The Great Façade: The Regime of Novelty in the Catholic Church from Vatican II to the Francis Revolution* (Kettering, OH: Angelico Press, 2015), 19–20, 25–33, et passim.
24   Thaddeus Kozinski, *Modernity as Apocalypse: Sacred Nihilism and the Counterfeits of Logos* (Brooklyn, NY: Angelico Press, 2019), 181–82.

Old words that carry the gravitas of tradition and centuries of revered usage are reminted into other tokens. The reassignments will not at first be evident. To say this in other words, the meanings of terms within a counterfeit culture break down the semantic web established under the former dispensation to achieve newly desired ends. Words become weapons.[25]

It was Archbishop Marcel Lefebvre who, on October 13, 1974, gave the fullest and clearest exposition of this strategy:

> Satan's master stroke will therefore be to spread the revolutionary principles introduced into the Church *by the authority of the Church itself*, placing this authority in a situation of incoherence and permanent contradiction; so long as this ambiguity has not been dispersed, disasters will multiply within the Church.... Satan reigns through ambiguity and incoherence, which are his means of combat, and which deceive men of little faith.... We must acknowledge that the trick has been well played and that Satan's lie has been masterfully utilized. The Church will destroy Herself through obedience.... "You must obey!" Whom or what must we obey? We don't know exactly. Woe to the man who does not consent [to this false obedience]. He thereby earns the right to be trampled underfoot [by its agents], to be calumniated, to be deprived of everything which allowed him to live. He is a heretic, a schismatic; let him die, "that is all he deserves."[26]

---

25 Ryan N. S. Topping, *Thinking as Though God Exists: Newman on Evangelizing the "Nones"* (Brooklyn, NY: Angelico Press, 2023), 76.

26 Quoted in the Editorial of *Le Sel de la terre* 94 (Autumn 2015), translated into English at https://dominicansavrille.us/satans-master-stroke-2/. Lefebvre continues: "Satan's master stroke, by which he is bringing about the auto-destruction of the Church, is therefore to use obedience in order to destroy the Faith: [pitting] authority against Truth." A Polish film released on YouTube on May 13, 2023, *The Hidden Treasure of the Church*, interviews a priest who gives a similar account: "In the name of obedience towards the pope, modernism is destroying the Catholic Church. In the name of [the] commitment of Catholics, hierarchy and laity, to the pope, this mechanism is used as a weapon by hostile supporters of modernism. After Vatican II they introduced reforms which were widely accepted in the name of obedience towards the Holy See. And that is a paradox and proof of how cunning the evil spirit is, since we know that all enemies of the Church are led by the devil, and this is what happened in the name of obedience towards the pope." The devil has succeeded in pitting our Catholic instinct for authority against our Catholic instinct for truth. When truth and authority conflict, we should follow truth, since the purpose of authority is to

The anti-traditional actions of Pope Francis and Cardinal Roche, among others, reveal anew one of the deep sicknesses of the Roman Catholic Church at this time – a multilayered sickness that places law above persons, legalism above devotion, compliance above pastorality, uniformity above unity, micromanagement above prudence, presentism above tradition. This sickness thrives on the blindness of blind obedience and the passivity of the (supposedly postconciliarly "reactivated") laity and clergy. It is a sickness fed by those who tolerate it, exonerate it, or surrender to it, which they do on account of ignorance of what is at stake, laziness in pushing back, fear of consequences, opportunism, or despairing resignation.

In the current assault on the immemorial Roman liturgy, blind obedience and legal positivism will reveal their deadliest potential as instruments by which the common good of the People of God is directly assaulted and wounded, yet under the guise of mere administrative regulation, done by "proper authority" with "proper forms." Canon law in the hands of unscrupulous ideologues too easily becomes a tool of dehumanization, depersonalization, and decatholicization. As a modern philosopher writes:

> Where was there ever a regime that did not have a host of lawyers at its disposal, to help it, as it were, to "legalize" itself? The same lawyers who served the revolutionary republic in France later worked for the Emperor Napoleon in order to create his *code civil* and to put it into practice. But even when Louis XVIII was restored to the throne there was no lack of compliant lawyers who supported *his* rule by means of law just as Napoleon's rule had earlier been supported, and just as, before that, the mob's and the demagogues' reign of terror had been represented as lawful and been advocated for by means of legal concepts. One might truly say: only lay your hands on power, on people who can construct a legal basis for your power, and you will never lack for anything! Hard and unbending in petty matters, in formalities; spineless and servile with respect to great matters, with respect to

serve truth. And since we have Scripture plus two thousand years of tradition, as witnessed by the constant teaching and practice of the Church over that span of time, we can know both what truth is, and when authority is failing to serve it – at least in egregious cases.

what is essential—this is how a lawyer who is a product of a law that has emancipated itself from an ethics that is itself without religion is shown to be in the light of day.[27]

"WOE TO YOU LAWYERS!"

In the Gospel of Luke, chapter 11 (vv. 11–13), Our Lord says:

> If a son shall ask bread of any of you that is a father, will he give him a stone? or if he ask a fish, will he for a fish give him a serpent? Or if he shall ask an egg, will he offer him a scorpion? If ye then, being evil, know how to give good gifts unto your children: how much more shall your heavenly Father give the Holy Spirit to them that ask him?

Even bad parents still want to give their children good things, and do give them good things (at least, what seems good to them, even if they are mistaken). So if there were a father who actually deprived his children of good things or who gave them evil things in place of good, he would be, on Our Lord's account, *worse* than evil. What could that mean? We would in that case be looking at *satanic* evil—at a diabolic pride that seeks to cut people off from what is good, fruitful, holy, nourishing. Is the word "diabolic" too strong? No. *Diabolos* means, in Greek, "the one who divides." A pope who acts against the tradition of the Church and against the faithful attached to it is *dividing the Church from herself*, dividing the faithful from what is rightfully theirs as members of the Body of Christ.[28] Is

---

27 Valentin Tomberg, *The Art of the Good: On the Regeneration of Fallen Justice* (Brooklyn, NY: Angelico Press, 2021), 39.

28 Like Balaam's donkey being made to speak beyond what a donkey could do by nature, the Instruction *Redemptionis Sacramentum* from the quondam Congregation for Divine Worship and the Discipline of the Sacraments uttered a wisdom that transcends (and, in a way, subverts) its Novus Ordo framework: "It is not possible to be silent about the abuses, even quite grave ones, against the nature of the Liturgy and the Sacraments as well as *the tradition* and the authority of the Church, which in our day not infrequently plague liturgical celebrations in one ecclesial environment or another. In some places the perpetration of liturgical abuses has become almost habitual, a fact which obviously cannot be allowed and must cease. The liturgical words and rites . . . are a faithful expression, *matured over the centuries*, of the understanding of Christ, and they teach us to think as he himself does; by conforming our minds to these words, we raise our hearts to the Lord... [A]rbitrary actions are not conducive to true renewal, but are detrimental to the right of Christ's faithful to a liturgical celebration that is an expression of the Church's life *in accordance with her tradition* and discipline. . . .

the word "satanic" too strong? No. *Satanas* means the accuser, and here we have a man, Jorge Mario Bergoglio, constantly accusing Catholics who love the Lord, love the Faith, love the traditions of the Church—accusing them of divisiveness, of rejecting the Holy Spirit, of rigidity, of lovelessness, of worshiping ashes, of mental illness, and on and on. Pope Francis should hold a mirror up to himself and discover the one who divides, the one who accuses.

One may imagine Christ our Savior speaking to the successors of His apostles and to their compliant, manipulative, and pharisaical canon lawyers the same words he spoke to the Jewish lawyers of his day: "Woe to you lawyers! For you took away the key of knowledge. You did not enter in yourselves, and those who were entering in, you hindered" (Lk 11:52). Ye corrupt canon lawyers: you take away the key of the knowledge of divine worship in accord with tradition and truth. You do not enter in yourselves, and those who were entering in—young and old, singles and married, families with children, the future priestly and religious vocations—these you hindered. Ye hierarchs, you refused to humble yourselves before the truth of history, the truth of tradition, the truth of the Holy Spirit's work in the traditional movement; you failed to seek the spiritual good of the people of God, and, on the contrary, you worked *against* their good, which is the sole justification for your authority. In the words of the Book of Daniel, in the story of Susanna: "Iniquity came forth from Babylon, from elders who were judges, who were supposed to govern the people. . . . And they perverted their minds and turned away their eyes from looking to Heaven or remembering righteous judgments" (Dan 13:5, 9).

As we have seen, a bishop—*every* bishop, including the bishop of Rome—is entrusted with the care of the common good: that is the sole rationale for his authority. If he acts against the spiritual nourishment that the faithful receive from the old rites, if he acts against the continuity of the Church's received and approved rites,

---

The Catholic people have the right that the Sacrifice of the Holy Mass should be celebrated for them in an integral manner, according to the entire doctrine of the Church's Magisterium" (nos. 4, 5, 11, 12; emphasis added). The logic here calls for the restoration of the authentic Roman Rite. Indeed, the effort to restore Eastern rites to their pristine condition by a process of delatinization is based on the concept of an identifiable authentic tradition as well as a reasonable claim on it, on the part of those whose tradition it is; the same concept exists in and for the Western rites, which need to undergo "demodernization" and "debugninification."

he is acting unjustly and *ultra vires*, and any such determinations do not bind us in conscience. They bind neither the priests nor the people. Like Christ, who came not to be served but to serve, so too should our priests continue to serve God's people first and foremost; and the pope, above all, is required before God to live up to his title, *servus servorum Dei*: the servant of the servants of God.

It is already a sign of divine mercy, of the fulfillment of God's promise that the Church would never fail until He comes again, that there are Catholics everywhere in the world – a minority, to be sure, but not negligible, and growing in every nation – who have been given the grace to recognize the anti-tradition for what it is, and to hold fast to the tradition (or to rediscover it later in life) so that it may continue. Such Catholics see that many are in the grip of a distorted and harmful notion of obedience, which injures the clergy even more than it does the faithful. If your concept of obedience is such that you will be ready to change your opinions at the whim of the pope or the bishop, that can only mean that your attachment is solely to obedience itself; there is no content behind it. You will never be able to truly love something, because you may be asked to reject it at any moment, and you will be expected to reject it with as much willingness as that with which you once accepted it. This is how we end up with psychologically damaged automatons instead of shepherds who, with intelligent and loving hearts, care for the souls entrusted to them.

The system described here is self-perpetuating; it is *designed* to be unbreakable, inescapable. This destructive cycle can be broken in only two ways, both of which are needed, as they complement one another. The top-down solution, for which we ardently pray, is a future pope's root-and-branch reform of the Church, clearing out the episcopacy of its cowards, modernists, and homosexuals and reinstituting traditional liturgy and doctrine. (Needless to say, this may require a whole series of popes, as was the case with church reform in the sixteenth century.) The bottom-up solution is what clergy and laity can do right now: exercise their God-given rights to live according to faith, reason, and tradition, ignoring penalties administered by and in service of the self-perpetuating closed system of false obedience, and thus clearing the way for the healing and rejuvenation of the Church. This is not doing evil that good may come of it; it is doing good by adhering to truth and tradition, and rejecting the evil of complicity with destroyers of the vineyard.

One of my favorite writers from the period right after the Council is the great American publisher and conservative pundit Neil McCaffrey (1925–1994). Here's what he was telling his fellow Catholics when the revolution against them first erupted – and his words from 1967 ring out with a strange relevance in 2023:

> Traditional Catholics find themselves bewildered, in disarray. Part of the disarray, I suspect, springs from an error most of us fell heir to. Not much burdened with a knowledge of Catholic history, we have assumed that Authority could do no wrong; well, very little wrong; well, at least nothing *seriously* wrong. And so we found ourselves disarmed. . . .
>
> I hope no one will read this [appeal to non-conformity] as an invitation to schism, even an oblique invitation. This is *our* Church. Like a family, we may not always be proud of its elders or its members. But it is still ours, we owe it filial love, it is our hope. We owe it loyalty, too: and not just in fair weather. Once the loyalty came easier. Once the yoke was sweet, the burden light. Now we are in a tunnel – or, rather, a madhouse. The consolations are gone. Our home is in the hands of strangers. Strangers who hate us, who tell us to conform or die.
>
> Let us turn their own non-conformity against them. If they have the freedom to preach contempt of the Church we know and love, surely we have the freedom to defend, to resist, to cherish what is part of ourselves. As Americans we are accustomed to exercise generous freedoms in the temporal sphere. We are not used to having to use them in the Church. Now we must, or be swept away. And the radicals do mean to sweep us away. They preach freedom – but only their own brand. They leave in their wake a totalitarian stink.[29]

CAUSES FOR HOPE

A great and courageous Dominican priest who stalwartly resisted the conciliar and postconciliar revolution until his death in 1975,

---

29 *And Rightly So: Selected Letters and Articles of Neil McCaffrey*, ed. Peter A. Kwasniewski (Fort Collins, CO: Roman Catholic Books, 2019), 152, 155.

Fr Roger-Thomas Calmel inspired and comforted French traditionalists with his words of wisdom. Having posed the question "What
can we do?," he writes:

> Obviously, hold fast to Tradition, be it the Mass—the
> Mass of St Pius V, Latin in the liturgy, the Catechism,
> the tried and true customs of Catholic prayer, especially
> the Rosary, and temporal Christian institutions, at least
> whatever remains of them.
>
> Even so doing, it is not out of the question that we
> may experience the temptation, *What's the use?* What
> *is* out of the question is that we should take this temp-
> tation seriously, or let it gain a foothold in our hearts,
> or impinge on our resolutions by a fraction of an inch.
> It is impossible to say *What's the use?* when one knows
> that it is always good to prove to God our love, the first
> proof of love being to persevere in the Faith and to keep
> Catholic Tradition.
>
> All the reasons we have for losing heart—the pro-
> longed fight, the extensive betrayal, increased isola-
> tion—should only be considered in the supreme light
> of faith. The greatest misfortune that could befall us is
> not to be bruised in the depth of our soul by the woes
> of the present times and the scandals from on high; it
> would be to lack faith and consequently to fail to see
> that the Lord makes use of the present distress to urge
> us to turn our gaze towards Him, to invite us to show
> Him more than ever our trust and love. So... the first
> thing to do is to look at the Lord, and then to keep this
> supernatural contemplation inseparable from consider-
> ation of the attacks to be repulsed and the struggle to be
> engaged till the end.[30]

May God grant us the grace to be faithful to His righteousness
as taught and lived in traditional Catholicism, clear, strong, and
beautiful as it is, and may He keep us from succumbing to the
poisons offered by the world—including the worldliness within the
Church. As the last book of the Bible exhorts us: "Here is a call for
the endurance and faith of the saints" (Rev 13:10).

---

30   First published in *Itinéraires*, April 1972; English translation from *The
Angelus*, vol. 38, no. 1 (January-February 2015): 43.

11

The Pope's Authority over Liturgy: A Dialogue

*T*HE FOLLOWING FICTIONAL DIALOGUE *between hyperpapalist "Rockmeteller" (apologies to P.G. Wode-house for stealing the name) and papal critic "Traddeus" is based on many real dialogues conducted online. It's not intended to be systematic but merely to provoke thought about key issues (pun intended) that will grow in importance as the blight of synodality — a delivery device for a certain brand of papally-shoved progressivism — continues to afflict the vineyard of the Church.*

Rockmeteller: Traddeus, you're always talking about "limits" to the pope's authority over the liturgy. But what do you make of Pius XII's *Mediator Dei* where he says in no. 58: "It follows from this that the Sovereign Pontiff alone enjoys the right to recognize and establish any practice touching the worship of God, to introduce and approve new rites, as also to modify those he judges to require modification."

Traddeus: As "no. 58," this passage has a context. Before and after it, Pius XII is talking about how the Church has used her authority to accommodate and incorporate devotional trends, "to protect the purity of divine worship against abuse from dangerous and imprudent innovations introduced by private individuals and particular churches," to defend "the legitimate rites of the Church," to "prohibit any spurious innovation," and to reprove severely "the temerity and daring of those who introduce novel liturgical practices or call for the revival of obsolete rites." Most basically, the Church "has organized and regulated divine worship, *enriching it constantly with new splendor and beauty, to the glory of God and the spiritual profit of Christians*"; thus she "add[s] what appeared more likely to *increase* the honor paid to Jesus Christ and the august Trinity." You see, there's a tendency and a purpose noted here: through the devotion of the faithful and the encouragement of the pastors, the liturgy grows richer over time, more perfect at doing what it is supposed to do. The idea of chopping away the heritage of centuries or dumbing things down or turning the focus away from God to the "people of God," as in (say) a *versus populum* communitarianism — all of that would be entirely foreign to the spirit of the Church, as we find it described in *Mediator Dei*. Whatever "new rites" might be introduced, such as the blessing of automobiles and airplanes, will, naturally, be in harmony with the entire existing body of traditional liturgy. That is obvious from everything else said in the encyclical.

Rockmeteller: What you are overlooking, it seems to me, is that Pius XII limits the role of everyone else in the Church to passive recipients of whatever the Apostolic See hands down to them: the bishops are to enforce it, and the laity are to accept it. Period.

Traddeus: If we took this to be truly the point of view of Pius XII, it would not make it right; it would make it simply the peak moment of ultramontanist concentration — clericalism on steroids. Nothing like that view was practiced for the first 1,500 years of Catholicism. It overlooks entirely the way in which episcopal subsidiarity operates, as well as the genuine right that the faithful have to their liturgical inheritance. The liturgy does not belong only to the pope, it belongs to the entire Church. He can be a shepherd but not a tyrant.

Rockmeteller: Let's take an example. I've heard you say that it was tyrannical for Paul VI to displace the Roman Canon by adding multiple neo-anaphoras cobbled together from bits and pieces of old sources. But who made the Roman Canon such a big deal? It was only a big deal because the Church used it, and the pope in particular; and if the pope decides he wants to use a different prayer, or wants to make us use a different prayer, who cares? As long as it hits the main points...

Traddeus: We have to ask ourselves why this was *never* the attitude of anyone, anywhere, throughout all of ecclesiastical history for which we have records. Nobody questioned the continuing and exclusive use of the Roman Canon in the Western rites and uses. Either people in the past were stupidly uncreative and stubbornly attached (almost sinfully so, it would seem) to doing things a certain way — or they had *good reason* for their conservatism. To me, it seems self-evident that the longer the Church prays a certain way, the better it is to continue praying that way.[1] But I suppose that requires having supernatural faith in God's guidance of the Church and her leaders over time. That's why I wonder, at times, if the supporters of a newly-fashioned modern liturgy have some obscure agnosticism or atheism in their mental makeup: God's Providence seems strangely absent from their assessment of the history of the Church and her liturgy, and no more present is the immense confidence our predecessors had in speaking of the *divine* liturgy, the *sacred* rites, as if they were bequeathed to us by God or, at very least, with God's abundant favor upon them. When did that attitude of pious respect disappear—and why?

Rockmeteller: It seems to me that what is missing here is the doctrine/discipline distinction. Doctrinal truth is per se immutable. Disciplinary matters, however, such as which orations are prayed on the Feast of Christ the King (or even whether or not there is to be such a feast), are not immutable. Therefore, the pope has the authority to change them. Now, one might find a particular disciplinary change imprudent, and one can ask the pope to change his mind or to give a dispensation for those who want to continue using the older discipline, but there is an essential difference between the pope (in a non-infallible statement) contradicting infallible doctrine (in which case his words are actually false) and the pope, as supreme legislator, changing discipline, even if he does so in an imprudent manner. We are usually bound by the commands of our superiors, even when they seem foolish to us. Of course, we ought to explain to the superiors why their commands are foolish, but we cannot actually disobey them. The promulgation of the Novus Ordo and the restriction of the old rite may have been foolish, but such things are within the scope of the pope's authority, so the proper response is to ask the pope for permission to continue using the old Mass, not simply to disobey him.

Traddeus: Two points in response.

First, I've often wondered if so sharp a distinction between doctrine and discipline can be maintained—especially in the area of liturgy. Some have argued that Pius V's *Quo Primum*, to take an important example, was no merely "disciplinary" document,

---

1   See Kwasniewski, "From Extemporaneity to Fixity of Form."

because its intention was to canonize (as it were) a traditional form of the Mass known with certainty to be a confession of the Catholic Faith and free from error. It would be difficult to maintain that there are not doctrinal ramifications of this move that go beyond "this Mass validly confects the Sacrament." Put differently, the tight connection between *lex orandi* and *lex credendi* suggests that, whatever freedom the Church may have to introduce *new* rites, the abolition of *traditional* rites is quite beyond the power of prelates.

Second, some prudential decisions can be so catastrophically bad that they lack the power to oblige subjects. So even if we admit the technical legality of a document like *Traditionis Custodes*, it may still fail to be binding on consciences because of its egregious violation of the common good. Deep waters here, but I recommend reading Fr Réginald-Marie Rivoire and Thomas Pink, who shed much light on these questions.[2]

Rockmeteller: I'll admit that most people out there who have given any careful thought to the current liturgical situation in the Latin-rite Church agree, on a practical level, that Francis has done something terribly imprudent and indeed reprehensible – something that should be annulled. Still, it seems to me that you're going too far when you say that a pope doesn't have ultimate authority over liturgical rites.

Traddeus: I find it striking that the Creed of Pius IV (which is a *de fide* document) includes the sentence "Receptos quoque et approbatos Ecclesiae catholicae ritus in supradictorum omnium Sacramentorum solemni administratione recipio et admitto": "I receive and admit the received and approved rites of the Catholic Church [used] in the solemn administration of all of the aforesaid sacraments." That looks to me as if it would make the suppression of any existing rite by any putative ecclesiastical positive law altogether *ultra vires*.

Rockmeteller: It seems to me that both *Quo Primum* and the Creed of Pius IV show that the older form of the Roman Rite is doctrinally sound, and that its ceremonies have a certain fittingness for divine worship. One cannot reject that form, therefore, in the sense in which some liberal theologians do who claim that it is doctrinally defective, or that its ceremonies are ridiculous. But I don't see how

---

2   See note 11 on page 64.

either of those documents precludes ecclesiastical authority from making changes to the form, even extensive changes. Abolishing the prayers at the foot of the altar, for example, does not imply that there was anything doctrinally suspect or ridiculous in those prayers; it only implies that the authority abolishing those prayers thought it more opportune to have the rite of Mass shorter and simpler. Now, we can think that that was a foolish decision; I personally do. But I don't think it was *so bad* that one can apply the principle "an unjust law does not bind." It was certainly *intended* by the legislator to promote the Church's common good, even if, as a matter of fact, it did not contribute to that good. The proper response, therefore, seems to me to petition the Holy See to restore those prayers and to give permission for the use of the older Rite more generally. But it would be blameworthy disobedience to use the older form in cases when permission is not granted.

Traddeus: It's easy to isolate a singular thing (like the Last Gospel) and ask: "Is this *really* necessary for the integrity of the Roman Rite?" To which the answer is likely to be "No." It's quite another, however, to select a great many characteristic features of the Roman Rite from long periods of its use in the Church and to ask: "If we remove all of these things, and modify all of the rest, do we still have the Roman Rite?" The sheer multitude and magnitude of the changes that were made to the Roman Rite could have been seen by any intelligent person to be grievously harmful to the common good. The fact that there *were* many observers at the time who came precisely to this judgment, plus the millions who "voted with their feet," indicate that this is no exaggerated assessment.[3]

If we want to ask about what popes may and may not do, we must take into account not only their legislative authority to make "some change," but the rate and scope and nature of the changes. We would not want to say that a mere *intention* to do something "for the common good" — or a statement that such was the intention, whether it was or not — suffices to make it credible or defensible. That is, if the pope said: "I am liquidating the entire patrimony of the Vatican museums for the Church's common good," one could simply refuse to accept the statement as true or capable of being true. And the liturgy is worth far more than the museums are.

---

3 See especially Shaw, *Latin Mass and the Intellectuals*.

Rockmeteller: By the way, that line you quoted from the Creed of Pius IV wouldn't support your argument if the Novus Ordo is, as its defenders claim, a revision of the Roman Rite rather than a replacement of it.

Traddeus: That's what they attempt to claim; but it flies in the face of all the evidence. As you can read in a book called *The Once and Future Roman Rite*, there is a concrete, historically definable thing called "the Roman Rite." We can identify the many characteristics that distinguish it from other rites. The Novus Ordo lacks these characteristics by design, and, in fact, has even less in common with the Roman Rite than the Eastern rites have with it. The changes made in the liturgical "reform" were so extensive that they brought into being a different rite; and the intention voiced by Pope Francis is to extinguish the Roman Rite completely and replace it with the new rite. That would be the equivalent of suppressing the entire Byzantine ritual Church, which Vatican II implies in solemn language is impossible and which would mean no longer accepting one of the Church's received rites, contrary to the *de fide* Creed of Pius IV. Thus, the entire affair would fall outside of the domain of legitimate ecclesiastical positive law.

Rockmeteller: But aren't you overlooking the rather obvious fact that all of the popes since the institution of the Novus Ordo have referred to it in their official documents as "the revised and reformed Roman Rite" (or some such language)? Even Pope Benedict XVI spoke of "two usages of the one Roman rite" (*Summorum Pontificum*, Art. 1). You are making a mighty claim by saying that the Novus Ordo is demonstrably *not* the Roman Rite!

Traddeus: Within limits, popes can create legal fictions if they think these fictions will help them with an intractable situation; and that, I believe, is what Benedict XVI did in order to promote liturgical peace.[4] But I'm interested not so much in the legal positivism angle as I am in the *ontological* angle. Ontologically, there is simply no way to claim that the rite of Paul VI is the same rite as the Roman Rite. They are too different from each other for that to be the case; as many have shown over the years, there is not one single thing that is proper to and characteristic of the Roman

---

4   See Gregory DiPippo, "The Legal Achievement of *Summorum Pontificum*," *New Liturgical Movement*, July 5, 2017.

Rite that survives intact, as it was formerly done, in the modern rite. At the level of ontology, the only alternative is to let my brain turn into tapioca by becoming an Ockhamist, and declaring that the word "rite" has no intrinsic meaning; therefore, any two rites which are not the same at all can somehow nevertheless be "the same rite."

By the standards of the strictest legal positivists – those who know of no law other than "The Lord Pope wills it so" – the Church may have the power to declare that the modern rite IS the Roman Rite *legally*, but the Church simply has no authority to declare that such is the case ontologically. It has no authority to constrain us to believe something that goes against all the facts of history and the evidence of our senses (i.e., to believe that two things radically different are actually the same), any more than it can constrain us to believe that Charlemagne was the Emperor of Russia or that the moon is made of cheese.

Note well: I am *not* contending that the lawgiver has no authority over the law. I am contending (because it is true) that the lawgiver does not have such authority over reality that he can legally require us to believe things that are manifestly not true. For example, adoption is a legal fiction; it establishes that *in law*, the absence of a genetic relationship between two persons is not meaningful, and that a parent-child bond does exist. Yet it does not accomplish this by *creating a genetic relationship* between them, which is ontologically impossible. By analogy, the papacy can establish *in law* that the absence of a real "genetic" relationship between the Roman Rite and the rite of Paul VI is not meaningful, and that all priests of the Roman Rite can celebrate either one; but it cannot as a matter of fact and history make the two rites the same rite, any more than it can as a matter of fact and history declare that the Byzantine Rite and the Mozarabic Rite are "two usages of the same rite."

Rockmeteller: But what do you make of the YouTube apologists who cite papal text after papal text declaring that the pope is the one in charge of everything liturgical . . . that he virtually *creates* liturgical rites (even over the 1,500 year period when no pope ever did – but he *might* have done it, if only he had thought of it!) . . . that we must all bow and submit to his rule, which is identical with Christ's . . . that anyone who questions him is guilty of "defiance" of his "office"? They even say canon law targets people like you for "stirring up animosity against the Apostolic See"!

Traddeus: Such apologists treat papal authority totally in abstraction: they are looking at nothing *except* authority, as if it can be understood in a vacuum. But authority always has a context: a community, a common good, a set of duties and responsibilities, a history and tradition – all the more (it should hardly be necessary to point out) in the case of the Catholic Church.

The errors of hyperpapalists are of a philosophical order. They know their "proof texts" well, but they seem to have a poor grasp of the concepts involved in *any* exercise of authority whatsoever. Their view amounts to saying that anything a pope does is (indeed, must be) both legal and right, and his subjects have no role but to be passive recipients of his action. He has no boundaries, no requirements, no duties, and they have no good of their own, no rights, no "ownership." Indeed, hyperpapalists dismiss the statements of great theologians who talk about resisting popes when they are "tearing the Church apart" or "going into schism" or "overthrowing rites," maintaining either that those theologians are simply wrong or that they were talking about purely hypothetical, extreme, and impossible situations.

The irrational views of the hyperpapalists can have no possible place in Catholicism precisely because faith is not contrary to reason, even as grace does not contradict nature. In general, it would help if people who wish to wade knee-deep into theology would also have some serious political philosophy under their belts, not to mention the basics of anthropology, psychology, and sociology. After all, an understanding of man, society, culture, and tradition facilitates an understanding of the things that presuppose and operate on them.

Rockmeteller: Perhaps you're not being entirely fair. Surely, the apologists in question could reply: "We're not saying the pope *couldn't* royally mess something up; but only that if he did, it would be tough luck for you, because you'd have to grin and bear it. You could respectfully protest and say 'Your Holiness, you had the legal right to do this, but not the moral right; please reconsider.' And if you won him over, splendid; but otherwise you're stuck."

Traddeus: Do you think this makes sense?

Rockmeteller: Well, there *are* situations where we have to accept imperfect laws until we can obtain their rectification…

Traddeus: No, it doesn't make sense, and here's why. The view of the papacy implied in that stance would be like having a marriage in which the husband has all authority and the wife none: even if he morally abuses his authority, she must accept it, and nothing she thinks or says or does needs to be taken into account by him.[5] Really, any authority-subject relationship has the same analogous structure: husband/wife; parent/child; president/citizens; pastor/parishioners. There is a God-given authority in each case that nevertheless can be used well or badly, and the subjects themselves have a certain dignity that must be respected, which includes respecting their access to the goods that Providence has bestowed upon them for their use. If the ruler in each case is not ruling for the actual benefit of the subjects, then his commands or prohibitions lose, to that extent, their validity.

Rockmeteller: I don't know what to say; you've certainly given me a lot to think about, and challenged my conceptions.

Traddeus: Iron sharpens iron, and all that. Oh, look at the time! I need to get going to schola practice for the feast of Saints Peter and Paul. Can you make it to the solemn High Mass tomorrow at noon?

Rockmeteller (smiling): Yes, as a matter of fact, I heard about it and was planning on it. The ancient Roman Rite seems a most fitting way to celebrate the apostles of Rome. I'll be there. See you then!

---

5   See Julian Kwasniewski, "Do to Your Wife as You Would Have Your Bishop Do to You," *Crisis Magazine*, September 26, 2023.

12

Cursed Cultus or Worthy Worship[1]

ET US TAKE AS OUR POINT OF DEPARTURE two quotations from Sacred Scripture: "Cursed be he that doeth the work of the Lord with slackness" (Jer 48:10, ESV), or as some other translations have it, "negligently" (cf. ASV); and "Worship the Lord in the beauty of holiness" (Ps 29:2, KJV).

The first verse, taken from the Prophet Jeremiah, speaks of a terrible danger that faces mortal man in this life: the danger of neglecting the *opus Dei*, the work of divine worship for which we and the entire cosmos have been created and redeemed, the sin of performing it carelessly or fraudulently. In the tradition, "religion" names the virtue by which we give to God what we owe Him — the best we can, in the best manner, according to the Book of Sirach: "When you glorify the Lord, exalt him as much as ye can; for even yet will he far exceed: and when ye exalt him, put forth all your strength, and be not weary, for ye can never go far enough" (43:30). As St Thomas Aquinas teaches, religion is the highest of all moral virtues.[2] Offering right religious worship is the most important task we have, ranking only behind the acts of the theological virtues of faith in God, hope in gaining heaven by God's help, and charity for God and for those who belong to Him. Jeremiah is warning us against a "cursed cultus," in which either what we are offering or the *manner* in which we are offering it is displeasing to Almighty God, and brings upon us not blessing but curse.

The second verse, taken from Psalm 28,[3] speaks positively of the blessed obligation we have to "worship the Lord in the beauty of holiness." The beauty required for worship is first and foremost

---

1 This chapter began as an address given at the launch of Bishop Athanasius Schneider's book *The Catholic Mass: Steps to Restore the Centrality of God in the Liturgy* (Manchester, NH: Sophia Institute Press, 2022) in Arlington, Virginia, on October 18, 2022.
2 *Summa theologiae* II-II, Q. 81, art. 6.
3 Psalm 29 in the Hebrew enumeration.

an internal spiritual beauty, that of holiness, of being in the state of grace; but since we are creatures of soul and body, the beauty of the invisible God and of the invisible soul in which He deigns to dwell are also meant to be reflected outwardly in the beauty of *how* we worship as rational animals – in the beauty of our churches, our liturgical ceremonies, our sacred music, our vestments, vessels, furnishings, paintings, sculptures, and windows. These things can teach us and tell us, often wordlessly, that God is the ultimate beauty for which we long; that His beauty is luminous, radiant, ravishing, attractive, comforting, and calming, yet also demanding, severe, strange, incomprehensible, mysterious. He is the God among us and the God beyond us: Emmanuel, but also the One "dwelling in light inaccessible, whom no man hath seen nor can see," as St Paul says to St Timothy (1 Tim 6:16).

Catholic worship always found ways to express this paradoxical mystery of God's immanence and transcendence, His supreme holiness that is both fearful and fascinating to us and calls forth from us a response of utter seriousness that encompasses our entire being, mind and heart, flesh and psyche, senses, imagination, memory. We offer to Him, moreover, not only what we are individually, not only what we are as a community at a particular time and place, but also what we have been and will be as members of the one Church of Christ stretching from Abel the just until the last breath of the last man to confess Christ before the world ends.[4]

In particular, we owe Him the worship of our forefathers, of our ancestors, our "precursors," the ones who have run the race before us and reached the kingdom ahead of us, and who are therefore more advanced than we are. The continuity of tradition, in other words, is part of what we offer to God in our worship: it is the combined voice of the departed and the living, the many generations

---

4 See St Augustine: "Our Lord Jesus Christ, like a whole and perfect man, is Head and body. . . . His body is the Church, not simply the Church that is in this particular place, but both the Church that is here and the Church which extends over the whole earth; not simply the Church that is living today, but the whole race of saints, from Abel down to all those who will ever be born and will believe in Christ until the end of the world, for all belong to one city. This city is the body of Christ. . . . This is the whole Christ: Christ united with the Church" (*In Ps. 90*, serm. 2, quoted in Emile Mersch, SJ, *The Whole Christ: The Historical Development of the Doctrine of the Mystical Body in Scripture and Tradition* [n.p.: Ex Fontibus Company, 2018], 415).

speaking, singing, keeping silence as one social-spiritual entity before the face of God. To worship God with novelties, inventions, fabrications, in a spirit of momentary spontaneity, is to deprive Him of the beauty of united, collective, time-embracing and time-transcending holiness. It is to deprive Him of the best that He Himself has inspired over the ages, the gifts He intended to be given and received among ourselves and under His gaze, for His glory.

Tradition is not the lazy repetition of the past on the part of a present generation lacking in creativity or adaptability. Our love for tradition is not a nostalgic hankering after something we no longer have but wish we did; it is, rather, an immediate sympathy with what is intensely solemn and piercingly beautiful, mingled with an attitude of humble receptivity that welcomes, cherishes, and rejoices in the treasury of the Church as the family of God and the people of God, on pilgrimage through time, carrying in their arms and hearts all the riches bestowed upon them. It is only the rootless, individualistic, self-centered, arrogant modern man, thinking himself to be self-sufficient, who cares nothing for his family heritage – for the history, customs, heirlooms, books, memories, and stories of past generations that, so far from being "dead and gone," remain supremely *alive in God* and form the most perfect worshipers in His Church, the ones in heaven. They have run ahead and we are far behind. It is perfect folly to imagine that the saints of the past are less qualified than we are to determine how divine worship should be conducted. Or, to put it the other way around, it is perfect folly to imagine that *we* are more qualified than the saints of the past to determine how divine worship should be conducted. On the contrary, their cumulative testimony is the model, measure, and motivation for our discipleship to Christ, our action and suffering, our divine worship. This is the Catholic mentality, and it is the exact antithesis of the modern one. Tragically, the violent contradiction between these two mentalities entered into the bloodstream of the Church on earth with the vaunted *aggiornamento* of the Second Vatican Council and the subsequent modernization of the sacred liturgy, and we have been suffering the effects of civil war ever since.

In truth, we receive what the Greek tradition calls "the divine liturgy" from God through the Church – not the Church of a single day or a single moment, much less the churchmen intoxicated with the Zeitgeist, but the Church throughout history – and we hand it down faithfully. Thus did the Israelites, having received their worship from the hand of God, who revealed the inflexible principles that govern all worship on earth and in heaven;[5] thus did Israel's Messiah when He said to His apostles, the first priests of the New Covenant: "Do this *in memory of me*," that is, imitate me, follow what I do, and pass it on as a living memory, as a making-present of this one sacrifice. Thus did St Paul when he told the Corinthians: "I commend you because you remember me in everything and maintain the traditions even as I have delivered them to you" (1 Cor 11:2), and who told the Thessalonians: "Brethren, stand firm and hold to the traditions which you were taught by us, either by word of mouth or by letter" (2 Thess 2:15).

Not even the apostles rejected the traditional Hebrew liturgy they received; they maintained the daily cycle of the Psalms of David and united the worship of the synagogue and the temple by means of the Mass of the Catechumens and the Mass of the Faithful. Jesus no more came to abolish the synagogue and temple worship than He came to abolish the law and the prophets (cf. Mt 5:17); quite the contrary, as He fulfilled or brought to completion the law and the prophets, so He fulfilled and brought to completion the verbal worship of the synagogue and the sacrificial worship of the temple.[6] He Himself, the Word of God, the Word made flesh, the Son offered on the Cross for the life of the world, became the substance of the Holy Sacrifice of the Mass – the Mass of the Catechumens taking up the synagogue's prayer, and the Mass of the Faithful taking up the temple's holocausts. The tradition of Hebrew worship finds its ultimate point of arrival in, and yet is surpassed by, the unspeakable gift of the Savior's divine life. So too, the gift first given sacramentally at the Last Supper and ratified in the once-for-all bloody sacrifice of Calvary finds its full ecclesial manifestation in the organically developed liturgical rites of East and West, wherein the concentrated meaning placed by Our Lord into a few compact and powerful

---

5   See my lecture "Enter His Courts With Praise: Liturgical Reverence for Christ the King," *New Liturgical Movement*, May 2, 2022.
6   See the chapter "Gregorian Chant: Perfect Music for Christian Worship" in my book *Good Music, Sacred Music, and Silence: Three Gifts of God for Liturgy and for Life* (Gastonia, NC: TAN Books, 2023), 88–115, esp. 88–89.

words, gestures, and materials is unfolded by Holy Mother Church under the guidance of the Holy Spirit for our greater access, our better engagement, our further instruction, our spiritual exercise and indeed our astonishment and confoundment.

For fifteen centuries, the Church did exactly this – striving to worship the Lord in the beauty of holiness, and striving also, by the guardrails of custom, canon law, and rubrics, to avoid doing the work of the Lord negligently – and she did this, for fifteen hundred years, *without papal intervention*. The missal that sat on every Christian altar from one end of Christendom to the other had been put there not by a pope, not even necessarily by a bishop, but by the hands of many generations of clergy and religious, copying out their missals line by line on the skins of animals, binding them stoutly in leather. When St Pius V issued *Quo Primum* in 1570, he was merely codifying – or better said, canonizing – what the Church in Rome had already traditionally been doing for centuries. So far from being a vindication of any supposed freedom to dispose of liturgy as he pleased, this great pope rather vindicated the prior unassailable dignity of immemorial tradition – what the Council of Trent called "the received and approved rites."

In general, although gradual liturgical development is normal and healthy, especially in the direction of addition or expansion for the fuller expression of truth and the better evocation of divine beauty, the *lex orandi* or law of prayer already in place is to be jealously guarded and religiously maintained, and novelty in the sense of sudden and drastic change is to be avoided.[7] This is the Catholic attitude; it has always been and will always be the Catholic attitude. When Pope Benedict XVI famously stated: "What earlier generations held as sacred, *remains* sacred and great for us too, and it cannot be all of a sudden entirely forbidden or even considered harmful. It behooves all of us to preserve the riches which have developed in the Church's faith and prayer, and to give them their proper place," he wasn't asking us to be obedient to his or anyone's whimsical dictate or condescending pastoral provision; he was asking us to recognize and remain faithful to a true principle, one that has always been true and will always be true. If it is not true,

---

7   For thorough discussion of this double claim, see Kwasniewski, *Once and Future Roman Rite.*

then we have no reason to trust the Church of yesterday, today, or tomorrow. If, on the contrary, we trust the Church, then we must embrace her tradition. It's as simple as that.

In the Church today, Bishop Athanasius Schneider stands out for his forthright defense of that primordial principle. In his book *The Catholic Mass*, he explains with great simplicity, elegance, and thoroughness the true Catholic understanding of the Holy Sacrifice, and insists on "restoring the centrality of God in the liturgy." For, as Joseph Ratzinger pointed out, liturgy in modern times is often conducted as if God does not even exist, or as if He has been utterly domesticated and subordinated to our (supposed) needs, conveniences, and political agendas. God has been marginalized. In the post-Vatican II Church He is the most marginalized of the marginalized. Bishop Schneider sets out to demonstrate how and why the liturgy must be centered on God—becoming once again "the divine liturgy."[8]

His Excellency helps us to see what liturgy is *in its essence*, and what attitudes or dispositions are appropriate for it. To do so, he must tell us all the dimensions of worship. Instead of taking an historical approach, as does Michael Fiedrowicz in *The Traditional Mass: History, Form, and Theology of the Classical Roman Rite*, or a phenomenological approach, as does Romano Guardini in *The Spirit of the Liturgy*, or a systematic approach as does Joseph Ratzinger in his own *The Spirit of the Liturgy*, Bishop Schneider adopts a thematic and spiritual approach. Like the legend that has the twelve apostles each uttering one of the articles of the Apostles' Creed, or like a question in St Thomas's *Summa theologiae* divided into articles, the twelve chapters of Bishop Schneider's book establish the fundamental "articles" or aspects of the Mass. These are: the Mass is Prayer; the Mass is Adoration; the Mass is Ritual; the Mass is Sacrifice; the Mass is Splendor; the Mass is Sacred Action; the Mass is Thanksgiving; the Mass is Listening; the Mass is the Church's Life; the Mass is Salvation's Source; the Mass is Sacred Service; the Mass is the Wedding Feast.

---

8   The treatment of liturgy in Bishop Schneider's catechism, *Credo: Compendium of the Catholic Faith* (Manchester, NH: Sophia Institute Press, 2023), can also be highly recommended for study. See my article "Bishop Restores, Develops Traditional Theology of Liturgy," *New Liturgical Movement*, December 4, 2023.

Some of these aspects may seem to be obvious – do we not all know that the Mass is prayer? – but the obvious has never been *less* obvious than it is today (in many places, the way Mass is celebrated makes "prayer" the last word that would come to mind!), and, more to the point, mystery is infinitely susceptible to meditation. We need to draw forth what is implicit in our faith and allow it to form our minds and hearts more actively. New lights are to be had if we ponder anew the great truths handed down by tradition. This, in fact, is how theology and spirituality grow over time: it is not the truth that changes, but our apprehension and communication of it.

One way in which this genuine progress occurs is by the bringing-together of an abundance of diverse, well-chosen sources to illuminate that which we already know but wish to understand more deeply. Bishop Schneider, an expert in patristics and a widely-read former professor, pulls out all the stops in *The Catholic Mass*, regaling us with quotations from Church Fathers like St Justin Martyr, Tertullian, Origen, St Cyril of Jerusalem, St Ambrose, St Augustine, St Jerome, St Leo the Great, St John Chrysostom, and St John Damascene; Doctors of the Church like St Thomas Aquinas, St Bonaventure, St Francis de Sales, St Alphonsus Liguori, and St Thérèse of Lisieux; medieval or early modern authors such as St Francis of Assisi, William Durand, Johannes Tauler, Denis the Carthusian, St Leonard of Port Maurice, and Bishop Bossuet; modern writers like Dom Prosper Guéranger, St John Henry Newman, St Peter Julian Eymard, Nicholas Gihr, Bl. Columba Marmion, Bl. Ildefons Schuster, Paul Claudel, Dietrich von Hildebrand, Charles Journet, Romano Guardini, Klaus Gamber, Evelyn Waugh, Fulton Sheen, Joseph Ratzinger, and Martin Mosebach; and magisterial sources like the Council of Trent and a host of popes who teach *una voce*, as well as altogether neglected gems from the discussions that took place at Vatican II. A book like this is an education unto itself – a veritable symphony orchestra of instruments of tradition that surrounds us with the rich sound of Catholicism, the same yesterday, today, and forever (cf. Heb 13:8).

Most refreshing of all is Bishop Schneider's fearlessness in bringing forward the traditional Latin Mass as the gold standard, the benchmark, the exemplar and paradigm of what Holy Mass is, how it is to be celebrated, how it should be understood and approached and *lived*. The continuing and permanent value of the traditional Roman rite is taken for granted, as it was taken for granted by Benedict XVI in the face of the liturgical revolution of the 1960s that divorced the Church's life of worship from its own past by the creation and universal imposition of a new rite. Although Bishop Schneider accepts the validity of the Novus Ordo (as would traditionalists in general) and sees a place for it in the Church (a view, in contrast, that many traditionalists would not share), he does not vainly imagine it to be adequate as it stands, nor does he think that it can rise above soul-deadening mediocrity without the beneficent influence and powerful "gravitational force" of the classical Roman Rite alongside it. Accordingly, Bishop Schneider emphasizes the exemplary perfection of the Latin Mass in regard to Eucharistic reverence and adoration, the complementary roles of music and silence, and the correct understanding of all-male sanctuary ministry in its sevenfold realization (porter, exorcist, lector, acolyte, subdeacon, deacon, and priest).

Whoever attacks this traditional form of the Mass, which truly merits the name "Roman Rite," is attacking all that is Catholic — the historical, traditional, ancient, and ancestral rituals that express, inculcate, and transmit the orthodox faith that comes to us from Christ and the Apostles. Such a person is attacking the host of saints, the cloud of witnesses, whose faith and charity were nourished on the Church's traditional liturgical rites. From an ecclesiological point of view, nothing could be more self-contradictory than expunging, or even limiting in any way, the use of the immemorial Roman Rite. Thus, when Bishop Schneider explains the improvements or changes that must take place to restore the centrality of God in the liturgy, he effectively tells us to traditionalize, to tridentinize (as it were), what we are doing. Anything that is right with our liturgy necessarily has its roots in tradition. We must become familiar with tradition and give it a warm welcome, as befits a Catholic. There is, indeed, no Catholicism without it. Traditionalists are on hand to point out that the simplest, unfussiest, best and noblest way to do what the good bishop counsels is to restore the traditional Roman Rite in the Church, utterly and completely.

Here I cannot avoid adding that it is absolutely absurd for the hierarchy of the Church to discourage or to prevent the faithful from attending the traditional form of the Catholic liturgy that attracts them and nourishes them. As Benedict XVI recognized in the letter that accompanied *Summorum Pontificum*:

> Immediately after the Second Vatican Council it was presumed that requests for the use of the 1962 Missal would be limited to the older generation which had grown up with it, but in the meantime it has clearly been demonstrated that young persons too have discovered this liturgical form, felt its attraction and found in it a form of encounter with the Mystery of the Most Holy Eucharist, particularly suited to them.

May I say something obvious? Liturgy is *supposed* to attract us and nourish us in the mysteries of Christ. Only a pagan or an infidel or an apostate or a demon would wish to see the suppression of "a form of encounter with the Mystery of the Most Holy Eucharist particularly suited" to young people – and obviously not only to young people, but to all ages! All the more is such an attack unjustifiable and intolerable when it targets not some kind of wild, experimental, charismatic liturgy, but the most venerable rite of Christendom, the immemorial Roman Rite, which is so ancient that its Roman Canon predates the Byzantine anaphoras of St John Chrysostom and St Basil the Great. Yes, the Second Vatican Council called for a *moderate* reform, but what came afterward was by no means a moderate reform – not by any stretch of the imagination. Moreover, in contrast with a dogmatic declaration that is and must be true (such as we find in the decrees of the Council of Trent), a prudential program of reform such as we have in the Second Vatican Council is neither true nor false, but either wise or unwise, successful or unsuccessful. It has no *guarantee* of success and must be evaluated precisely by its practical outcomes. By that criterion, the pope should be reining in the Novus Ordo, not the Latin Mass.

There is nothing more urgently needed in the Church today than the overcoming of false notions of obedience, which play into the hands of the enemies of Christ who wish for nothing more than to sever the Church *once for all* from the faith and morals and liturgy she once upheld and treasured. It cannot be denied anymore that many of the Church's rulers are abusing their authority.

Our principled resistance to those who are themselves disobedient to divine law, natural law, and ecclesiastical tradition – whether this resistance of ours takes the form of open confrontation or a more subtle, indirect effort to bypass and undermine their agendas and enactments – is not a matter of "being disobedient." It is recognizing what is inherently right, using the twin gifts of faith and reason, and then *doing* it in the fear and love of God. Obedience is grounded always in reason and in the *sensus fidei*. It must never contradict them, cancel them out, or trample on them. Bishop Schneider himself, having grown up in a Soviet Union that relied on blind obedience to the diktats of the controlling Communist Party, and having later experienced the still more insidious forms of cultural conformism and social pressure at work in liberal Western democracies even unto the liberalization and secularization of Catholicism, understands very well the use and abuse of obedience – its role as a tremendous virtue, founded upon the truth and aspiring to perfection, or its inverted image, a treacherous vice wedded to self-interest, cringing before power, and resulting in a dead conscience.

Returning, in conclusion, to Bishop Schneider's book, I would like to draw attention to its remarkable cover, which was specially chosen by the author. Here we see a photograph of St Paul's Cathedral in Münster, Germany, in 1946, after the Allied bombing of the city. The church has been gashed open by explosions. A gaping wound lets the light of day stream in to the apse. Like the Lord Jesus in His Passion, the church is despised, abject, acquainted with infirmity (cf Is 53:3). This is our situation at the sixtieth anniversary of the promulgation of Vatican II's Constitution on the Sacred Liturgy *Sacrosanctum Concilium*: the Catholic Church in the West is in ruins. A new iconoclasm swept through and destroyed the beauty of countless churches and their furnishings. Above all, the icon of the Holy Mass and the other sacramental rites were vandalized almost past recognition. The liturgy was violently removed from its bimillenial arc of providential development.

Yet all the same, Tradition carries on. In this moving photograph we are astonished – and then consoled – to discover that Holy Mass, the great Mass of the Roman Rite, is taking place, in spite of everything. The priest, deacon, and subdeacon continue to offer the *Missa Solemnis*, heedless of the rubble, the missing walls, the absent faithful, the cold and damp conditions, or whatever other inconveniences or obstacles beset them. They will be faithful to the *opus Dei*, the work of God, the sacred liturgy, the *divine* liturgy. They have not forgotten the centrality of God. They will not be cursed in their negligent *cultus*. They are striving to worship the Lord in the beauty of holiness, as best they can, in spite of the odds against them, in spite of the hostile environs. After Bugnini's bombardment, after Bergoglio's backwardism, after whatever this or that bishop has done or failed to do, our local church might feel a lot like that bombed-out cathedral, and we, by the grace of God and by the true obedience that takes the form of courageous adherence to the truth and determined fidelity to tradition, can be like those intrepid ministers in that cavernous church, carrying on with the work of God that saves souls and glorifies Him.

Bishop Schneider's *The Catholic Mass* is, you might say, a kind of "how-to" manual: it teaches us how to avoid the curse of negligence, slackness, and fraudulence, and how to ensure the beauty of holiness—how to offer the pleasing sacrifice of Abel instead of the displeasing one of Cain.

PART II

13

Clandestine Ordinations Against Church Law

O NE OF THE MOST REMARKABLE EPISODES in the life of Karol Wojtyła – and one from which we can learn a great deal today – took place during his time as cardinal of Kraków. It is astonishing to me that, with all the attention lavished on John Paul II, this incident has failed to attract notice, much less commentary. The same is true of a momentous event in the life of the great Cardinal Josef Slipyj.

CLANDESTINE PRIESTLY ORDINATIONS

For readers who may be unfamiliar with it, *Ostpolitik* refers to the Vatican's Cold War strategy of conceding certain demands of the Communists in Eastern Europe in return for supposed tolerance of an ongoing minimal ecclesial existence. George Weigel has been a candid and severe critic of *Ostpolitik*.[1] Weigel's authoritative biography *Witness to Hope* presents the salient facts accurately, albeit with a bit of sugar-coating:

> Cardinal Wojtyła never doubted the good intentions of Paul VI in his *Ostpolitik*, and he certainly knew of the Pope's personal torment, torn between his heart's instinct to defend the persecuted Church and his mind's judgment that he had to pursue the policy of *salvare il salvabile* ["to save what could be salvaged"] – which, as he once put it to Archbishop Casaroli, wasn't a "policy of glory." The archbishop of Kraków also believed he had an obligation to maintain solidarity with a persecuted and

---

1   See George Weigel, "The *Ostpolitik* Failed. Get Over It," *First Things* online, July 20, 2016; idem, "The Casaroli Myth," September 29, 2021. Weigel does not appear to have read *Windswept House* or he would be less naïve about Cardinal Agostino Casaroli (Cardinal Cosimo Mastroianni in Martin's thinly-disguised fiction) or, for that matter, about Paul VI. See Gregory DiPippo, "Paul VI Did Not Exist: A 'Nostalgic' Response to George Weigel on Vatican II," *OnePeterFive*, October 24, 2022.

deeply wounded neighbor, the Church in Czechoslovakia, where the situation had deteriorated during the years of the new Vatican *Ostpolitik*.

So Cardinal Wojtyła and one of his auxiliary bishops, Juliusz Groblicki, clandestinely ordained priests for service in Czechoslovakia, in spite of (or perhaps because of) the fact that the Holy See had forbidden underground bishops in that country to perform such ordinations. The clandestine ordinations in Kraków were always conducted with the explicit permission of the candidate's superior—his bishop or, in the case of members of religious orders, his provincial. Security systems had to be devised. In the case of the Salesian Fathers, a torn-card system was used. The certificate authorizing the ordination was torn in half. The candidate, who had to be smuggled across the border, brought one half with him to Kraków, while the other half was sent by underground courier to the Salesian superior in Kraków. The two halves were then matched, and the ordination could proceed in the archbishop's chapel at Franciszkańska, 3.

Cardinal Wojtyła did not inform the Holy See of these ordinations. He did not regard them as acts in defiance of Vatican policy, but as a duty to suffering fellow believers. And he presumably did not wish to raise an issue that could not be resolved without pain on all sides. He may also have believed that the Holy See and the Pope knew that such things were going on in Kraków, trusted his judgment and discretion, and may have welcomed a kind of safety valve in what was becoming an increasingly desperate situation.[2]

Notice how Weigel tries to side-step the significance of the facts he has presented. In the midst of a mid-century Church held in the grip of an unquestioned ultramontanism, Cardinal Wojtyła simply defied the papal interdict on such ordinations and proceeded nonetheless, with the involvement of an auxiliary bishop and with the knowledge of the superiors in question. If a cardinal who knew he was acting against the will and law of the pope did not inform the pope, can one truthfully say "he did not regard them as acts of

---

2   George Weigel, *Witness to Hope: The Biography of John Paul II*, rev. ed. (New York: Harper Perennial, 2020), 233.

defiance of Vatican policy," when that is precisely what they were?[3]
Obviously he did not raise the matter with "the authorities" because
he believed they were in the wrong in this case. Moreover it is
purely gratuitous to assert, in a sanitizing effort, that Wojtyła "may
also have believed that the Holy See and the Pope knew that such
things were going on in Kraków." Where is the evidence for this?
It was *because* the pope and his Secretary of State at the time did *not*
trust the judgment and discretion of such heroes and confessors of
the Faith as Cardinal Stefan Wyszyński or (as we shall see below)
Cardinal Josyf Slipyj that the Vatican had forbidden ordinations,
whether above-ground or underground. Weigel should just stick to
the truth: as he rightly says, the cardinal knew he had an *obligation*
in the sight of God, and a *duty* to suffering fellow believers. That is
all that needs to be said.[4]

According to another biographer:

> Wojtyła had a greater connection to the Prague Spring
> than he could let on. Over the years, he had gradually
> expanded his secret ordination of underground Czech
> priests. By 1965 he was also training and ordaining covert
> priest candidates from Communist Ukraine, Lithuania,

---

3 Some say that the prohibition against clandestine ordinations applied only
to Czechoslovakia, so that Wojtyła, by having the seminarians come to him in
Kraków, was cleverly sidestepping the issue, and not in fact acting in disobedience of any rule. This much is clear, however: the reason for the prohibition
was to placate the Communist authorities, who would surely not have been
pleased to learn that seminarians were heading over the border to get ordained
elsewhere (according to Jonathan Kwitny, Wojtyła was also ordaining secretly
for the Church in the Ukraine, Lithuania, and Belarus). Hence the Vatican's
Ostpolitik would surely have stopped what Wojtyła was doing, had they found
out about it. One could say, then, that what he did was contrary to the known
or inferable intention of the lawgiver, but not contrary to the purpose of any
ecclesiastical law, namely, the salvation of souls. And that is my main point in
all the examples discussed in this second part of the book. Just as man is not
made for the sabbath, but the sabbath for man, so the Church is not made for
canon law, but canon law for the Church.

4 The fact that Weigel learned of these ordinations only from a personal admission of John Paul II in 1996, as a footnote in his book at this place tells us, shows
that Wojtyła's conscience remained untroubled by what he had done: he had no
intention of hiding it, at least after the dust had settled. It is also worth pointing
out that if Wojtyła had received some kind of hint or indication from Rome
that he should proceed (as Weigel gratuitously imagines), he would surely have
mentioned this to Weigel when relating the story. But he did not, and it is in
fact much more believable that there would have been no discussion between
Rome and Wojtyła on this point.

and Belarus, where seminaries had also been closed. Some candidates sneaked across the border to Poland, while others arranged for secular jobs that allowed them to travel legally; for example, one was a psychologist who regularly visited a Polish health institute. Wyszyński, in Warsaw, was aware of the nature, if not the details, of these activities. Had authorities known of them, they might well have jailed Wojtyła.[5]

Whether or not we are among those who laud "John Paul the Great," one thing is clear: what he did in Kraków was entirely justified, and adds to, rather than detracts from, the luster of his character.

CLANDESTINE EPISCOPAL ORDINATIONS

The life of Cardinal Josyf Slipyj (1892–1984), whose cause for canonization has been introduced in Rome, offers a parallel case for consideration. He one-upped Wojtyła by performing forbidden *episcopal* ordinations because of his inner conviction that the good of the Ukrainian Greek Catholic Church (UGCC) in the Soviet Union required it. As Fr Raymond J. De Souza summarizes:

> In 1976, the head of the UGCC, Cardinal Josef Slipyj, living in exile in Rome after 18 years in the Soviet gulag, feared for the future of the UGCC. Would it have bishops to lead it, given that Slipyj himself was now over 80? So he ordained three bishops clandestinely, without the permission of the Holy Father, Blessed Paul VI. At the time, the Holy See followed a policy of non-assertiveness regarding the communist bloc; Paul VI would not give permission for the new bishops for fear of upsetting the Soviets. The consecration of bishops without a papal mandate is a very grave canonical crime, for which the penalty is excommunication. Blessed Paul VI—who likely knew, unofficially, what Slipyj had done—did not administer any penalties.[6]

---

5   Jonathan Kwitny, *Man of the Century: The Life and Times of Pope John Paul II* (New York: Henry Holt, 1997), 220.
6   Fr Raymond J. De Souza, "Ukrainian Cardinals Husar and Slipyj are heroes to Church community," *The Catholic Register*, June 22, 2017. According to another source, the year was 1977. At the time of writing, De Souza apparently recognized the beatification of Paul VI as legitimate; many traditional Catholics question both it and his "canonization." See Peter Kwasniewski, ed., *Are Canonizations Infallible? Revisiting a Disputed Question* (Waterloo, ON: Arouca Press, 2021), esp. 219–41.

I was recently discussing this matter with a knowledgeable source who had read the *Memoirs* of Cardinal Slipyj, which are not yet available in English. He told me that the cardinal was lured to Rome under the pretext of "having a meeting" and was then told he could not leave Rome to return to the Soviet Union to live among and suffer with his people, even though he was quite willing to go back to the Gulag. It was a source of great suffering to him to be living in comfort in Rome while his flock labored under Communist and Eastern Orthodox oppression. As Jaroslav Pelikan writes in *Confessor Between East and West*:

> Here in exile, here in the Rome for which he and his church had sacrificed so much, the Ukrainian metropolitan felt increasingly hemmed in by what he called, in one of the subtitles of a document submitted to the pope, the "negative attitude" he continued to encounter from "the sacred congregations of the Roman curia." Sometimes, in his exasperation at that attitude, he would even resort to the hyperbole of declaring that he had never experienced such mistreatment from the atheists in the Soviet Union as he was experiencing now from fellow Catholics and fellow clergy in Rome.[7]

According to my aforementioned source, Paul VI certainly knew of the secret episcopal ordinations but declined to punish the cardinal because he was widely revered as a Confessor of the Faith. One of the bishops secretly ordained was Lubomyr Husar; John Paul II later officially recognized his consecration, appointed him Major Archbishop of the Ukrainian Greek Catholic Church, and created him a cardinal in 2001.[8]

---

7 Jaroslav Pelikan, *Confessor Between East and West: A Portrait of Ukrainian Cardinal Josyf Slipyj* (Grand Rapids, MI: William B. Eerdmans, 1990), 173. Interesting examples of *Ostpolitik* may be found throughout this book; see, e.g., 182–86.
8 The UGCC is a story of hope in its own right. Consider the following statistics and then apply them analogously to the state of the Latin-rite Church and its liturgical "death and resurrection" from the 1960s to the present: "In 1939, the UGCC had some 3,000 priests in Ukraine. In 1989, after 50 years of war and persecution, the priesthood was reduced by 90 per cent, to just 300. At an average age of 70, the priesthood of the UGCC was just a generation away from extinction. Then came divine deliverance and the resurrection of a Church of martyrs. Nearly 30 years later, the UGCC has again 3,000 priests with an average age of 39. There are some 800 seminarians for five million Ukrainian Greek Catholics globally" (De Souza, "Ukrainian Cardinals").

It bears noting that Cardinal Slipyj's action took place at a time when the Pio-Benedictine Code of Canon Law (1917) was still in force. Can. 2370 of the 1917 Code reads: "Episcopus aliquem consecrans in Episcopum, Episcopi vel, loco Episcoporum, presbyteri assistentes, et qui consecrationem recipit sine apostolico mandato contra praescriptum can. 953, ipso iure suspensi sunt, donec Sedes Apostolica eos dispensaverit" (A bishop who consecrates someone as a bishop; bishops who are present [when this happens], or assisting priests who take the place of bishops; and a person who receives consecration without apostolic mandate, contrary to what is prescribed in canon 953, are suspended by virtue of the law itself, until the Apostolic See dispenses them). The language of the Code makes it clear that such clergy are suspended not in virtue of an announcement of the penalty but simply on account of what they have done, namely, to consecrate without an apostolic mandate — something Paul VI never granted to Slipyj. A legal positivist would say that the suspension he incurred would have had to be expressly removed later on. Yet the fact that the suspension was never lifted is an eloquent testimony to the role of *epikeia* in interpreting and applying law. In short: a situation existed in which the canon simply did not take effect. This ought to give us pause about the limits of legal positivism.

A NEW LENS FOR VIEWING ÉCÔNE

When the Church is under attack and her survival is at stake, or when her common good is gravely threatened, flagrant "disobedience" to papal commands or laws can be justified — indeed, not only justified, but right, meritorious, the stuff of sanctity. No one has ever questioned that rules concerning episcopal consecrations are the pope's right to establish, and that Wojtyła and Slipyj unquestionably and knowingly violated ecclesiastical law, which should have merited them a place of opprobrium alongside Archbishop Lefebvre. Instead, we celebrate them as heroes of the resistance against Communism.

The reason we do so is that we recognize a more fundamental law than that of canonical dictates: *salus animarum suprema lex*. As I said in chapter 10, the entire structure of ecclesiastical law exists for the salvation of souls; it has no other purpose than to protect and advance the sharing of the life of Christ with mankind. In normal circumstances, ecclesiastical laws create a structure within which the Church's mission may unfold in an orderly and peaceful way. But there can be situations of anarchy or breakdown, corruption or apostasy, where the ordinary structures become impediments to, not facilitators of, the Church's mission. In these cases, conscience dictates that one should do what needs to be done, in prudence and charity, for the achievement of the sovereign law.

As the years pass and I watch the Catholic Church descend ever further into doctrinal, moral, and liturgical chaos, I can no longer accept the opinion that Archbishop Marcel Lefebvre was guilty of "wrongful disobedience."[9] He was caught in a terrible situation, with a hostile Vatican that seemed to care nothing for tradition (how 2021 brought us right back to that place!) and a worldwide diaspora of traditional Catholics looking to him for a semi-stable solution. The imposition of the Novus Ordo and the *aggiornamento* launched by the Council was a kind of "*Ostpolitik* with Modernity" against which Lefebvre was rightly protesting, and against which he was willing to take a decisive step when the Faith appeared to be threatened like never before.

The actions of Wojtyła and Slipyj place Écône in a new light. That is not to say all difficulties evaporate, for on anyone's accounting, friend or foe, it is not normal to have a society of priests operating in dioceses around the world without official jurisdiction, and one must pray for a happy resolution to an emergency situation precipitated by those who, derelict in their duty, allowed the smoke of Satan — and now, rather obviously, heaps of burning faggots — to pervade the Church of God. When a building is burning down,

---

9   I recommend the sympathetic but not uncritical treatment of Lefebvre found in Sire, *Phoenix from the Ashes*, 410-30. I still believe, as I first argued in an article at *OnePeterFive* published on April 3, 2019 ("Is It Ever Okay to Take Shelter in an SSPX Mass?"), that the SSPX chapels should be frequented if no other traditional parish or chapel in unblemished communion with the local ordinary is available within a reasonable radius. I say this as one who has no animus toward SSPX-goers, some of whom are friends of mine, and nothing less than the highest respect for the priests who continued to say Mass and administer the sacraments throughout the Covid-19 "pandemic" when the mainstream response was scandalously inadequate. I would also add that in my opinion Latin-rite Catholics should assist in their *own* rite, that is, the (traditional) Roman Rite, even if this means going to a Society chapel, in preference to seeking refuge in an Eastern-rite parish. If no TLM is available at all, and an Eastern rite is available, then it would make sense to choose it over the Novus Ordo. See chapters 20 and 21.

one tries to put out the fire and rescue victims with any means to hand, rather than waiting until the fire brigade arrives—especially if one knows from bitter experience that the fire chief is absent from his post, or sleeping, or intoxicated, or convinced that fires are beneficial, and that most of the firemen are bumbling idiots whose methods don't work, or, worse, are paid saboteurs who spray gasoline on the fire.

This much is clear: those who, conscious of an obligation in the sight of God and a duty to suffering believers, have responded to a preexisting crisis as best they can are by no means to be blamed, for they have taken up the bright weapons of obedience to the ultimate law that governs all others: *salus animarum suprema lex.* If anyone at this point, after more than a decade of Bergoglian-ity, really believes that Communism in Eastern Europe was more of a threat to the integrity, orthodoxy, and sanity of the Catholic Church than the liberalism, progressivism, and modernism that have infiltrated parishes, chanceries, and academies around the world, they deserve a headshake of pity and a prayer that the scales would drop from their eyes. Just because an evil is more subtle, more "winsome,"[10] does not mean it is less pervasive or less harm-ful. On the contrary, the parasite that silently and invisibly mul-tiplies within is far more dangerous than the hateful persecution that rages from without.

LESSONS FOR OURSELVES

If the Vatican, following on the heels of *Traditionis Custodes*, should dare to prohibit traditional priestly ordinations, it would be entirely justifiable for a bishop who understands what is at stake[11] to con-tinue to ordain priests traditionally but clandestinely, without any

---

10   The word Bishop Robert Barron used to describe the spiritual theology of Fr James Martin, SJ.

11   Arguably no part of the liturgy suffered graver damage than the rites of ordination, which pertain most intimately to the existence and well-being of the Church on earth. A classic on this subject is Michael Davies's *The Order of Melchisedech: A Defence of the Catholic Priesthood*, published by Roman Catholic Books but distributed by Sophia Institute Press. Davies shows the Protestantizing and modernizing distortion in the new rites of ordination and argues for the urgency of retaining and restoring the traditional ones. For a close comparison of the new and old rites of ordination with some striking conclusions, see Daniel Graham, *Lex Orandi: Comparing the Traditional and Novus Ordo Rites of the Seven Sacraments* (n.p.: Preview Press, 2015), 159–85.

permission requested or obtained. Even if the new rite of ordination is valid (as is the new rite of Mass), it is severely defective, unfitting and inauthentic in liturgical terms.[12] The authoritative witness, priority, and superiority of the *lex orandi* of the traditional rite must be maintained in the life of the Church until such time as the Tridentine *Pontificale Romanum* can be universally restored. The same is arguably true of episcopal consecration, as Antonio Francés argues in a convincing essay "May a Bishop in Extraordinary Circumstances Ordain Another Bishop Without Papal Consent?"[13] He cites an example reminiscent of the consecration of Lubomyr Husar, who, as mentioned, though illicitly consecrated, was later formally recognized as a bishop and eventually made a cardinal. Francés narrates:

> Pope John Paul II had himself erected the Apostolic Administration of St John-Mary Vianney at Campos in Brazil (2002), and it was Cardinal Castrillón Hoyos who furnished it with a bishop as its superior, by ordaining Bishop Fernando Rifan. That had in fact been the first step made in the direction of those who had been close to Archbishop Lefebvre and to the Society of St Pius X (SSPX). Indeed, the bishop at Cardinal Hoyos' side during Bishop Rifan's episcopal consecration, acting as co-consecrator, was Bishop Licinio Rangel, the successor of Bishop de Castro Mayer, the bishop who had participated as co-consecrator in Archbishop Lefebvre's consecrations of the SSPX bishops in 1988. Bishop Rangel had himself been consecrated bishop by three of those bishops: Bishop Tissier de Mallerais, assisted by Bishop de Galarreta and Bishop Williamson. The links, then, between this Apostolic Union of St John Mary Vianney and Archbishop Lefebvre's Fraternity were strong, and rooted in a common combat dating back many years.

Here, a series of "illicit" consecrations, done in order to protect a local church from modernism and to preserve living tradition, culminated in a regularization in which one of these "renegade" bishops, welcomed back into communion without having to forego

---

12   See my article "The Four Qualities of Liturgy: Validity, Licitness, Fittingness, and Authenticity," *New Liturgical Movement*, November 9, 2020.
13   *OnePeterFive*, October 23, 2023.

tradition, in turn co-consecrated his successor. In an emergency, heroic steps must sometimes be taken *praeter legem*, with trust in the overcoming of difficulties by the workings of Divine Providence.

At the same time, we see that Wojtyła and Slipyj acted clandestinely, which gives us a hint that actions like theirs do not need to be publicly announced and, as it were, made a spectacle of. They were responding to an immediate and desperate situation, as decisively *and* as inconspicuously as they knew how to do. In saying this, I am not implying the impossibility of a situation in which such actions could not rightly be done in broad daylight, but rather, pointing out that when material disobedience is required, *normally* the clandestine route is preferable to the public one.

This has obvious implications for our present situation. If a priest in good conscience chooses not to comply with unjust mandates or requirements emanating from ecclesiastical authority, he should not necessarily announce to the world that he will not be complying, but should simply carry on with his pastoral and priestly work. If and when he is penalized, he should not make a big fuss about it, but ignore it and continue his ministry. Again, the key word is *normally*: there may be times when open resistance is the best route, as in the possession of the church of St Nicolas du Chardonnet in Paris under the leadership of Msgr. Ducaud-Bourget and the repossession of the boarded-up church of Saint Louis du Port Marly.[14]

Unquestionably, the temptation to have instant recourse to social media, with the pros and cons of the popular support it generates, makes good discernment about the most prudent course of action (which might turn out to be "acting under the radar") more difficult than ever.

CONCLUSION

One of the many ways in which Archbishop Lefebvre is being vindicated is this: he saw that he had to keep ordaining priests (and, for that matter, bishops) in the traditional rite. The *usus antiquior* is all

---

14   To read more about the heroism of this postconciliar generation, see "Resistance is never futile: An interview with Christian Marquant, founder of Paix Liturgique," *Rorate Caeli*, December 16, 2020. On St Nicolas du Chardonnet, see Theresa Marie Moreau, "Recaptured Paris Church Preserves True Mass," www.theresamariemoreau.com/blog/archives/09-2017; on Port Marly, see chapter 24.

of a piece – an inherited, unitary, coherent *lex orandi* embodying the *lex credendi* of the Catholic Faith. Yes, there are priests who were validly ordained in the new rite (as was archtraditionalist Fr Gregory Hesse) who later came to join the FSSP, SSPX, etc., and the same thing happens today, as a steady trickle of Novus Ordo clergy move to the TLM institutes. But it is more important than most people realize to keep the old rites of ordination, at all levels, intact and alive.

If the Dicastery for Divine Worship and the Discipline of the Sacraments or the Dicastery for Institutes of Consecrated Life and Societies of Apostolic Life were to demand that the old rites of ordination be no longer used, that, too, would have to be for us a *"non possumus"* moment: this we simply cannot accept. But even more, it would be a time for the greatest challenge of all in the years ahead: will there be cardinals, archbishops, bishops, who, under such circumstances, are willing to confer Holy Orders clandestinely in the traditional rites? Our Lord who, in His Providence, bestowed upon us the glorious patrimony of the Church of Rome will surely arrange for its preservation in the hour of need.

14

Why a Bishop Should Ignore His Unjust Deposition by a Pope[1]

SERVIDEUS: PAULINUS, POPE FRANCIS HAS "relieved" Bishop Joseph Strickland of his office (what a euphemism!), even as he went after Bishop Daniel Fernández Torres in Puerto Rico, whom he removed from office at the age of only fifty-seven. That bishop allowed for conscientious objection

---

1   The following dialogue is based on a real interview that took place between John-Henry Westen and me, the video of which can be seen at *LifeSiteNews*. The transcript has been edited for brevity, clarity, and literary effect – changing names of the speakers, dividing up the speeches, adding interjections, etc. In his article "Why a Good Bishop Should Not Ignore but Obey His Unjust Deposition by a Pope" (*OnePeterFive*, October 17, 2023), José Antonio Ureta attempts to refute my position as articulated in this chapter and the next. While I understand the classic arguments he presents, I am not convinced he is in the right. First, throughout much of Church history, bishops were chosen in different ways than by direct papal appointment and functioned without his express grant of jurisdiction. Second, if the crisis of our times is of a qualitatively unique character, it is not clear to me that the right way forward is simply to emulate the past and to fall back on the thinking of the past. That is a paradox of traditionalism in general: there are many things we say and do that have no precedent. For example, we resist a liturgical rite published by two popes and intended for the whole Church, even if it was never technically *mandated*. Surely, the same people who defend papal primacy in jurisdiction would defend papal primacy in liturgical law; yet traditionalists (including Ureta) assert the rights of immemorial and venerable custom and the rights of the faithful against papal legislation. So we are obviously willing to push back against the pope when he does something egregiously harmful to the good of the Church. It seems to me, similarly, that allowing a heretic like Francis to remove orthodox bishops is exactly such a case, where the harm of submissive acceptance massively outweighs the harm of direct resistance. Third, could it not be the case that the hypertrophic expansion of the papacy, the absolutization of its monarchy to the denigration and destruction of other poles of authority in the Church (liturgy, episcopacy, tradition in general), is precisely what needs to be challenged and stymied in order for health to return to the body? In short: the Ultramontanes, like Ureta, assume that the one and only solution to every ecclesiastical difficulty is the absolute power of the pope (that is, as long as a saintly orthodox pope is someday elected, who can right all wrongs); yet it is exactly this Maistrean assumption that the anti-Ultramontanes call into question. Today's ultramontanists are looking for a conventional solution along

to the Covid vaccines, and he was summarily dismissed from his diocese by the pope. The same thing happened with the less-well-known case of the bishop of San Luis in Argentina, Pedro Daniel Martínez Perea, who was removed by the Vatican at the age of 64, not long after he prohibited altar girls in the diocese.[2] Similarly, the seminary of San Rafael was shut down after its bishop refused to allow Communion only in the hand.[3] What do we do in situations like this? Is a bishop just supposed to pack up his bags and leave? Should such a seminary be shut down? I remember Bishop Schneider talking about what bishops and priests should do in light of the severe restrictions on the Latin Mass: he said it's wrong to follow these directions, and it's right to disobey them because they're unjust.

Paulinus: The most important principle to begin with—it's a principle of natural law, something that belongs to the structure of reality as God created it—is that all authority exists for a certain purpose. It doesn't exist as a free-floating, arbitrary imposition that can coerce people to do whatever it wants them to do. No; authority's purpose is to promote and foster the common good of the society over which a wielder of authority is placed. That common good is also something *definite*. For example, in a country it might be the peace of the country, good laws, good morality. These are the things that the ruler is supposed to see to. And if the ruler acts against the good of the people in an extreme way, they can either refuse to consent to what he's doing or even rise up against him. Now, in the Catholic Church, we don't rise up against popes and bishops—we don't take out pitchforks and run after them. Although in the Middle Ages some people might have done that...

Servideus: They probably did!

Paulinus: But it's still true that, as with any authority, the pope is placed by Christ in the Church to serve a given function, which is to promote the common good of the Church. He does that by preaching the true faith, teaching the deposit of faith revealed by Christ

---

nineteenth- and early twentieth-century lines. We are looking for a recalibration of the network of authorities and obediences.

2   See "El obispo de San Luis prohibió la presencia de mujeres en los altares," *Clarín*, November 1, 2019, www.clarin.com/sociedad/obispo-san-luis-prohibio-presencia-mujeres-altares_0_OSD-mgCY.html.

3   See Andrea Zambrano, "Seminario cerrado y sombras sobre Roma: 'El obispo se ha equivocado,'" *Brújula Cotidiana*, August 3, 2020, https://brujulacotidiana.com/es/seminario-cerrado-y-sombras-sobre-roma-el-obispo-se-ha-equivocado.

through the Apostles; by fostering good morals and good discipline; by appointing worthy bishops or at least bishops that he thinks are worthy. He might be mistaken, everyone can be mistaken at times. But what a pope wouldn't have the authority to do, even though he has supreme authority in the Church, is thwart Catholic doctrine, undermine Catholic morality, or appoint men as bishops wickedly, as occurred with nepotism or simony — when popes in the Renaissance were appointing their fourteen-year-old nephews as cardinals and so forth. When they do this kind of thing, they are acting *ultra vires*, outside their powers, outside their authority, contrary to the nature of what their authority was given for.

Servideus: That raises the really interesting ecclesiological question: Is it possible for a pope to act *so* contrary to the common good and to justice in a given situation that his act is invalid, that it has no force — it's not merely an imperfect law or command, but not a command *at all*, not a law *at all*? Is that possible?

Paulinus: The answer of the tradition of the Church is yes, that *is* possible. St Thomas says an unjust law is no law at all, it doesn't have the rationale of a law. I would argue that if a pope removed a bishop arbitrarily, that is, for no good cause, without a due canonical process, with no reason given and no reason discoverable — and especially if there was evidence that the reason that bishop was removed is because he was conservative or traditional, teaching the faith, upholding good discipline and morals — then that act would be null and void, an act that should be ignored. The bishop in question should assume that he is still the bishop of that place, because he *is*. The pope can remove somebody only for just cause, he can't arbitrarily remove people. The papacy is not a tyranny, it's a monarchy. And we have to remember that.

Servideus: Bishop Strickland was a hero for American Catholics, for Catholics around the world. Even though there are a good number of bishops who are faithful and who every once in a while will make their voices heard, no one was doing that like Bishop Strickland. He ruffled feathers. His conscience urged him to proclaim the Faith, including its hard teachings that run against the modern secular consensus (shared by all too many of his fellow bishops), and a lot of the faithful rallied around him. So, let's say it's for that reason — for his being outspoken, for his going to Los Angeles to do the procession of reparation, his bold pro-life and pro-family stance, his taking to task Father James Martin for his homoheresy — it's for that reason that Bishop Strickland was targeted.

Paulinus: Exactly so. I want to address a point you've raised, because I think it's important. Is it legitimate for Bishop Strickland or for Bishop Schneider, an auxiliary bishop in Kazakhstan, to speak about issues all over the world, to address issues outside of their dioceses, to be teaching the Catholic faith to a very large audience, you might say a global audience? There are some people out there who want to say, no, every bishop should restrict himself to his own diocese and only concern himself with local affairs. You know I'm not the biggest fan of Vatican II who's ever lived, but that objection is completely contrary to what Vatican II says in *Lumen Gentium* section 20:

> Just as the office granted individually to Peter, the first among the apostles, is permanent and is to be transmitted to his successors, so also the apostles' office of *nurturing the Church* is permanent, and is to be exercised without interruption by the sacred order of bishops.

Then it goes on to say in section 23:

> The individual bishops, who are placed in charge of particular churches, exercise their pastoral government over the portion of the People of God committed to their care, and not over other churches nor over the universal Church. But *each of them, as a member of the episcopal college and legitimate successor of the apostles, is obliged by Christ's institution and command to be solicitous for the whole Church*, and this solicitude, though it is not exercised by an act of jurisdiction, contributes greatly to the advantage of the universal Church. For it is the *duty of all bishops* to promote and to safeguard the unity of faith and the discipline *common to the whole Church*, to instruct the faithful to love for the whole mystical body of Christ, especially for its poor and sorrowing members and for those who are suffering persecution for justice's sake, and finally to *promote every activity that is of interest to the whole Church*, especially that the faith may take increase and the light of full truth appear to *all men*. (emphases added)

I mean, it's as if the council fathers are trying to double-underline this point: even though the bishop's proper territory over which he has immediate jurisdiction is his own diocese, he's still concerned with and should be promoting actively the good discipline and the faith of the entire Church in whatever ways are suitable for him.

Servideus: A good example of that would be the way Bishop Fulton Sheen preached over the radio and television to millions of people. Although I'm sure he ruffled some modernist feathers back then, most people were happy to have Bishop Sheen on prime-time television preaching the gospel.

Paulinus: Well, this is what Bishop Schneider is doing, this is what Bishop Strickland was doing on Twitter, YouTube, and other such media pulpits. Such bishops look outrageous, not because of what they're saying, but because of how *few* are saying the things that they're saying. If you rewound the clock by fifty or a hundred years, what they're saying would be perfectly obvious: "Of course — that's what the *Baltimore Catechism* says." So we're not talking about outlandish opinions, as if these bishops are saying things from outer space. They're saying what's in the traditional catechisms.

Servideus: To get back to my main question, what if one day a bishop's just told: "That's enough. You're gone. As with Bishop Fernández Torres and Bishop Strickland, we're going to replace you with someone else. Pack your bags." If we assume that this is an unjust act, what do you think should happen next?

Paulinus: Unquestionably it would be an unjust act. I find it noteworthy that Bishop Daniel Fernández Torres published a statement saying: "I have done nothing wrong. They've never told me I've done anything wrong. And in fact, they offered me another position if I would resign my diocese." That shows that he hadn't done anything wrong, because if you're guilty of some wrongdoing, they're not going to say, okay, here's another plum position over here that we'll give you. Basically they were trying to bribe him to leave his diocese because the other bishops didn't like him. And it wasn't just about vaccinations. It was about him not wanting to send his seminarians to an iffy interdiocesan seminary. He didn't want to suppress the traditional Latin Mass. None of these things could be called *faults,* let alone delicts or any kind of serious cause for as grave a step as removal. Similarly, Bishop Strickland admitted that it was, in part, his refusal to implement the unjust demands of *Traditionis Custodes* that got him sacked. He said that he could not, in good conscience, "starve part of his flock." His rationale here is perfectly sound, based on divine and natural law.

Servideus: How, then, should a bishop respond in that situation?

Paulinus: He could say: "With all due respect, Holy Father, I pray for you, I want to be in communion with you. But although it was a pope who appointed me bishop, when I was consecrated a bishop it was *Jesus Christ Himself* who established me as a bishop. And that's also the teaching of the Church. It's not the pope who makes a bishop a successor of the apostles; it is Jesus Christ. Once someone is a bishop, he's a bishop forever, just like a priest is a priest forever. Since there are no suitable grounds for removing me, I remain the bishop of this diocese, and intend to continue my work here, for the benefit of my presbyterate and my people."

Servideus: But the pope is the one who named him the bishop of that place...

Paulinus: Yes, but since the pope is not the source of his episcopacy, the pope doesn't have complete arbitrary authority over a bishop's continuing to serve his flock, once he has been placed there. His power to rule and care for the flock comes from Christ, not from the pope. The pope says, "you go to this diocese, I'm appointing you to this diocese"; but it's Christ who gives him the rights and duties of the episcopate. This is very important to grasp.

Servideus: Of course, these two spheres sort of collide, or better, overlap, don't they?

Paulinus: The pope has immediate and supreme universal jurisdiction in the Church, which means, in practice, he can do whatever is within his ambit of authority to do, and nobody can stop him and nobody's over him. But again, *within the ambit of his authority*, within the sphere of it.

Servideus: So, if a bishop dug in his heels, what would happen next?

Paulinus: Maybe the pope would excommunicate him and assign another bishop to the place. Then there would be, so to speak, two bishops in this area. But there would be only one true bishop, because there's *already* a bishop there – he's going to be there as long as he lives unless he's removed for just cause, retires, or dies. That means the new bishop will be a usurper or an imposter.

Servideus: What a mess!

Paulinus: Absolutely. Has Church history seen these kinds of messes before? Yes. If you read about the history of the Church of Constantinople, for example, patriarchs were deposed and reinstated, they went back and forth and there were conflicting patriarchs. We don't *desire* that situation. But we should be willing to tolerate such a messy situation rather than compromise on this point—namely, that the bishops are not the "vicars of the pope." Recall the strong words of *Lumen Gentium*, section 27:

> The pastoral office or the habitual and daily care of their sheep is entrusted to them [the bishops] completely; *nor are they to be regarded as vicars of the Roman Pontiffs*, for they exercise an authority that is proper to them, and are quite correctly called "prelates," heads of the people whom they govern. Their power, therefore, is not destroyed by the supreme and universal power, but on the contrary it is affirmed, strengthened, and vindicated by it, since the Holy Spirit unfailingly preserves the form of government established by Christ the Lord in His Church.

Could the Council have emphasized any more clearly that the power of the pope is for edification, not for destruction; that the Holy Spirit wants to preserve the dignity of the episcopacy rather than allowing it to be effectively absorbed into a singular autocracy; that the bishops are not delegates of the pope, as if they were all nuncios, but are proper authorities in their own right and, as the medievals saw it, wedded to their local church? Arbitrary removal would be an ecclesiastical "no-fault divorce," which is incoherent.

Servideus: Many nowadays *do* think of bishops as vicars of the pope. We have to recover the truth that their authority to govern comes from *Christ*. It helps to remember this when you have a dictator pope.

Paulinus: I think what happens is that, as long as a pope is exercising his monarchy in a reasonable way—a way that doesn't give cause for scandal or for alarm—most people are content to assume that he is completely in charge of everything. And if he doesn't do anything to make you *question* your understanding, maybe you will never find out that you have a false understanding. But Pope Francis is so extreme in his actions and in his teachings – his opinions on marriage and family, LGBTQ, the death penalty, sacraments, liturgy, I mean, there are so many alarm bells ringing, you're in danger of ear damage – that he makes us start to look at these issues more closely until we realize, oh, wait a minute, the papacy actually *has* limits.

Servideus: It's obvious once you *say* it, because it's a created authority and the only authority that is absolute is God's.

Paulinus: And, needless to say, any created authority can be resisted if he abuses his authority. This is something you can find in the whole canonical and theological tradition. Torquemada says this, Aquinas says it, Bellarmine, Suárez... They all say that when an authority abuses his office, he can be fraternally corrected and even resisted and disobeyed. These views were part of our tradition, but they tended to be forgotten in the wake of Vatican I and the ultramontanist spirit that swept through the Church.

Servideus: Tell me what you mean by "ultramontanist" here?

Paulinus: After the French Revolution, the Church was on the run in Europe – anticlericalism, Freemasonry, rising socialism, eventually communism... All of these ideologies were forcibly acting against the Church, trying to suppress it, trying to destroy Catholic schools, trying to obliterate the clergy. And in the face of that kind of pressure against Catholicism, Catholics had a very natural instinct to rally around the pope. The pope is our head, our father. He's our universal leader. He's our general, in a sense – the general of the Catholic armies. And we have to rally around him. A strong pope can lead us in this modern battle against all of these ideologies. That's legitimate. People needed the pope to be that way for them.

But the problem is, this attitude, born of peculiar historical circumstances and magnified by modern media, can morph into a cult of personality, with the pope as "the Great Leader": the faith *is* the pope; the faith is all about the pope. It's not. That's a caricature that Protestants play upon quite a bit, because they would *love* to be able to say, "oh, you Catholics don't follow Scripture, you just follow whatever the pope says." We know that that's false, but the ultramontanism that's looking over the mountains to the pope for everything all the time *suggests* this error – suggests that our faith is wrapped up in the person of the present pope and in what he's teaching right now, as opposed to being something that's been handed down by all of the popes and all of the bishops from the beginning until now.

Servideus: How does the issue of ultramontanism relate to the reduction of bishops to "vicars of the pope"?

Paulinus: As we saw earlier, *Lumen Gentium* 27 tells us that the church is not like a multinational corporation in which the bishops are branch managers and the pope is the CEO. In a corporation, the CEO could just ring up Daniel Fernández Torres or Joseph Strickland and say, "You know what, Daniel (or Joseph), it's been good having you on the team, but you're fired. Incompatible visions." And the CEO of Vatican, Inc. puts another manager in there. No, it's not like that. The managers, the *prelates* of this Mystical Body, this Mystical Corporation (so to speak), are put in place by *Christ* and are permanently in place unless they actually do something to forfeit being in their place. They're like the professors who have tenure, whom you can't get rid of unless they burn down a building or murder a colleague.

Servideus: Well said!

Paulinus: I'll tell you a story that shows how seriously the episcopal dignity used to be taken. It has to do with Pius XII.

There was almost nobody who was more fiercely anti-Nazi than Pius XII, Eugenio Pacelli. Although he was engaged in diplomacy with the Third Reich, he quickly realized he was dealing with a liar and a psychopath. And that's why he drafted the text of one of the most passionate encyclicals ever, *Mit Brennender Sorge*, published by the pope at the time, Pius XI. So if you know your history, you can't justly accuse Pius XII of being sympathetic to Hitler or the Nazis, although some people have maliciously said that. Anyway, after World War II, a bunch of people in the French government – people who had been fighting for the Free French and had been against the Vichy regime – asked the pope to remove not only the papal nuncio, who had been sympathetic to Vichy, but also dozens of French bishops who had been in cahoots with the Vichy regime. They wanted the pope to remove *all* of them from office.

Well, how did the pope reply? Did he say, "Oh, I understand, it's just terrible. I'll remove them all." No! He sent word of his displeasure with the attitude of the French government, which he regarded as offensive, discourteous, and injurious. He agreed to change the nuncio, but not without misgivings. And as for purging the episcopacy, he declared that there can be *no question* of changing the bishops. That has never been done. That will not be done. That would be an injustice without precedent. Inadmissible. What his reaction shows is that for him, it was unthinkable to remove bishops, *even if* they had been in cahoots with the Nazis.

But we have Daniel Fernández Torres removed for not going along with highly debatable Covid protocols, choosing to send his seminarians elsewhere than an interdiocesan seminary, and allowing the venerable Latin Mass to continue. We have Joseph Strickland "relieved from pastoral governance" because he "did his duty in preaching and defending with *parrhesia* the immutable Catholic faith and morals and in promoting the sacredness of the liturgy, especially in the immemorial traditional rite of the Mass," as Bishop Schneider said.[4] Pius XII would be sickened.

Servideus: So far, we've been discussing a situation where a good bishop is removed unjustly from his flock. But it's even worse if the reason the pope removes a good bishop is to install a bad bishop, that is, a wolf, who will prey on the flock. Can a good shepherd abandon his sheep to the wolves? Could the sitting bishop, knowing or suspecting his replacement will be someone in the mold of Cardinal Cupich or Cardinal McElroy – could he leave his flock without sinning? Or must he remain at his post, no matter what?

Paulinus: I don't think that's a difficult question. It *seems* to us to be a difficult question because our hyperpapalist instincts or habits of thought make us never want to think about somebody disagreeing with the pope in such a major way, on such a major issue as the episcopacy. We also tend to downplay or underestimate the obligation that a bishop has to his own flock, *because* we have gotten used to thinking of them as branch managers who can be moved around. Eric Sammons has frequently made this point (but so have many others): ever since it's become customary to move bishops

---

4 "Bishop Strickland's Removal is a 'Blatant Injustice,' says Bishop Schneider," *LifeSiteNews*, November 11, 2023.

around, to advance them from a (so to speak) "lesser" diocese to a "greater" diocese, we've had a terrible plague of ambition, of career climbing. It's like going up the corporate ladder, from lower management to higher management, with increasing perks and power. That mentality has crept into everybody's minds to such an extent that we don't think of a bishop anymore as a *father*. The medievals talked about the bishop as the *bridegroom* of the local church, just as Christ is the Bridegroom of the whole Church. What does it say when a bishop is then "promoted" to another local church? This is like ecclesiological polygamy, or divorce and remarriage.

Servideus: But it's not *impossible* to move a bishop...

Paulinus: I'm not saying that it's impossible; only that it's weird and unhealthy, seen against the backdrop of church history, where, for very sound reasons, theoretical and practical, that was never the custom. The bishop is the husband of the local church, and therefore the father of his faithful. They're his spiritual children, right? And isn't it beautiful to think about how, in pre-modern times, the image of a father was something that people thought of with the warmth of affection. Now, everybody attacks patriarchy and fatherhood is dismissed or seen as an arbitrary social construct. But in reality, the fatherhood of God is the source of all authority: "For this cause I bow my knees to the Father of our Lord Jesus Christ, of whom all paternity in heaven and earth is named" (Eph 3:14-15). The *highest* title of a bishop, in a way, would be "father of his spiritual children" and then "shepherd of his flock," to use another metaphor. So, it's not difficult *in itself* to say that a bishop should be prepared to die rather than abandon his children and his flock, especially if he believed they were in danger of having sacraments, or the traditional liturgy they know and love, or sound doctrine and moral guidance, removed from them.

Servideus: For me, that says all the hassle, all the awkwardness, is worth it. Like the possible removal of buildings: a canceled bishop is going to have his residence and his chancery taken over by the usurpers. He will have to get a new place and have a new office.

Paulinus: That's right.

Servideus: It seems to me that your position rests on recognizing a crisis in the Church. Would you say that's true? I mean, if things were peaceful and stable, none of this would be happening.

Paulinus: Correct. We are living in times when a different gospel, a false gospel, is being preached. As St Paul sternly taught us: "But though we, or an angel from heaven, preach a gospel to you besides that which we have preached to you, let him be anathema" (Gal 1:8), that is, accursed, condemned.

Servideus: But Pope Francis and his supporters tell us that there isn't a new gospel, just a better, more developed understanding of the gospel, and so the bishops need to get behind this "fuller" gospel and not be stuck in the past. It's serious enough that apparently some bishops ought to be removed if they are not "on board" with the program!

Paulinus: That's their approach.

Servideus: What's wrong with it?

Paulinus: We can let one of the Fathers of the Church answer that question. Saint Vincent of Lérins was the first to articulate the truth that the deposit of faith can never essentially change. Even if the way that we grasp it and formulate it develops over time, the essence of the faith, the substance of it, never changes. This Church Father is often misquoted by Pope Francis as if he's some kind of an evolutionist, so that, doctrinally speaking, you can start with a microbe and end with a mammoth. But that's not what Vincent teaches; he says there is growth (*profectus*), not a radical change (*mutatio*).

The verse I mentioned from St Paul's Epistles to the Galatians is quoted again and again by Vincent, to drive home that the deposit of faith given by Christ our Lord to the Apostles is so rock-solid, so definite and definitive, that neither the Apostles nor even the angels who are above the Apostles – the angels in heaven, who see God face to face! – not even *they* have the authority to change it. Paul's assertion is a counterfactual: *even if* an angel from heaven were to come down (not that any of them would) and preach something other than the gospel you received, you shouldn't, you mustn't follow that angel. Follow the original, hold fast to the faith once delivered to the saints.

What I find most pertinent to our situation is that Paul emphasizes: if *we* – that is, the *Apostles*: himself, Peter, Andrew, James, John – if *we* should preach a gospel other than the one we originally preached, let us be accursed, and whatever you do, don't follow us. There's no verse in Scripture that more beautifully highlights the fact that the pope and the bishops are subordinate to the truth handed down, not superior to it. They're not in control of it, they can't mold it however they wish to fit it to a humanist, modernist, globalist, or whatever agenda. They have no authority to do that. Let them be accursed who try to do it.

Servideus: Unfortunately, it does seem that that's where we're at. So many teachings of this pope and his supporters contradict Scripture, Tradition, and the preceding Magisterium. This can't be from the Apostles; it's surely not from God.

Paulinus: Right. One of the themes I insist on over and over in my writing is that God gave us two powerful and precious gifts — John Paul II called them two wings with which we rise up to the contemplation of truth: reason and faith. We can see with our reason that certain acts are contrary to the natural law. Even pagan philosophers like Plato and Aristotle saw that homosexuality was contrary to human nature. Aristotle unquestionably rejects it, classifying sodomy as a form of bestiality or subhuman vice.[5] And these men lived without any benefit of divine revelation! We have the gift of reason, we have the gift of faith. The gift of faith gives us access to the teaching of Christ and the teaching of the Church for all the ages. There's no question whatsoever about the uninterrupted, constant, universal ordinary magisterium on issues of sexual morality.

Modernity is characterized, in general, by irrationality, irrationalism, the exaltation of the ego, the exaltation of the will or voluntarism: *I want what I want.* Reality is what I want to make it. That kind of thinking has been around in the writings of philosophers for centuries now, long enough to have trickled down and permeated a vast number of minds. Reason, you might say, is having a terribly hard time right now. And as for faith, how many people really take pains to learn their faith? When you read the good old catechisms — hundreds of catechisms going back hundreds of years — they all taught the same thing about matters of importance. When we study them side by side, we can see very clearly what the

---

5   See *Nichomachean Ethics*, Bk. 7, ch. 5, where, after calling sodomy brutish, a "diseased state or habit," Aristotle notes that homosexual tendencies form in people who have been sexually abused since childhood.

Church teaches. We can see how Pope Francis is departing from the Faith; how somebody like Victor Manuel Fernández, Prefect of the Dicastery for the Doctrine of the Faith, departs from it.

Servideus: His being put in charge is like Pope Francis rubbing salt into the wounds that all of us have suffered for the past decade.

Paulinus: Absolutely. That appointment in and of itself—if that isn't a supreme wake-up call for all of the conservatives or all of the moderates who are still sitting on the fence, I'm afraid they're just going to die on the fence. They must be glued to it, because if you can't see that this man is totally unsuitable for the office he has, with his questionable morality, his record on clerical abuse, and his ideas that are contrary to Faith, can you see anything at all?

Servideus: So we are in a state of crisis. In a crisis or an emergency, certain steps are more defensible or more necessary than they would be in times of peace. This is an accepted moral principle.

Paulinus: There are things we can do when a house is burning down—like break down a door, enter in uninvited, shoot water all over the place, remove people without consent—that we can't do when a house is not burning down.

Servideus: So, granting all the chaos that would ensue from a bishop not stepping down when told to do so, it is still better that he remain than for him to further enable the abuse of papal authority, lend support to the heretical faction in charge, and abandon the flock to the wolves.

Paulinus: Exactly.

Servideus: I'm curious: would you say this scenario could play out at the parish level as well? Let's say you have a dictatorial bishop who removes a priest in charge of a parish for doing good things, and that priest has reason to believe his successor at the parish will be a wolf. Could the priest refuse to leave his position?

Paulinus: To give a detailed answer we would have to make some canonical distinctions between a pastor and a parish administrator, but we can answer the question generally. It seems to me that it's much more grave when you're talking about the pope unjustly removing a bishop than when you're talking about a bishop moving a priest around. Because the priests are not equipped by Christ with a "pastorship" when they are ordained. They are simply given assignments by the bishop. Essentially, the way to think about the presbytery of a diocese is that all of the priests are an extension of the bishop because he can't be everywhere at the same time. That's certainly the way it developed in the ancient church. Early on, when the flock was small, it was the bishops who celebrated Mass and the other sacraments. As the Church grew and grew during the early centuries, and especially after the fourth century when Christianity was legalized and it took off like wildfire, the bishops became overwhelmed. They couldn't possibly be everywhere they needed to be.

Servideus: If the priests are like an extension of the bishop, he can move them around as he pleases.

Paulinus: Yes. That doesn't mean, however, that he should move them with no consideration for their aptitudes, personalities, and gifts, as if they were unfeeling chess pieces, nor is it to say they shouldn't push back respectfully if they believe a big mistake has been made or seek canonical recourse if they are *unjustly* attacked, removed, or disciplined. There's a lot of that kind of injustice going on, and it *is* injustice that should be identified publicly so that bishops can at least be shamed into acting better, or undoing some of the damage they've done.

Servideus: That's why something like the Coalition for Canceled Priests exists.

Paulinus: Quite so. Still, you couldn't ever say "I'm a pastor by Christ's divine institution." You can't say that. You are a pastor solely because your bishop made you one. The bishops, on the other hand, are not, as it were, an extension of the pope simply because the pope can't be everywhere in the world at once. For that to be true, Christ would have to have appointed only *one* apostle, Peter, who, after being bishop for a while, said, "I'm way too busy. I can't go to every city in Asia Minor, so I'm going to appoint other people who represent me." That would be the "vicars of the pope" or "nuncios" model of the episcopacy that we just rejected and that *Lumen Gentium* rejected. From the beginning, Christ said: I want there to be *many bishops*. That is by divine institution.

Servideus: It's amazing to think that there is a way forward. It might be messy, but there's a way forward amidst all the confusion. We just need to find those bishops who are willing to stand up. We really need to pray hard for God to raise them up.

Paulinus: Let me add one final point. In church history, the fourth century is extremely valuable to study. What a lot of people don't realize about the Arian crisis is that it spread so widely that in some dioceses there were two men claiming to be bishop: an Arian one and a Catholic one. Sometimes there was a Catholic bishop and an attempt was made to bump him out by appointing an Arian bishop; or a Catholic bishop died and an Arian bishop replaced him. Meanwhile, a Catholic bishop like St Athanasius might pass through to minister to the orthodox (i.e., Catholic) faithful. There were wildly different scenarios in different places. The point is, it was extraordinarily messy. But St Athanasius didn't ever say "It's just too messy. Let's not do this. We'd better wait for better times." No, he just *dealt with the mess*, threw himself into it, because he could never abandon the Catholic flock. Even if it's a flock outside your proper diocese, you don't abandon the sheep of Christ. He didn't say, "Well, you know, the pope is letting it happen this way, so who are we to judge? The pope excommunicated me, so I'll stop saying divine liturgy and stop acting like a bishop." No! Even when he was excommunicated, he continued to act like a bishop and he continued to do the liturgy. God gave us St Athanasius for a reason: He wants him to be a permanent example for other crisis periods in church history.

Servideus: The faithful laity will play a big role, too. You have to support your true bishop at a time when a lot of people will be saying: "He's not the bishop. He's been kicked out. Stop already. You're being so divisive. You're schismatics!"

Paulinus: Exactly. Don't give in to their simplistic views. Reject what you know is wrong, and stick to what you know is right. As Newman said, the laity were the great supporters of the minority of orthodox bishops during the Arian crisis. We are seeing the same scenario in our times.

Servideus: Time to fast and pray.

Paulinus: Amen to that.[6]

---

6   For further reading on the Strickland case and its ecclesiological implications, see Fr Gerald Murray, "Strickland's removal was against canon law," *Daily Compass*, November 22, 2023; Antonio Francés, "Pope Francis does not have the right to dismiss Bishop Strickland without cause," *LifeSiteNews*, November 23, 2023; idem, "The Pope Cannot Depose Bishops Without Grave Cause," *OnePeterFive*, November 28, 2023.

15

Do Not Go Gentle into That Good Retirement

ON NOVEMBER 11, 2023, THE FEAST OF THE great bishop St Martin of Tours, the Vatican announced: "The Holy Father has relieved from the pastoral governance of the Diocese of Tyler H.E. Msgr. Joseph E. Strickland and appointed the Bishop of Austin, H.E. Msgr. Joe Vásquez as the Apostolic Administrator of the vacated diocese."

In last chapter's dialogue, "Paulinus" explained why a bishop should not only refuse to retire under pressure if he is guilty of no wrongdoing, but also refuse to acknowledge his deposition if Rome proceeds to that dire step. As we saw, the Second Vatican Council teaches that "the apostles' office of nurturing the Church is permanent and is to be exercised without interruption by the sacred order of bishops. Therefore, the Sacred Council teaches that bishops by divine institution have succeeded to the place of the apostles."[1] Moreover,

> The pastoral office or the habitual and daily care of their sheep is entrusted to them completely; nor are they to be regarded as vicars of the Roman Pontiffs, for they exercise an authority that is proper to them, and are quite correctly called "prelates," heads of the people whom they govern. Their power, therefore, is not destroyed by the supreme and universal power, but on the contrary it is affirmed, strengthened, and vindicated by it, since the Holy Spirit unfailingly preserves the form of government established by Christ the Lord in His Church.[2]

Finally, the Council affirms that a bishop, although governing only the portion of the flock of Christ entrusted to him, nevertheless has a responsibility to and for the whole Catholic Church.

---

1 Second Vatican Council, Dogmatic Constitution on the Church *Lumen Gentium*, no. 20.
2 *Lumen Gentium*, no. 27.

In short: a bishop is a bishop because Jesus Christ has made him a high priest of the Church and a successor of the apostles. He is not a "vicar of the pope," that is, one who stands in for the pope like a branch manager beholden to Vatican, Inc., but a vicar of Christ in his own diocese, receiving his episcopacy from God at the pope's delegation.[3] In the absence of a just cause for the grave step of deposition – historically used for cases of heresy or other notorious crimes – the bishop remains bishop of his see by divine authority. Nor can he be faulted for addressing and assisting the faithful who dwell beyond the borders of his own diocese even if he has no immediate pastoral care over them, for in bearing witness to Christ and the sacred deposit of faith, he is simply doing his job, according to his discernment of what the times demand.

The reader may well ask: "Is there any *precedent* for resisting a deposition?"

Let me tell you the story of Isidore Borecky (1911–2003). Born in Ukraine, he studied for the priesthood in Lviv and in Munich between the wars, and was ordained on July 17, 1938. He then worked in Canada for ten years until Pope Pius XII appointed him apostolic exarch of the Apostolic Exarchate of Eastern Canada. Ten years later, he was appointed eparchial bishop of the newly-created Ukrainian Catholic Eparchy of Toronto, an office he held until his retirement on June 16, 1998. He was a father at the Second Vatican Council, and, as the founding bishop of his eparchy, much beloved.[4]

So far, so good. But you see, he was *supposed* to stop being bishop when he reached the "mandatory retirement age" of 75. At least, that's what Rome thought. Bishop Borecky, however, refused to retire, saying that this rule applied to the Latin church and not to the Eastern churches, that he was exempt from it, and that he would

---

3   See Kwasniewski, *Hyperpapalism to Catholicism*, 2:266–71; cf. chapter 4 above.
4   It must be admitted, in the interests of fairness, that Bishop Borecky had his critics: those who said he was clinging to power as if the eparchy was his personal fiefdom, or that he was fixated on bringing married clergy into the eparchy and pushing a sort of "Ukrainian nationalist" agenda. My point here is not to argue that Borecky was entirely right in what he did, but simply to point out *what he did*, and that it may be time for such action on the part of faithful bishops vis-à-vis a faithless Rome. In general, it seems to me that if a significant number of laity, priests, and bishops in any given territory pushed hard against the wayward governance of their superiors, the superiors in turn would be compelled (or at least given adequate reasons) to back down and negotiate instead of assuming they can lord it over their subordinates.

remain in his office until he died. "We have, as the Ukrainian Catholic Church, to fight for our rights," the bishop told a reporter.[5] The Vatican eventually appointed a successor, Roman Danylak (1930–2012), but Borecky refused to acknowledge him as the new bishop.

The above-cited news article continued:

> The dispute has immobilized and divided the eparchy, which has about 100,000 members as well as 125 priests, most of whom are married. Some laypeople and priests, along with Borecky, stayed away from Danylak's consecration as bishop. . . . For his part, Danylak did not attend the celebration of Borecky's 45th anniversary as bishop in June. . . . The dispute between the two bishops appeared to come to a head in a letter of June 28 from the Vatican. It affirmed that Danylak has "all rights and duties" in spiritual and temporal matters. It said Borecky "retains only the prerogative of a liturgical character," and that his decisions about the eparchy were "void of every judicial effect." The letter came at the request of Danylak after both he and Borecky issued letters to the eparchy claiming authority over its affairs.
>
> The Vatican letter was from Cardinal Achille Silvestrini, prefect of the Congregation for Eastern Churches. He said the pope had given Danylak the authority over the eparchy and pointed out that Borecky "has already completed his 81st year of age." Borecky countered in an Aug. 5 letter to Silvestrini, "I have taken the position, based on advice, that there is some question" whether Vatican II's "resignation requirement" applied to bishops appointed before the council, especially an Eastern-rite bishop. . . . "Unfortunately, I did not have the courtesy of a direct communication from Your Eminence either advising me of the appointment of the apostolic administrator or outlining the specific reasons which would constitute the 'serious and special reasons' for the appointment," wrote Borecky.

I was told by an elderly gentleman living in that eparchy that a majority of the clergy supported Bishop Borecky.[6]

---

5   See Art Babych, "Ukrainian bishop fights to hold eparchy: he claims Vatican II rule does not apply," *National Catholic Reporter*, September 24, 1993.

6   Those who are interested in reading some articles from the midst of the events may consult *The Ukrainian Weekly* of Sunday, January 3, 1993 (https://archive.ukrweekly.com/print-media/1993/The_Ukrainian_Weekly_1993-01.pdf)

How did the story end? As an entry on Danylak notes, after six years of standoff Bishop Lubomyr Husar of Lviv "negotiated a resolution whereby Borecky retired and Danylak was reassigned to 'special responsibilities in Rome,' resulting in the vacancy of the Toronto eparchy effective June 24, 1998. Bishop Cornelius Pasichny of Saskatoon was appointed the new bishop on July 1 of that year."[7] Bishop Borecky stuck to his post till 87, and died five years later. Although he didn't die in office, he relinquished it of his own volition, as befits the dignity of a successor of the apostles.

"This is all very interesting," you may be thinking, "but after all, the Borecky case was a dispute between a prelate of an Eastern Church *sui iuris* and the bishop of Rome, so of course there was more room for such a protest. There isn't really any lesson here for us Latin Catholics, since the pope is the undisputed head of our own rite-church."

There's some truth to that point. Nevertheless, we mustn't forget the language of the magisterial text that hyperpapalists appeal to more frequently than to any other:

> Wherefore we teach and declare that, by divine ordinance, the Roman Church possesses a pre-eminence of ordinary power over *every other Church*, and that this jurisdictional power of the Roman Pontiff is both episcopal and immediate. Both clergy and faithful, *of whatever rite and dignity*, both singly and collectively, are bound to submit to this power by the duty of hierarchical subordination and true obedience, and this not only in matters concerning faith and morals, but also in those which regard the discipline and government of the Church throughout the world.[8]

What this Ukrainian bishop did was certainly contrary to a narrow or positivistic reading of this passage in Vatican I, and yet he did it nonetheless, convinced that he was defending prior and legitimate rights, rooted in apostolic succession, that papal authority is required to respect, *regardless* of its primacy. Is it not possible that the Church has, for a long time, been overlooking the inherent dignity of the

---

and Sunday, February 7, 1993 (https://archive.ukrweekly.com/print-media/1993/ The_Ukrainian_Weekly_1993-06.pdf).
7   See https://en.m.wikipedia.org/wiki/Roman_Danylak.
8   First Vatican Council, Dogmatic Constitution *Pastor Aeternus*, ch. 3, emphases added.

episcopal office after two ecumenical councils (Vatican I and II) that *both* overemphasized the papal primacy at the expense of – or at least to the eclipse of – other elements of ecclesiastical life, or formulated it in a way that has allowed erroneous extrapolations?[9]

Many speak of "the spirit of Vatican II," but there is also a "spirit of Vatican I."[10] Indeed, it may be argued that every influential council emanates or fosters a spirit, and this can be good, bad, or a mix of the two depending on whether or not it aligns with the letter of the Council's teaching and pastoral intentions. The spirit of the Council of Trent was overwhelmingly good, for it became the animating force of the Counter-Reformation that pushed back Protestantism and revitalized the Church in Europe and well beyond. The spirit of Vatican II was overwhelming bad, for it became the animating force of a Counter-Counter-Reformation that systematically undermined the handing-on of the Faith, a reversal exemplified in the attempt to replace (in an abuse of papal authority[11]) the Roman Rite canonized after Trent – the *lex orandi* corresponding to the Roman Church's *lex credendi* – with a modern papal rite diluted by Protestant, modernist, and secular influences.

The spirit of Vatican I, however, was decidedly mixed: on the one hand, ultramontanism raised the dignity of the Apostolic See and recognized the authority of the common father of Christians at a time when the Catholic Church was everywhere under attack and the faithful needed a shining beacon to look to; on the other hand, a tendency to absolutize papal monarchy and infallibilize papal statements took hold throughout the Church, paving the way for an increasing pastoral passivity among bishops and a thoughtless, almost mechanical obedience in their flocks. This strange evisceration of hierarchy and infantilization of the faithful was, of course, unsustainable, and a tidal wave of opposing errors submerged the Church after Vatican II, in which bishops frequently ignored traditional teaching emanating from Rome (of the many examples that might be cited, recall John XXIII's *Veterum Sapientia*, Paul VI's *Humanae Vitae*, John Paul II's *Veritatis Splendor*, and Benedict XVI's *Summorum Pontificum*) and the laity, egged on by those renegade

---

9   See chapter 4. Cf. Darrick Taylor, "Can We Learn Anything from the Critics of Vatican I?," *OnePeterFive*, November 13, 2023.
10   See chapter 3.
11   See chapters 5, 9, and 11.

bishops, claimed exemptions of conscience from any teaching they preferred not to follow, if they still bothered to practice at all.

We have come full circle now, with a progressivist pope who nevertheless employs ultramontanist tactics and surrounds himself with curial and episcopal sycophants who have quite suddenly rediscovered, after decades of dormancy, an almost latreutic devotion to the supreme pontiff, while the orthodox are few in number and beleaguered. It is in this precise context that we must understand the possibility and indeed the necessity of some bishops digging in their heels to say (whether it be to politically-motivated demands for resignation, manifestly ideological depositions, the schismatic Synodal Way, the heretical rewriting of catechisms, or the ongoing demolition of matrimonial morality): *Non possumus. Non licet.* We cannot do it. It is not allowed.

The shameful treatment of Bishop Daniel Fernández Torres set a precedent for what happened to Bishop Joseph Strickland. Sadly, both bishops lost their opportunity to stand firm against papal overreach, as Bishop Borecky stood firm, and, indeed, as Cardinal Slipyj and Cardinal Wojtyła had done decades earlier.[12] It may seem as if allowing an injustice to be done to oneself and not resisting it is the more Christian path, but this is true only if "turning the other cheek" does not contradict one's God-given vocation and one's responsibilities to others. An individual may let himself be struck and not strike back, but a father of a family may not allow his wife or his children to be struck without striking back; he must defend them. A president may allow himself to be inconvenienced but he may not allow his country to be unjustly assaulted by the enemy without fighting back. Emperor Charles I of Austria refused to lay aside his crown and took whatever steps he could to continue ruling, although he was unsuccessful (in earthly terms). So, too, with a bishop whom the Vatican "cancels" with neither due canonical process nor published evidence of grave wrongdoing: he has obligations to his people and his brother bishops that make it necessary to resist a papal tyranny that would deprive the flock of orthodox governance and violate of the dignity of the apostolic college. Placid cooperation with a dictator pope and toleration of manifest grave injustice is not for the benefit of the Catholic Church.

---

12   See chapter 13.

16

When a Bishop Outlaws or Restricts Private Traditional Masses[1]

IN A THREE-PAGE LETTER DATED AUGUST 20, 2021, and addressed to "Dear Brothers in Christ," Most Reverend David A. Zubik, bishop of Pittsburgh – apparently in an effort to show that he is more Bergoglian than Bergoglio – took a hearty step beyond what a strict interpretation of Pope Francis's motu proprio *Traditionis Custodes* would require (on the dubious assumption that it possesses legal standing).[2] In spite of the fact that Pittsburgh is one of the United States' most depressed and collapsing dioceses—as can be seen from relentless parish closures that have left the city pockmarked with churches converted into restaurants, bars, penthouses, and other secular venues – the infusion of spiritual energy from the wellsprings of tradition is evidently too risky to allow. Better a dead church than a traditional one.

The bishop's letter was one of many disturbing signs of the damage caused by bishops who lack understanding of or sympathy with Catholic tradition and who fail to grasp the pastoral wisdom of delaying implementation, setting up "study groups," formulating plausible excuses, discovering clever canonical loopholes, and, the most ecological of all, recycling unwanted mail from the Vatican. Zubik declared that there will be only one "full-service" traditional Roman Rite parish in the entire city, namely, The Most Precious Blood of Jesus, run by the Institute of Christ the King Sovereign Priest. At two other named parishes, Masses are to be

---

1   The first part of this chapter (until the section "Can a bishop restrict a private Mass?") was published, in a slightly different form, in Kwasniewski, *From Benedict's Peace to Francis's War*, 327–32.

2   See Rivoire, *Does "Traditionis Custodes" Pass the Juridical Rationality Test?*; Pink, "Is *Traditionis Custodes* Lawful?"; Kwasniewski, "Does *Traditionis Custodes* Lack Juridical Standing?," in *From Benedict's Peace to Francis's War*, 74–78; Lamont, "Dominican Theologian Attacks Catholic Tradition."

allowed occasionally, but expressly *not* on Christmas, Easter, and Pentecost. The other sacraments (Baptism, Confirmation, Confession, Marriage, Extreme Unction) are permitted *only* for registered parishioners of the Institute's apostolate; any other use is forbidden.

Worst of all, diocesan priests were forbidden to offer private Masses in the traditional Roman Rite. The bishop wrote:

> With the promulgation of *Traditionis Custodes* on July 16, priests no longer have general permission or faculties to celebrate the Eucharist or the other sacraments according to the Roman Missal of 1962, not even in private. Instead, they must be expressly given the faculty to do so by their local diocesan bishop (or his delegate). Furthermore, the Holy Father has made it clear that permission for the celebration of the Eucharist according to the Roman Missal of 1962 is not meant to be for the personal devotion of any particular priest; rather, it is only to be given for the benefit of groups of the faithful. . . . Once again, this faculty will not be granted to priests who request permission to celebrate privately according to the Roman Missal of 1962.

Let us think for a moment about the implications of this step.

The Latin Mass of the Roman Rite that has never ceased to be offered, at whatever stage of its development, from the fourth century until today (even after 1969 there was never a total break in the celebration of the *usus antiquior*) – this is now deemed so harmful to Church unity, so dangerous to souls, that even a priest who, on a given day, has no other pastoral responsibility is to be forbidden its use? Even the priest who finds great spiritual nourishment in the rich *lex orandi* of the traditional Mass, who knows from experience that it unites him in a special way to the Sacrifice of the Cross and helps him to pray fervently for the intention of the Mass – he must be deprived of this food, this more profound union, this more intense grace of devotion, which (as we know from St Thomas Aquinas) wins greater fruits from the Mass?

RENOUNCE A SOURCE OF PRIESTLY IDENTITY AND GRACE?

Over the years, I've heard from many priests whose discovery of the Latin Mass has transformed their priesthood and their entire spiritual life.[3] In his book *Cor Iesu Sacratissimum*, Roger Buck quotes from a letter sent to him by just such a priest, who readily celebrates the reformed Mass but especially values his contact with the old rite:

> These [traditional] Masses are special to me, and so great a privilege to be united with Christ as His Priest, and offer with Him the sacrifice of Calvary, for the living and the dead. It is through using the Tridentine form that I have come to appreciate something of the great significance of what I am doing each morning. Can there be anything more important than this?[4]

Archbishop Carlo Maria Viganò movingly testifies:

> Many priests discover the treasures of the venerable Tridentine liturgy only when they celebrate it and allow themselves to be permeated by it, and it is not uncommon for an initial curiosity towards the "extraordinary form" – certainly fascinating due to the solemnity of the rite – to change quickly into the awareness of the depth of the words, the clarity of the doctrine, the incomparable spirituality that it gives birth to and nourishes in our souls.
>
> There is a perfect harmony that words cannot express, and that the faithful can understand only in part, but which touches the heart of the Priesthood as only God can. This can be confirmed by my confreres who have approached the *usus antiquior* after decades of obedient celebration of the *Novus Ordo*: a world opens up, a cosmos that includes the prayer of the Breviary with the lessons of Matins and the commentaries of the Fathers, the cross-references to the texts of the Mass, the Martyrology in the Hour of Prime...
>
> They are sacred words – not because they are expressed in Latin, but rather they are expressed in Latin because the vulgar language would demean them, would profane them, as Dom Guéranger wisely observed. These are the words of the Bride to the divine Bridegroom, words of the soul that lives in intimate union with God, of the soul that lets itself be inhabited by the Most Holy Trinity. Essentially priestly words, in the deepest sense of the

---

3   See my articles "Discovering Tradition: A Priest's Crisis of Conscience" and "Not Abandoning the Flock – Not Abandoning the Truth."

4   Roger Buck, *Cor Iesu Sacratissimum: From Secularism and the New Age to Christendom Renewed* (Kettering, OH: Angelico Press, 2016), 302.

term, which implies in the Priesthood not only the power
to offer sacrifice, but to unite in self-offering to the pure,
holy, and immaculate Victim.[5]

For all these reasons, the effort to extinguish the priest's right to
offer the traditional Mass, or to deprive him of the full panoply of
the spiritual resources of tradition, can have only an infernal origin—it could never be of the Spirit of God. For this is what an enemy
of Christ and His Church would do. No one but an enemy would seek
to outlaw this consolidator of priestly identity, this font of fervent
prayer, this haven of refreshment and copious graces for the soul.

Priests are entirely within their rights before God and Holy
Mother Church to refuse to comply with such restrictions or prohibitions (as previous "disobedience" to unjust liturgical commands
has been twice exonerated by the Holy See itself).[6] Priests in the
diocese of Pittsburgh or any other diocese that has implemented a
policy as cruel and anticlerical as Pittsburgh's should continue to
celebrate the Latin Mass and to utilize the other traditional sacramental rites whenever it is possible to do so, e.g., if they go somewhere on retreat, or are visiting trustworthy family and friends.
(I will return, below, to the canonical justification for continuing
to offer private Masses.)

ARRIVING AT A PARTING OF THE WAYS?

Yet this watershed might also be a priest's providential moment of
realization. Could the Lord be calling him, especially right now, to
continue calmly doing what he was doing before, in defiance of a

---

5   See Carlo Maria Viganò, "Lapides Clamabunt," in Kwasniewski, *From Benedict's Peace to Francis's War*, 190–202; here, 193. My quoting of the controversial
archbishop is by no means to be construed as a blanket endorsement of all his
positions, especially his unconscionable stance on Vladimir Putin's war of aggression against the nation of Ukraine with the collusion of the Russian Orthodox.
Nevertheless, intellectual honesty demands that we recognize the value and
incisiveness of many of the archbishop's writings, such as those collected in *A
Voice in the Wilderness: Archbishop Carlo Maria Viganò on the Church, America,
and the World*, ed. Brian M. McCall (Brooklyn, NY: Angelico Press, 2021).
6   See Timothy Flanders, "Why the Term 'Extraordinary Form' is Wrong," *The
Meaning of Catholic*, August 9, 2019. It is crucial to understand that, in the
Catholic tradition, obedience has precise requirements and limits, as the other
chapters in this book explain in detail. As St Thomas Aquinas teaches, an unjust
law does not have the rationale of law and therefore should not be followed. In
this case, the one who does not follow it is not guilty of the sin of disobedience
but rather is to be praised for obedience to a higher law.

manifestly unjust prohibition? Such a course of action is almost certain to result in his being sacrificed ("canceled") like a lamb led to the slaughter. Perhaps it is time for many priestly grains of wheat to fall into the ground and die, so that they may bear a greater fruit of holiness than collaboration with abusive chanceries would allow. They will quickly find laity who will support them in their needs. More home chapels than ever are being built; the lay faithful are busy preparing for this next phase of resistance to wayward pastors' attacks on the Church's common good.[7]

Let us recall that traditional Catholic worship and the way of life it sustains was saved in the late sixties and seventies by priests and laity willing to do exactly this, and nothing less, to remain true to what they knew to be true.[8] It was initially a tiny minority who kept the flame burning and who spread it, one person at a time, across the world. Very often they had to do so outside of the official structures of the Church, or rather, outside of the self-endorsing legal fictions of churchmen and their self-destructive "renewal." They were, for a time, "pastors out in the cold,"[9] but they would never exchange their clear conscience, Catholic integrity, pastoral fruitfulness ("unless a grain of wheat falls into the ground and dies . . ."), and spiritual consolation for any emoluments from a corrupt and corrosive system.

Stuart Chessman of the Society of St Hugh of Cluny analyzed the transition from cold war to hot war:

> Everywhere there's a sense that a boundary has been crossed, that the Church has moved into new and uncharted waters. War does have the advantage of clarifying issues and power relationships, of advancing from mystification to reality.
>
> However, the "fortunes of war" are inherently unpredictable. A nation, like France in 1870, may enter into war, as its prime minister at that time, Émile Ollivier, said, "with a light heart." So did all Europe in 1914, Germany in Russia in 1941, Japan at Pearl Harbor later that same year, and the United States subsequently in Vietnam, Iraq,

---

7 See chapter 25.
8 See my Foreword to Chessman's *Faith of Our Fathers*.
9 See M. Jean-Claude Dupuis, "A Tribute to Father Yves Normandin (1925–2020), Hero of the Traditional Mass in Canada," *Rorate Caeli*, February 7, 2021.

and Afghanistan. In all these cases, the confrontation that emerged was unimaginably different from the assumptions governing at the beginning. The Roman Catholic Church will shortly be experiencing the same.

Moreover, Pope Francis has declared his intent to conduct that most difficult of martial undertakings, an aggressive war of annihilation. As Martin van Creveld points out, such a war, by leaving the enemy only two outcomes: victory or extinction, dramatically solidifies the enemy's will to resist regardless of what his previous political or military weakness may have been. In this respect, TC is the "Operation Barbarossa" of the Church.[10]

"Operation Barbarossa" was the code name for Hitler's invasion of Russia in 1941. It commenced with the German Reich at a high tide of power and confidence, with wave after wave of soldiers and fearsome military equipment. Surely this campaign could not fail. But fail it did, and rapidly. The fortunes of war turned against the Reich's hunger for hegemony.

For its part, *Traditionis Custodes* marks a similar attempt on the part of the progressive faction that holds most of the Church's offices. They have gambled everything on a final assault against the last outposts withstanding their wintry "new Pentecost." Those who comply with unjust decrees will place themselves by that very fact on the side of the would-be extinguishers of Catholic tradition. Those who find ways to resist, be it secretly or openly, will have the merit and glory of fighting for the Faith of our fathers, which, so far from being our possession to treat as if it were raw material for exploitation, is to be gratefully received as a fully-formed gift, which we humbly benefit from and faithfully hand on.

This is the true Spirit of Pentecost, which those who have been touched by the Pentecost Octave (abolished in the Novus Ordo),[11] who have savored each day the honeysweet words of the *Veni, Sancte Spiritus*, have come to know as their source of unconquerable fortitude in the midst of a conflict for which all human forces are inadequate.

---

10   Stuart Chessman, "*Traditionis Custodes*: Dispatches from the Front," *The Society of St. Hugh of Cluny*, August 18, 2021.
11   See my article "What's the Big Deal with the Pentecost Octave?," *The Remnant*, May 22, 2021.

To quote Archbishop Viganò once more:

> How many of you priests—and certainly also many lay
> people—in reciting the wonderful verses of the Pentecost
> Sequence were moved to tears, understanding that your
> initial predilection for the traditional liturgy had noth-
> ing to do with a sterile aesthetic satisfaction, but had
> evolved into a real spiritual necessity, as indispensable
> as breathing? How can you and how can we explain to
> those who today would like to deprive you of this price-
> less good, that that blessed rite has made you discover the
> true nature of your priesthood, and that from it and only
> from it are you able to draw strength and nourishment
> to face the commitments of your ministry? How can you
> make it clear that the obligatory return to [exclusively
> using] the Montinian rite represents an impossible sacri-
> fice for you, because in the daily battle against the world,
> the flesh and the devil it leaves you disarmed, prostrate
> and without strength?... It is not a question of nostalgia,
> of a cult of the past: here we are speaking of the life of
> the soul, its spiritual growth, ascesis and mysticism. Con-
> cepts that those who see their priesthood as a profession
> cannot even understand...

CAN A BISHOP RESTRICT A PRIVATE MASS?

In other dioceses, too, *Traditionis Custodes* is being "applied" in
ways that go well beyond what would be required by the letter of
the law (such as it is). One offensive tactic is when bishops attempt
to redefine "private Mass" as a Mass at which only a priest and a
server are present, *and no one else.*

Let's begin with a preliminary canonical matter. If a bishop
merely *tells* his priests that this will be his policy, or has it communicated to them in an informal way, then it is neither valid nor
legally enforceable, the reason being given in a series of canons:

> **Can. 49.** A singular precept is a decree which directly
> and legitimately enjoins a specific person or persons to
> do or omit something, especially in order to urge the
> observance of law.

> **Can. 51.** A decree is to be issued in writing, with the
> reasons at least summarily expressed if it is a decision.

Can. 54. §1. A singular decree whose application is entrusted to an executor takes effect from the moment of execution; otherwise, from the moment it is made known to the person by the authority of the one who issued it. §2. To be enforced, a singular decree must be made known by a legitimate document according to the norm of law.

Can. 55. Without prejudice to the prescripts of cann. 37 and 51, when a very grave reason prevents the handing over of the written text of a decree, the decree is considered to have been made known if it is read to the person to whom it is destined in the presence of a notary or two witnesses. After a written record of what has occurred has been prepared, all those present must sign it.

What is to be gathered from these canons is that the bishop would have had to present such a limitation on the rights of a priest *in writing*, then properly promulgate it. If a bishop intends to ban something that a priest is otherwise entitled to, he must issue it in writing, because it has to be the sort of thing capable of being challenged by those affected by it. Otherwise, it would just be a form of bullying: "You gotta do this because I *say* so," with no paper trail. Now, in the case at hand (where a bishop attempts to redefine a private Mass), what right of a priest is being infringed?

Can. 906. Except for a just and reasonable cause, a priest is not to celebrate the Eucharistic sacrifice without the participation of at least some member of the faithful.

Note that Can. 906 normally *requires* that there be "at least some member of the faithful," which is deliberately open-ended: it could logically and legally include several people, indeed it could include a large church packed to the rafters. This remains true for a Mass that an unimpeded priest offers on any day of the week in any legitimate place for any legitimate reason. That would include a Mass held, for appropriate reason, in a side chapel, at a school or a retreat center, in a rectory chapel, at a house, etc.

Now, Pope John XXIII in the 1960 *Code of Rubrics*, no. 269 (and after him, Paul VI in the encyclical *Mysterium Fidei*, nos. 32–33) rejected the *term* "private Mass" because a Mass *of its very nature* is a social act — even when said by a priest with a server and no one else. Historically and juridically, a "*Missa privata*" meant a

Mass "deprived" of solemnity or ceremonial – a low Mass at a side altar in contrast with a solemn conventual Mass. Only later and colloquially did it acquire the sense of "unofficial, unscheduled, unadvertised." Nevertheless, we can reasonably describe a Mass that is said on private property (not in a diocesan property) and not advertised to the public, and without pomp and circumstance, as a "private Mass."[12] There is and can be no canonical rule against such a Mass, nor, for the reasons given, could a bishop's merely verbal instruction not to do it suffice.[13]

It is arbitrary to limit servers to a single one. There is no canonical basis for such a limit. A priest could have one, two, or three servers, or as many as seemed *conveniens*. Similarly, it is arbitrary to specify that a server can be present but not, say, three lay people who are simply attending and praying. Unless the server is ordained to the minor order of acolyte or installed in the "ministry" of acolyte, the server is simply a layman wearing a cassock and surplice and offering some assistance. There would be no objective basis for the aforementioned limit. Indeed, since the very term "private Mass" is to be avoided as per the 1960 *Code of Rubrics* (no. 269), one might consider any policy couched in terms of "private Mass" to be theologically unsound, and therefore deserving to be ignored.

Prior to 1958, the term "*missa privata*," when used by the Holy See, carried with it various valences of meaning: conditions of privacy, lack of solemnity or music, etc.[14] I can only assume that a bishop today might use it in the sense of Mass "*sine populo*," a concept that exists in the *Novus Ordo* texts.[15] This concept of a

---

12 O'Connell lists several kinds of private Masses. See Fr John Fenton, "What is a 'Private Mass'?," May 15, 2021, https://cum-angelis-et-archangelis.orthodox-westblogs.com/2021/05/15/what-is-a-private-mass/.
13 Let us be clear about this point: *any* implementation of *Traditionis Custodes* that is not formally committed to writing in such a way that it might be canonically evaluated and challenged is invalid on the face of it and cannot be enforced.
14 Cf. Frederick R. McManus, *Handbook for the New Rubrics* (Baltimore: Helicon, 1960), 106–7. Fr McManus would go on to be one of the destroyers of the liturgy, but this work is a useful reference tool.
15 "The revised edition of the Roman Missal that was promulgated by Pope Paul VI in 1969 presented two forms of the Order of Mass: *Ordo Missae cum populo* and *Ordo Missae sine populo*. . . . The 1970 General Instruction of the Roman Missal dealt with the first of these forms of celebrating Mass under the numbers 77-152, and with the second under the numbers 209-231. The latter section began with the explanation: 'This section gives the norms for Mass celebrated by a priest with only one server to assist him and to make the responses.' In the revised and

Mass *"sine populo"* does not, however, exist for the *usus antiquior*, and is therefore inapplicable.

Since current legislation does not define "private Mass," a bishop could argue that it's up to him to make distinctions (invoking the somewhat spurious and nearly always exaggerated notion of the bishop as the "chief liturgist" of his diocese),[16] though the counter-argument would be that such distinctions are *praeter legem* and beyond the authority of the bishop. Practically speaking, it is usually sufficient to state something like the following: "Father N. will be offering a private Mass at 8:30 a.m. in the school chapel. The doors of the chapel will be unlocked as usual; all are welcome to visit the chapel at any time for personal prayer."

Incidentally, if a bishop dared to prohibit priests from saying the ancient Mass *by themselves*, this prohibition would be null and void. Pursuant to Can. 906 (and this is a change from Can. 813 in the 1917 Code), a priest is permitted to celebrate Mass *without a server or anyone else* for a "just and reasonable cause."[17] This has long been understood canonically to include simply the great good, for himself and for the Church, of the priest saying daily Mass.

Thus, taking all the forgoing into consideration, hypothetically in a diocese where a bishop attempted to limit "private Masses" to a priest and one server, it would be permissible for a priest to celebrate a *"Missa sine populo"* without a server (i.e., a *Missa solitaria*) for a "just cause" as per Can. 906 (what more just cause than pursuing sanctity and the honoring of God according to the sound ritual tradition of the Church?), but in such a way that some of

---

expanded 2002 edition of the General Instruction, the term *Missa cum populo* remains as the heading for the information given under numbers 115–198, but the other section (numbers 252–272) speaks of *Missa cuius unus tantum minister participat* (Mass in which only one server participates). Corresponding to the latter form, the Missal presents the *Ordo Missae cuius unus tantum minister participat* (Order of Mass in which only one server participates)." Information from https://en.wikipedia.org/wiki/Sine_populo.

16   The text of *Sacrosanctum Concilium* nos. 41 and 45, usually adduced as evidence for this concept, does not use the phrase "chief liturgist." For animadversions and a clear explanation of what the bishop's responsibilities are in reference to liturgy, see Archbishop Alexander K. Sample, "The Bishop: Governor, Promoter, and Guardian of the Liturgical Life of the Diocese" and Raymond Leo Cardinal Burke, "Liturgical Law in the Mission of the Church," in *Sacred Liturgy: The Source and Summit of the Life and Mission of the Church*, ed. Alcuin Reid (San Francisco: Ignatius Press, 2014), 255–71 and 389–415.

17   See Fr John Zuhlsdorf, "Can priests say the 'Tridentine Mass' alone, without a server?," *Fr Z's Blog*, December 30, 2016.

the faithful happened to be there at the same time for an unrelated reason (say, for instance, they gathered to pray the Rosary). In this case, everything would be canonically correct and the bishop's ruling – already incorrect for other reasons – would not even find matter to which it could apply.

THE MOUNTING THREAT OF
COERCIVE CONCELEBRATION

Within religious communities, in schools or houses of formation, in parishes, and in other situations, the campaign is intensifying to forbid priests from offering their own daily Masses (when they are otherwise free of the obligation to celebrate Mass with and for a congregation) and to compel them to concelebrate with confreres.[18] The same policy has been (more or less rigorously) enforced in St Peter's Basilica itself, to the great detriment of pilgrim groups and visiting priests.[19]

Clearly, the modernists and progressivists are fuming and plotting against the young priests who piously make a proper use of side altars to say Mass, or the parochial vicars who set up dignified altars in their rooms for their day off, or the clergy who with curious consistency absent themselves from the sacramental jamborees that pass for special occasions like the Chrism Mass. They can see the writing on the wall. There comes a time when the threat of tradition looms too large to ignore – and then, all kindness, real or simulated, is laid aside. The spread of the traditional Mass and the many customs it has revived is indeed a threat to the postconciliar house of cards that many have substituted for the rock-solid Church of Christ and its perennial doctrine and liturgy. The older generation, still paddling and splashing in a lake of Kool Aid, wants to thwart the offering of private Masses above all because these Masses are so often in the *usus antiquior*.

18   We first got wind of this back in July 2017 when a document circulating around Colleges in Rome attempted to intimidate clergy into concelebrating, contrary to their canonical rights. The inimitable Fr Hunwicke commented on it and related matters extensively at his blog *Fr Hunwicke's Mutual Enrichment* in a series called "Concelebration in the Roman Colleges."
19   See Edward Pentin, "'Like a Museum': Dead Silence in St. Peter's Basilica as Suppression of Individual Masses Comes into Force," *National Catholic Register*, March 22, 2021; idem, "After Outcry, Vatican Eases Restrictions on Individual Masses in St. Peter's Basilica," *National Catholic Register*, June 22, 2021.

Let us, then, be as clear as we can be. It is illegal and abusive to require a priest to concelebrate, or to establish that he should "as a rule" do so. It is still more impossible, as we have seen, to exclude the *usus antiquior* for a priest's "private" Mass—that is, when he is not scheduled to offer Mass in public with a congregation.

1. **Canon 902** guarantees the right of each priest to celebrate individually with the sole condition that this offering of the Holy Mass not take place in the same church or oratory in which another concelebration is taking place. (Some English translations simply say "in which another celebration is taking place." The Latin, however, is clear: *non vero eo tempore, quo in eadem ecclesia aut oratorio concelebratio habetur.*) Thus, having many simultaneous Masses at side altars is fully permissible even according to the 1983 Code.

2. **Canon 904** recommends the daily offering of the Holy Mass by priests "since, even if the faithful cannot be present, it is the act of Christ and the Church in which priests fulfill their principal office/duty [*munus*]." The standard English translation of the 1983 Code translates *munus* as "function" in this canon, a translation certainly not felicitous.

3. **Canon 906** prohibits a priest from offering the Holy Mass "without the participation of at least some member of the faithful"—"except for a just and reasonable cause." It is clear from context that the fulfillment of the recommendation of Canon 904, that is, the recommended daily offering of the Holy Mass by priests, is a just and reasonable cause.

4. These canonical points are well supported by recent magisterial documents. According to Pope John Paul II in the Encyclical Letter *Ecclesia de Eucharistia* (no. 31):

> If the Eucharist is the center and summit of the Church's life, it is likewise the center and summit of priestly ministry. For this reason, with a heart filled with gratitude to our Lord Jesus Christ, I repeat that the Eucharist "is the principal and central *raison d'être* of the sacrament of priesthood, which effectively came into being at the moment of the institution of the Eucharist."... We can understand, then, how important it is for the spiritual life of the priest, as well as for the good of the Church and the world, that priests follow the Council's recommendation to celebrate the Eucharist daily: "for even

if the faithful are unable to be present, it is an act of Christ and the Church." In this way priests will be able to counteract the daily tensions which lead to a lack of focus and they will find in the Eucharistic sacrifice – the true center of their lives and ministry – the spiritual strength needed to deal with their different pastoral responsibilities. Their daily activity will thus become truly Eucharistic.

The same teaching is reaffirmed in Pope Benedict XVI's Post-Synodal Apostolic Exhortation *Sacramentum Caritatis* (no. 80):

The Eucharistic form of the Christian life is seen in a very special way in the priesthood. Priestly spirituality is intrinsically Eucharistic.... An intense spiritual life will enable him [the priest] to enter more deeply into communion with the Lord and to let himself be possessed by God's love, bearing witness to that love at all times, even the darkest and most difficult. To this end, I join the Synod Fathers in recommending "the daily celebration of Mass, even when the faithful are not present" (*Propositio* 38). This recommendation is consistent with the objectively infinite value of every celebration of the Eucharist, and is motivated by the Mass's unique spiritual fruitfulness. If celebrated in a faith-filled and attentive way, Mass is formative in the deepest sense of the word, since it fosters the priest's configuration to Christ and strengthens him in his vocation.

Both of these magisterial documents renew the recommendation of the daily offering of the Holy Mass even when a member of the faithful cannot be present. It is, of course, important always to bear in mind that the Holy Mass is never in fact offered "alone," for there is always the participation of the choirs of angels and of the communion of the saints. Indeed, as Fr Bryan Houghton relates in his autobiography:

I had another strong impression from my first Mass and which has never ceased to grow. It was perfectly obvious that Jesus was the celebrant and I was merely a concele-brant. He, not I, was the active partner. When the pres-ent fashion of concelebration of Mass by a plethora of priests became the norm I failed to understand it. Their participation could only dim the basic fact that I was concelebrating with Jesus.[20]

5. In connection with the Mass of Paul VI, The *General Instruction of the Roman Missal* provides rubrics for the offering of Holy Mass when only one minister participates (nos. 252–72), and for the offering of Holy Mass without the participation of a minister (no. 254). There would be no point in furnishing such rubrics were this situation not anticipated as a normal occurrence in the life of the clergy.

Priests who find themselves victims of the attempt to exclude private Mass or to require concelebration should resist by respectfully – and, if necessary, repeatedly, and in writing[21] – pointing out the provisions in Church law, as summarized above, avoiding attribution of motives or expressions of rancor, and leaving the judgment of hearts to Almighty God. Since we know there are wicked men in high places, at times this self-defense may precipitate a larger confrontation. Such confrontations are never pleasant affairs but they can be occasions of greatly-needed clarification on the limits of authority and obedience, and even moments of grace in discerning whether a given diocesan or community situation is sustainable over the long term.

A number of *good* men in high places have given this advice to individuals: Be strong and stand your ground: *esto vir, esto sacerdos Christi.*

---

20   Houghton, *Unwanted Priest*, 40.
21   Bullies rarely want to write anything down on paper, because they either know or have an intuition that if they write down their demands, they can be challenged canonically, and defeated or embarrassed. So a key defense is to insist that any demand or request be put into writing so that one can be certain of what is being requested and why. If they will not do so, then one can plausibly claim later on that one did not understand what they were asking or had not been given a sufficient reason or had doubts in one's conscience about the validity of their requests, etc.

17

Why Traditionalist Priests Should Avoid Concelebrating the Chrism Mass

HEN POPE FRANCIS TOLD A GROUP OF French bishops that *all* priests in a diocese, regardless of affiliation, should be present to concelebrate the Chrism Mass with their bishop each year,[1] the ever-simmering question of concelebration once more came to a boil. Traditionalist commentator Michael Charlier published an article in which he opined that, even if normally concelebration may and should be refused by traditional clergy, the Chrism Mass is a special case where a refusal *in principle* would be unreasonable and where it would be prudent to go ahead in a spirit of compromise and as a minimal sign of unity with the local bishop, at whose sufferance these traditionalist communities function in the diocese.[2] I shall argue that this is a mistaken conclusion, and that it is important for traditional clergy to avoid concelebration *tout court*, even on this occasion.

HISTORICAL-LITURGICAL RATIONALE

As Bishop Athanasius Schneider has demonstrated in his unsurpassed study on the subject—"Eucharistic Concelebration: Theological, Historical, and Liturgical Aspects"[3]—the rite of concelebration as it was "drawn up" after the Second Vatican Council, and even more as it has been "lived" in the Church, is a sheer novelty that bears no substantive relation to the Western tradition or to the Eastern tradition.[4] It is, in short, another fabrication of the liturgical

---

1 See "Pope insists traditionalist FSSP priests must concelebrate new rite Chrism Mass: French archbishop," *LifeSiteNews*, April 26, 2022.
2 See Michael Charlier, "Concelebration as compromise?," *Rorate Caeli*, May 3, 2022.
3 Published at *New Liturgical Movement*, August 11, 2021.
4 See also Gregory DiPippo, "Concelebration in the Byzantine Rite," *New Liturgical Movement*, September 6, 2014.

innovators. It therefore deserves to be avoided for exactly the same reasons for which traditional clergy refuse to use the new missal, the other new sacramental rites, the new liturgy of the hours, the new "book of blessings," the new pontifical ceremonies, and so forth.

ECCLESIOLOGICAL RATIONALE

If what is desired of the traditional clergy is that they should freely and publicly express their communion with the local bishop and the presbyterate, it is obvious that concelebration is not the only way to express it. An important article by Clemens Victor Olden-dorf is worth quoting *in extenso* on this point:

> What is interesting in the wording of the question [number 3 of the Roche *Dubia*] is the talk of recognizing the validity and legitimacy of concelebration, and the implicit presupposition that such recognition can consist *only* in occasionally concelebrating in person, and especially at the Chrism Mass with the local bishop in whose diocese one resides and ministers. The explanatory note speaks of the validity and legitimacy of the liturgical reform, so "concelebration" and Pope Paul VI's postconciliar "liturgical reform" are, as it were, used synonymously. In other words, the practice of concelebration is seen as an exquisite achievement of this liturgical reform, like an emblem. And although current canon law guarantees the right to individual celebration, as is well known, one should not be surprised at such an interpretation, since in St Peter's itself, individual celebrations even according to the postconciliar missal have been de facto abolished in favor of concelebration. . . .
>
> [Yet] concelebration is not the only way to express one's hierarchical communion with the bishop. . . . By receiving from the local ordinary the sacred oils conse-crated in the new rite, a priest also accepts its validity, and furthermore – with the exception of the Apostolic Administration of the Holy Curé of Ars in Campos, Bra-zil – none of the former Ecclesia Dei communities have their own bishops, consecrated according to the old Pon-tifical. Even if the priests themselves have been ordained according to the old Pontifical up to now, from this point of view, none of the priests of these communities is, so to speak, "purely Tridentine" because the prelates ordaining

them were ordained using the 1968 Pontifical; and even the SSPX accepts into its ranks priests ordained in the new rite, or at least collaborates with them....

Furthermore, it can be pointed out that probably the majority of the Masses celebrated on the basis of *Summorum Pontificum* using the Tridentine Missal were celebrated in churches and chapels where otherwise the post-conciliar Missal is predominantly used, and moreover, that at such Masses, in the Vetus Ordo, Communion for the faithful may be taken from ciboria in the tabernacle whose hosts were consecrated in celebrations according to the new missal. Such a thing would certainly not be possible if there was a denial of the validity and legitimacy [N.B.: see below for a qualification] of the new rite.

In the *dubium* about concelebration under closer consideration here, therefore, an unrealistic construct is present, one which, strictly speaking, cannot have existed in the case of anyone who has ever applied to benefit from an old-rite indult, or who, from September 14, 2007 to July 16, 2021, celebrated Masses on the basis of *Summorum Pontificum* according to the *Missale Romanum* of 1962, or assisted at Masses celebrated on this legal basis. In short: a much higher threshold of evidence than could possibly be necessary has been introduced, which gives the response a punitive character....

The faithful who feel committed to the liturgical tradition of the Latin Church and who want to be nothing but Roman Catholics are thus pushed out, and it becomes clear: Pope Francis and the Congregation for Divine Worship are obviously not really concerned with the high good of genuine ecclesial unity, but at most with a positivist loyalty to authority.[5]

The Latin Mass Society of England and Wales' "Some Notes on the Congregation for Divine Worship's *Responsa ad Dubia* in light of Canon Law" rightly points out:

Ecclesial communion can be manifested in many ways: intercommunion with the bishop, mention of the bishop in the Canon, presence at the Chrism Mass in choir, use of the oils blessed by his bishop at the Chrism Mass, etc.

---

5 Clemens Victor Oldendorf, "Who Actually Delegitimizes the *Novus Ordo Missae?*," *New Liturgical Movement*, December 30, 2021.

CANONICAL RATIONALE

The third rationale is canonical. As such, it is closely bound up with the preceding, since canon law exists to facilitate unity in the truth and the communion of charity. Chartier calls into question the fittingness of applying Canon 902 to the Chrism Mass, yet any sidestepping of Canon 902 raises a deeper problem. The requirement of an annual concelebration can be seen as a way of insisting that modern Church customs and pontifical preferences surpass and relativize tradition and canon law, which has been the pattern throughout Francis's pontificate and indeed throughout all postconciliar pontificates, back to Paul VI's surrender to northern European pressure regarding Communion in the hand, or John Paul II's surrender on the question of female altar servers. Being pressured into concelebrating, even for the "best" of reasons, is the first step on a slippery slope of giving up other rights and traditions. It opens the door to other demands and requirements, other new "wishes" and "expectations" and "exceptions" and "accommodations." It is better to say no at the start than to begin sliding down that slope. One might even say that the traditional clergy are doing the entire Church a favor by reminding everyone of the limits that exist and of the theological truths these limits are meant to safeguard.[6]

As Christopher Altiere remarks:

> Priests have a right – enshrined in law – not to concelebrate. In fact, canon 902 of the Code of Canon Law is written in a way to give permission for *concelebration* – i.e., when more than one priest celebrates the same Mass – precisely because the practice was virtually unheard-of in the Latin West until the second half of the last century. How can a healthy mind see in the exercise of a right, any evidence of anything except knowledge of one's right?[7]

Fr Pius Pietrzyk goes further, showing that the response to question 3 in the *Responsa ad dubia* flatly contradicts more authoritative teaching:

---

6   See the section on "The Mounting Threat of Coercive Concelebration" in the preceding chapter.
7   Christopher R. Altieri, "Trying to make some sense of the *responsa ad dubia*," *Catholic World Report*, December 19, 2021.

The *Responsa* does seem to lack a sufficient understanding of the legal and ecclesiological norms of concelebration. Like the question of episcopal dispensations, this is not simply a legal norm but was a part of the teaching of the Second Vatican Council. In *Sancrosanctum Concilium*, where the Church opened the Latin Church to the wider ability to concelebrate, the conciliar fathers made clear: "each priest shall always retain his right to celebrate Mass individually" (*SC*, 57). This has been consistently interpreted by the Church as the right of priests not to be required to concelebrate. The notion that the exercise of this right, given in a Constitution issued by an Ecumenical Council and enshrined in universal law, may be the basis for the restriction of other rights and privileges is impossible to square with the provisions of law and Conciliar teaching. The stated goal of the *Responsa ad dubia* is to foster conformance to the liturgical reforms of the Second Vatican Council. That goal is compromised by a statement in these *Responsa ad dubia* that seems to repudiate one of the express liturgical directives of that Council.[8]

In an extensive interview on the *responsa ad dubia*, Fr Gerald Murray, also a canon lawyer, expands on the dangerous lawlessness of the CDW response and of the course of action Pope Francis suggested to the French bishops:

> The clear presumption . . . is that a priest who chooses not to concelebrate at the Chrism Mass or at other Masses, as is his right, is suspected of not recognizing the validity and legitimacy of concelebration itself. . . . That is an unwarranted suspicion and presumes that it is likely that the priest rejects concelebration as valid and legitimate, rejects the liturgical reform as a whole, and lacks ecclesial communion with the bishop in addition. Such rash conclusions about the intentions of priests who choose not to concelebrate Mass cast these men in the position of being presumed guilty of grave offenses for simply exercising their canonical right to celebrate Mass individually.

---

8 Fr Pius Pietrzyk, OP, STL, JD, JCD, "A Dominican Canonist Responds to the *Responsa ad Dubia*," February 8, 2022, at https://edwardpentin.co.uk/a-dominican-canonist-responds-to-the-responsa-ad-dubia/.

No priest can be canonically compelled to concelebrate Mass, as canon 902 states that "priests may concelebrate the Eucharist; they are, however, fully entitled to celebrate the Eucharist individually." Thus, a decision to *not* concelebrate Mass is *perfectly lawful in itself*, and should not form the basis for a suspicion that any particular priest who makes the choice not to concelebrate does so because he "does not recognize the validity and legitimacy of concelebration." Only direct evidence that a priest believes that concelebration of the Mass is invalid and illegitimate should lead to that priest being asked by his ecclesiastical superior to correct this erroneous contention or face canonical sanctions. Concelebration [nevertheless] remains a free choice of every priest, with the possible exception of the Mass celebrated at his priestly ordination where the ritual presumes that the newly ordained priest will concelebrate the Mass with the ordaining bishop from the point immediately following his ordination.[9]

Worthy of note is Fr Murray's reminder that *even if* a bishop had evidence and reason to correct a priest about his opinions, there would still be no basis for requiring concelebration at the Chrism Mass. It is not legally translatable into a requirement.

MORAL RATIONALE

For a priest to make use, essentially for political reasons only, of a rite of which he internally disapproves and which he will find in practice disedifying and distressing, is a true example of "politicizing the Eucharist," making of the holiest and highest mystery of the Church a punchcard, a token, a litmus test. (Needless to say, the greater guilt for this abuse would be that of the bishop who demanded it *contra legem* as a new law, like a Pharisee multiplying observances while neglecting larger matters of justice.) To go along with this is to agree to subordinate the liturgy to politics – precisely one of the besetting vices of the postconciliar Church, a vice one should wish to avoid feeding in any way. If one does not personally wish to enter into a given liturgical act, then one would be doing it in order to be seen by others – a scenario about which Our Lord has some pointed

---

9   Fr Gerald Murray, "Guarding the Flock: A Canon Lawyer's Advice to Bishops on Latest Vatican Crackdown on Tradition," *The Remnant* online, February 15, 2022.

words in the Gospel. One might almost say it verges on sacrilege to make the Eucharist into a sign not so much of ecclesial unity as of ideological conformity, employee verification, or party loyalty.

When Charlier says: "It is difficult to justify refusing to participate in it [the Chrism Mass] . . . since even the Old Rite communities (including the Society of St Pius X) recognize in principle the validity and legitimacy of the liturgy according to the 1969 books," he is misapprehending the issue at stake. Apart from the minority view held by such figures as Fr Anthony Cekada, the traditionalist movement broadly speaking has never had a difficulty admitting the bare sacramental *validity* of the new rites of the sacraments. But legitimacy is another matter entirely.

If the reformed/"renewed" liturgical rites and offices were acknowledged as "legitimate," on what basis would the traditionalists refuse to accept them and to use them, at least sometimes? Would not their choice of the old rites be reduced to mere aestheticism, sentimentality, or church politics? Of course this is not so. The liturgical reform is called into question and rejected because of its serious internal flaws, which extend from the *lex orandi* into the *lex credendi*. As a result, I think it is no exaggeration to say that traditionalism rejects the legitimacy of the liturgical reform.

Moreover, anyone who reads widely in traditionalist literature, past and present, can see that even the question of licitness is by no means a foregone conclusion. If the licitness of a rite relies on its having been duly and appropriately promulgated by the competent authority acting on the basis of his God-given authority and for the common good of the society in question, most traditionalists should find themselves denying, with one nuance or another, the licitness of the reformed rites.[10] The licitness, the lawfulness, of Paul VI's rupture with liturgical tradition is a vexed and vexing question that cannot be resolved with an ultramontanist shrug of the shoulders. To quote Oldendorf once again:

> The traditionalists whom *Traditionis Custodes* is targeting have never asked for "permission" to hold on to the traditional liturgy—they consider it a patrimony prior

---

10   Dr John Lamont has argued twice in the negative: see "Is the Mass of Paul VI Licit?," *Dialogos Institute*, March 20, 2022, and "Dominican Theologian Attacks Catholic Tradition." Cf. chapter 21.

to and deeper than the whim of the pope – and will not now suddenly allow it to be taken away and forbidden by Pope Francis. However, many of those who, until now, have attached importance to the requesting and receipt of such permission may now start to think it over again, and, possibly even more, to rethink the basic legitimacy of the liturgical reform, including the Pauline *Pontificale Romanum* of 1968 and the Pauline *Novus Ordo* of 1969 – especially since the postconciliar liturgical books have now been claimed to be the sole (!) expression of the *lex orandi* of the Roman Rite. So great an unreality handicaps this declaration that it compels a re-examination of the delicate (and, some might say, unsustainable) peace on which *Summorum Pontificum* was constructed.

In short: however *valid* the new sacramental rites are, their legitimacy and licitness should not be assumed a priori. If there were even a slight doubt in the mind of a priest in this regard, he should not concelebrate the new Mass, for there would be a kind of dissimulation or dishonesty at work, and his conscience would rightly reproach him for it.

I am sure that still further points could be made, but the foregoing arguments suffice to show why it would be a mistake to "shimmy from compromise to compromise" in order to avoid "the danger of failure." We do heartily agree with Charlier, however, when he says at the end of his article that traditional clergy should "prepare themselves materially and theologically for the fact that a point may arrive when such communion [with a Rome moving away from tradition] no longer *de facto* exists."

Thanks be to God, apart from Rome, and even arguably in Rome, there are still bishops who believe the Catholic Faith or who at least are willing to tolerate "diverse expressions" of it – particularly when they bring in large numbers of faithful and generous donations to diocesan coffers. Traditional clergy have often been able to establish and maintain good relations and a certain mutual understanding or *modus vivendi* with these bishops. In this case, the *communio ecclesiae* is better achieved in personal informal meetings than in artificially inflated liturgical celebrations.

18

Priests Who Want Holy Water Must Use the *Rituale*— Despite Episcopal Prohibition

AS IS WELL KNOWN BY NOW, THE *RESPONSA ad Dubia* from the Congregation for Divine Worship, published on December 18, 2021, try to make the continued use of the *Rituale Romanum* contingent on episcopal permission. This is but one of many falsehoods contained in the document,[1] which, in addition, violates the rights of bishops on numerous points of canon law. Bishops who truly care for the good of their presbyterate and people will either leave undisturbed the priests who already use the great *Rituale Romanum*, or will – if they are legalistic in mentality – freely grant them the supposed "permission" required to use it.

In some dioceses, however, bishops are forbidding their clergy any use of the *Rituale Romanum*. This is often accompanied by a decision that a local personal parish run by the FSSP or the ICKSP will become the solitary place in the diocese where the *Rituale* is still allowed to be used. In dioceses where several or even dozens of parish priests have been using the *Rituale* for years, this creates an absolute pastoral nightmare, especially now that the more educated among the faithful are aware of the vast differences between the old and new rites across the board. How can a single personal parish possibly be expected to handle all of the requests for blessings and sacraments that will now be directed exclusively to them? This consideration alone should prompt a bishop to hesitate before restricting and ghettoizing.

The prohibition of the *Rituale* to diocesan clergy is problematic on numerous points, but here I wish to focus on one very particular problem: holy water.

---

1 See my article "'O, What a Tangled Web . . .': Thirty-Three Falsehoods in the CDW's *Responsa ad Dubia*," *OnePeterFive*, January 5, 2022.

The *Rituale Romanum* authoritatively blesses objects, that is, it calls upon God in the name of Jesus Christ to bless the object itself, to make *it* holy and thereby to help sanctify those who make use of it, as well as to endow it with power to expel evils. With more important blessings – above all, that of water – the priest first exorcises the element in the name of Jesus in order to remove it totally from the dominion of the Prince of this world (cf. Jn 12:31, Eph 2:2, 2 Cor 4:4) and to give it a sacred status and use. The *Rituale* does the same with the baptism of infants and adults: they are duly and properly exorcised prior to their incorporation into Christ as members of His Mystical Body.

The new rite of baptism has no proper exorcism,[2] and the new "blessing" of holy water doesn't even pretend to do an exorcism because the new theology doesn't believe that the devil has any power over the world after Christ has come; all things are already fine (the theory of the "anonymous Christian" slots in nicely here), and what we do with our rituals is a form of "salvation theater" to manifest to ourselves what we believe has already happened – not what needs to happen *here and now* to separate, sacralize, and sanctify fallen reality.[3]

Accordingly, the new "blessing" of holy water doesn't bless *the water itself*; it simply blesses *those who will use the water*. As Fr Zuhlsdorf has pointed out many times over the years, when you use the "Book of Blessings" to "bless" holy water, you don't end up with blessed water; the water's just the same as it was before, because God was never asked, by His sanctifying power, to give it a new relation to Himself and thus a new objective power to affect other things – especially demons.[4]

---

2   The Dave Armstrongs of the world will pull out their hair and quote the new rite of baptism's "exorcism," as wimpy as it is; but that is because they have not done the heavy lifting required to see that its quasi-exorcism reflects a wholly different (in fact, Rahnerian) theology, as Pink demonstrates in his "Vatican II and Crisis in the Theology of Baptism."

3   The denial of a difference between "sacred" and "profane," a commonplace in contemporary sacramental and liturgical theology, is pertinent here as well. For the various claims in this and surrounding paragraphs, see, in addition to Pink, the following authoritative studies: Daniel G. van Slyke, "The Order for Blessing Water: Past and Present," *Antiphon* 8:2 (2003), 12–23 (which may also be found in U. Michael Lang, ed., *The Fullness of Divine Worship: The Sacred Liturgy and Its Renewal* [Washington, DC: Catholic University of America Press, 2018], 169–95) and U. Michael Lang, "Theologies of Blessing: Origins and Characteristics of *De benedictionibus* (1984)," *Antiphon* 15.1 (2011): 27–46.

4   See Fr John Zuhlsdorf, "QUAERITUR: Is water blessed with the newer rites really holy water?," *Fr Z's Blog*, June 4, 2012.

Let's have a look at some excerpts from the contrasting liturgical books, just to drive home the point. Here's what the old prayers of exorcising and blessing water look like:

> O water, creature of God, I exorcise you in the name of God the Father Almighty, and in the name of Jesus Christ His Son, our Lord, and in the power of the Holy Spirit. I exorcise you so that you may put to flight all the power of the enemy, and be able to root out and supplant that enemy with his apostate angels, through the power of our Lord Jesus Christ, who will come to judge the living and the dead and the world by fire. . . .
>
> May this, your creature, become an agent of divine grace in the service of your mysteries, to drive away evil spirits and dispel sickness. . . May the wiles of the lurking enemy prove of no avail. Let whatever might menace the safety and peace of those who live here be put to flight by the sprinkling of this water, so that the health obtained by calling upon your Holy Name may be made secure against all attack. . . .
>
> Humbly and fearfully do we pray to you, O Lord, and we ask you to look with favor on this salt and water which you created. Shine on it with the light of your kindness. Sanctify it by the dew of your love, so that, through the invocation of your Holy Name, wherever this water and salt is sprinkled, it may turn aside every attack of the unclean spirit, and dispel the terrors of the poisonous serpent.

Now *that's* how the Catholic Church used to pray — and still does, where the Faith survives. The language of the old prayers, which is efficacious by the power of Christ and His Church, makes it perfectly clear why St Teresa of Avila could write in her *Autobiography*: "From long experience I have learned that there is nothing like holy water to put devils to flight and prevent them from coming back again. They also flee from the Cross, but return; so holy water must have great virtue."

In painful and scandalous contrast, the new rite reads like this:

> Blessed are you, Lord, all-powerful God, who in Christ, the living water of salvation, blessed and transformed us. Grant that, when we are sprinkled with this water

or make use of it, we will be refreshed inwardly by the power of the Holy Spirit... (etc.)

Nowhere is there an actual blessing *of the water*.[5]

Consequently, most Catholic churches for the past fifty years have welcomed the faithful with the ecclesiastical equivalent of birdbaths. You dip your hand into dihydrogen monoxide with germs. And while there's nothing wrong with playing in water, as children are wont to do, it doesn't carry any of the demon-dispelling, passion-quelling, venial-sin-remitting power that the Church attributes to the potent sacramental of holy water.[6] No wonder people raised on such ersatz came up with ideas like putting sand in the stoops for Lent, or leaving them empty during Coronatide.

One of the most remarkable moments of my life as a liturgist was when I sat in the audience at the 2019 Sacred Liturgy Conference in Spokane, Washington, listening to Archbishop Salvatore Cordileone deliver a lecture entitled "What Makes Water Holy? Reflections on the Rites for the Blessing of Holy Water."[7] The talk was remarkable because His Excellency, unlike most prelates, didn't beat around the bush, hemming and hawing: he agreed with van Slyke, Lang, Zuhlsdorf, and others, who hold that the new blessing of water doesn't make water holy, while the old one—the one in the *Rituale Romanum*—does.[8]

---

5   For those who wish to do a deep dive, see the side-by-side comparison of the old and new rites in "How long does holy water stay blessed?," *Fr Z's Blog*, January 3, 2018; Kevin Losleben, "Holy Water in the Time of Coronavirus: Old and New Compared," *OnePeterFive*, March 16, 2020. Reading one or the other of these comparisons is so revealing of the dastardly work of the liturgical reformers that it may forever change your way of thinking.

6   See my articles "St. Thomas on the 'Asperges' (Sprinkling Rite)," *Views from the Choir Loft*, August 7, 2014, and "Things That Remit Venial Sins – The Traditional Liturgy Is Full of Them," *New Liturgical Movement*, February 8, 2016.

7   The text has been removed from the Archdiocese of San Francisco's website, where it used to be located, but I have shared the PDF at https://rb.gy/o2k3u. The video of the talk is still available (for now) at YouTube at the Sacred Liturgy Conference channel under the title "Archbishop Salvatore Cordileone – What Makes Holy Water Holy?"

8   To be fair, he also notes that the (very rarely used) Asperges blessing in the new missal does in fact state that the water is the object of the blessing, even if the Book of Blessings definitely does not say this. I stand by my position that it was wrong and harmful for churchmen to have abolished the traditional blessing of water and that this form of blessing is the only way in which one can be absolutely certain that the object is indeed blessed and prepared for all the uses for which Holy Mother Church intends it.

Where does that leave us? The conclusion should be obvious. If a priest wishes to prepare holy water for his own use and for the benefit of his people, as the Church has always done in her implacable warfare against the Evil One until the end of time, he must bless it with the *Rituale Romanum*. There is no other way.

What, then, of the question of "obedience"? Ah, the virtue the enemies of Christ love to abuse for their own purposes, twisting and defiling it to suit their wicked agendas! Here is where we need the "supernatural common sense" called the *sensus fidelium*.

Our Lord Jesus Christ could never wish His clergy and faithful to be deprived of the powerful weapon and consolation of holy water. Neither could Holy Mother Church, His immaculate Bride, who wills what He wills. It could only be the devil who would want to see holy water disappear from our churches, rectories, and homes, as it gives him more freedom to prowl about the world, seeking the ruin of souls. Therefore, any prohibition on the blessing of holy water can *never* have its origin from God or the Church, but only from the devil.

Priests have a grave obligation, in conscience, to obey God and the Church of all ages, and to seek the salvation of souls and their liberation from the Evil One. They will therefore know what to do in such alarming circumstances: if they cannot bless holy water from the *Rituale* in public, they will do so in private. They will never deprive themselves or their people of this sacramental. And they will avoid altogether the "Book of Blessings"—an ineffective substitute for the real tools of the trade.

19

The Need for Mutual Humility and Support

I N RESPONSE TO POPE FRANCIS'S DECISION IN January 2019 to suppress the Pontifical Commission *Ecclesia Dei* and let its functions be absorbed by the then Congregration for the Doctrine of the Faith, the Priestly Society of St Pius X issued a snubbing statement:

> One conclusion is evident: as the so-called Ecclesia Dei communities have preserved "their spiritual and liturgical traditions," they clearly do not count in this discussion. If they remain attached to a section of the Congregation for the Doctrine of the Faith, it is incidental. They can have the Mass, the "spiritual and liturgical traditions," but not the whole doctrine that goes along with them. That has always been the Society of St Pius X's great reproach against Dom Gérard [Calvet] and all those who thought they should break the unity of Tradition in order to negotiate a purely practical agreement. The crisis of the Church cannot be reduced to a spiritual or liturgical question alone. It is deeper, for it touches the very heart of the Faith and the doctrine of Revelation, Christ the King's right to reign here below over men and over societies.

This statement is curious, to say the least. If the liturgy really is the primary theology of the Church and we truly believe the axiom *lex orandi*, *lex credendi*, then maintaining the *usus antiquior* and the ascetical-mystical spirituality that sustains and surrounds it is, in practice, already to maintain "the very heart of the Faith and the doctrine of Revelation," which, incidentally, includes a primacy of honor and jurisdiction on the part of the supreme pontiff. In fact, everything Catholics believe—including "Christ the King's right to reign here below over men and over societies," on which the reformed liturgy is virtually silent[1]—can be directly deduced

---

1 For a further explanation of how the new (post-Paul VI) version of the feast of Christ the King differs notably from the preconciliar one of Pius XI, see my

from the preconciliar Roman liturgy that *all* "Ecclesia Dei communities" treasure.

We might, in fact, turn the tables by noting that it is the "so-called Ecclesia Dei communities" that are recovering the ancient liturgical tradition found in the pre-1955 Holy Week ceremonies and other aspects of the Roman Rite's earlier traditional practice (e.g., abundant octaves, additional collects, doubling the readings, folded chasubles, proper last Gospels), while the SSPX, as far as I know, continues merrily on with the suppressions and distortions of Pius XII and John XXIII. Whatever his other magnificent qualities, Archbishop Lefebvre was somewhat naïve about the extent of the damage that had already been done to the liturgy prior to 1962. If he held on to this "last missal" in order to stem the tide of incipient sedevacantism, it sounds to me like a different version of "breaking the unity of Tradition in order to negotiate a purely practical agreement."[2]

---

articles "Should the Feast of Christ the King Be Celebrated in October or November?," *Rorate Caeli*, October 22, 2014; "Between Christ the King and 'We Have No King But Caesar,'" *OnePeterFive*, October 25, 2020; and "May His Kingdom Come: Catholic Social Teaching, Part VII – The Kingship of Christ, Source and Summit of the Social Order," *Catholic Family News* online, October 25, 2020; cf. Michael Foley, "A Reflection on the Fate of the Feast of Christ the King," *New Liturgical Movement*, October 21, 2020.

2   Thus, we are not surprised in the least to find certain original members of the FSSP, who were once under the wing of Archbishop Lefebvre, praising him for his "pastoral approach" to liturgy. They use this to justify aberrations like reciting the readings in the vernacular facing the people instead of chanting them in Latin facing eastwards or northwards at a *Missa cantata* or even a *Missa solemnis.* "Pastoral," indeed – and so strangely reminiscent of the aspirations of Jungmann, Parsch, Bouyer, Bugnini, and countless others whose cumulative "pastoral wisdom" birthed the Novus Ordo Missae in all its celebrated pastorality.

Lefebvre landed on the 1962 books simply because they were the last *editio typica* he believed to have been promulgated by lawful authority prior to the devastations unleashed by the Council. The Instructions of 1964 and 1967 were not to be followed because they expressly referred to *Sacrosanctum Concilium*, which Lefebvre, although a signatory in 1963, had come to see as a Trojan Horse, and especially because they implemented the program of the Consilium. It is possible that Lefebvre – like Pope John XXIII himself, who still celebrated the Liturgy of the Presanctified Gifts even after his predecessor had set it aside – would have preferred the pre-1962 rites but judged that he, as bishop or superior, would not have the right to make such a momentous choice on his own, and that it would have obscured his position on the papacy.

Again, there is a certain irony here: the very proximity of the "Ecclesia Dei" communities to their Roman contacts (which is considered "selling out" by their critics) facilitated their use of the older (pre-Pius XII) form of Holy Week, whereas the SSPX, standing at a greater distance, was never given (an admittedly

On the other hand, members of the FSSP have not hesitated to launch broadsides over the years at the wayward parents from whom the children have departed. One of its founders stated rather bluntly: "I pray very much for my old, good friends [in the SSPX] to join the Church" (!) and to "come in without any conditions," but to "accept the authority of the living magisterium."

I do not and would not criticize the judgments of conscience that led to the founding of the FSSP in July 1988. Good-willed Catholics have disagreed and will continue to disagree in their interpretations of Archbishop Lefebvre's dramatic step, but there is no question that he freely acted against the provisions of canon law and a solemn papal injunction to desist. If one is given the option, one should attend an *usus antiquior* Mass offered by a priest in "good standing" with the Church.[3]

It is disappointing to see the one priestly Fraternity attacking, or speaking dismissively of, the other. I understand why this happens, as there are serious issues at stake; but it still leaves me wondering if they realize the direness of an ecclesial situation in which "all hands on deck" should be the prevailing motto. Laity, in my experience, have a stronger sense of the importance of being flexible and "tradumenical" in this cancer phase of the postconciliar disease.

ST PIUS X AND THE SSPX

We might ponder a divine irony in the Fraternities' very names, which suggest two faces, like that of the ancient Roman god Janus.

---

unnecessary) "permission" to do so. They could at some point formally request the right to revert to an earlier edition of the missal, but given the sensitive nature of the ecclesial situation, this issue would be far down on their list.

As Fr Hunwicke recently pointed out, our liturgical hindsight is 20/20. In the 1950s and even through the 1960s, the trajectory from Pius X's breviary to Pius XII's Holy Week to Paul VI's Novus Ordo was not clear to most observers. At the time, Lefebvre and others may have considered all of Pius X's actions mantled in his sanctity, and all of Pius XII's reforms to have been moderate and worthy of acceptance. It was only subsequently, when the full horror of the constructivism, presentism, utilitarianism, rationalism, and papal voluntarism of Paul VI's "reform" became apparent, that a more comprehensive critique of the twentieth-century reformist program began to emerge. Today, this critique is increasingly widespread, but in 1965, 1970, or 1975 one would have looked for it largely in vain. For an overview of the superiority of the pre-55 Roman Rite, see Kwasniewski, *Once and Future Roman Rite*, chapter 12.

3   A fuller treatment of this topic, with some important qualifications, is provided in the following two chapters.

First, the Priestly Society named after St Pius X. Every true Catholic admires Pius X for his authoritative condemnation of Modernism, that "collection of all heresies," and his vigorous (although unfortunately unsuccessful) efforts to suppress the Modernists; for his unequivocal condemnation of the principle of the separation of Church and State in his encyclical *Vehementer Nos*; for his promotion of Gregorian chant in *Tra le Sollecitudini* and his condemnation of the use of pianos in church (still in effect, although widely ignored); for his encouragement of a lower age for First Communion and of the practice of frequent Communion for the well-disposed.

However, there is one blotch on his papal escutcheon: the violence he did to the Roman Breviary with his radical reforms of 1911.[4] Many popes have added this or that small feature to the liturgy – a new feast, a new preface, a new octave, the prayers at the foot of the altar and the Last Gospel; many have modified the rubrics; very occasionally they have pruned elements deemed overgrowths, such as Pius V's removal of certain obviously legendary saints from the calendar of the 1570 *Missale Romanum*.[5] But never had a pope dared to alter in such a radical and thoroughgoing way any of the Latin Church's ancient liturgical offices. When Pius X had the *Breviarium Romanum* dismantled and reconfigured in the early twentieth century, he was not merely setting aside something that had been constructed in the sixteenth century, as liturgists can be found to assert; he was altering a rule of prayer so old its origins cannot be discerned. Indeed, there is strong reason to think that the daily recitation of the Laudate psalms (148–150), from which the

---

4 See Gregory DiPippo, "Compendium of the Reforms of the Roman Breviary, 1568–1961: Part 7.2 – The Breviary Reforms of St. Pius X (Continued)," *New Liturgical Movement*, November 3, 2009.

5 The claim that Pope Pius V "removed lots of sequences" is something of an urban legend (see Gregory DiPippo, "What Really Happened to the Sequences?," *New Liturgical Movement*, May 5, 2022). Unlike other uses around Europe, which added Sequences with abandon, the Missal of the Roman Curia, the medieval predecessor of the Missal of St Pius V, had not (out of classically Roman conservatism) added any more beyond the four great ones it already contained (*Victimae Paschali laudes*, *Veni sancte Spiritus*, *Lauda Sion*, and *Dies Irae*; the *Stabat Mater* came much later). After 1570, whenever local churches voluntarily adopted the use of Rome, this had the effect, arguably unfortunate, of losing the regional Sequences. The same thing happened with some who, though retaining their proper uses, like the Premonstratensians, recast them in imitation of the Roman Missal.

very hour of Lauds derives its name, is traceable to the Jews of the time of Christ and therefore, with great likelihood, was practiced by Our Lord Himself in His prayers on earth.

There *were* problems with the breviary at the turn of the twentieth century; no one disputes this point. But Pius X's solution was *not* to retain the office as it stood while modifying its rubrics so that (e.g.) the weekly *cursus* of 150 psalms would be prioritized over the festal psalms, or perhaps some hours, such as Matins, would become optional for secular clergy, in order to conserve the integrity and harmony of the breviary as a whole. Instead, Pius X became the first pope in the history of the Latin Church who, freely spending the abundant capital of ultramontanism, threw the weight of his office behind the construction of a new Divine Office. In this way he provided the very premise of papal contructivism that offered Pius XII the precedent for revamping Holy Week in similar fashion from 1948 to 1955, and Paul VI for transmogrifying everything from 1964 to the mid-1970s.[6] Paradoxically, the pope who fought valiantly against doctrinal modernism exemplified liturgical modernism by rupturing the principle of the inviolability of longstanding tradition in the name of easing up pastoral burdens. If this sounds eerily familiar, it should.

Bishop Athanasius Schneider had the courage to address this issue in an interview, which is worth quoting from at length:

> The reform of the breviary under Pius X, in 1911, was unfortunately also a revolutionary reform. It is for me an enigma how he could do this, Pope Pius X, because he changed completely the entire structure of the psalm distribution, which the Roman Church kept almost inviolably since the times – even before – of Pope Gregory I. So, already from the sixth century, maybe even earlier – substantially, through at least 1,300 years – the Roman Church had always kept the order of the distribution of psalms in the breviary during the week. The order of psalms was called the *cursus romanus* (*cursus*, meaning the course or sequence): the psalms are running through the week, from Sunday to Saturday. It was very harmonious, very

---

6   By "papal constructivism" I mean a Cartesian attitude of *technē* whereby the pope sees himself as the "master and possessor" of the liturgical rites, losing the attitude of profound piety towards the family inheritance.

logical, when you observe it. And Pius X completely, radically, changed the entire distribution of psalms. It never happened thus in the Roman Church. This is for me an enigma. How could he make such a revolution?

Of course, he had some pastoral motives about unburdening the secular priests, to lighten their burden. But this could be done in a way not touching, substantially, the order of psalms, which the Roman Church always kept. The problem was Matins, because it had 12 psalms in the weekly office, and for some diocesan priests it was too much. The pope could have avoided touching the *cursus romanus psalmorum* and allowed the diocesan priests to pray maybe only half of them, six for example. So Matins would already be lightened. But the religious priests and the nuns who have to pray as their first duty, they would pray all of it. Unfortunately, the pope changed everything, even for the nuns and for all religious, maybe with the Benedictines as the only exception, who were allowed to keep their traditional psalmody. So I repeat: it would be sufficient to make a provision specifically for the clergy who are in pastoral work to lighten the burden of praying the amount of psalms, without changing substantially the order or structure of the millennium-old Roman liturgy of the Divine Office.

I hope that in the future, the Church will return to the traditional Holy Week, pre-'55, substantially, maybe with some slight modifications that will not touch the substance. And the same with the breviary — to return to the pre-Pius X breviary, which I call "The Breviary of All Ages," with maybe some modifications that would be reasonable. But I repeat: not touching the substance of it. I shall repeat: the Church has to do all these things very carefully, and she had always done this wisely in the past. The popes have to be conscious that they are not the owners of the liturgy and the rites, but the keepers and the guardians of them.[7]

Thus, the very saint to whom the SSPX is dedicated shows us two sides in tension: the zealous promoter of Catholic dogma, and the activist reformer who treated part of the liturgy as if it were a

---

7 "Bishop Schneider on Chastity vs. a Society 'Becoming Ever More Cruel,'" *OnePeterFive*, September 21, 2018.

mechanism to be rebuilt rather than a living organism to be nurtured or an inheritance of the saints to be treasured.

ST PETER AND THE FSSP

The heavenly patron of the Priestly Fraternity of St Peter also offers us two sides in tension: the Peter who confessed Christ as the Son of God and received the keys of the kingdom of heaven; and the Peter who tried to remonstrate with Christ and received His rebuke: "Get behind me, Satan." We see in the New Testament the Peter who preached the first homily on the first Pentecost and won over thousands of souls to the Church; we also see the Peter who, from human respect, denied his Master in the Passion, and later declined to associate with Gentile converts, for which he merited the sharp rebuke of his fellow apostle Paul. As Joseph Ratzinger pointed out, the long course of Church history has displayed both faces of Peter, when his successors have acted as a stable rock of doctrinal orthodoxy and sure-handed governance, or as men acting on their own fallible initiative, ambitious, worldly, profligate, compromising.[8]

Leaving aside this pervasive duality between office and incumbent, we may say that the patronage of St Peter is likely to take one of two forms in the Catholic Church of the Tridentine and especially post-Vatican I period. The saint can symbolize either adherence to authentic apostolic tradition, which will pit him against Protestantism and its offspring in matters of dogma, ethics, and worship; *or* he can symbolize the spirit of ultramontanism – a false exaltation of the pope, a papal personality cult, which some have named hyperpapalism or papolatry.

Manifestations of contemporary hyperpapalism can be obvious or subtle. For obvious manifestations we need only look to the circle of sycophants who applaud a pope's every word and gesture. For a subtle manifestation, consider the deafening silence on the part of many traditionalists to the pope's most appalling statements and actions; the desire to project an image of "toeing the line" in public, while rejecting it in private. One understands why, in a time of persecution, members of traditional religious communities would

---

8 Joseph Ratzinger, *Called to Communion: Understanding the Church Today*, trans. Adrian Walker (San Francisco: Ignatius Press, 1996), 47–74, esp. 61 and 72–74; cf. Kwasniewski, *Hyperpapalism to Catholicism*, 1:28–53, 71–76.

keep their lips sealed, for fear of reprisal; but one would think that, out of self-respect, members of such communities would then refrain from speaking against Catholics who *do* raise their voices to protest open deviations from dominical, apostolic, and ecclesiastical tradition.

The irony, then, is that one community, which has fallen out of favor with the popes on account of its outspoken battle against modernism, is dedicated to a pope who was himself both an anti-modernist and, in a way, a proto-modernist; while another community, which has always retained papal favor on account of its willingness to refrain from explicit criticism of any pope, is dedicated to the first pope, who was himself a rock of faith and a stumbling block, and has become, in our times, a symbol claimed for the permanent charism of truth as well as for the pseudo-charism of *fiat voluntas mea.*

These sobering reflections, it seems to me, should prompt in everyone – whether persevering quietly under the patronage of the Church and the tiara of Peter, or fighting manfully on the open field while bleeding from the wounds of irregularity – a deep humility in thanking God for any and all of the gifts He has given to tradition-loving Catholics in this time of ever-intensifying spiritual warfare. It is a time for making alliances on behalf of perennial doctrine, sound morals, and authentic liturgy, not for waging battle on two fronts.

20

On the SSPX and the Situation of Catholics in the Trenches

DEDICATION OF THE IMMACULATA

O N MAY 3, 2023, A MAGNIFICENT NEW CHURCH was dedicated in St Marys, Kansas. It surely counts as one of the most ambitious traditional churches built since "The Council"; indeed, it is said to be the second largest church in the state of Kansas. Its other claim to fame is more intriguing: it was built by the Society of St Pius X (SSPX) for their burgeoning flock. Needless to say, the church was bursting at the seams with faithful,[1] and, subsequent to its dedication, settled into a rhythm of four Sunday Masses and three Masses on weekdays.[2]

Of particular interest was a statement from the archdiocese of Kansas City that sent a mixed message: though discouraging Catholics from attending Mass at the Immaculata because its Masses are "not licitly offered," the archdiocese wished it to be known that "it does not consider the SSPX to be schismatic," that "one may fulfill one's obligation to participate at Holy Mass on Sundays and Holy Days of obligation by attending an SSPX Mass," and that SSPX marriages done at the Immaculata are valid because faculties for witnessing them are requested from, and granted by, the archdiocese. This may not be a warm welcome, but it's not exactly the cold shoulder treatment either.

---

1 The video of the consecration and dedication ceremony was livestreamed on YouTube; the resulting five-and-a-half hour video is available there. Photos are easy to find online. Two articles on the Immaculata event are worth reading: Eric Sammons, "Our Incurious Bishops," *Crisis Magazine*, May 8, 2023, and Kennedy Hall, "Little Christendom on the Prairie," *OnePeterFive*, May 9, 2023.
2 Mass schedule taken from www.anewimmaculata.org on November 13, 2023.

A RETIRED DIOCESAN BISHOP SPEAKS OUT

The SSPX has never *not* been in the news, but I would venture to say attention to it skyrocketed after July 21, 2021, when Pope Francis issued his declaration of war against the traditional Latin Mass and the faithful who attend it.

It is therefore of more than minor interest that the emeritus bishop of Chur, Switzerland, the Most Rev. Vitus Huonder, who had been appointed by then-Prefect of the then-Congregation for the Doctrine of the Faith Cardinal Müller to investigate the SSPX — discovered upon closer examination that he basically agreed with Lefebvre's positions. Having received permission to retire in an SSPX community (complete with Pope Francis's blessing), he has taken to the screen to offer a remarkable commentary on what he has learned. Filmed on March 31, 2023, the well-produced three-part series is entitled *The Great Wound* (in German, with English subtitles). Each part is well worth watching and pondering.

A lot of people made a big deal of Bishop Huonder's claim, in part 1, that Pope Francis said to him outright: "They [the SSPX] are not schismatics." Let's be both honest and consistent here. If Pope Francis is indeed one of the worst popes in history, with a catastrophic track record in doctrine and governance, we shouldn't suddenly applaud when he says something we happen to like. I wouldn't trust Francis to recognize heresy or schism (or their opposites, for that matter) if they stood up and hit him over the head with a shovel. Perhaps someone might say it's a good rhetorical strategy to toss Francis's *obiter dicta* like so many grenades at the anti-traditionalists, but we should be merciful to those who are already tormented by their own internal contradictions. Besides, they are likely to say: "A stray remark doesn't count as magisterial." And they would be right.

THE SOCIETY'S ANTAGONISTS

Anyone who has "gone into the weeds" knows that there is a vast literature by now on the SSPX, ranging from those, on one extreme, who accuse it of schism plain and simple, to those, on the other, who defend it as a redoubtable bastion of straight-up Catholicism.[3] I have generally kept quiet on this debate, although I follow it

---

3   The former perspective has become the obsession of John Salza and Robert Siscoe; the latter perspective is elegantly represented by Kennedy Hall.

with keen attention and occasionally make an observation where it seems warranted.

Opponents of the SSPX typically rest their case on the notions of "full communion" and "canonical mission."[4] Their argument requires one to believe that if the pope outlawed the Latin Mass entirely, tradition-loving Catholics would have no choice but to swallow that decision and go back to the Novus Ordo. Indeed, Catholics would be required, by the force of logic, to believe that a Fr James Martin or a Fr Michael Pfleger are "in full communion" – that they act with the Church's mandate and their Masses bear the stamp of approval – while Fr Gladtrad Fiddleback, SSPX, down the road, offering the Mass of the Ages "outside of communion," robs the sheepfold and prevents Catholics from fulfilling their obligations.

Such arguments are very easy to come by. They are, in my opinion, specious at best and injurious at worst, as they ignore the prescriptive rights of tradition, the prior duties of the hierarchy toward the faithful, and the normal requirements of orthodox Catholic communal life. In short, they treat authority and obedience in an absolutist and positivist way, and fail to grasp their intimate relationship with the common good.[5]

The militant and legalistic attacks on the Society have provoked a number of responses worth pondering. *OnePeterFive* has run a long series of articles pro and con, in which (in my opinion) the pro side has gotten the better of it. Kennedy Hall published a book, *SSPX: The Defence*, which is well worth reading. Paul Casey, in his article "SSPX Masses and Fulfilling the Sunday Obligation,"[6] furnishes a detailed defense of the claim implied in the title; you might say Casey is providing the arguments that undergird the archdiocese of Kansas City's assertions.

A friend of mine attempted to put in a nutshell the logical shape of the case for the SSPX. He did not do this to support the case (or, for that matter, to attack it), but to manifest its essence. I find his syllogistic presentation helpful for this reason, since the search for clarity on this subject is often hampered by clouds of emotion.

---

4   See Brian McCall, "The Ordinary Mission of the SSPX – Reply to Salza," *OnePeterFive*, January 17, 2022.
5   See chapters 7–10.
6   *Catholic Family News* online, April 28, 2023.

The SSPX position can be boiled down to the following argument:

1. In an emergency, rules that correspond to the nature of the emergency cease to bind.[7]

2. The Church is in an ongoing state of emergency.

3. Therefore, the rules that correspond to the nature of the Church's ongoing state of emergency do not bind.

4. Violations of non-binding rules are entirely permissible.

5. The SSPX violates certain ecclesiastical rules that correspond to the rules that are non-binding.

6. Therefore, the SSPX's violations of certain ecclesiastical rules are entirely permissible.

It should be noted that any arguments demonstrating that the SSPX is breaking rules are arguments that are undisputed by, and even baked into, the SSPX's argument.

As lines 1 and 4 are undisputed principles of moral theology, and as lines 3 and 6 are logically-following conclusions, the entirety of the SSPX question can be boiled down to the veracity of minor premises 2 and 5. In other words:

· Is the Church in an ongoing state of emergency?
· If so, which rules are suspended?
· Do the rules that the SSPX is breaking correspond to the rules that are suspended?

Let us bear the foregoing analysis in mind as we proceed.

ARE THE ORDINARY FAITHFUL WORTH ANYTHING?

One point I especially appreciated in the first part of Bishop Huonder's interview was his emphasis on how the faithful, after the Council, were left abandoned, confused, and scandalized by novel teachings and liturgical wreckage, and *no one seemed to care* — they were like the sacrificial meat that had to be offered to the mouth of the insatiable idol of Progress. Archbishop Lefebvre actually cared about them, cared enough to feed them with truth and grace. He was not the only one, certainly, but he was among

---

7   In the case of a dangerous house fire, the rule forbidding jaywalking would not bind; however, the rule forbidding killing would still bind.

the most courageous and uncompromising. And his "cancellation" was nothing but the modernist-progressivist organism defending itself against the virus of orthodoxy.

I am quite sick and tired of people who, for all intents and purposes, ignore the plight of the ordinary faithful, even today; who seem to think the only thing that can possibly matter is for Catholics to "stay in communion" with whomever and do whatever, even if it's false or harmful, unworthy of Our Lord and of souls purchased by His Blood, even if it's likely to lead their children to exit a lame-duck charade they will soon grow bored with. No: this attitude is insulting, irrational, inhuman, intolerable. Parents, in particular, have an obligation to seek out tried and true ways of supporting their own life of faith and the transmission of faith to the next generations.

In an email to me, a "convert" to tradition told the following familiar story—one that I have heard (in its many accidental variations) so many times by now that I could recite it like a schoolboy discharging his assigned poetry:

> I had hoped our local parish community would offer the support we needed in reinforcing the Catholic morals and values we are teaching at home but, as you can imagine, this has not been my experience. We have met a couple of families who have become dear friends, but the experience as a whole—from the lack of reverence in dress, the behavior in Mass, the lack of reverence in how we receive our Lord, let alone how the pastor "expects us" to receive our Lord—left me deflated and exhausted. After many cringeworthy liturgies filled with cheesy songs and uninspiring (at best) homilies, I knew there *had* to be something else out there. Initially I only found the "something else" online. I don't even remember how it started but it went somehow from Dr Scott Hahn to Fr Chad Ripperger, to the FSSP, to listening (during Covid) to the homilies of traditional priests: all this led me to researching reverent Masses in our area. We tried to visit an FSSP parish but they are 2+ hours away from us. So, I was left with the SSPX priory that is only a half-hour from our home. I did not know much about them but knew about the "controversies." I decided I would see for myself. I went to

one Mass . . . and found myself weeping like a child. The beauty of the liturgy, the reverence of the priests and people, the Gregorian chant – it made my heart swell with love and the fire of the Holy Ghost. Their orthodox preaching, their confessions, it all now made sense. It felt like home. Traditional Catholicism feels like home to me.

There it is. The *sensus fidelium* at work. Who can seriously criticize this person's motivations: the hunger for truth without any watering-down, the thirst for reverence with which to honor God and refresh the soul, the sense of divine beauty finally encountered, the coherence of a Catholic community and way of life? All of this is just as it should be: we *ought* to have these motivations. They are from God and lead us to Him.

WHAT SHOULD BELIEVERS DO IN A TIME OF CRISIS?

Granted: intuitions and experiences like the foregoing do not instantly translate into "therefore the SSPX"; but they categorically rule out: "just accept the status quo as it's dished out to you," with pervasive desacralization and ragged ruptures from tradition, liberalism and cultural conformism, numbing tepidity and indifference, gaslighting and hypocrisy, and the rest of the traits that, in varying combinations, make up the masonic mosaic of what many, impervious to the evidence of their own senses, are still pleased to call the "Catholic Church."

Instead: go to where you find Catholic Tradition loved, honored, preserved, passed on. That is the fundamental instinct of the *sensus fidelium* when it has not been stifled by a false Jesuitical notion of blind obedience. It is the grace of baptism and confirmation surging up to the surface and cutting through the self-serving nonsense of prelates who, like the Pharisees, multiply burdens while not lifting a finger to help.

If members of the hierarchy (or their eager-beaver apologists) expect the laity to "pay, pray, and obey," then let them *man up*, let them "apostle up" as it were, and provide something worth paying for, a liturgy worth praying with, and an authority worth obeying. Otherwise, shut up and shutter up, and let the rest of us build *as* Catholics and *for* Catholics.

As a father of a large family wrote to me:

> I don't have twenty or thirty years to wait around while Bishop Weathervane, Auxiliary Bishop Rainbow, Pastor Getalong, Parochial Vicar Sadtrad, and all the Karens and Susans in the parish, work out their problems and get back to something that kinda functions like Catholicism again. I don't have time or even ability to be a grassroots reformer. Canonical niceties are above my pay grade. It's hard enough to be a serious Catholic in the modern world, and even harder to keep your kids in the Church, without having to fight internal battles all the time.
>
> We go to a chapel that provides me and my family with sound preaching, beautiful liturgy, and like-minded families doing the same thing. There's nothing like it anywhere else for a hundred miles. To me, it's an absolute no-brainer that this is where we should go. When I stand before the Judgment Seat, Christ will not ask me: "Did you check off the canonical boxes?" He will ask: "What did you do with the souls I entrusted to you? And how did you keep the flame alive in your own soul?"
>
> If there is something "irregular" about our current situation, so be it; I trust Jesus to work it out. The cause of this crisis does not rest with the laity, but with the hierarchy. It is *their* mess, *their* responsibility, and they will answer for it. When my local bishop shows himself supportive of a traditional Catholic way of life, then by all means I will be right there at his side. Meanwhile, we pray for him and for the pope every night in our family rosary.

That pretty much sums up where a lot of good Catholics are nowadays. Not only do I *not* blame this father, I *praise* him for being a good, clear-sighted, loving, valiant, and disciplined father.

"AS FOR ME AND MY HOUSE, WE WILL SERVE THE LORD"

I attend a chapel of the Priestly Fraternity of St Peter (FSSP) and love it. I don't agree with certain SSPXers who claim that the "Ecclesia Dei" institutes are full of cowardice and compromise. On the contrary, I find the Ecclesia Dei clergy to be generally of stellar quality and orthodoxy. If they choose to focus their preaching on the Creed, the Commandments, and other basic themes of the spiritual life,

I don't put that down to some kind of unwillingness to confront modern errors. The pulpit is not the lecture podium. For that matter, apart from some excellent interventions by Fr Davide Pagliarani, the SSPX has been strangely quiet during the last ten years, and has shown itself sluggish, not to say closed-minded, about recovering the fullness of the traditional (that is, pre-55) Roman liturgy. [8]

I believe that it is better to have *as many positives* (so to speak) as one can have: traditional liturgy; orthodox preaching; vibrant community; full communion with the pope and local ordinary. Therefore, given a choice, I will always go to the FSSP or ICKSP rather than the SSPX. But if I were traveling and the only traditional Latin Mass available were a Mass offered by the SSPX, I would gladly and gratefully attend it.

We should be adamantly opposed to reducing all goods to one alone: "full communion." We should be opposed to the laity being treated like expendable cannon fodder. We should be opposed to simplistic and superficial "solutions" that amount to giving Fr James Martin or Fr Michael Pfleger more "official standing" in Christ's Church than Fr Gladtrad Fiddleback, SSPX; that amount to giving the rupturous Novus Ordo at a regular parish more "official standing" than the rapturous Mass of the Ages at a mission chapel. Anyone who thinks this kind of thing "makes sense" because "canonical" (check box) and "approved by neoscholastic manuals" (check box) will, I solemnly predict, prove to be a ready recruit for the final synodal push of the modernist onslaught. Such a person can, if he wants, offer himself and his children as cannon fodder, but I won't ever do it, and I will defend to the death the right of my fellow Catholics not to do it.

If anything is a notorious scandal, it would have to be this: that the flourishing chapels of the SSPX — brimming with men, women, children, future religious and priestly vocations, all striving to serve the Lord as best they can with the treasures of tradition, holding their own against a ferociously secular, irreligious, anti-Christian age — have not, long since, been fully integrated into diocesan life as flagships of Catholicism. Such an outcome seemed distinctly possible under Benedict XVI, but the wolves that always surrounded him successfully outmaneuvered him on that front.

---

8 See the preceding chapter.

WHO, EXACTLY, ARE THE SCHISMATICS?

Many consider the SSPX to be "in schism." Since the SSPX is by definition a clerical association, this could only mean that the *clergy* who staff the chapels are in schism. Thus, these critics fear that assisting at Society liturgies and listening to their clergy's preaching will induce a "schismatic mentality."

But what if the real problem we are facing is a *pope* who has become schismatic vis-à-vis the Faith and the Church? Canonists and theologians for centuries took seriously the possibility that a pope could either fall into heresy or become schismatic. Ever since Vatican I, people have falsely (and lazily) assumed that neither is possible. That is a premature and imprudent curtailment of Catholic theology, and it has caused us immeasurable harm. We are now handicapped by inadequate tools, by an idealism that hides behind mammoth implausibilies and twisted rationalizations.

It is not hard to see that the peculiar push for "synodality" as wielded by its proponents (e.g., Cardinals Grech and Hollerich) has schismatic and heretical characteristics, even if only the Germans and Belgians have taken steps to formalize them, rushing ahead to smooth out the path for the rest. Above all, it is not hard to see that Pope Francis has sown not only ambiguities – that weasel word with the versatility of a Swiss Army knife – but also *errors*; that he has, to a greater extent than any other pope in history, weakened Catholic faith and morals in a host of well-documented ways.[9]

In short: it is far easier to see schism or a schismatic mentality in Pope Francis and the German bishops than in any bishop or priest of the SSPX. The former have deviated from dogma, tradition, and liturgy; the latter adhere to them inflexibly while accepting an irregular status resulting from the unwillingness of ecclesiastical authorities to rule for the common good. Even in this dreadful scenario, however, there is nothing that undermines Vatican I's (narrow) teaching on the infallibility of the pope or on the *actual purpose* of the pope's office, which is to hand down the Catholic Faith he himself has received; there is nothing in our ecclesial crisis that undermines the indefectibility of the Church, understood rigorously and not romantically.

---

9 See Lamont and Pierantoni, *Defending the Faith*; Lamont, "Pope Francis as Public Heretic."

Moreover, nearly everything I have read by Lefebvre has struck me as more Catholic, more sane, more truthful, more accurate, than nearly anything I have seen in the words or writings of Pope Francis. Again, bracketing the 1988 consecrations, Lefebvre was far less defective and controversial in his episcopal conduct than Roncalli, Montini, Wojtyła, or Ratzinger, because, as he often said, he continued to believe and to do what everyone had believed and done until the collective hysteria that took hold after Vatican II. What a poignant memory is shared in this reflection by a French priest:

> My grandfather was a Lefebvrist.... He had organized dozens of retreats for men. He ran the village choir. Overnight, his parish priest told him not to sing a single word of Latin and ordered work to be carried out to break up the beautiful marble altar and replace it with a roughly squared cube of wood, in homage to Christ the worker against bourgeois oppression. *In extremis*, the bishop prevented the massacre. The sacred vessels disappeared, replaced by rough-hewn pottery, and the ornaments were rotting in the empty, moth-eaten confessionals. He spoke to me of those difficult years for the rest of his life, like a wound that never healed. He couldn't bear the violence of the liturgical change. Many had left religious practice. He had found in Archbishop Lefebvre what he had always known. [10]

The archbishop's key role in moderating the victories of progressivism at the Council should, all by itself, win him the respect and admiration of all Catholics who still believe in the Deposit of Faith. [11]

Yes, at times Lefebvre seems to have suffered from paranoia. He had a tendency to give certain texts, persons, or situations the worst possible interpretation. I agree with Henry Sire in *Phoenix from the Ashes* that Lefebvre acted hastily in the matter of the 1988 consecrations (and this judgment is from an historian who, at the end of his book, predicts that Lefebvre will one day be canonized!). Nevertheless, in his career as a bishop, superior general, and

---

10   Fr Luc de Bellescize, "The True Meaning of Our Liturgies," *Rorate Caeli*, June 6, 2023.
11   See Jerome Stridon, "The Coetus: Trad Godfathers at Vatican II," *OnePeter-Five*, December 12, 2022.

archbishop, Lefebvre was characterized by better, more realistic, more pastorally charitable, and more courageous decisions than (*mutatis mutandis*) John XXIII, Paul VI, John Paul II, or Benedict XVI. If any of those hierarchs deserves to be canonized, Lefebvre deserves it more. The fact that the poster-children of the Council are rushed to the honors of the altar while Lefebvre is vilified only shows the extent to which church affairs remain in the hands of ideologues and apparatchiks (not to mention nihilists, sodomites, Freemasons, and Satanists, who are all represented at the Vatican and in the upper echelons of ecclesial power).

DON'T BOX ME IN

A careful reader of this chapter will not be able to "claim" me definitively for any particular side in the traditionalist "wars." This isn't a matter of my wishing to enjoy a perch on the fence, with a nice 360-degree view. I have plenty of skin in the game and many definite commitments I do not shy away from stating and defending. But when I do not have sufficient certainty about something, I will not bluff or bluster my way ahead. I don't see it as necessary, much less desirable, that I should defend *this* traditionalist group *against* that one. You could sum up my attitude as "tradumenical."

In this essay I have upheld the reasonableness of the *ordinary faithful* wishing to attend SSPX chapels, and the unreasonableness of those who would hold them back without providing a concrete alternative to the disaster from which the faithful are often fleeing. Yet my saying this does not translate into a complete and total endorsement of the Society or its positions. I have indicated that I assist at a chapel run by one of the Ecclesia Dei institutes and have said why.

For reasons of space, I haven't even broached the far more complicated topic of diocesan traditional Latin Mass communities, which from 2007 (sometimes much earlier) down to 2021 had played an ever-increasing role in a positive and constructive response to the crisis in the Church, but which are now under severe attack in many places by the "prison-guards of treachery" (as one might translate "*custodes traditionis*"). Diocesan priests, in particular, have been thrust into a crucible of hierarchy-inflicted suffering from which many outcomes can be expected, ranging from great holiness to nervous breakdowns, from SSPX crossovers to lost vocations.

What is clear to me is that, in a situation as confusing and chaotic as the present one, the laity must do what their conscience judges right before God — and this is not a decision that can be "outsourced" to anyone else. We must form our consciences as best we can, with reference to Scripture, Tradition, and the Church's Magisterium, while seeking advice from those we trust, and *always* praying for light, staying close to the Blessed Virgin Mary. When the time for acting is at hand, we must act on whatever moral certainties we have, and on the intuitions and inclinations born of the Catholic Faith. Let no one dare to condemn anyone for doing just that.

21

The Sunday Mass Obligation in a Time of Liturgical Crisis

THE SUNDAY MASS OBLIGATION – IN PARTICular, the circumstances under which it may cease to bind – is a topic of considerable practical importance in our times. Resisting the language used by many bishops during the Covid shutdowns, Raymond Leo Cardinal Burke emphasized that the objective duty to worship God in the way He has specified – namely, through participating in the sacramental renewal of the sacrifice of Christ on the Cross – can never cease in this life, although this duty can cease to bind *subjectively* under certain circumstances. In other words, instead of saying "The obligation has been dispensed/has ceased," one should rather say "the circumstances are such that the obligation does not bind me in this case." It belongs to *the faithful* to make the discernment of these circumstances, guided by correct principles. In a case of serious doubts, one should consult a trustworthy and knowledgeable priest, religious, or layman, but it's important to be aware that in this present time of confusion, opinions are likely to range widely (and sometimes wildly).

DIFFERENT KINDS OF COMMANDMENTS

Catholicism for a long time has tended to be rule-oriented, regarding the do's and the don'ts as a black-and-white list that admits of little to no flexibility. There is, nevertheless, a key difference between negative precepts and positive ones.

Negative commandments – thou shalt not kill (as in: murder), thou shalt not commit adultery, thou shalt not steal – admit of no exceptions, because they specify acts that are *intrinsically evil*, and evil may never be chosen or done, regardless of the situation or the outcomes.

Positive commandments, on the other hand, are binding *when and as* they can be *rightly followed*. For example, one should always honor one's father and mother, but exactly when and how to do this admits of considerable variation, nor is one obliged at every moment to be showing this honor in specific ways, as one is perpetually obliged to avoid evil. Typically we say that positive precepts must be fulfilled *at some time* – or, as Aristotle would say, at the right time, in the right place, in the right manner, etc. These are acts that should by no means be neglected, and we must carry them out often enough to maintain the underlying habit of virtue.

The same is true of the worship of God. It is a positive precept of the Church that we must attend or assist at or hear Mass on Sundays and Holy Days of obligation. (N.B.: This does *not* include receiving Holy Communion; we are obliged to confess and commune only once a year, even if, for our spiritual good, we should seek to do so more often, indeed much more often.) As a positive precept, the commandment to go to Mass is to be followed *when and as* it can be *rightly followed*.

When I began to look into this question more deeply, I was surprised at the broad-minded attitude that older (preconciliar) moralists took on the question of circumstances that make the obligation to attend Mass not binding on an individual or a family. I suspect that in the atomic wasteland of postconciliar Catholicism, conservatives simplified and hardened the black-and-white rules in order to hold on to whatever bits and pieces they could salvage and thus prevent further disintegration. That's understandable. But given the stubborn survival of the 1960s revolution right down to the present day and the worsening liturgical situation in many places, it's time we recover the more supple analysis of our forefathers, who were much more realistic than we tend to be. This, I believe, will help to ease the troubled consciences of laity who feel crushed between a rock and a hard place.

In the first section of this chapter, I will share the plain counsel of widely-read preconciliar moral theologians. This will lay the groundwork for the second section, concerning what the faithful should do in the case of irreverent Masses or the lack of availability of traditional Masses. That will segue into the third section, on why the Novus Ordo should be avoided as a matter of principle. The final section, more in the nature of an appendix, presents some pertinent quotations from Bishop Athanasius Schneider's *Credo: Compendium of the Catholic Faith*.

§1. MORAL THEOLOGIANS

"Spiritual harm to oneself or to another..."

My first source is the Capuchin Fr Heribert Jone, who writes:

> *Excuses from assisting at Mass.* Any moderately grave
> reason suffices to excuse one from assistance at Holy Mass,
> such as considerable hardship or corporal or spiritual
> harm either to oneself or to another. Therefore, the fol-
> lowing are excused: the sick, convalescents, persons who
> cannot endure the air in church (e.g., certain neurotic
> persons and sometimes pregnant women in the first or
> last months of pregnancy); those that have a long way
> to church; people hindered by the duties of their state
> (e.g., shepherds, watchmen, policemen on duty, cooks,
> and those working in mills that may not shut down over
> Sunday); women or children who would incur the grave
> displeasure of their husbands or parents by attending
> Mass; servants whose masters do not permit them to
> attend Mass (should this happen consistently the servants
> should seek other employment); those that care for the
> sick, rescue workers in time of fire or flood; and those who
> have reason to think that by staying home they can hinder
> sin; or who would suffer injury to their good name or
> possessions by going to Church. (Thus: unmarried women
> who are pregnant may remain at home if by doing so they
> can avoid disgrace; similarly, those who lack clothing
> becoming to their social standing; those on a journey;
> those who would suffer the loss of extraordinary gain
> by attending Mass.) One may miss Mass for the sake of a
> pleasure trip once or twice if he has no other opportunity
> during the year, or if it is the last opportunity he will ever
> have for a certain excursion. Finally, custom in certain
> localities excuses such as, for example, lying-in women,
> widows in the first days of their bereavement, engaged
> persons whose marriage banns are published in the only
> Mass they can attend.[1]

I am convinced that very few today would be able to offer so many
(and such) examples of when Catholics are dispensed from the

---

1   Fr Heribert Jone, OFMCap, JCD, *Moral Theology*, trans. Fr Urban Adelman,
in accordance with the eighteenth German edition (Westminster, MD: The
Newman Press, 1962), no. 198, pg. 125. The very first edition of *Moraltheologie*
came out in 1929 and was quickly translated into many languages.

precept, or rather, when the precept ceases to bind. Some of these phrases deserve to be underlined: "spiritual harm either to oneself or to another [think of children![2] . . . those that have a long way to church . . . those who have reason to think that by staying home they can hinder sin . . . those on a journey . . ." I don't know about you, but I can think of plenty of Masses I have experienced or heard about over the decades that either involve sin or constitute proximate occasions of sin!

"Moderately grave inconvenience . . ."

According to Jesuit moralist Fr Henry Davis:

> Any moderately grave inconvenience to mind or body, or to temporal goods, either of oneself, or of another, excuses from the precept. . . . Those are excused who are sick or whose presence is required for care of the sick, or who tend infant children at home, or who do necessary domestic work, or who have no suitable clothes (an excuse rather easy to magnify), or who would have to hear their banns of marriage called (if this prove disconcerting), or those who live at a distance from the church of three miles or an hour's walk, or even less, if the weather is bad, or if they are infirm; the distance that excuses would be greater for those who can use cars, tramway, railway, cycles, without incurring expense which they can ill afford. Servants also are excused, if forbidden by non-Catholic employers to go to Mass, but they should find another place [i.e., job], if reasonably possible, where they could have the opportunity of hearing Mass. A wife is excused, if by going to Mass she would give great offence to her husband; under similar circumstances, children and servants are excused. It is not expected by the Church that servants or labourers should deprive themselves of reasonably necessary sleep that they may be able to assist at an early Mass. Those are excused who would normally remain at home during a period of mourning; mothers, too, after childbirth for some weeks, and of course some weeks before childbirth. It is held that those are excused who would have to forgo – occasionally, but not as a general rule – a good stroke of business or considerable gain,

---

2 See Kwasniewski, *Reclaiming Our Roman Catholic Birthright*, 235–80.

such as would be the case with merchants, and during the lambing season with farmers.[3]

In a 1908 publication, fellow Jesuit Fr Thomas Slater notes:

> We have here to do with a positive precept, and any serious inconvenience or loss, spiritual or temporal, affecting one's self or one's neighbour, which would follow from hearing Mass, will excuse the faithful from fulfilling the obligation. So that the sick, the convalescent who could not venture out of doors without danger, those who have to take care of the sick, mothers of families who have little children to attend to, those who live at such a distance that it would take them more than an hour to walk to church, all these are excused from hearing Mass regularly.[4]

Lastly, consider this passage from two Dominican fathers, John A. McHugh and Charles J. Callan:

> Impossibility or serious inconvenience excuses from hearing Mass – e.g., those who have to walk an hour's journey to church or ride a two hours' journey, regarding which, in terms of distance travelled, it has been suggested that the figures should be more than *three miles* each way if one must walk, more than *thirty miles* if a car is available and the roads are good; those who will suffer great detriment to health, honor, fortune, etc., if they go; those who are kept away by duties of charity or employment or office that cannot be omitted.[5]

I highlight "three miles" and "thirty miles" to draw attention to the fact that enormous car trips in order to get to the nearest traditional Mass are by no means obligatory, even if the desire to go to this Mass in particular is laudable, and even if one has concluded that no other closer Mass is an acceptable option (more on this point in the next section).

---

3   Fr Henry Davis, SJ, *Moral and Pastoral Theology*, sixth edition, vol. 2, Commandments of God and Precepts of the Church (London/New York: Sheed and Ward, 1949), 64-65. First published in 1935.

4   Fr Thomas Slater, SJ, *A Manual of Moral Theology for English-Speaking Countries*, vol. 1 (New York: Benziger Brothers, 1908), 263.

5   John A. McHugh, OP and Charles J. Callan, OP, *Moral Theology: A Complete Course Based on St. Thomas Aquinas and the Best Modern Authorities* (New York: Joseph F. Wagner, 1958), no. 2584, p. 583, emphasis added. This work's first edition dates to 1929.

In other words, taking the advice of the moral theologians, one may find oneself in a situation in which there is *no reasonable way to fulfill the obligation*; and in that case, it ceases to bind, and one should rather engage in some other suitable work of piety, such as reading aloud from the missal,[6] with perhaps a homily on the Gospel by a Father of the Church,[7] and saying the Rosary.[8] At the same time, people in this situation should seriously consider what steps they might take to relocate, in time, to a place where they would be able to fulfill their Mass obligations with relative ease.

McHugh and Callan go on to say:

> Though the Church does not impose excessive Sabbatarianism, neither does she admit laxity in the important matter of the Lord's Day. Hence, not every reason excuses from the church precept. Thus, those are guilty who unnecessarily place themselves in the impossibility of observing the law (e.g., *by moving to a place where there is no church,* by taking a position that requires work all Sunday morning, by starting on a vacation or auto trip to a churchless region), or whose excuses are frivolous (e.g., those who stay away from Mass because they dislike the priest, or who work on Sunday merely to keep busy).[9]

In other words, it is not spiritually healthy to continue to live in a place where attending Mass is very difficult or even (morally or physically) impossible. This is simply not a sustainable situation.

"Seek first the kingdom of God" means living near good liturgy

As hard as it is to change jobs or move one's family, the words of the Savior resound from the pages of the Gospel: "Seek ye first

---

6   For suggestions on how to do this in the family circle (and for a printable resource), see my article "Your Local Mass Canceled? Try Meditating on the Texts of the Traditional Mass," *OnePeterFive*, March 20, 2020.

7   There are many resources one could use, but an especially helpful book is Rev. D. G. Hubert's *Sundays & Festivals with the Fathers of the Church: Homilies on the Gospels of the Ecclesiastical Year* (Waterloo, ON: Arouca Press, 2019), which is already keyed to the traditional Roman Rite.

8   A tremendous aid for doing this in a way closely related to the Mass and the Divine Office has been provided in *The Liturgical Rosary: Meditations for Each Hour, Day & Season of the Liturgical Year,* compiled by the Slaves of the Immaculate Heart of Mary (Waterloo, ON: Arouca Press, 2023).

9   McHugh and Callan, *Moral Theology,* no. 2585, p. 584, emphasis added.

the kingdom of God and His righteousness, and all the rest shall be given to you." Even as the virtue of religion is the highest of the moral virtues, so is the right worship of God our primary obligation – the duty around which we should organize our lives. When God delivered Israel from Egypt and brought them into the promised land, He did so precisely to free them to offer Him right worship. Israel had to suffer a huge amount of inconvenience, upheaval, and disorientation to leave behind the land to which they had grown accustomed (as downtrodden slaves, no less!), but this is what the Lord asked of them, for their own benefit.

To speak from my life experience for a moment, my family and I have made many sacrifices over the years to ensure that we could worship the Lord in continuity with Catholic tradition. As a student at Thomas Aquinas College, I attended secret off-the-record Latin Masses with a chaplain who had a rocky relationship with the administration. In graduate school in Washington, D.C., I took inconvenient public transportation to get to Old St Mary's in Chinatown, and later, while working on my dissertation at a dilapidated farmhouse in Gordonsville, Virginia, drove a big distance to go to the Mass at Old St John's in Silver Spring, Maryland. When we lived in lower Austria, we drove on most Sundays either into Vienna, where the FSSP offered Mass at the Kapuzinerkirche, or into Linz, where the FSSP offered Mass at the Minoritenkirche. At Wyoming Catholic College, which opened its doors only a month after *Summorum Pontificum* was promulgated, a Sunday *Missa cantata* was eventually added to the chaplaincy schedule, but it dried up every summertime when the chaplains vanished to other assignments. That summer drought prompted some long drives to Powell, Wyoming, or to Fort Collins or Littleton in Colorado. The number of miles clocked on the various automobiles from grad school onward would be hard to calculate – and I know there are plenty of families out there doing even more than we did!

Many of these trips were supererogatory – that is, above and beyond what duty demanded, as per the moral theologians quoted above – yet at the same time they confirmed, deep in my heart, the beauty and rightness of assisting at the authentic Roman Rite. Eventually, I came to realize that this good had to be given maximum priority in my life. This led, in 2017/18, to a search for a new home in a place where the classical Roman Rite would be available *daily* and *nearby*. The search started with a map of the USA on which every location of the FSSP and the ICKSP had been duly noted. Passing over some road-bumps along the way, we finally found a house located less than a mile from a chapel run by the FSSP, with solemn Masses most Sundays of the year and the best Gregorian schola I have ever sung in. To say we are grateful to Divine Providence would be a colossal understatement.

Although there are many reasons why it was good for us to live at the various places we lived and to be a part of the great things that were happening in each of them, I can also see, in retrospect, that there was a slow development in my own understanding and feelings that necessitated this final step: a complete break with the modern rite, and a full embrace of the traditional rite. Talking to and corresponding with a large number of people has shown me that many Catholics today are reaching the same conclusions I did—but are reaching them far more quickly, and with less hemming and hawing.

In my opinion, Catholics who are trapped in a liturgically unhappy situation should start making plans now for an eventual relocation to a fully traditional Catholic community.

§2. MAKING DIFFICULT DECISIONS

We have looked at what old manuals of moral theology said about circumstances that may excuse someone from attending Mass on days of obligation, such as "spiritual harm either to oneself or to another," "a long way to church," being on a journey, and the hindrance of a sin that would likely be committed if one attended. I quoted several authors but many more can be found who speak along the same lines, including famous figures like St Alphonsus Liguori.

With these principles in mind, let's look at a letter I received from a friend.

> Dear Dr. K.,
>
> I am hoping that you can reference some Church teaching on the current issue we are facing here. I am well aware that our problem is not (unfortunately) a unique one in the Church today. During the past year and a half, in all the parishes of our city, we have seen infuriating and

The Sunday Mass Obligation in a Time of Liturgical Crisis

heart-stopping behavior: heretical homilies, the words of consecration changed, desecration of the Eucharist, being denied Communion on the tongue. Our bishop ignores all letters, will not take calls, and refuses to see us.

My husband continues to search for a job in a place that has a Latin Mass, but until then we are stuck here, making trips to Masses when we can.

I do not think I can go to Mass here anymore. The Novus Ordo is indescribably painful and I cannot stand to take my children to witness the evil. Covid has definitely been a catalyst for some of the abominations we see, although we are also just waking up to certain evils that have always been there. During a visit a few months ago, Fr N. spoke on how the Novus Ordo retards the progress of souls and said in some cases there can be a moral obligation *not* to go, especially if one has children. However, he was hesitant to give specific advice.

Do you have any thoughts/resources to help guide us through the discernment of not attending Mass here? What are the moral implications?

God Bless,
Catholic in Distress

My Response

Dear Catholic in Distress,

I'm very sorry to hear about the situation that you face. The fact that so many others face it too doesn't make your own suffering any less. The evil of the situation is compounded by a cold and uncaring bishop who, as far as I can tell from reports, does not even believe the Catholic Faith in the Eucharist and the Mass as solemnly defined by the Council of Trent. That would (at least partly) explain why you are receiving no response to your pleas.

In what follows, I will recommend articles that support the various points I will be making.

The starting point in responding to your questions is *the obligation to worship God*. Corresponding to the obligation prescribed by the Church (namely, to assist at Mass on Sundays and certain Holy Days) is a *duty* on the part of the Church to provide a *suitable* Mass for the faithful — not a blasphemy that is destructive to faith and imperils our salvation. Catholics have a magisterially defined *right* to worship according to the Church's tradition and according to the rubrics of the liturgical books. [10] You are right to be seeking a Mass that is totally free of abuses and heresy, [11] nor should you accept the sophistry that "we are called to suffer with Christ when we attend a bad liturgy." [12]

Moral theologians agree that when there is an impossibility, physical or moral, of assisting at Mass, one's obligation is removed. A *physical* impossibility is caused by something like being sick, the car not starting in the winter, or the lack of availability of a Mass at all, say in a time of war or plague. [13] A *moral* impossibility refers to a situation where a given action is physically possible but should be treated as impossible for the purposes of decision-making. For example, since a Mass that violates the liturgical norms with impiety and irreverence or a Mass in which heresy was preached is objectively offensive to God and sinfully unjust to the faithful, whose rights are thereby violated, it would be morally impossible to attend it, that is, not something that one is able rightly to choose. [14] Esteemed canon lawyer Msgr. Markus Graulich speaks in this case of a genuine form of abuse:

> The question that arises here is: what are we guided by? By doctrine and law, that is, by objective criteria, or by the attitudes of the day, of the moment or the spirit of the times?... The law—including criminal law—protects the

---

10   See my article "Fidelity to Liturgical Law and the Rights of the Faithful," *OnePeterFive*, March 1, 2023; cf. note 28 on page 140.
11   See my article "If your Mass is defective or abusive, find another one," *LifeSiteNews*, November 7, 2019.
12   See the articles referenced in note 34 below.
13   See chapter 24.
14   Another way of defining a moral impossibility is when it is unreasonable, or contrary to another legitimate good, to fulfill an obligation. Obviously there is wiggle room here for prudential judgment. Precisely because missing Mass for this or that "legitimate reason" is a prudential judgment (and cannot be otherwise), there can be disagreement about the reason, depending on whether someone is more rigorist or more relaxed. (Neither of those attitudes is inherently wrong; it's not as if the Church has said we must always be as rigorous as possible, or on the contrary, always as relaxed as possible.) It seems to me that the only possibility is to lay out the principles and recognize that different people (and priests) are going to come down in different places. Nor should that be surprising when dealing with *particulars*, which are the proper concern of prudence. Just how sick must a person be to not have to go to Mass? Just how vulnerable? How far is too far to drive to a TLM? and so forth. On all these points, it seems to me that if a person/family is making a good-faith effort to get to Mass regularly and to take their obligations seriously, one should assume they are where they need to be, and that God is not, as it were, looking to trip them up on a technicality.

sacraments by regulating what is required for their valid and licit celebration. . . . Among the rights of the faithful in the Church is "to celebrate divine worship in accordance with the prescriptions [rubrics, etc.] of their own rite, approved by the competent pastors of the Church" (can. 214). Therefore, when priests or other pastoral workers begin to "knit" their own rite, invent Eucharistic prayers, etc., they violate this right of the faithful. They are committing, as we would say today, spiritual abuse.[15]

If one knows from experience and by a reasonable conjecture that a certain parish Mass is likely to be an occasion of abuse, sacrilege, or heresy, one should not attend it. In such a case there is no need for a dispensation from anyone, since we are dealing with matters of divine and natural law.

If the abuses are such that they can reasonably be judged to spring from a disbelief in some part of the Catholic Faith, or from contempt for God or the Church or religion, a person is at least exempted from the obligation to attend. If the abuses are such that there is no other possible explanation of them, then one would have an actual *duty to stay away.*

When such a situation obtains, here is what the faithful should do.

1. Seek out another Mass in the greater vicinity, including Masses offered by the SSPX or by visiting priests. According to the moral theologians, if one has to travel more than is reasonable, the obligation to attend Mass ceases to bind. It would seem that nowadays a one-hour drive is a reasonable outside limit. Of course, one could *choose* to drive further out of devotion, and that would be meritorious, as long as it did not cause other difficulties in the family.

2. If you will not be able to get to Mass on a given Sunday or Holy Day, the day does not cease to be a day on which worship ought to be given to Almighty God. It is therefore highly appropriate to perform some other act of religion – preferably, something weighty, and different from one's weekday routine. Examples: make a holy hour, in a chapel or at home; pray Lauds or Vespers from the Roman Breviary or Monastic Diurnal; do some *lectio divina*; pray a Rosary,

---

15　"Was bringt das reformierte Strafrecht der Kirche? Interview mit Monsignore Markus Graulich," *CNADeutsch*, June 1, 2021. On the inventing of rites, see my article "The 'Unique Expression of the Roman Rite' in the Wild: New Zealand Priest Ad-libbing Eucharistic Prayer," *Rorate Caeli*, October 9, 2023.

perhaps all fifteen decades; read the prayers and readings out of a daily traditional Missal. In this way, one is doing one's best to fulfill the Third Commandment, *to keep holy the Lord's Day*, in the absence of the possibility of doing so sacramentally, since the local Church is failing to provide what it is obliged to provide and what Our Lord has a right to receive (which you, too, have a right to receive, as a member of His flock). Our Lord will see that you have given Him what you can, and He will supply for the rest.[16]

3. It's not uncommon for people—even Catholics who are striving to live by tradition—to think that a grave or very grave reason is necessary to dispense from going to Mass, while simply a just reason or no reason at all suffices for doing servile work on a Sunday or Holy Day. Both views are false. In reality, only a *just* or *moderately grave* cause is necessary to dispense from Sunday Mass, while a *grave* cause is necessary if the prohibition on servile work is not to bind. We have gotten things upside-down: we'll grit our teeth at a jamboree hootenanny Mass because we think we "have to go," but then we'll mow the back yard when we get home, even though we could have done it on Saturday or some weekday evening. It would be morally right in that case both to skip Mass and to refrain from mowing the lawn.

4. You mentioned moving elsewhere. This is the only decisive solution to the problem: a Latin Mass parish, where you know just what you are getting, and you know it is pleasing to God, and will be edifying to you and your family. I hope and pray that you can make this move at some point.

Yours in Christ,
Dr. Kwasniewski

Distillation

As I reflected on the matter subsequently, I distilled it to a few basic principles.

1. The duty to worship God (Third Commandment) is fulfilled by attending Holy Mass on Sundays and other specified days, as per the Church's determination of the precept.

---

16 For further thoughts about "aliturgical" days and how to think about their spiritual value, see the chapter "Sorting Out Difficulties in Liturgical Allegiance" in Kwasniewski, *Reclaiming Our Roman Catholic Birthright*, 281–88, and my article "Living Corpus Christi in a Liturgical Desert," *OnePeterFive*, June 7, 2023.

2. To this duty on the part of the faithful corresponds a duty on the part of the clergy to offer Mass reverently, in accord with all rubrics and texts, and in harmony with tradition. The laity have a right to such a Mass, as *Redemptionis Sacramentum* clearly states.

3. The lack of a suitable Mass—let us say, for the sake of argument, either in the form of the authentic Roman Rite or in the form of the Novus Ordo—is, so far from being the fault of the laity, squarely a fault of the clergy, who alone are empowered to offer it. *The laity, therefore, can never be at fault for not attending a liturgy that offends God and harms the people, especially children.*

4. When abuses or heresies exist in or during the Mass, laity are obliged to inform the bishop and to request his intervention, since he alone is in charge of his clergy. If the bishop refuses to respond or will not take action within a reasonable time-frame (one might estimate three months), the laity have done all that they can do to correct the problem; they are not responsible for the lack of a solution. All the guilt falls on the shoulders of the bishop who did not act rightly when he was informed. As St John Chrysostom writes: "Do not tell me that the priest or the deacon is at fault. Their guilt comes upon the head of those who ordained them. . . . I speak not otherwise than it is, but as I find it in my own actual experience. I do not think there are many among bishops that will be saved."[17]

5. Reasonable efforts should be made to attend a suitable Mass elsewhere, meaning, with efforts that are not disproportionately burdensome to the family (this is why moral theologians say if it takes more than X amount of time to reach Mass, or if Mass is more than X miles away, or if buying the fare or the gas will bring financial hardship, etc., one's obligation ceases to bind).

Three questions

On another occasion, a Catholic reached out to me to ask three questions prompted by the cancellation of the local Latin Mass by a bishop hell-bent on implementing "Prison-Guards of Treachery" (*Traditionis Custodes*). Since these questions and my answers are pertinent to the overall topic of this article, I include them here.

1. *Are we (as some people claim) in "material heresy" when we blatantly ignore the wishes of the Holy Father and the local Ordinary?*

---

17 *Commentary on the Acts of the Apostles*, 3:5–6.

Heresy means that one departs from a dogma of the Faith, for we are obliged to believe all of them. Particular disciplinary decrees of bishops and popes do not fall under this category. Those who disobey legitimate policies or commands *might*, in rare and extreme cases, be guilty of the sin of schism, but again, there are many requirements before such a grave crime can be said to have been committed.[18] The desire to hold fast to the apostolic and orthodox Catholic Faith and to worship in accordance with it is not only *not* heretical or schismatic, it is right, virtuous, and meritorious—indeed, the lack of such desire and such worship would be more wrong than disobeying any pope or bishop who attempted to eradicate them.

2. Are we fulfilling our Sunday obligation by going to an underground Latin Mass?

The Mass obligation is fulfilled by assisting at the Eucharistic Sacrifice offered in a Catholic rite by a Catholic priest. If a priest is offering the Holy Mass privately, and there is no better alternative, that would surely fulfill the layman's obligation. Moreover, a bishop who forbade a priest to offer Mass solely because it is the traditional Latin Mass would exceed his remit; the priest would remain free to offer it and the laity free to attend it.

3. Can a "canceled priest"—i.e., one who has no pastoral assignment but has not been suspended for a just cause—hear confessions?

The answer one gives to this question depends on one's view of the kind of crisis or state of necessity that exists in the Church on earth at this time. If one believes that "basically things are okay," then one will expect canon law to be followed punctiliously. If one believes that "all hell's broken loose" (which is my point of view), then one would regard a priest who holds the Catholic Faith and who has never been disciplined for canonical crimes as an ordinary and legitimate dispenser of all the sacraments for which a priest usually has faculties.

In particular, it seems to me that a priest who has unjustly lost his faculties for confession—that is, who was guilty of no crime that would merit such a loss—may continue to hear confessions of the faithful who are "in danger of death," that is, either in danger of dying physically, or in danger of the second death of damnation

---

18   See Boniface, "Stop Using This Word So Recklessly," *Unam Sanctam Catholicam*, August 10, 2023.

because they are in a state of mortal sin. Such souls have the most dire need of the Church's mercy, and thus, the norm of all norms — *salus animarum suprema lex*, the salvation of souls is the supreme law — dictates that the confession be heard. As it would be awkward to announce to a group that "only those in mortal sin may come to confession," a priest might let it be known ahead of time that whoever is in serious need may approach him for confession.

§3. SHOULD THE NOVUS ORDO BE AVOIDED IN PRINCIPLE?

I understand there is a diversity of opinion on this question and that many readers may disagree with me, by having either a more generous attitude toward the Novus Ordo, or a stricter disapproval of it.[19] My disapproval is already rather strict, as will be seen, but I do not believe it is possible for a Catholic to maintain that the Novus Ordo is *necessarily or in itself* invalid, heretical, or sacrilegious.[20] Rather, it carries with it a continual *risk* of having one or another of these defects, and, in any case, it always lacks fittingness or suitability against the backdrop of Catholic tradition and in view of the dignity of the Most Holy Sacrament; and that is cause enough to avoid it altogether.

There is not — and in my opinion could not *in principle* be — any actual (positive) heresy in the Novus Ordo. Its texts are often inadequate and vague, but they *need* not be construed in a heretical

---

19   For those who are tempted to believe the Novus Ordo invalid: the late Fr Anthony Cekada's argument that there is not a proper consecration in the Novus Ordo but rather a simple narrative of the Last Supper, told in the manner of an historical commemoration (as can be found among some of the Protestants), is false. Sacramental words say what they do and do what they say. The magisterial documents leave no doubt about the intention of the Church to confect the Body and Blood of Christ using just those words found in any of the Church's missals, including the new missal of Paul VI. Even when that pope modified the words of consecration, nothing that St Thomas Aquinas had argued was essential to the forms was removed (and Paul VI knew that as well as anyone). Although we should lament the neoscholastic reductionism that led to such wild experiments, nevertheless there is truth in the analysis of a sacrament in terms of its form and matter. The problem arises, instead, from not recognizing that we owe to God (by the virtue of religion) and to ourselves (in recognition of the needs of human nature) a certain providential fullness of liturgy that serves as the fitting "repository" or "context" in which the sacramental mystery is to be enacted. We do not want "in vitro transubstantiation." See Kwasniewski, *Once and Future Roman Rite*, 150–55.

20   My argument here about the *Novus Ordo Missae* can be applied, *mutatis mutandis*, to all the novel liturgical rites.

way. It is unfortunate that some less educated traditionalists jump to hasty conclusions in this regard, owning to the fact that many modern Catholics, clerical and lay, undoubtedly *do* hold heretical views, and sometimes even attribute them to the Novus Ordo. But if one simply takes the liturgical texts one by one and examines them, a Catholic sense can always be given to them. The real problems lie elsewhere – in the massive insufficiency of the texts, rubrics, signs, and music to convey the fullness of the Catholic Faith, and to do so in harmony with the particular ways in which this fullness providentially unfolded in the West.

Having read and pondered much on this question, and having discussed it with other specialists in the field, I still cannot see a "smoking-gun" argument that makes it *per se* wrong to *ever* attend the Novus Ordo. But it stands to reason that one can be justified in attending it only if one has a reasonable certainty, ahead of time, that it will be done *not only* "by the books" – a difficult enough condition to find fulfilled, although it is required by church law! – *but also* with the signs of reverence that Our Lord deserves, e.g., Mass offered *ad orientem*, with only male ministers, proper sacred music, Communion kneeling and on the tongue, etc. People call this the "unicorn Novus Ordo" because it's so rarely sighted. The liturgies conducted by conservative Oratorians come to mind: people who go to *their* Novus Ordo *know just what they're getting*, as it never varies from the highest standards. Assisting at such a Mass now and then would hardly skew one's faith or damage one's children.

Reasons for avoiding the Novus Ordo

And yet . . . there is the deeper level: the Novus Ordo, even in its most formal attire, is premised on a rejection of much of the Western tradition of divine worship as if it were inherently flawed – a position either heretical or proximate to heresy. Its euchology (prayer content) is defective. Its variability or "optionitis" is contrary to any mature liturgical rite, Eastern or Western. It is a Trojan Horse for modern theology, which reinterprets the whole of Christian tradition through modern lenses. It is a fateful marriage of the antiquarianism condemned by Pius XII and the ecumenism condemned by Pius XI. In no way can it be considered one of the "*received* and approved rites of the Catholic Church" that the Council of Trent holds up as normative.[21] It embodies and inculcates rupture with nearly our entire heritage.[22]

As you come to see these things by lived experience and comparative study of the Roman Rite and the modern papal rite of Paul VI, you come to understand the danger of letting the latter be the normative and formative liturgy you attend. *Once you see it, you can't unsee it.* The Novus Ordo is not just a prayer offered sincerely by some of its users (and, in that respect, a good thing); it is *also* a moral and intellectual habituation in rejecting, repudiating, and rupturing: a rejection of the Church's past, a repudiation of her bimillennial tradition, a rupture with the teaching of Trent as well as (ironically) of Vatican II. It cannot possibly be spiritually healthy to assist on a regular basis at what is effectively a parody of the Roman Rite; nor does it benefit the Church when the faithful perpetuate this rite's existence by supporting it with their presence (let alone their donations). This rite has harmed countless millions who have walked away in disgust or boredom, or who, sticking with it, are chronically undernourished and malformed in divine worship.

Moreover, the unicorn version is *not* "what the Novus Ordo was supposed to be," since Paul VI made it very clear that that's exactly *not* what it was supposed to be.[23] Rather, the unicorn is the triumph of subjective good taste in choosing an array of options (and sometimes, inventing options where they don't exist).[24] In other words, it's an accomplishment, not a given. This is unhealthy both for the priest and for the people: it flatters the priest, who can easily think of himself as the one personally responsible for "good liturgy," and it makes the laity too attached to a particular priest when their attachment should be to the traditional liturgy and to the priesthood as such.[25]

---

21 Session VII, canon 13; cf. the *Professio fidei Tridentina*, also called the Creed of Pope Pius IV.

22 Those who are interested in the full argument for this conclusion will find it in two books: my *Once and Future Roman Rite*, and the anthology by eight authors that I edited, *Illusions of Reform.*

23 For abundant documentation, see *Once and Future Roman Rite*, 109–43 and 381–97.

24 See, e.g., "A Primer for a Tradition-Minded Celebration of the OF Mass," written by Fr Richard Cipolla and published by Gregory DiPippo at *New Liturgical Movement*, September 14, 2017; cf. my article "Two 'Disobediences' Compared," *OnePeterFive*, January 18, 2023.

25 To read more about the problem of the "reverent Novus Ordo," see, for starters, my articles "Why the 'Reform of the Reform' Is Doomed," *OnePeterFive*,

Worst of all, it is impossible for the Novus Ordo to exclude *all* bad practice, because it itself *permits bad practice* and so the clergy are in no position to prevent it.[26] To take perhaps the most notorious example, although a particular priest might promote Communion on the tongue at the altar rail, if a layman comes up, remains standing, and sticks out his or her hands, the priest cannot refuse to give the host into the hand, and we know that this will mean, over time, particles scattered and trampled on.

In short: it would be difficult to maintain that *occasional* attendance at a Novus Ordo Mass celebrated in the most tradition-friendly manner possible would be spiritually harmful to oneself or one's children. Yet as that opportunity is rarely available, it is a moot point for most people. Furthermore, after one has made the transition and adjustment to the classical Roman Rite, one grows accustomed to its traditional calendar of seasons, feasts, and fasts, its potent means of cultivating an array of virtues, and its highly consistent methods for enticing and rewarding actual participation. For a person thus habituated, the Novus Ordo, even in optimal conditions, brings with it distraction, irritation, anguish, a plethora of near occasions of sin.

Ultimately, the two rites are different worlds with different worldviews. Participating means imbibing the spirit of the rite and consenting to its continuation, with all the consequences that follow in its wake.

Rules for deciding what to do

Building on what has been said so far in this chapter, I argue as follows.

1. No one is obliged to attend a Mass at which Our Lord is treated irreverently (taking longstanding Catholic tradition as the measure of what counts as reverence) or at which one will be provoked to

---

April 22, 2020; "Men Must Be Changed by Sacred Things, and Not Sacred Things by Men," *OnePeterFive*, September 15, 2021; "The 'Latin Novus Ordo' Is Not the Solution," *OnePeterFive*, August 24, 2022; "Can a Case Still Be Made for Reforming the Reform?," *OnePeterFive*, May 3, 2023. Also recommended are two articles by "Boniface" at *Unam Sanctam Catholicam*: "The Problem of the 'Reverent Novus Ordo,'" September 10, 2020, and "Reform of the Reform: Liturgical Russian Roulette," December 5, 2022.

26   See my article "No Eucharistic Revival without Restoration," *Tradition & Sanity* [Substack], April 20, 2023.

sin or to participate in the sins of others by complicity. Indeed, it is not good for one's own faith or for the faith of one's family even to *witness* such a liturgy, let alone take an active part in it. Therefore, to fulfill one's Sunday or Holy Day obligation properly, one ought to have, ahead of time, a reasonable certainty that the Mass one will be attending will not be defective in the aforementioned ways.

2. A liturgical rite that is radically variable, subject to the control of the priest (or a parish committee, or a liberal bishop, etc.), and captive to subjectivist notions of "reverence" – try getting any two Catholics who attend the Novus Ordo to agree about what counts as a "reverent Novus Ordo," or "how much reverence" can be taken as the minimum – such a rite *cannot* provide the faithful with that reasonable certainty. According to its own design, the intentions of its architects and promoters, the history of its reception and customary use, and the by-now nearly ubiquitous set of assumed practices that can be met with in nearly every diocese in the world, normally there cannot be *sufficient probability* of a Novus Ordo Mass that fulfills the conditions necessary for obligatory divine worship.

3. With any traditional liturgical rite, Eastern or Western, *that sufficient probability exists*: in other words, before going, you have the reasonable certainty that the worship will be sound in content, correct in practice, and reverent according to the measure of tradition.[27]

Think of how well the above points "track" with experience. If you go to a random Novus Ordo Mass while traveling or on vacation, it is likely to be bad (most Catholics have their fair share of horror stories). If you go to a random traditional Latin Mass, however, it is likely to be good – not only good owing to its inherent goodness, but also good in relative ways too: the demeanor of the celebrant, the decorum and modesty of the congregation, the orthodoxy of the preaching, the beauty or at least non-offensiveness of the sacred music, and so forth. In other words, if you gamble on the Novus Ordo, you're extremely likely to lose; and if you gamble on the traditional Latin Mass, you're extremely likely to win. This is a hard fact of modern Catholic life.

---

27 There are some odd exceptions even in this realm: for example, the reformed [sic] Maronite rite is celebrated *versus populum* and with severely redacted propers, making it inauthentic and a poor choice. See my article "The Maronite Liturgy's Corruption under Modern Western Influence," *New Liturgical Movement*, September 27, 2021.

In sum:

A. No Catholic is obliged to attend an objectively irreverent Mass, [28] and no Catholic is required to drive enormous distances to get to a reverent Mass.

B. The Church's clergy are obliged to provide Catholics with their own rite properly celebrated, which means, for Latin-rite Catholics in the Roman tradition, the Tridentine Mass done according to its rubrics. It is the clergy, not the laity, who are culpable for the lack of availability of this rite and therefore the lack of possibility of attending it.

C. *All* Catholics are required to take the steps needed to live within reach of a worthy Mass to attend; and for the occasions when (or the span of time during which) this is not possible, they are required to set aside time to worship the Lord at home.

Why is it such a big deal to assist at a *traditional* rite?

It used to be taken for granted (and frankly I do not see how a believing Catholic can withhold assent) that the Holy Spirit leads the Church throughout her history to an ever-fuller expression and veneration of the mysteries of Christ in her solemn public worship.

From this premise it follows that once a major prayer or cere-mony has become a regular part of our worship, *it would be wrong to remove it*: specifically, a sin against the virtue of religion. It is *wrong* to have a modern rite claiming to be "Roman" but lacking the prayers at the foot of the altar, the traditional lectionary, the Offertory rite, the required Roman Canon (with its many signs of the cross), [29] a thorough preparation for Holy Communion, ade-quate ablutions, and the Last Gospel. Having no prayers of prepa-ration—Psalm 42, the double Confiteor, the versicles, the "Aufer a nobis" and "Oramus te"—before mounting the steps to kiss the altar and recite the Introit makes the liturgy fundamentally unserious. The removal of an oblative Offertory has become a fruitful cause of sacrilege, inasmuch as the priest's failure to establish with clarity his sacrificial intention more readily allows for the abuse whereby

---

28   As I argued earlier in this chapter, the same is true for a Mass at which the preaching is, or is highly likely to be, heretical, or even merely, in the language of the old theological censure, *piarum aurium offensiva* (offensive to pious ears), as is much of the preaching of Pope Francis.

29   See my article "The Many Meaningful Signs of the Cross in the Roman Canon," *Tradition & Sanity*, August 17, 2023.

the Mass is treated as, and even considered to be, primarily a meal. And so forth and so on.

To put it as briefly as possible, sacrilege means treating holy things with contempt, inappropriately, perversely, or negligently.[30] The liturgical tradition of East and West grew organically over the millennia toward ever greater and more careful signs of reverence for the Blessed Sacrament and all holy things (the book of Scripture, sanctuaries, holy images, vessels, vestments, etc.). The Novus Ordo abolishes or excludes much of this, and therefore deprives God of the worship and honor, and deprives the faithful of the palpable helps, that He Himself moved the Church to institute over the centuries.

It may not have been irreverent for a Christian ca. AD 100 to receive Communion in the right hand and bow to take it with his mouth as if it were a paten; but it *is* irreverent for a Catholic to imitate that *in a mangled way* today by receiving in his left hand and then feeding himself with his right. It may not have been irreverent for a priest ca. AD 500 not to genuflect before *and* after the consecration, but it is a different matter to *cancel out* this double genuflection after it has already been done for practically a millennium. *Our place in history is very important*: we cannot abstract from the concreteness of Christian history. God gives *more*, liturgically speaking, to those who come later, and as it says in the Gospels: "From everyone to whom much has been given, much will be required; and from the one to whom much has been entrusted, even more will be demanded" (Lk 12:48).

The fullness of the liturgy is our "compensation," so to speak, for living further away from the time when Christ actually dwelt on the earth. His apostles and disciples had the maximum physical proximity but a fairly simple liturgy, whereas we, who are far removed from the "historical Christ" who walked the roads of Galilee and Judea, are greatly privileged to behold Him and worship Him in liturgical signs, prayers, and ceremonies that are more fully

---

30   The creators and enforcers of the Novus Ordo were guilty of facilitating an institutional sacrilege, inasmuch as the Novus Ordo is a monument to and a vehicle of iconoclasm: they committed a direct, immediate, grave attack on the common good of the Church. Yet the people using this rite today usually do so in good faith and in a state of profound ignorance that makes it exceedingly unlikely they would meet the criteria required for being voluntary agents of sacrilege.

developed than they were in ancient times, and, in that way, more expressive in signifying the realities of the heavenly Jerusalem toward which we are journeying ("further up and further in," one might say). Even as the more precise doctrinal formulations that were developed over time are binding in conscience not simply because they are customary but above all because they are true, so too is the traditional liturgy that developed over time binding in conscience not only because of the force of immemorial custom but even more by the force of its inherent truth, which cannot be denied without denying the Holy Spirit as the soul of the Church at prayer, the agent in her liturgical action.

This argument from custom points to the objective value of the concrete history of use, reception, and transmission embedded in liturgical forms.[31] The rite in its totality, first given germinallly by Christ through His Apostles, remains sacrosanct as it unfolds in history – not by way of bare juridical authority (there was no papally approved missal for three-quarters of the Christian era!) but *by its outgrowth in and from His Mystical Body*, worshiping precisely as a corporate entity; and its violation is, consequently, something immoral: impious, superstitious, and sacrilegious, to use all the pertinent scholastic terms.

It is never enough merely to point to a Mass's *validity* or *licitness*; one must also take into account fittingness, continuity with tradition (which we can also call authenticity or legitimacy), and correct external and internal dispositions. All of these elements ought to be present. They are either necessarily or far more often present in and with the *usus antiquior*; tragically they are either necessarily or frequently absent from the Novus Ordo. Its very genesis, content, structure, operative rules, and habitual abuses constitute acts *contrary* to the virtue of religion. One runs the risk of displeasing the Lord by assisting at it.[32]

This, then, is a way of broadening the argument made earlier: not only is the Novus Ordo far more likely to be irreverent in this or that respect, it has a primordial irreverence "baked into it," hard-wired, coded into the genes (pick your metaphor). Therefore, one

---

31 See chapter 5.
32 See the chapter "Pouring the Argument into the Soul" in Kwasniewski, *Good Music, Sacred Music, and Silence*, 245-50.

cannot be obliged to attend it, even for Sundays or Holy Days. One is obliged to assist at the Roman Rite in its integrity (or another traditional Catholic rite), as long as no moderately grave reason excuses one from such assistance.[33]

Commonly-heard rejoinders like "We should be willing to suffer through a bad Mass—look how much Jesus suffered for us!," or "As long as Jesus is present at Mass, nothing else should make a difference," though undoubtedly pious-sounding and well-intentioned, in fact express a point of view that is deeply erroneous and overlooks both offenses to God and harm to our souls.[34]

Postscript: Illicit?

The same conclusion would be reached with lightning speed if someone believed the Novus Ordo to be an *illicit* rite—that is, valid, but a legal abuse as introduced or enforced; thus, incapable of being mandated; thus, incapable of being attended to fulfill an obligation. An extended argument for this conclusion is made by Dr John Lamont.[35] I am sympathetic to Lamont's conclusion, and his argument contains many flashes of insight (especially his interpretation of the reasons behind the catastrophic decline of the Church); but to my mind there are gaps or leaps in his argument that leave me unconvinced.

Nevertheless, it has planted a doubt, or rather, watered a doubt already existing in my mind, about the liceity or legality of the introduction of a new rite by Paul VI, and this doubt counts as an additional reason to avoid the new rite, based on the axiom that one should not perform an action if one has a well-founded doubt about its morality. For example, if one has a doubt about whether a certain action is chaste or compatible with the virtue of chastity,

---

33 It is obvious that attending Mass at an SSPX chapel or a religious community affiliated with it fulfills this obligation. See Paul Casey, "SSPX Masses and Fulfilling the Sunday Obligation."

34 To understand why, see my articles "The Mass Should Not Be a Torture Device," *New Liturgical Movement*, February 7, 2022; "Finding Christ in Present Sufferings Does Not Mean Embracing Abuse, Error, or Deformation," *OnePeterFive*, February 8, 2023; "'All That Matters at Mass is Jesus': Responding to Liturgical Heresy," *OnePeterFive*, February 16, 2022; "Why I Couldn't Go Back... to the Novus Ordo," *OnePeterFive*, April 14, 2021.

35 See "Is the Mass of Paul VI Licit?" and "Dominican Theologian Attacks Catholic Tradition."

one should not do it lest one be guilty of unchastity. So too, if, based not on feelings but on facts, one is doubtful about the lawfulness of the new rite, one has an obligation either to clear up or to confirm one's doubts, and meanwhile avoid attending it. Speaking for myself, when I tried to clear up my doubts by further study, the things I learned only multiplied and intensified them! Hence, I personally would not attend the Novus Ordo, even if it were the only liturgy available.

It also bears noting that any rite that is so indeterminate, so poorly equipped for the exigencies of worship, so inadequate vis-à-vis its lineage, and so easily abused by clergy and laity alike, may very well be illicit for that reason alone. No lawful rite can be so deeply, intrinsically, and irremediably flawed.[36]

Weddings and funerals of relatives at which one's presence would be legitimately expected can be exceptional cases in which one might tolerate the Novus Ordo as long as one's intention is to support the family and to pray for the couple being married or for the soul of the departed—not specifically because it is the new rite, which is tolerated for a greater good. One is present for love of persons, yet under silent protest in regard to the liturgical imposition. But even here, if one had good reason to believe ahead of time that the liturgy was going to be egregiously deficient in reverence, one would be obliged to make polite excuses and avoid it, perhaps joining the group for the reception, the burial, etc. (provided that these, too, are in accord with basic Christian morality). We have to recognize with gritty realism that in a world—and a Church—ever more secularized and emptied of common decency (let alone any connection with Catholic tradition), the faithful will be confronted with more and more situations in which their participation is simply ruled out, regardless of the "offense" that may be taken by those who invite them to take part. This is a regrettable consequence of accelerating dechristianization, largely unresisted by civil and religious leaders for decades.

---

36 Here is where Fr Gregory Hesse's observation is worth recalling: Paul VI did not promulgate or mandate the Novus Ordo, he merely published it (the Latin text of his apostolic constitution *Missale Romanum* is rather different from the muscled-up vernacular versions); therefore, the indefectibility of the Church was not compromised, as no one was required either to use or to attend Paul VI's rite. See note 30 on page 94.

§4. A SUCCESSOR OF THE APOSTLES' *CREDO*

It is in the nature of moral reasoning in a contingent, fallen world that it cannot always give black-and-white answers. Yes, a direct sin against any of God's commandment is evil. But in anything *less than* divine commandments (and that non-divine category would include the Church's precepts), there are situations that call for prudential decisions, for discernment of circumstances, assessment of gains and losses, balancing of obligations and risks. For that reason, it is impossible for me to tell any reader, short of knowing a lot of details, what he or she "must or must not" do when it comes to fulfilling the Church's days of obligation for attending Mass. The best I can do is to share valid principles of moral reasoning and insights into the liturgical mess we are dealing with, as I have done in the preceding three sections, in order to help with the decision-making process. It is one's *conscience*, well-informed – and that means, not fed on half-truths, lazy rationalizations, and extravagant gaslighting – that will issue directives. It is on these directives, and on one's efforts to make them righteous, that one will be judged by Almighty God.

Given the seriousness of the issues under discussion, I deem it highly appropriate to crown this chapter with the wisdom of a successor of the apostles, Bishop Athanasius Schneider, admired around the world for his clarity of judgment, serenity of spirit, and undaunted courage. Bishop Schneider's new comprehensive catechism, *Credo: Compendium of the Catholic Faith* – a book I cannot praise with too many superlatives and that I recommend you acquire instantly and use diligently – contains helpful points on divine worship and our obligations thereunto. Bishop Schneider's clear teaching breathes the spirit of the Church Fathers and shines with the light of supernatural common sense, the *sensus fidelium*. [37]

368. What is superstition?

Acts of worship that are sinful in either their *object* or *mode*; i.e., the worship of a false god, or the worship of the true God in an undue manner. "Superstition is a vice contrary to religion by excess,

---

37 I quote each of the following points in full, but without the internal citations that may be found in the endnotes of *Credo*. Emphases have been added.

not that it offers more to the divine worship than true religion, but because it offers divine worship either to whom it ought not, or *in a manner it ought not.*"

372. What kinds of superstition involve undue worship of the true God?

False worship, which contains something contrary to natural truth or divine revelation, as when false revelations are maintained; *impious worship, as when a man-centered worship is established in violation of the Church's constant liturgical tradition.*

375. Why do man-centered forms of worship violate the Church's constant liturgical tradition?

Because only "the received and approved rites of the Church" offer to God the worship that He has prescribed, and only her constant liturgical custom best safeguards the truly God-centered form of worship.

376. What is the most common form of man-centered worship today?

Drastic liturgical innovations and abuses, by which one introduces into the worship of the Church something contrary to her traditional doctrine or custom, e.g., a Protestant and banquet-style celebration of the Mass as in a closed circle, dances, show performances, tokens of secular organizations or pagan religions, etc.

378. Should we avoid a Mass in which liturgical abuses will foreseeably occur?

Yes. The presence of a valid Eucharist notwithstanding, ceremonies with liturgical abuses are objectively contrary to the divine and apostolic tradition, displeasing to God, scandalous, and often dangerous to faith.

379. Should we attend a Mass with liturgical abuses to fulfill our Sunday obligation?

This depends on the gravity of such abuses in each place. If a Sunday Mass would include practices like dances, heresies in preaching, or other serious liturgical abuses, we may not be obliged to attend such a Mass, even if it were the only one available in our vicinity, because we cannot be obliged to place ourselves or our families in a near occasion of danger to faith.

380. In this specific case, would we violate the third commandment?

No. The obligation to attend Sunday Mass is an ecclesiastical and not a divine law, and therefore subject to exemption and dispensation. If a Sunday Mass with liturgical abuses were the only available option, we should sanctify the Sunday in some other way; and in this way we are keeping the third commandment.

384. What is sacrilege?

The profanation of the sacred; it is the unworthy or irreverent use of something or someone consecrated to divine worship.

385. How do we learn the proper treatment of sacred things?

God Himself has revealed it, and the Catholic and apostolic tradition of the Church has retained it. Even natural reason instructs us here, as "it belongs to the dictate of natural reason that man should do something through reverence for God."

423. What works of religion should Christians perform on Sunday?

1. Worship of God, from which no cause excuses and no authority can dispense; 2. Assisting at Holy Mass, if we are able to observe this precept; 3. Other pious works.

424. Is everyone bound to perform all of these works on every Sunday?

No. The law of Sunday worship binds universally; the precept of attending Mass only binds Christians with the use of reason, and additional pious works are merely encouraged.

425. What is required to satisfy the precept of attending Mass?

1. Our bodily presence in the place where Mass is offered, at least from the Offertory to the priest's reception of Communion; 2. Our active participation in the rite itself.

428. Are we required to risk our life to fulfill the obligation of attending Mass?

No. Physical dangers like extreme weather, plague, or war automatically suspend this obligation, until we may do so without grave danger. Even so, it is praiseworthy to go to great lengths to attend Holy Mass.

429. What other causes automatically suspend the obligation to attend Mass?

1. *Physical impossibility*, as with the homebound, sick, prisoners, or those with no available priest; 2. *Moral impossibility* and *charity*, as with caretakers of small children or those treating the ill or disaster victims; 3. *Danger to reverence or faith*, as when a Mass is celebrated in an unworthy or heretical manner, being the only available Mass in the wider area.

430. If we have a legitimate reason not to attend Mass, what should we do instead?

The obligation of Sunday worship always remains, and may be fulfilled through other forms of private, family, or communal prayer, to which other works of piety may also be added.

431. What works of piety are recommended to help us sanctify Sunday?

Attending Sunday Vespers, Benediction of the Blessed Sacrament, and catechetical instruction, as well as reading devotional books and performing works of charity.

613. What does the first precept of the Church require of us?

It orders all the faithful who have the use of reason and are not justly impeded, to assist at the Holy Sacrifice of the Mass on Sundays and holy days of obligation.

614. Why does the Church order the faithful to attend Mass?

In order to: 1. Determine the specific way we must observe the third commandment of worshipping God; 2. Ensure that we worship as a community, and not merely individually; 3. Further motivate the faithful to participate in the sacrifice of the Cross.

615. Is assisting at Mass the greatest act of worship?

Yes. There is no religious act more agreeable to God and no prayer more efficacious, for it is the divine sacrifice and prayer of Jesus Christ together with the Church, His Bride and Mystical Body.

22

Pro-TLM Strategies in the Era of *Traditionis Custodes*

PEOPLE OFTEN ASK ME: "WHAT'S YOUR advice for Catholics living in a diocese where the traditional Mass has been limited or eliminated, or where there is a threat that this might happen? What should we do?" As rumors circulate of still more draconian measures, it is time to tackle head-on the question of what can be done concretely.

Here are some steps I would recommend – though obviously certain angles will work better with certain episcopal or parochial personalities or situations than others will. Not everyone will be comfortable or enthusiastic about every idea, nor is that surprising; this is meant as a buckshot list, to cover all the bases. The items listed are not meant to be in order of importance or chronological sequence. We have to multiply strategies going forward because we simply don't know what's going to work, and some of these strategies involve fairly lengthy timelines.

Before I go any further, it must be understood that everyone is doing three things: praying; fasting; and giving alms. As for prayer, the daily Rosary, with the restoration of the Mass as a specific intention; the First Five Saturdays and the Nine First Fridays; TLMs whenever you can get to them. Join the lay sodality called the Crusade of Eucharistic Reparation, which has for its secondary intention the restoration of the Latin Mass. As for fasting, Our Lord says that some kinds of demons come out only that way (Mt 17:21). As for giving alms, support traditional parishes, orders, and organizations. Don't give up: we were born for these times! God put us here to fight this fight.

1. Start an Una Voce chapter in your diocese. It can be helpful to have an umbrella organization that speaks "with one voice," on its own letterhead. For this reason it seems good to create an Una Voce chapter in your area, if one does not already exist. If you obtain for it charity or non-profit status, it can receive tax-deductible donations that can be put toward literature, vestments, Mass and server training camps, priest stipends, special events, property and chapel acquisition, and the like. An Una Voce chapter could organize an annual pilgrimage in the diocese (and if it does, the bishop should be informed of it). Seminarians and priests who show signs of interest in tradition should be supported in their TLM training, purchase of supplies, or attendance at TLM-friendly events. The internet is a great tool, but we need local in-person communication, networking, and events, and an Una Voce chapter is well-positioned to meet that need.

2. Help the bishop to understand his canonical rights. Try to obtain a meeting with the bishop and explain to him (straightfor-wardly, tactfully, and kindly—bishops don't like to be instructed about their rights and duties by laity!) that canon law permits him to make his own discernment about the local situation and the needs of the faithful, as Fr Gerald Murray explains.[1] The Dicastery for Divine Worship (DDW) in Rome serves in an *advisory* capacity toward him, not in a *legislative* one. The DDW has no authority to command a bishop to terminate the ancient Roman Rite; they may only tell him he "should," which is quite a different matter. This remains true even after the infamous "rescript" of February 2023, in which Cardinal Roche sought to neutralize appeals to canon 87 of the *Code of Canon Law* by reserving all dispensations from *Traditionis Custodes* to the Holy See. In fact, by making this move, Francis and Roche undermined *TC* itself, since the *raison d'être* of that document—as can be seen by reading its text—is nothing other than restoring control over the regulation of the old rite to diocesan bishops, as they are claimed to have requested. In other words, if Roche's rescript is right, *TC* is wrong and need no longer be followed, since the two are contradictory; but if *TC* is right (at least in regard to granting bishops oversight), then Roche's rescript is wrong, as conflicting with its basic premise.[2] Beyond that mon-

---

1 See his interview "Guarding the Flock."
2 Edward Condon's commitment to legal positivism prevents him from draw-ing the same obvious conclusion, in spite of the fact that he brings together all of the pieces of evidence necessary to do so: see "Does Roche's rescript dispense with Vatican II?," *The Pillar*, February 22, 2023. For further canonical aspects, see my article "Newly Ordained Priests and Permission to Offer the Traditional Latin Mass," *OnePeterFive*, May 11, 2022. The last-mentioned article predates the rescript, but much of its content is unaffected thereby.

umental illogic, there are – as I have argued throughout this book – still more fundamental questions about the truthfulness of *TC*'s claims and the lawfulness of its implementation.[3]

Your arguments should be boiled down to the shortest possible number of pages and sent to him in advance of the meeting. Even better if you know a sympathetic priest who is a canon lawyer. The bottom line: even after "Roche's rescript," there are still work-arounds of which a bishop can avail himself, such as naming an unused church an "oratory" or a "shrine" where the traditional Latin liturgy may be used.[4]

3. Meet in person with your bishop. When you meet with the bishop, have both men and women present, and explain how much the old Latin Mass means to all of you in terms of loving God and practicing your faith in your day-to-day life. Leave out the arguments about liturgical form because he likely offers exclusively the Novus Ordo and is thus likely to have neither experiential background nor patience for any arguments that even remotely suggest the superiority of one form over the other; go instead for the heartstrings.

When the bishop says "I can't do anything else, this is what Rome requires," remind him of the content of the letter you sent showing him that he *does* have the freedom; remind him of his rights under canon law and of the behavior of many other bishops who are letting the traditional Mass continue, often in multiple locations and also in parish churches. If the time and the atmosphere seem right, you could also propose to him inviting the Priestly Fraternity of St Peter into the diocese, because the pope expressly approved the continuation of their work wherever the bishop welcomes it.[5] Perhaps a church building that is on the chopping block for a parish merger or a closure could be taken over by the FSSP. (This papal "deal with the FSSP" would seem to apply *mutatis mutandis* also to the Institute of Christ the King Sovereign

---

3 See the articles in note 11 on page 64.
4 Sometimes chancery officials want to keep bishops in the dark about their options; and sometimes threats are made by various people to the bishop ("you know, if you actually *do* this, then . . . "). Much depends on whether you have a man of principle and courage or not.
5 See "Decree of Pope Francis confirming the use of the 1962 liturgical books," www.fssp.org/en/decree-of-pope-francis-confirming-the-use-of-the-1962-liturgical-books/.

Priest and smaller traditional communities; certainly that is the way things are being perceived and handled everywhere, except in the gravitational field of Chicago.[6])

One of the great challenges of our time is the distance that has grown between bishops and faithful in general; it can be difficult to build up mutual trust and good will when the head of the diocese seems remote, inaccessible, and uninterested in the laity. Nevertheless one must try to do what one can. I was speaking with a lady who said she was inspired one day to call the chancery and invite the bishop over for dinner. To her shock, the bishop agreed, and came over!

4. Organize a letter campaign. Have TLM attendees, families, and especially children send letters to the bishop. Don't flood him with letters all at once unless the situation calls for it. Instead, agree among yourselves to spread them out so that he's always getting some mail. After a time, you may wish to pick certain seasons or dates of the year when everyone in the community will resume sending in mail (Advent, Lent, etc.). This way the mail doesn't just drop off and never return.

It's not necessary to write more than a sentence or two: "We are heartbroken at what has happened in our lives / to our parish . . ." "We feel as if we are being singled out for punishment, and why? Because we love our Faith and its traditions?" "Our boys loved serving the Latin Mass . . ." "We used to pray the Rosary together for the pope's intentions, and now everyone has scattered . . .") Have people send the bishop spiritual bouquets from their families. We are trying to reach his *heart* and make him feel bad about what he has done or is threatening to do (or is being bullied into doing); we want to make him regret it, rethink it, walk it back quietly.

True, such letters may not change his mind. They may not move him to change his policies. But a bishop still has a heart, even if it has hardened toward some of his faithful; he still has a conscience, even if it needs to be awakened. A steady flow of letters may soften that hard heart, may stimulate that dormant conscience. Over time, he might, for example, decide not to enforce his policies, or to enforce them inconsistently and weakly. He might decide to leave

6   See Trevor Alcorn, "Chicago: The Saga of a Canceled Parish," *OnePeterFive*, September 2, 2022.

untouched a Latin Mass that has sprung up somewhere without approval, even though he has heard about it. He might intercept or sideline a damaging assault started by a more zealous fan of *Traditionis Custodes*. There are many things that go on behind the scenes that most of us will never hear about, and we cannot judge from appearances only. When we send in letters, it is part of an effort to move things slowly in a better direction. The same is true when we pray: sometimes the results are dramatic and obvious, but at other times, even most of the time, the results are hidden to our eyes. Nevertheless, we still have faith and we still pray with hope and confidence.

One might worry: "What if the letters will annoy the bishop?" Truth be told, even that's not a bad outcome. Remember the parable of the persistent old woman who so bothered the wicked judge that he finally granted her what she asked, so that she would finally leave him alone (see Lk 18:1–8)? We very definitely want the hierarchy to get it through their heads that we are not going away and we won't change our minds or our goals.

One cautionary note: Some bishops are actively hostile to or contemptuous of the traditional Latin Mass and all that goes with it. For such reprobates, the normally persuasive strategy of identifying all the good fruits of *Summorum Pontificum*—the army of altar servers, the numbers of births and baptisms versus funerals, etc.—can backfire. Because of their firm conviction that the TLM represents "the past" and not "the future" (a conviction obsessively repeated by Pope Francis), all the evidence that suggests the opposite is not, as far as they are concerned, an occasion for reconsideration or encouragement but rather a cause of alarm. The more the tradition grows, the more such bishops will become convinced that the Catholics of their dioceses are being misled into a dangerous dead-end. Attempts to get on the good side of bishops like this may have the unfortunate result of stimulating their malformed consciences to impose *further* restraints on your activities. Thus, some discernment will be required in determining what kind of communication may or may not be fruitful with the local Ordinary.

5. Take canonical action. There are sometimes canonical recourse steps that Catholics who are being deprived of goods to which they have a right can take. Here, time is of the essence:

the moment a chancery or episcopal decree goes out restricting the traditional Mass or old-rite baptism, confirmation, marriage, funeral, etc., you need to file with a canon lawyer ASAP. There is no risk to the individual faithful and there is a chance that the legal intervention will throw a wrench in the works.

Some Catholics say: "Taking canonical action will upset the bishop and he will retaliate by being even meaner to us." This is the beaten wife syndrome: if I complain about my husband beating me, he will beat me even more. It is *because* the laity have been so passively "obedient" that the authorities can so easily get away with abusing us and attacking the good of our souls and our families. I regret to say that the villains in the Church are counting on us *not* to fight back, to be good *sheeple* whom they can cancel out, as they cancel out good priests. This is part of the whole gaslighting structure. It's crucial that people see through it. The only thing a bully can be made to understand is fighting back, because then he has to deal with it. Otherwise, he will ride roughshod over everyone.

Now, your local bishop may not be a bully; he might very well be a gentleman and even somewhat sympathetic. Yet he is probably a victim of the same false understanding of obedience as that under which many priests operate, where, e.g., if Francis says "give Communion to remarried Catholics" or "teach that the death penalty is wrong," they think they have no choice but to do it. St Thomas makes it very clear that we are under immediate and exceptionless obedience to no one but God; all His human representatives must follow divine and natural law and reverence ecclesiastical law and custom, as earlier chapters in this book have demonstrated.

In all your formal or argumentative communications directed to the bishop (as opposed to spiritual bouquets or personal notes), it should always be made clear that *you* are well aware, from close study of the matter by canonical experts, that a bishop is by no means required to shut down parish traditional Masses or other sacramental rites. He has room to maneuver.

6. Show up in public places. Gather at the cathedral and/or the chancery and pray the Rosary, holding posters with nice messages.[7] No personal attacks on the bishop, just messages like "We are

---

7   See what is being done in Chicago and Arlington for ideas: Savannah Dudzik, "We Know that God is on Our Side in This Fight," *OnePeterFive*, April 8, 2022;

faithful Catholics who love the Latin Mass!" and "Don't take our beloved Latin Mass away from us!" It's especially important to try to interest local media in covering these peaceful protests, since there is no bishop who enjoys negative publicity. Pray the Rosary and sing lots of Catholic chants and hymns. Prepare a piece of paper or half a piece of paper with a simple explanation on it of who you are and what you stand for and what you are asking for, so that you can hand it to curious bystanders going in and out or passing by. In short: don't let your existence be forgotten.

Another way of showing up is to take a table at a diocesan event, e.g., if there is an annual Diocesan Catechists Workshop or a Men's Conference or a Women's Conference. You can distribute free informational materials and set up books or other items to sell.

7. Educate the clergy about the battle. Meanwhile, parallel to all of the foregoing, talk one-on-one or in small groups with the TLM-celebrating and TLM-favorable priests. Be sure to give them copies of the book *True Obedience in the Church*, which argues that priests may and must keep the Latin Mass and other traditional sacraments and sacramentals alive *regardless* of what their bishop may allow or prohibit, and if they respond well to it, give them (or suggest to them) this present book, which is the successor to it. There are profound theological issues at stake here; it's no mere "matter of discipline" over which the pope and bishops have unlimited powers of discretion or disposal. On the contrary, the ban on traditional sacramental rites goes to the *root* of the Catholic Faith; it concerns the Church's consistency and coherence with herself and with Christ's action over history and in the magisterium. A book that draws out these points in detail is *From Benedict's Peace to Francis's War*, but Fr Rivoire's book *Does "Traditionis Custodes" Pass the Juridical Rationality Test?* is also excellent (and much shorter). Get your priests a quality traditional calendar so they can be better aware of its ins and outs. Above all, encourage them to keep offering private Masses, at least on their days off, in order to retain a lifeline to the TLM. Similarly, encourage your priests who don't already know how to offer the TLM to learn it for their own benefit, and with a view to the "second spring" that is bound to come when the

Noah Peters, "The National *Summorum Pontificum* Walking Pilgrimage," *OnePeterFive*, September 21, 2022.

281

hateful and unpopular policies of Francis have been reversed in better days to come.

8. Try to persuade priests to offer *underground private Masses* if need be. Be ready to support a priest, in friendship and in practical/financial assistance, if he is unjustly stripped of a position in the diocese and is given no assignment (in other words, if he becomes what is called a "canceled priest").[8] At that point he can become your local underground chaplain. Bishop Athanasius Schneider has supported this course of action in a case of necessity. Remember: the suppression of the ancient Roman Rite will be successful to the degree that priests and bishops allow themselves to be coerced. Those who refuse to be coerced may be visited with unjust penalties, but they will retain a clear conscience and fulfill the pastoral ministry to which Christ the High Priest has called them, and they will help pave the way for the future restoration of tradition.

9. Acquire and renovate property. We have to think long-term, because the crisis that has reached fever pitch under Pope Francis is still going to be with us for some time. We must be realistic: long gone are the days when we could expect the institutional Church—i.e., the churchmen of the moment—to anticipate our needs and to provide for them. On the contrary, some churchmen seem to specialize in new forms of discrimination and marginalization, and in stomping on the spiritual needs and canonical rights of the faithful.

It is therefore time to meet the fire of hatred with the fire of a love that surmounts every obstacle. If a group of laypeople can find an old Catholic church or a closed Protestant chapel, they should buy it and convert it into a usable chapel.[9] This is a smart step for the difficult times that may be coming (and have already come in certain places).[10] All things being equal, it is better to have a church in which to celebrate the Holy Mass and other

---

8   See Fr John P. Lovell, "What is a Canceled Priest?," *OnePeterFive*, October 4, 2021.

9   It is advisable for them to keep hidden the reasons for which they would like to acquire the property. Sometimes Catholics create a legal entity that can serve as a front in business transactions.

10   A word of advice: don't blow a ton of cash on a chapel that never or rarely gets used, unless you have concrete reasons to believe your chapel will become a Mass center for your surrounding area, and you have some assurance of a priest who will visit or stay for that purpose. Whatever you do, before taking large steps, seek the direction of a trustworthy traditional priest.

sacraments than to limit oneself to living rooms, basements, or hotel ballrooms, as often occurred in the 1970s. If you have no success finding a chaplain locally, you may be able to get a priest from the Coalition for Canceled Priests to come in and say Mass there. Sadly, if things keep going as they have been going, other priests will become available in due course.

10. Drive and carpool. Some people have the option to drive an hour or two into a neighboring diocese for a traditional Mass offered by diocesan clergy, an Ecclesia Dei group, or the SSPX. This is obviously not a long-term solution but it can be a temporary strategy, especially for the sake of children who should not be exposed to liturgical deviations.[11] It is also possible that a drive like this could be done once or twice a month. Carpools or vanpools to help the elderly or those with no vehicles get to Mass could be considered; it would be an outstanding work of mercy.

If the Sacrament of Baptism or Confirmation is unavailable in your vicinity, see if you can bring your child to a neighboring diocese where the FSSP or ICKSP (or even, in some rare cases, a diocesan church) can take care of it. Policies vary but there have been places that welcome outsiders for the sacraments of initiation. If the Vatican were to cut off Catholics from any and all access to traditional-rite sacraments, it would then be necessary to reach out to the SSPX.

11. Start a Traditional Catholic Homeschool Co-op. Unlike an Una Voce chapter or other (perhaps clandestine) group, a homeschool co-op can be an effective vehicle for openly educating the traditional Catholic youth and for collaborating to advance traditional Catholic values within the diocese. It would be best if a priest can offer the ancient Mass on, say Friday mornings in the local church, with the co-op students meeting afterwards for religion or other classes. Such a co-op doesn't have to limit itself to children's offerings; it might also offer fellowship and enrichment for the adults by offering evening talks on various topics, from spiritual formation to experienced homeschoolers teaching those new to homeschooling which curriculum and materials they've had the

---

11   See the preceding chapter, and Fr Michael Gurtner, "The Current Crisis of Faith in the Church Has Its Ground in the New Mass," *Rorate Caeli*, December 15, 2022.

most success with. Keeping the group traditional and Catholic so that it is not overrun by a majority of Novus Ordo and/or Protestant homeschoolers is essential; this could be done with bylaws that call for voting and non-voting members, with the former having to meet certain traditional Catholic criteria.

12. Begin the SSPX conversation. If your bishop has canceled every accessible Tridentine Mass in your diocese and/or other sacraments in the old rite, and nothing else avails – if a bishop will not relent in his cancellations, if he will not be reasonable in providing for the needs of his sheep, if he will not establish a shrine or oratory, if he refuses to invite in the FSSP, etc. – then it is time to consider the "nuclear option," namely, contacting and inviting the Society of St Pius X into your area. It is your way of saying, unequivocally: "We are playing for keeps and will not back down." Given the ever-growing demands on their limited personnel at this time, the Society is not likely to be able to respond to your request right away; but if you can assure a chapel and funding, and if there is a decent number of faithful in question, they may come.

Here is not the place to go into detailed questions about the status of the SSPX; I will limit myself to saying the following. If the Church is in a state of unprecedented and anomalous institutional crisis, a historical meltdown next to which the Arian controversy and the Protestant revolt are as puff-pastry – and that is the view I have, and, I would think, most of those who are reading this – then it is infinitely more necessary to retain the fullness of Catholic orthodoxy, which means both *right teaching* and *right worship*, than it is to check off all the boxes of canonical propriety and to satisfy the desiderata of scholastic manuals written in saner times and without even the remotest conception of the situation we are passing through. [12]

Plus, on a pragmatic note, and sad as it is to say it, nothing better motivates certain bishops to provide diocesan-sponsored Latin Masses than the possibility of an SSPX presence! To protect yourself against the counterargument that "you were schismatics all along, because look how you are reaching out to the SSPX!," make it absolutely clear: "We never thought of seeking the help of the Society until we were painted into a corner by unreasonable and unjust

---

12 See chapter 20 for further thoughts on the SSPX.

actions. Since there is absolutely no good case that can be made for withdrawing the traditional sacramental rites from baptized Catholics and flourishing communities, it is clear that, in reality, the local shepherd has decided to stop feeding his sheep; and the sheep therefore turn to where they may be fed."[13]

In this connection I would urge traditional Catholics to recognize sedevacantism for what it is, namely, a trap set by the Devil to capture those who are too quick to judge, overzealous and unequipped with the spiritual and theological resources needed to make some sense of our chaotic times (which, it is only fair to point out, will never *completely* make sense, since we are dealing with the *mysterium iniquitatis*, the mystery of iniquity, which is inherently irrational). Even when we legitimately protest against and refuse to follow the directives of our pope and our bishop, we do so regretfully, under duress, and for the sake of greater goods that must be defended by true Catholics. We do not stop acknowledging and praying for the pope and the clergy in general, nor do we seek to escape from the confines of the visible Church. Our goal is the restoration of tradition *within* the Church, its natural and supernatural home.

13. Education never stops. It is crucial to educate yourself and your fellow ancient Mass attendees on why we love this long-matured form of the Mass and all of the other traditional rites and customs. It's not just about "smells and bells." It goes far deeper than that. My book *Reclaiming Our Roman Catholic Birthright* is perhaps the most immediately useful "apologetics manual" for the TLM; Joseph Shaw's *Sacred and Great* pamphlet is a much shorter read, perfect for newbies. You could start up one or more reading groups. We have to educate ourselves about what we are fighting for and why. For a deep dive, take up *The Once and Future Roman Rite: Returning to the Latin Liturgical Tradition after Seventy Years of Exile* (TAN, 2022). Those who prefer the video format will find many educational lectures at my YouTube channel and at many other traditionalist channels. Organizing viewings of the "Mass of the Ages" documentaries, with conversation afterwards, is

---

13   For those in your community who fear that this is a "Protestant" way of thinking or acting, see chapter 1 above, as well as my article "Are Traditionalists Guilty of 'Private Judgment' Over the Popes?," *OnePeterFive*, December 22, 2021.

particularly effective for integrating newcomers into the community. Another good book club choice would be Stuart Chessman's
Faith of Our Fathers, a short but inspiring read about the history
of the traditionalist movement in America, what it has had to go
through, and how by God's grace it has overcome obstacles.

14. Last but not least: let us endeavor to *carry our cross well*. It
may be that Almighty God is asking us to carry a heavier cross than
before. If He asks us to do so, it means He knows we can handle it
with His grace, and that we will be sanctified by it. Maybe He is asking us to bear it on behalf of those who reject and insult the Cross.

Bishop Athanasius Schneider in *Christus Vincit* and other works
talks about the suppression and rarity of the Mass during his childhood in the Soviet Union. He used that cross for his personal sanctification, and ultimately it led him to accept his priestly vocation.
Look how the Lord is using him today, to preach the truth in season
and out of season, around the world. The same will be true for us:
God does not allow evil unless He will draw forth good from it. Let
our own growth in virtue and sanctity be the good that He draws
forth from the evils unleashed by *Traditionis Custodes*.

How Catholic Laity Can Influence the Church for Good

ILLIONS OF AMERICANS VOTE EACH YEAR for their public officials. We live in a democratic age where such opportunities are taken for granted. While there are problems with certain *theories* of democracy (especially when it is understood in terms of the so-called "social contract"), on a practical level it is hard to dispute that the people of a nation should have *some* say in how their government operates and how their society is shaped.

Things are obviously and intentionally quite different in the Catholic Church. Founded as a perfect society by Our Lord Jesus Christ, the Church is governed by a sacred hierarchy consisting of bishops and their subordinate clergy, all of whom are subject to the universal and immediate jurisdiction of the sovereign pontiff, the pope of Rome. Although the laity are overwhelmingly the majority in terms of membership in the Church, their contribution to building up the Kingdom of God has always been understood to be primarily the Christianization of the secular sphere in which they live and work.[1]

Thus, at one level, laity have no "power" in the governance of the Church, and certainly no "vote." But on another level, laity have a remarkable amount of power, and we should exercise it to the fullest. We can, so to speak, vote in five ways. I shall rank them here from the least to the most important.

First, we vote with our wallets. Having seen the doctrinally questionable and morally corrupt uses to which diocesan money is put, Catholics understandably react by keeping their wallets

---

1   For a thorough explanation, see Peter Kwasniewski, *Ministers of Christ: Recovering the Roles of Clergy and Laity in an Age of Confusion* (Manchester, NH: Crisis Publications/Sophia Institute Press, 2021).

bolted shut against "diocesan appeals" and the like. Do I want my money to go into huge pay-offs for legal damages? Into dubious catechesis, out-of-date "hipster" youth programs, episcopal residences, or wonky liturgies? Into support for clergy who are not actually providing the faithful with the traditional Catholicism they desperately need *and desire*? No thanks, we will keep our money – and spend it only on good causes. This may include, of course, a good bishop or a good local parish, but we no longer *assume* that "the diocese" deserves our support. Support now must be *earned*, every penny of it.

Second, we vote with our feet. If the local parish is not providing for our spiritual needs, then, when a better option is available within some reasonable distance, we go there instead. The reason is simple. Our first obligation after loving God, say the saints, is to love our own souls by becoming holy.[2] Therefore, we must never put some abstract or ideal or future "community good" ahead of the nourishment *we* individually need in order to live the Christian life and to worship God as He deserves to be worshiped. In this way, as can be seen everywhere, good parishes grow stronger and bad parishes grow weaker. It is a sort of supernatural version of the survival of the fittest. Lay Catholics have no obligation to allow themselves or their families to be liturgically malnourished, pastorally mistreated, musically assaulted, or given the short end of the stick in any other way. If this is happening to you, please, for the love of God and the good of your soul, go elsewhere.[3]

Third, we vote with our voices. Countless lay-run initiatives (think of the online media) have made a huge difference in the Catholic Church in recent decades. Writers have been willing to stick their necks out and say "Enough is enough!," as they exposed the darkness of cowardice, heresy, and turpitude with a brightly shining spotlight. Magazines, websites, petitions, and open letters have pursued truth and accountability with a "game-changing" relentlessness. Bad bishops, bad cardinals, and bad popes cannot hide their machinations any more. Why is this important? It creates a network of well-informed Catholics who will know whom

---

2 See St Thomas Aquinas on the "order of charity": *Summa theologiae* II-II, Q. 26, especially art. 4.
3 See chapter 21.

to support or oppose, which programs to adopt or avoid, and, in general, how to navigate the complicated and chaotic situation of Church life after Vatican II. It inspires new efforts, informs strategies, encourages the lonely and downtrodden, and best of all, strengthens genuinely Catholic clergy with the knowledge that they are riding the crest of a growing wave.[4]

Without this chorus of orthodox voices and blazing spotlights, our Church would be even more deeply morassed in stagnant vice. We cannot change things overnight but we can document, analyze, clarify, network, move forward with open eyes and ready hands. Included in this category are letters written by the faithful to their shepherds – polite and respectful in tone, of course, but no less forceful for that. It is a work of charity to speak hard truths to those who need to hear them, and to make legitimate demands of those who are entrusted by God with our welfare.

Fourth, we vote with our protests. A public protest is, in a way, a super-concentrated form of using one's voice. What I have in mind is something like the rallies across the world at nunciatures and chanceries protesting anti-TLM measures. The annals of history record protests that have brought about significant change, as with the civil rights movement. If a large number of Catholics descend on the offices and residences of prelates, the bishops will be reminded of how angry the faithful are, and how tired of being put off with the usual flabby-authoritarian response: "We're very sorry. We will devise new policies and procedures. You just have to trust us." Laity are thoroughly sick of self-indulgent bureaucratic posturing. History remembers those who protest injustice. Whether they were successful or not, they stood for the truth at the right time. This is not fruitless as a form of evangelical witness. Let it never be said of ourselves: "Thus and such colossal evil was done, and Catholics did nothing to protest it; everyone accepted it without demur."

Fifth, we vote with our prayers. In our worldly, unconverted mentality we think of prayer as the weakest and last resort, when in reality it is the most powerful, for the simple reason that God is all-powerful and can move human hearts directly from within,

---

4   See Chris Tomlinson, "Traditionalism and Conservatism Thriving Among Young U. S. Catholic Priests," *European Conservative*, November 12, 2023.

which is not something any of us creatures can do. You can try to persuade someone to be reasonable, but God can *make* him reasonable. You can try to get him to see the beauty of the Faith, but God can make him fall in love with it. God is on the side of Catholics who love the Lord, His Mother, the saints and angels, and traditional dogmas, morals, and liturgies, since He gave us all these good things. He is expecting us, then, to redouble our prayers and penances, as a sign that we really believe He is the source of all good, the one who can restore to us what is lost, repair what is broken, scourge what is evil, and magnify what is holy.

I like to think of prayer this way: How badly do we want something? If we want it a little bit, we'll work for it on our own; if we want it more keenly, we'll get someone else's help; if we're smarter, we'll add a quick prayer to God; but if we want it *a lot*, we'll pray and sacrifice in a serious way to get it. God looks at our prayers to see what actually matters to us. Will we be like St Monica, who prayed for many years for the conversion of her son St Augustine? Will we be like the Catholics from the 1960s onward who never stopped praying and working for the restoration of the traditional liturgy, in spite of everyone telling them to quit and move on?

God will answer the prayers of those who put their trust in Him and beg Him to intervene. But He will do so in response to *persevering* prayer, because it demonstrates that we are more attached to *Him* than to quick results. He permits delays and setbacks to test our faith and to make it stronger – indeed, unconquerable. As long as there are loyal friends of Christ, the evil in the Church will never have the final word. In this way, the laity cast a "vote" that has divine power behind it.

When we ask ourselves what we can do to live out our Catholic Faith more fully during the current crisis in the Church, and how can we better share the Faith with others in spite of the many obstacles that surround us, the answer is not remote or recondite. By far the most important thing is simply to *live the Faith* with all of the resources it places at our disposal. Concretely, this means: staying close to Our Lord by means of the sacraments, His greatest gifts to us in our pilgrimage to heaven; staying close to Our

Lady by praying her Rosary, which is *her* greatest gift to us in this vale of tears; wearing and using sacramentals like blessed rosary beads, holy water, the brown scapular, the St Benedict medal; daily prayer; participation in the Holy Mass and recitation of some part of the Divine Office; spiritual reading or *lectio divina*; fasting and abstinence; almsgiving.

While we may not be able to take advantage of all of these things every day (and, moreover, we should always do what is in keeping with our state in life), we can and indeed *must* build a personal regimen, somewhat like a monastic horarium or schedule, by which we give structure and purposefulness to our days. "The life of man upon earth is a warfare," as the Book of Job tells us, and we need to be equipped to fight (Job 7:1; cf. Eph 6:11-17). All masters of the spiritual life concur that without an intentional *daily plan*, we will not achieve holiness. We would be like soldiers who, surrounded by armor and weapons, never take them up, and therefore make themselves vulnerable and incompetent in battle.

The restoration of the Church, as Dr John Rao writes,

> will only happen if we reject the temptation to despair; the temptation to flee from a battle that grows more and more unseemly as the years go by. . . . It will only happen if we continue to study our Faith more deeply, practice it more fervently, and . . . call unceasingly upon the aid of the truly living help of Christians: Mary and the saints in heaven.[5]

A pacifistic age like ours shies away from such military imagery.[6] Is it still appropriate?, we wonder. Apart from the fact that Scripture is full of this imagery—reason enough to retain it—we would do well to remember that the sacrament of Confirmation has been understood, since ancient times, as the sacrament that strengthens us for confronting the world and its prince, the devil, and triumphing over every power that sets itself against Christ the King. We are enrolled in His army by the holy chrism. If we are attacked, the Spirit is at hand to fortify us; if we are wounded or troubled, the

---

5   "The City of Light and the Regime of Darkness: Historical Meditation on Current Events," *Rorate Caeli*, September 3, 2018.
6   See my lecture "Christian Militancy in the Prayer of the Church," *OnePeter-Five*, March 16, 2022.

Spirit comforts us; if we grow weary, the Spirit is ready to sustain and energize us; if we make use of His strength, the Spirit will crown us with victory.

But a full answer to the question "what should we do?" must go beyond the individual. As political and social animals, *we need one another*, and we need to form *intentional communities*. Thus, to take an example, young professionals should create social opportunities for themselves, whether a monthly book club with dinner; a time for conversation at the local café every other weekend; watching a good artistic movie, followed by a discussion of it; an art class taken together; traditional dancing; a day of recollection led by a priest; a visit to a pumpkin farm in the autumn; horseback riding; playing board games or sports with other Catholics, with some good beer to top it off.[7] Other categories of people will find the social activities that befit and benefit them the most.

A book club is generally a great way to go, as everyone needs the opportunity (and incentive) to learn more, especially at a time when so much of our reading is confined to bits and pieces of news and commentary that rarely offer a broad integrated view of the Faith or a deep analysis of an issue. Examples of the sort of books I have in mind would be Bishop Athanasius Schneider's *Christus Vincit*, Frank Sheed's *Theology for Beginners*, Michael Kent's *The Mass of Brother Michel*, or Brian McCall's *To Build the City of God: Living as Catholics in a Secular Age*. Of course, there are many good choices out there for a discussion group; most of my books end with a carefully curated bibliography that will offer lots of ideas.

One last comment to make about books. Not everyone is fond of historical reading, but there are few things more helpful than the study of history for developing a realistic perspective on our present situation. It is both wise and comforting to remember what a variety of very good and very bad things have happened to Christians and the Church before, and how neither complacency nor despondency is ever warranted. Reading history may sound like a

---

7 See Leah Libresco, *Building the Benedict Option: A Guide to Gathering Two or Three Together in His Name* (San Francisco: Ignatius Press, 2018), and the articles by Julian Kwasniewski, "Money is for Coffee," *Salvo*, May 8, 2023; "The Enjoyment of Persons is Man's True Happiness," *OnePeterFive*, May 12, 2023; "Hilaire Belloc's List of Eight Manly Activities," *Crisis Magazine*, April 18, 2023; "Eight Activities of the Renaissance Woman," *Crisis Magazine*, April 26, 2023.

distraction from living in a community with other Catholics in the here and now, but I'm convinced from experience that it is no such thing. One of the problems we all face in the Church, and more widely in our social-media-driven society, is *ignorance* of the past, with a consequent lack of perspective on the present that can easily leave us vulnerable to simplistic "answers" or bouts of despair.

Let me give a concrete example of what history shows us. John McManners' two-volume *Church and Society in Eighteenth-Century France* (sadly too expensive for many) documents a fascinating time that ended in 1789 in a catastrophe that would have been utterly terrifying to those living (or dying) through it, but was then followed by the amazing recovery of the Church in France in the mid-nineteenth century, which led to a flourishing surpassed only by the Middle Ages. St John Vianney started off his life at forbidden underground Masses held in barns. Strange things can and do happen in the history of Christ's Church in her 2,000-year sojourn on the Earth. A perfect book-group read in this regard would be Henry Sire's *Phoenix from the Ashes: The Making, Unmaking, and Restoration of Catholic Tradition* (Angelico Press, 2015). It is eminently readable and thought-provoking, and the second part of the book—Sire's analysis of the Vatican II era—is simply brilliant. The writings of Dr John Rao and of Prof. Roberto de Mattei are also highly recommended.

There is no reason not to invite well-intentioned non-Catholics to any of the activities mentioned above; and while it is true that in ancient times the Mass was meant to be visited only by the baptized, this limitation has long since passed, and we can in fact lead souls into the Catholic Church by inviting well-disposed men and women to join us for a beautifully celebrated traditional Mass. Many conversions have taken place through exposure to this Mass, which, contrary to the doom pronounced upon it by the progressives in the '60s and '70s, is proving itself to be a major powerhouse of evangelization in our times—and this, precisely because it does not aim at evangelizing, but at something far greater, deeper, more absolute: the worship of the thrice-holy God.

24

Shutting Down Sundays and Sacraments: Never Again!

A FRIEND ONCE ASKED ME WHAT I THOUGHT about Catholic clergy who "went rogue" during the Covid-19 lockdown and continued offering Masses and other sacraments—even when "forbidden" to do so by "legitimate authority." She asked me what I thought of laity who encouraged them, assisted them, and benefited from their ministrations. Is this defensible behavior? Is it even, perhaps, *required* behavior?

The topic continues to be relevant because our Western so-called democratic governments are now drunk with the new, more intimate and more extensive power they gained over citizens by tapping into the primal emotion of fear prompted by mightily exaggerated danger. Whatever the next government-sponsored virus will be, we can be sure of seeing a return of restrictions of every kind, including limitations on religious activities and gatherings. We can expect the world-managers of anxiety and panic to milk any "health crisis" for all it's worth, and to extend it for as long as they possibly can – particularly in populations whose native irascibility has been all but neutralized by decades of socialist conditioning.

I was and continue to be sympathetic to every effort by clergy and laity to circumvent and ignore episcopal diktats that severely limit the sacramental life of the Church. My thinking on the question stems from a few basic principles.

The sacraments are not a privilege for the deserving, or a symbolic "window dressing" for the "real" Catholic life that goes on purely interiorly or domestically, as one of the cardinals of the Church seems to think,[1] but rather a *necessity*, a reality integral to the Christian spiritual life, as well as a genuine right of the faithful, understood in reference to our membership in the Body

---

1 See Antonio Spadaro, SJ, and Simone Sereni, "Bishop Mario Grech: An interview with the new secretary of the Synod of Bishops," *La Civiltà Cattolica*, October 23, 2020.

of Christ. The Eucharist is our elementary food for soul and body. Confession is our (blood)bath. Extreme unction is our lifeline, our immediate preparation for death, judgment, and eternity. Fasting from spiritual goods of this magnitude should be a last resort, of brief duration; therefore, limitations on them must also be a last resort and of brief duration, manifestly prompted by an undeniable emergency (think: bodies dropping dead all around us in the streets). A *total* lack of access *at any point* is indefensible.

It is one thing when a totalitarian regime hostile to the Church hauls priests away to a concentration camp in an effort to take the sacraments away from the people; then there is little choice on anyone's part. It is quite another thing for the Church's own shepherds to order priests to stop giving the sacraments to the faithful. In doing so, they short-circuit their own authority, function, and mission; they cancel themselves out. It is the equivalent of a bishop preaching that Christ has not come in the flesh (cf. 1 Jn 4), or denying the *homoousios* of the Creed: that Christ is consubstantial with the Father and thus has authority and power to impart the divine life, *His* divine life, to the poor and needy of the Church here below. Regulations there must be; strangulations there must never be. The dam may regulate the flow of waters, but the waters must indeed flow.

The same holds true of the public offering of the sacred liturgy and our participation in it. Thanks to the blundering of bishops chained to insurance companies and lawyers, there are today millions of Catholics who now believe that their obligation to worship God on Sunday can be summarily dispensed with. But this is not true. God commanded that He be worshiped in a formal, public *cultus*, for which He instituted a weekly Sabbath among the Chosen People. With the resurrection of Christ on the first day of the week, Sunday was sanctified as the firstfruits and the symbol of the new creation in which righteousness dwells (cf. 2 Pet. 3:13); therefore, Sunday, the *Dies Domini*, the "little Easter," is a solemn day of formal, public *cultus* that must be offered to God. This is how Christians best fulfill the Third Commandment, from which there can be no dispensation, as noted by Cardinal Burke. That strong view explains the odd absence of precedent for general, *standing* Sunday Mass "dispensations" — even in the midst of much worse famines, wars, plagues, and disasters than anything we have experienced in recent times. The obligation to join personally in the perfect sacrifice of Christ on Sunday remains in place for all of the baptized, and no bishop can alter that one bit, nor can virtual "livestreamed" attendance substitute for it.

If it is *impossible*, physically or morally, for an individual to attend—his car breaks down on the way to church; he is sick or vulnerable to sickness; or the church has been locked shut and he has no choice—the obligation ceases to bind, and no sin is committed (at least, not by the layman!), but in no way is it waived. It stands. The only question is whether or not we have legitimate grounds to leave it unfulfilled. The actions of our bishops and some of our priests have given quite a different impression: attending Sunday Mass ends up looking more like a human custom, a mere "take it or leave it" practice, rather than the observance of a divine precept as determined by Christ and His Church in her unbroken tradition.[2]

Beyond these points about sacraments and liturgy, we should look at the big picture in the Church. We are dealing with a situation, built up over several decades, in which the bishops have lost credibility and trustworthiness. With a few exceptions, they do not teach sound doctrine; they do not celebrate reverent liturgy; they do not rid their dioceses of homosexuality and abuse; they are mammon-hungry. In all these ways, they have lost the "moral high ground" required for us to "just trust them" in their judgment calls. As Newman argued was the case during the Arian crisis, it is fair to say that the present-day magisterium of bishops is in many ways "in suspense," in a state of dysfunctionality, disengagement, and inefficacy.[3] In jungle circumstances of this kind, priests and laity must shift for themselves as well as they can. Where there is every reason to think that the salvation of souls is *not* respected as the highest law (*salus animarum suprema lex*), a Christian's obligations to His Lord and Master take precedence over his obligations to members of the hierarchy, no matter how exalted.

In a May 20 letter published at *LifeSiteNews*, Archbishop Thomas J. Rodi of Mobile, Alabama stated: "If any priest cannot follow

---

2 For a thorough explanation of when the obligation binds and does not bind, see chapter 21.

3 See Timothy Flanders, "Has the Magisterium Been Suspended?," *OnePeterFive*, August 1, 2023.

archdiocesan regulations [which, *inter alia*, forbade Communion on the tongue], it will be necessary for him to refrain from the celebration of public Masses. This matter is too serious for us to take any other approach than one of extreme caution for the safety of others."[4] Similar attitudes were at work in dioceses across the globe.

I could somehow imagine a different and more authoritative statement issued from the chancery of the court of heaven: "If any bishop cannot follow natural law and divine law in regard to the adoration, reverence, and care to be shown to the Son of God in the Most Holy Sacrament of the Altar, and if, moreover, he does not fight to keep churches open, liturgical worship accessible, and sacraments available to the faithful, it will be necessary for him to refrain from the hope of reaching eternal glory. This matter is too serious for us to take any other approach than one of extreme sacredness and total commitment for the salvation of souls."

The same is true for all the clergy and laity. In a time of pandemic (if a real one should come our way), we must make *more*, not less, use of prayer, processions, penances, liturgy, and sacraments. In a time of spurious pandemic, we must make war against exaggerated restrictions and unjust cancellations, supporting those who creatively and courageously work around them and behind them.

Catholics around the world admire Archbishop Sample for many things he has said and done. For example, he is one of a select few bishops in the world who has regularly offered traditional Pontifical Masses, at a time when that is definitely a way to ostracize oneself from the halls of power. He was also placed by Benedict XVI in one of the USA's most liberal dioceses, Portland, and has managed to keep a steady hand on the tiller. The same holds true for Archbishop Cordileone in San Francisco.

However, when during Covidtide Governor Kate Brown imposed heavily restrictive measures in Oregon, limiting attendance in *any* church to 25 people at a time — even if the building

---

4   Martin Bürger, "US Archbishop forbids priests to say public Masses if they offer Communion on tongue," *LifeSiteNews*, June 2, 2020. For examples and critique, see Peter Kwasniewski, *Holy Bread of Eternal Life: Restoring Eucharistic Reverence in an Age of Impiety* (Manchester, NH: Sophia Institute Press, 2020), 227–55.

can hold 300 or 1,000 – the reaction of Archbishop Sample was deeply disappointing. After freely admitting that the restrictions were unconstitutional, unjust, and wrong from a Catholic point of view, all he did was *verbally* protest it. There was to be no civil disobedience. Similarly, Archbishop Cordileone pushed a movement he called "Free the Mass," but the underlying premise was that we should assume good will on the part of civil authorities and always try to accommodate the health dictatorship, until they can be *persuaded* to relax their unjust limitations. Matthew Archbold insightfully commented:

> I applaud Archbishop Cordileone's efforts. He has done so much more than countless priests, bishops, and cardinals. But I plead with all of them right now. Catholics need a hero. The faithful are calling out to the clergy for one perhaps ridiculous and fruitless effort to show how important the Eucharist truly is. The American Church is desperate for some action. Catholicism must be heroic, brave, and countercultural. Or it is nothing. There's a time for lawyers and press conferences and petitions. This is not that time. Now is the time Catholics must be willing to draw a line in the sand and say *here, and no further*. Open the churches. Don't allow them to be closed. Let's be willing to go to jail. Let's be fools for Christ. Take a stand. Imagine the impact of seeing a priest put in jail for celebrating Mass. Yes, the media would ridicule that priest. Perhaps many in the Church would as well. But it would inspire millions to understand that ours is not a passive faith. We are different because we believe. Think of all the young men who might see that and be inspired. Force the secularists to put a priest, bishop, or cardinal in jail or rescind their anti-Catholic mandates. Force them to unmask themselves. Show the world who they really are. And let's show the world who we are.[5]

It was no different in Ireland, where the bishops instantly caved in; and in many other parts of the world. With this kind of "playing dead," pretty soon the Church will move past playing dead – it will just *be* dead. And thus does Christian faith go out . . . not with a

---

5 "No Abp. Cordileone, These People Wish Catholics Ill," *Creative Minority Report*, November 24, 2020.

bang, but with a whimper. We witness the unedifying spectacle of Successors of the Apostles crumbling under lady governors' sanitarian diktats.

The rejoinder quickly comes: "We are supposed to overcome evil with good. That means abiding by all the civil laws and regulations." But laws and regulations must be proportioned to the common good and not be – or appear to be – radically opposed to it.[6] Categorizing religious gatherings as "unnecessary" or "inessential" is manifestly contrary to the common good of society, which includes the public recognition of God's right to receive due worship, and the priority of our spiritual obligations and needs, as Leo XIII, Pius XI, and other popes taught with one voice. In his *Letter from a Birmingham Jail*, Martin Luther King Jr. memorably recalled the teaching of St Thomas Aquinas: an unjust law is no law at all (and the same holds for regulations, policies, and other government initiatives, whether officially passed in a legislature or not). To such "laws" we must give not obedience but civil disobedience, which is obedience to a higher law, indeed the highest law.[7]

Among the sad lessons learned in 2020, perhaps the saddest was that we cannot rely on most of our bishops to look out for our spiritual good, or even to exhibit a basic understanding of the non-negotiable and non-erasable priority of divine worship. We entered 2021 with a wide-eyed awareness that we are more or less left on our own to find whatever resources we can, where and when we can. Our good and holy priests need to carry the holy water, so to speak, and do the heavy lifting when push comes to shove. That will include – and here we come to the crux of the matter – a willingness to suffer suspension or other disciplinary measures for so doing, with no intention of ceasing their ministrations.

It is time to show forth in broad daylight the two kingdoms that currently occupy the same physical, liturgical, and juridical space. The servants of these respective kingdoms do not work for the same ends, and the gods of the new religion are hungrier by the day. A fundamental choice is inescapable. The traditional Latin Mass is part of it, but clearly not all. The priests of so-called "Ecclesia Dei" institutes (e.g., the Institute of Christ the King Sovereign Priest, the

---

6   See chapter 7.
7   See Kwasniewski, "The Kingship of Christ and the Anti-Kingdom of Modernity."

Priestly Fraternity of St Peter) have also been put to the challenge by *Traditionis Custodes*: what is their "bridge too far," their "line in the sand"? They must learn to die to their fears of the marauding "indy chapel" life. The whole canonically-regular edifice is going under; it is falling in line for subservience to Bergoglianity and its socialist-globalist-environmentalist ideology.

To all clergy, mainstream and traditionalist, the challenge has been sounded: continued compliance in bad policy may not, after all, be a tactful investment in a tomorrow when "things blow over." What will then be left to defend—a set of "church services" that can be canceled at the whim of a heathen governor or the still more despicable whim of a spineless bishop threatened by paper bombs from Cardinal Roche? Yet laity are simultaneously supposed to teach their children about the heroism of martyrs and how good it is to stand in the stream of sacred Tradition! Things haven't even begun to get really rough, and the fort's already been betrayed.

Dear Priests: If and when you decide to start offering underground Masses, here are some points of advice that have been shared with me by those who are experienced in such matters.

1. Do not communicate about anything via emails. This is a major mistake. Those emails are likely to end up in the chancery office.

2. In general, do not put things into writing. In-person communication is best, even traveling by car to tell people something. A phone is the next best thing, in spite of the fact that Apple or Google or someone will own your voice.

3. Be careful about who is taken into confidentiality. This is good advice for laity as well as clergy. It may sound harsh to say it, but we should not let our excitement about having Mass blind us to the malice that exists in demons or disordered souls, in people of poorly-formed conscience who might believe they have a "duty" to sniff us out and then snuff us out. We are living in a time of spiritual warfare, so we must know *well* who our allies are, and assume *nothing* about those whom we do not know well. If you are going to invite someone to a Mass, let it be someone that you know *agrees* with the reason why the Mass is being held and is capable of maintaining silence, rather than inviting someone who "might be interested in coming" but whose allegiance you're not certain

of. Yes, this might mean that deserving souls will be excluded for a time, but it is better thus than to put the entire endeavor at risk.

4. Be wise about how to gather, if you are using a church or chapel. A friend of mine in Eastern Europe described her experience in November of 2020:

> My visit to my family passed undisturbed. There was a beautiful All Saints Mass, and three Masses for All Souls, in a church locked with a key. The organizers opened the church fifteen minutes before the Mass, and again one minute before the beginning for possible latecomers. It was prohibited to gather near the door; we were told to walk about nonchalantly in the park, in case we came and the church was still closed. After the Mass, we left one by one, at random. It resembles the years of Communism all too much.

On the other hand, there may be situations where the most appropriate course of action is to seize hold of an unused or shut-down church and to claim it for one's community, as occurred among the Port Marly traditionalists in 1987 (of which more in a moment). As Christian Marquant says: "Piety and fortitude are not opposed."[8]

I think the challenge is making that first giant step of saying "I'm full in, no matter what." It seems to me that the comforts and conveniences of our modern Western life make that step nearly impossible for most people. Let it not be so for us. What a glorious opportunity Our Lord is giving us to demonstrate to Him – and even, in a way, to ourselves – that He is first in our lives, first in our hearts!

It is only fair to say that some bishops, especially in France, stood up to the civil authorities in a more forceful way. Gladden J. Pappin relates:

> Mgr. Marc Aillet, bishop of Bayonne, was one of five initial bishops to request that the Conseil d'État lift restrictions. In an interview with *Le Figaro*, Aillet suggested that in some circumstances, the common good of the Church outweighs obedience to civil mandates. "If Saint Paul exhorts us to obey the civil authorities," he said, "it is with respect to the common good – that of society, but

---

8 "Resistance is never futile: An interview with Christian Marquant, founder of Paix Liturgique," *Rorate Caeli*, December 16, 2020.

also the superior common good of the Church, whose supreme law is the salvation of souls."[9]

Jane Stannus narrates:

> Bishop Ginoux of Montauban has also spoken out loudly against the ban, tweeting on October 29 [2020], "It's easy to ask bishops to take the lead if no one stands behind them. Invade the churches at Mass times, ask for the Mass and bishops and priests will come to celebrate it... Actions, not words!" He said Mass himself on Sunday, November 15, in the presence of ten or so faithful, and publicly congratulated pro-Mass protestors.[10]

These Successors of the Apostles were not afraid to encourage the faithful to act openly against unjust or irreligious laws and regulations, and offered the support of their own example. This is a lesson all the bishops need to internalize in regard to the unjust and irreligious policies of *Traditionis Custodes*.

It's easy to understand some of the poor decisions that were reached in the first months of the outbreak of Covid-19. We did not know how harmful it would be or how quickly it would spread, and whether our medical facilities would be overwhelmed. However, as time passed, and the statistics became better known, we came to see quite clearly – or I should say, anyone who took pains to step past the *Pravda*-like unified mainstream media narrative – that we were dealing with something like a severe flu season.

Bishops have the God-given responsibility to apply their reason to evaluate the seriousness of the risks while at the same time preserving and promoting the essential goods of Christian life, which include liturgical worship and reception of sacraments. These are not only indispensable for the sanctification of individuals, which is reason enough to uphold them, come what may; they are also necessary for beseeching divine assistance and pardon. It would have required a great deal more danger than anything we witnessed to justify long-lasting restrictions on worship and sacraments;

---

9   "The Mass Is the First Necessity," *First Things* online, November 20, 2020.
10   "France Declares War on the Mass (Again)," *Crisis Magazine*, November 19, 2020.

nothing could have warranted their simple cancellation. It was unjust, *tout court*, for churches to be shut against the faithful, for public Masses to be eliminated, for Confessions or extreme unction to be lessened or unavailable, for Adoration to be suspended, and so forth. So much has been written on this subject that further commentary is not necessary here.[11]

Rather, what I wish to emphasize is the need for Catholics, both laity and clergy, to move into a more decisive phase of resistance against unjust determinations of either temporal or ecclesiastical authority. The tumultuous history after the Second Vatican Council offers us models. Christian Marquant, head of Paix Liturgique, speaks of two that occurred in France:

> Catholic resistance had not been completely asphyxiated [after the Council] – but that was no reason for its opponents to stop their persecutions. Everywhere, by calumny or even by force, they did all in their power to prevent Masses, catechisms, schools. Paradoxically, and contrary to every Vatican II principle of promoting the laity, this will to eradicate came from the clergy and attacked the people. Indeed, historians and sociologists have noted that the refusal of conciliar novelties was an essentially lay and popular phenomenon. The Catholic people was not taking it lying down. Two important popular events shook the Church of France during this time: first, in 1977, the storming of Saint Nicolas du Chardonnet by a crowd of Parisian faithful following Msgr. Ducaud-Bourget; they were sick and tired of attending Mass in rented halls. Later, near Versailles in 1987, there was the reaction of the parishioners at Saint Louis du Port Marly who refused to allow their community to be killed: they had been kicked out of their church, its doors had been walled up . . . and they simply kicked down the doors to move back in.[12]

The latter event in particular deserves to be better known among Catholics everywhere. A Catholic parish in Port Marly, twenty miles from Paris, had maintained the Latin Mass after Vatican II.

---

11   See Philip F. Lawler, *Contagious Faith: Why the Church Must Spread Hope, Not Fear, in a Pandemic* (Manchester, NH: Crisis Publications, 2021).
12   Marquant, "Resistance is never futile."

When the parish priest died, the bishop attempted to impose the new Mass in French. The people occupied the church, refused to welcome the new pastor, and maintained a priest of their own to continue the traditional Mass. The bishop retaliated by having fifty police officers come and take back the church, clubbing and dragging out men, women, and children from the pews. The police then sealed the doors of the church with cemented cinder blocks.

Two weeks later, for Palm Sunday of 1987, 3,000 traditionalists came back to the church in procession. A group of laymen with a battering ram smashed through the cinder blocks and the faithful took possession of the church. "If the police come to evict us again," said Francis Tommy-Martin, on guard duty at the church, "we can have more than 500 people in the streets in less than an hour." In spite of a continually rocky relationship with the local Diocese of Versailles, the traditional community in Port Marly remained steady to the present, and, in more recent years, was established as a parish under the care of the Institute of Christ the King Sovereign Priest.

A video of that memorable reconquest on Palm Sunday in 1987 is available online. Worthy of special mention is the segment during which the procession reaches the church and the battering ram breaks through the blocked entrances.

This video is a reminder of just how bad things had become in France (and nearly everywhere else except Campos, Brazil) after the Second Vatican Council—and of the courage and strength of faithful resistance. Just as the loyal Catholics of the Vendée opposed the Revolution in France, so loyal Catholics after the Council resisted the "revolution in tiara and cope";[13] and so must we do in our day. The Covid-1984 plandemic caught us quite unprepared for the rapid power-grab of civil and ecclesiastical authorities, who recognized a golden opportunity to stifle resurgent populism and traditionalism.[14] *Traditionis Custodes* followed in its wake. In response, we ought to emulate the more down-to-earth methods of our valiant predecessors.

---

13   See Brian Miles, "Revolution in Tiara and Cope: A History of Church Infiltration," *OnePeterFive*, May 10, 2016.

14   On this point, see Kwasniewski, *Holy Bread of Eternal Life*, 241–55.

25

In Uncertain Times,
House Chapels Proliferate

A GROWING NUMBER OF CATHOLICS ARE
interested in building, within or adjacent to their home,
a chapel with an altar.[1] Many have already done so. Their
reasons for doing it vary. Some would like to have a formal prayer
corner with icons or statues and they wish to give it still more dignity by the installation of an altar beneath the holy images. Others
have a spare room in the house that is well suited to becoming a
chapel where people can go to pray the Divine Office, meditate with
the Rosary, or read Scripture, and surely no chapel is complete
without an altar to remind us of Christ the Rock, the supreme
Sacrifice, and of our duty to make our hearts His altar. Still others
have priest friends who stay with them when traveling through
town or who might wish to have a quiet place to say Mass when
they are not otherwise obliged to offer it—or who are looking ahead
to darker and more difficult times, when good priests may be forced
to make the rounds from house to house, or go into hiding.

Whatever the reasons may be, we need to understand a few
things before we go about setting up such an altar.

First, while the family is indeed a domestic church, and the
home is a sanctified place once it has been formally blessed using
the *Rituale Romanum*, nevertheless an altar of this kind has not
received a solemn dedication, nor has a home chapel been consecrated for divine worship, and so its use should be seen as something of an exception, or at least, something that should have a
reasonable justification. Certainly, an emergency situation, such as
the State's unjust suppression of worship in churches, or a bishop's
cancellation of the traditional Mass, would easily qualify.

Second, the altar, if possible, should have a first-class relic in it

---

1   These house or home chapels may also be called oratories, prayer corners, or
shrines. The terminology is not particularly important, as long as one does not
call them "churches," a term that has a quite specific meaning.

or at least placed on it for the offering of the Holy Sacrifice of the Mass. Some priests travel with a Byzantine antimension, an altar covering with relics sewn into it. The very prayer said by the priest in the traditional Roman rite when he reaches the altar to kiss it before saying the Introit makes reference to relics in and near the altar: *Oramus te, Domine, per merita Sanctorum tuorum* [he kisses the sacred stone] *quorum reliquiae hic sunt, et omnium Sanctorum: ut indulgere digneris omnia peccata mea* (We beseech Thee, O Lord, by the merits of Thy Saints whose relics are here, and of all the Saints, that Thou wouldst vouchsafe to forgive me all my sins). A traditional priest should be able to assist in sourcing relics.

Third, once an altar is installed, it would be improper to use it for any other purpose, especially once Mass has been offered on it. It should not double as a dining room table or a television stand or a surface for cleaning rifles. Let the altar be an altar and nothing else.

Fourth, make sure that the altar is built according to correct specifications. Most regular tables are too low to be suitable for Mass, since they are made for sitting, not for standing. Although dimensions can vary considerably and still be acceptable, the following dimensions work admirably for a home altar and have been found by priests of my acquaintance to be suitable: 39 inches in height; 59 inches wide; 20 inches deep. This height, depth, and breadth allows room for everything needed for the traditional Latin Mass.[2]

When space and resources allow, it is optimal to place an altar atop three steps, but this is not always practicable in a home setting. While the steps are a beautiful symbol, clergy are accustomed to "making do" with whatever situation is at hand (e.g., many priests when traveling offer Mass in hotel rooms). I have also seen home altars fully dressed with an altar frontal in the appropriate liturgical color of the season or feast; this level of refinement may be considered when everything else is in place.

My view is that we *should* be building altars in our homes.[3] My wife and I commissioned a friend to build one, which we had the

---

2   Those who are interested in further details can read Matthew Alderman on the proper shape, dimension, and placement of altars: "On the Size of Altars," *New Liturgical Movement*, October 8, 2010.

3   Readers may draw inspiration from the many photographs of home altars and chapels featured at the website *New Liturgical Movement*. Seach for "newliturgicalmovement.org" and "home altar" or "home chapel."

privilege to see "inaugurated" by Holy Mass three days in a row when a priest friend was passing through town. Built of sturdy wood and stained a dark brown, it was set up in our living room against the eastern wall, with an icon hung above it, and two first-class relics on top of it.

A last point. There is absolutely no need for a home altar to be a "Cranmer table," that is, situated so that a priest can say Mass *versus populum* or toward the congregation. Historically and theologically, this is an incorrect way to offer Mass;[4] it is not even what the Novus Ordo assumes by its own rubrics;[5] and it is awkward in a liturgy done only a few feet away from the faithful. Any priest of the Roman rite should be able and willing to offer the sacrifice *ad orientem* (eastward). This, moreover, is usually necessary in a house because of the small space available, where an altar up against the wall will be of much practical advantage.

Priests who offer the traditional Latin Mass are usually well-equipped to offer it anywhere, carrying with them reversible chasubles and the other garments, as well as candles, altar cards, and a missal. However, it is a good idea for those who have a home altar to keep a supply of candles (preferably at least 51% beeswax), cruets for the water and wine, three layers of linen to dress the altar, and a small bell. It can't hurt to have the other items, too, in case one ends up giving shelter to a fugitive who has lost his belongings or who never owned them to begin with.

How ironic it would be if the "Christian house church"—that concept so dear to the antiquarianizing liturgical revolutionaries who took it as a pretext for their streamlined modern prayer-service—turned out to be the place where the Tridentine Mass in all its medieval and Baroque density, albeit in temporarily humble circumstances, survived the coming persecution of Catholics. Martin Mosebach relates how a priest of his acquaintance was exasperated with him for not attending a Novus Ordo at the cathedral with an orchestral Mass. Mosebach reflects: "I simply could not make him

---

4   See my articles "Mass 'Facing the People' as Counter-Catechesis and Irreligion," *New Liturgical Movement*, August 20, 2018; "How Contrary Orientations Signify Contradictory Theologies," *New Liturgical Movement*, November 5, 2018; cf. Michael Fiedrowicz, *The Traditional Mass*, 141–52.

5   See my article "The Normativity of *Ad Orientem* Worship According to the Ordinary Form's Rubrics," *New Liturgical Movement*, November 23, 2015.

see that a low Mass in the old rite, read silently in a garage, is more solemn than the biggest church concert with spiritual trimmings."[6]

Perhaps a time is coming when the words of St John Chrysostom will once again be as accurate as they were in the fourth century:

> As those who bring comedians, dancers, and harlots into their feasts call in demons and Satan himself and fill their homes with innumerable contentions (among them jealousy, adultery, debauchery, and countless evils); so those who invoke David with his lyre call inwardly on Christ. Where Christ is, let no demon enter; let him not even dare to look in in passing. Peace, delight, and all good things flow here as from fountains. Those [pagans] make their home a theatre; make yours a church. For where there are psalms, and prayers, and the dance of the prophets, and singers with pious intentions, no one will err if he call the assembly a church.[7]

In Western history, house chapels are a phenomenon associated mostly with aristocrats who lived on large estates and could afford to employ a resident chaplain. In times of persecution, these chapels often became important places of refuge, since their remoteness, together with the status of the family owners, introduced a kind of safety buffer between the outside world and the services that took place within. This buffer was not always enough, alas, to prevent priests from being surprised and captured by hostile state forces.

While some house chapels of the aforementioned sort are still in existence and functional, it is becoming more common to see modest chapels being built in the homes of ordinary Catholic laity. A basement renovation, a small spare room, an attic, all offer possibilities for building an altar and setting up a space that is appropriate for the Mass and other devotions in a time of necessity. Some families simply wish to create a prayerful space where they can gather for individual or group prayer, in an environment that reminds them of and connects them with the parish or chapel

---

6   *The Heresy of Formlessness: The Roman Liturgy and Its Enemy*, trans. Graham Harrison, rev. and expanded ed. (Brooklyn, NY: Angelico Press, 2018), 80.
7   St John Chrysostom, from the *Exposition of Psalm XLI*, in Oliver Strunk, ed., *Source Readings in Music History from Classical Antiquity through the Romantic Era* (New York: W. W. Norton & Co., 1950), 69.

where they usually go for Mass. Others, keenly aware of the grave and deteriorating situation of the Church in the West, have decided to "plan ahead" by making a suitable space for eventual underground or "canceled" priests. One diocese has already (illegally) outlawed private traditional Masses altogether, and there may be more that follow suit.[8] Priests in such dioceses will benefit from having places of refuge where they can bypass the unjust restrictions and offer Mass to God, in the presence of grateful laity.

Some Catholics may be inclined to scoff or raise eyebrows at Masses held in homes, as if it is a thing that should not be done. They would be right in this sense: in ideal circumstances, every parish church, every cathedral, every basilica, should be breathing the sacred silence of the Low Mass and should be ringing with the sounds of Gregorian chant and the pipe organ at the *Missa cantata* and the *Missa solemnis*. But that is not where we are – not even remotely. And in a time of growing hostility to the tradition of the Church, our patrimony must be preserved and handed on. In the 1970s, there were plenty of Masses in hotels and living rooms: that is a large part of the reason we have the traditional Mass today in churches and cathedrals.

Robert Hugh Benson's historical novel set in the reign of Queen Elizabeth, *By What Authority?*, furnishes the best fictional treatment (of which I am aware) of a secret Mass in a home. One of the principal characters, a Puritan lady named Isabel, who has become intimate friends with a Catholic recusant family and is drawn to their faith, experiences her first Mass, said by a priest who has been racked multiple times and who has nonetheless escaped with his life. Given the extremely dangerous circumstances, it has to take place in the middle of the night, in the living room of the manor. Here is the excerpt: it is one of the finest descriptions of the Holy Mass in all of English literature.[9]

The chapel at Maxwell Hall was in the cloister wing; but a stranger visiting the house would never have suspected it. Opening out of Lady Maxwell's new sitting-room was a little lobby or landing, about

---

8   See chapter 16.
9   The excerpt is taken from the unabridged newly typeset edition of *By What Authority?* published by Cenacle Press of Silverstream Priory.

four yards square, lighted from above; at the further end of it was the door into her bedroom. This lobby was scarcely more than a broad passage; and would attract no attention from any passing through it. The only piece of furniture in it was a great tall old chest as high as a table, that stood against the inner wall beyond which was the long gallery that looked down upon the cloister garden. The lobby appeared to be practically as broad as the two rooms on either side of it; but this was effected by the outer wall being made to bulge a little; and the inner wall being thinner than inside the two living-rooms. The deception was further increased by the two living-rooms being first wainscoted and then hung with thick tapestry; while the lobby was bare. A curious person who should look in the chest would find there only an old dress and a few pieces of stuff. This lobby, however, was the chapel; and through the chest was the entrance to one of the priest's hiding holes, where also the altar-stone and the ornaments and the vestments were kept. The bottom of the chest was in reality hinged in such a way that it would fall, on the proper pressure being applied in two places at once, sufficiently to allow the side of the chest against the wall to be pushed aside, which in turn gave entrance to a little space some two yards long by a yard wide; and here were kept all the necessaries for divine worship; with room besides for a couple of men at least to be hidden away. There was also a way from this hole on to the roof, but it was a difficult and dangerous way; and was only to be used in case of extreme necessity.

It was in this lobby that Isabel found herself the next morning kneeling and waiting for mass. She had been awakened by Mistress Margaret shortly before four o'clock and told in a whisper to dress herself in the dark; for it was impossible under the circumstances to tell whether the house was not watched; and a light seen from outside might conceivably cause trouble and disturbance. So she had dressed herself and come down from her room along the passages, so familiar during the day, so somber and suggestive now in the black morning with but one shaded light placed at the angles. Other figures were stealing along too; but she could not tell who they were in the gloom. Then she had come through the little sitting-room where the scene of last night had taken place and into the lobby beyond.

But the whole place was transformed.

Over the old chest now hung a picture, that usually was in Lady Maxwell's room, of the Blessed Mother and her holy Child, in a great carved frame of some black wood. The chest had become an altar: Isabel could see the slight elevation in the middle of the long white linen cloth where the altar-stone lay, and upon that again, at the left corner, a pile of linen and silk. Upon the altar at the back stood two slender silver candlesticks with burning tapers in them; and a silver crucifix between them. The carved wooden panels, representing the sacrifice of Isaac on the one half and the offering of Melchisedech on the other, served instead of an embroidered altar-frontal. Against the side wall stood a little white-covered folding table with the cruets and other necessaries upon it. There were two or three benches across the rest of the lobby; and at these were kneeling a dozen or more persons, motionless, their faces downcast. There was a little wind such as blows before the dawn moaning gently outside; and within was a slight draught that made the taper flames lean over now and then.

Isabel took her place beside Mistress Margaret at the front bench; and as she knelt forward she noticed a space left beyond her for Lady Maxwell. A moment later there came slow and painful steps through the sitting-room, and Lady Maxwell came in very slowly with her son leaning on her arm and on a stick. There was a silence so profound that it seemed to Isabel as if all had stopped breathing. She could only hear the slow plunging pulse of her own heart.

James took his mother across the altar to her place, and left her there, bowing to her; and then went up to the altar to vest. As he reached it and paused, a servant slipped out and received the stick from him. The priest made the sign of the cross, and took up the amice from the vestments that lay folded on the altar. He was already in his cassock.

Isabel watched each movement with a deep agonizing interest; he was so frail and broken, so bent in his figure, so slow and feeble in his movements. He made an attempt to raise the amice but could not, and turned slightly; and the man from behind stepped up again and lifted it for him. Then he helped him with each of the vestments, lifted the alb over his head and tenderly drew the bandaged hands through the sleeves; knit the girdle round him; gave

him the stole to kiss and then placed it over his neck and crossed
the ends beneath the girdle and adjusted the amice; then he placed
the maniple on his left arm, but so tenderly! and lastly, lifted the
great red chasuble and dropped it over his head and straightened
it — and there stood the priest as he had stood last Sunday, in crimson vestments again; but bowed and thin-faced now.

Then he began the preparation with the servant who knelt
beside him in his ordinary livery, as server; and Isabel heard the
murmur of the Latin words for the first time. Then he stepped up
to the altar, bent slowly and kissed it and the mass began.

Isabel had a missal, lent to her by Mistress Margaret; but she
hardly looked at it; so intent was she on that crimson figure and
his strange movements and his low broken voice. It was unlike
anything that she had ever imagined worship to be. Public worship
to her had meant hitherto one of two things — either sitting under a
minister and having the word applied to her soul in the sacrament
of the pulpit; or else the saying of prayers by the minister aloud and
distinctly and with expression, so that the intellect could follow the
words, and assent with a hearty Amen. The minister was a minister to man of the Word of God, an interpreter of His gospel to man.

But here was a worship unlike all this in almost every detail. The
priest was addressing God, not man; therefore he did so in a low
voice, and in a tongue as Campion had said on the scaffold "that
they both understood." It was comparatively unimportant whether
man followed it word for word, for (and here the second radical
difference lay) the point of the worship for the people lay, not in an
intellectual apprehension of the words, but in a voluntary assent
to and participation in the supreme act to which the words were
indeed necessary but subordinate. It was the thing that was done,
not the words that were said, that was mighty with God. Here,
as these Catholics round Isabel at any rate understood it, and as
she too began to perceive it too, though dimly and obscurely, was
the sublime mystery of the Cross presented to God. As He looked
down well pleased into the silence and darkness of Calvary, and saw
there the act accomplished by which the world was redeemed, so
here (this handful of disciples believed), He looked down into the
silence and twilight of this little lobby, and saw that same mystery
accomplished at the hands of one who in virtue of his participation

in the priesthood of the Son of God was empowered to pronounce these heart-shaking words by which the Body that hung on Calvary, and the Blood that dripped from it there, were again spread before His eyes, under the forms of bread and wine. Much of this faith of course was still dark to Isabel; but yet she understood enough; and when the murmur of the priest died to a throbbing silence, and the worshippers sank in yet more profound adoration, and then with terrible effort and a quick gasp or two of pain, those wrenched bandaged hands rose trembling in the air with Something that glimmered white between them; the Puritan girl too drooped her head, and lifted up her heart, and entreated the Most High and most Merciful to look down on the Mystery of Redemption accomplished on earth; and for the sake of the Well-Beloved to send down His Grace on the Catholic Church; to strengthen and save the living; to give rest and peace to the dead; and especially to remember her dear brother Anthony, and Hubert whom she loved; and Mistress Margaret and Lady Maxwell, and this faithful household: and the poor battered man before her, who, not only as a priest was made like to the Eternal Priest, but as a victim too had hung upon a prostrate cross, fastened by hands and feet; thus bearing on his body for all to see the marks of the Lord Jesus.

Lady Maxwell and Mistress Margaret both rose and stepped forward after the Priest's Communion, and received from those wounded hands the Broken Body of the Lord.

And then the mass was presently over; and the server stepped forward again to assist the priest to unvest, himself lifting each vestment off, for Father Maxwell was terribly exhausted by now, and laying it on the altar. Then he helped him to a little footstool in front of him, for him to kneel and make his thanksgiving. Isabel looked with an odd wonder at the server; he was the man that she knew so well, who opened the door for her, and waited at table; but now a strange dignity rested on him as he moved confidently and reverently about the awful altar, and touched the vestments that even to her Puritan eyes shone with new sanctity. It startled her to think of the hidden Catholic life of this house – of these servants who loved and were familiar with mysteries that she had been taught to dread and distrust, but before which she too now was to bow her being in faith and adoration.

After a minute or two, Mistress Margaret touched Isabel on the arm and beckoned to her to come up to the altar, which she began immediately to strip of its ornaments and cloth, having first lit another candle on one of the benches. Isabel helped her in this with a trembling dread, as all the others except Lady Maxwell and her son were now gone out silently; and presently the picture was down, and leaning against the wall; the ornaments and sacred vessels packed away in their box, with the vestments and linen in another. Then together they lifted off the heavy altar stone. Mistress Margaret next laid back the lid of the chest; and put her hands within, and presently Isabel saw the back of the chest fall back, apparently into the wall. Mistress Margaret then beckoned to Isabel to climb into the chest and go through; she did so without much difficulty, and found herself in the little room behind. There was a stool or two and some shelves against the wall, with a plate or two upon them and one or two tools. She received the boxes handed through, and followed Mistress Margaret's instructions as to where to place them; and when all was done, she slipped back again through the chest into the lobby.

The priest and his mother were still in their places, motionless. Mistress Margaret closed the chest inside and out, beckoned Isabel into the sitting-room and closed the door behind them. Then she threw her arms round the girl and kissed her again and again.

"My own darling," said the nun, with tears in her eyes. "God bless you – your first mass. Oh! I have prayed for this. And you know all our secrets now. Now go to your room, and to bed again. It is only a little after five. You shall see him – James – before he goes. God bless you, my dear!"

She watched Isabel down the passage; and then turned back again to where the other two were still kneeling, to make her own thanksgiving.

Isabel went to her room as one in a dream. She was soon in bed again, but could not sleep; the vision of that strange worship she had assisted at; the pictorial details of it, the glow of the two candles on the shoulders of the crimson chasuble as the priest bent to kiss the altar or to adore; the bowed head of the server at his side; the picture overhead with the Mother and her downcast eyes, and the radiant Child stepping from her knees to bless the world – all this burned on the darkness. With the least effort of imagination too she could recall the steady murmur of the unfamiliar words; hear the rustle of the silken vestment; the stirrings and breathings of the worshippers in the little room.

Then in endless course the intellectual side of it all began to present itself. She had assisted at what the Government called a crime; it was for that—that collection of strange but surely at least innocent things—actions, words, material objects—that men and women of the same flesh and blood as herself were ready to die; and for which others equally of one nature with herself were ready to put them to death. It was the mass—the mass—she had seen—she repeated the word to herself, so sinister, so suggestive, so mighty. Then she began to think again—if indeed it is possible to say that she had ever ceased to think of him—of Anthony, who would be so much horrified if he knew; of Hubert, who had renounced this wonderful worship, and all, she feared, for love of her—and above all of her father, who had regarded it with such repugnance:—yes, thought Isabel, but he knows all now. Then she thought of Mistress Margaret again. After all, the nun had a spiritual life which in intensity and purity surpassed any she had ever experienced or even imagined; and yet the heart of it all was the mass. She thought of the old wrinkled quiet face when she came back to breakfast at the Dower House: she had soon learnt to read from that face whether mass had been said that morning or not at the Hall. And Mistress Margaret was only one of thousands to whom this little set of actions half seen and words half heard, wrought and said by a man in a curious dress, were more precious than all meditation and prayer put together. Could the vast superstructure of prayer and effort and aspiration rest upon a piece of empty folly such as children or savages might invent?

Then very naturally, as she began now to get quieter and less excited, she passed on to the spiritual side of it. Had that indeed happened that Mistress Margaret believed—that the very Body and Blood of her own dear Savior, Jesus Christ, had in virtue of His own clear promise—His own clear promise!—become present there under the hands of His priest? Was it, indeed,—this half-hour action,—the most august mystery of time, the Lamb eternally slain, presenting Himself and His Death before the Throne in a tremendous and bloodless Sacrifice—so august that the very angels can only worship it afar off and cannot perform it?

26

When Nuns Are Persecuted: Lessons from the Russian Underground

T HOSE WHO HAVE BEEN PAYING ATTENTION to the mounting attack on the contemplative religious life and on traditional religious communities[1] may be wondering: What can be done about this evil? How can nuns or sisters defend themselves? What can they do? Are they helplessly at the mercy of Church authorities who would obliterate them from off the face of the earth?

The answer to the first question is grim: there is very little that can be *done* about the attack, which is under way *right now*; short of a dramatic divine intervention, the Vatican will lower the boom. Attempts will be made to discredit, dissolve, and disperse traditional communities, especially the contemplative Carmelite nuns who are the "heart" of the Church.[2] To the second question, the nuns may defend themselves by appealing to various dicasteries in defense of their centuries-old and consistently approved charism, by asking for the intervention of friendly cardinals and other influencers, even by directly calling on the pope to make exceptions for them.

But let us say these routes fail to deliver the goods, and a decree comes down saying: "Your monastery is closed." Or: "We are sending so-and-so as your interim superior until the problems we discovered have been resolved." What then?

There is a strategy that has worked before during times of persecution in Church history. And let us be clear about it: there *is* a persecution taking place—this time not from the State, as in Henry VIII's suppression of monasteries or the butchery of the French

---

1 Well documented by Hilary White: see "A Warning to the Carmelites of Fairfield," *OnePeterFive*, October 21, 2021, which provides further links to her research.
2 See my article "Contemplative Religious: The Heart of the Church and the Measure of Her Health," *OnePeterFive*, October 2, 2019.

Revolution, but from churchmen who dare, with diabolic pride, to lay violent hands on the apple of God's eye. This strategy aims at preserving the reality of the charism and traditional way of life by temporarily sacrificing some of its external manifestations. The step is taken under compulsion and therefore does not count in the sight of God as a blameworthy abandonment of these external manifestations; indeed, they are left aside precisely to continue adhering to what they signify.

The most basic presupposition is that the community's material possessions, including their land and buildings, must be owned by a lay organization, so that no religious entity, diocesan or otherwise, can lay hands on it as "spoils of war."

Assuming this to be in place, the nuns do not have to bend to unjust demands for their modernization, coerced federating, etc. Instead, they voluntarily "dissolve" the community by taking off their religious habits. The place will no longer be called a convent or monastery; signs, placards, and letterhead to this effect will have disappeared. The nuns adopt a form of simple lay clothing that suggests a religious habit, and remain in their buildings, *living exactly the same life of personal and liturgical prayer and penance that they were living before.*

The monastery has thus become, in the sight of the world, a center in which like-minded women voluntarily pursue a common interest. It's nothing other than a group of devout laity who have formed what might be called a "household of prayer," against which there are no prohibitions in either civil or canon law. They do not even have to ask to be "an association of the faithful" (*consociatio christifidelium*). They don't need to have any status whatsoever. They just do what they have always done, but without the labels. They know in their hearts that they are still nuns.

The most important "piece" in this scenario is the availability of a traditionally-minded priest who can serve as their chaplain. If the nuns are located in a diocese with a supportive bishop, that bishop could no doubt find or appoint a suitable priest to serve in this capacity, or welcome a priest from elsewhere who has the requisite background. If the nuns are located in a diocese with a hostile bishop or a bishop who, buckling under Vatican pressure, refuses to give these women a chaplain, then it will be time for a more radical step: the nuns would need to find their own chaplain—probably a "canceled priest"—who, though he may officially lack faculties, knows with a clean conscience and a spotless record that he has been canceled illicitly and invalidly, and is therefore free to give himself to this important work. That is a worst-case scenario, but in our times it may be necessary, until the pope and the Roman curia reverse their self-destructive course, and/or until the local ordinary grasps the necessity to act fearlessly for the benefit of his flock, regardless of bullying from above.

If worse comes to worst, the religious life can move entirely underground. I read an inspiring book a few years ago about Russian Orthodox monks and nuns that gave a lot of attention to their sufferings and survival under the Communists.[3] They were clever about how to manipulate or mislead or confound the authorities; and when they ran out of luck, they knew how to move into disguise, going underground and continuing their life under the very noses of their persecutors. When Communism fell, it was discovered that certain monks and nuns had kept their life intact and had passed it on to new members over the course of decades of official suppression.

The best chapter in this regard is "The True Story of Mother Frosya," of which I will now share some excerpts.

> In that little house on Lesnaya Street in Diveyevo where the relics of St Seraphim were kept, there lived a schema-nun named Margarita. Except that for many, many years nobody knew that she was secretly a nun. Everybody just called her Mother Frosya or just simply Frosya. She was as old as the century itself. When I met her in February 1983 on my first trip to Diveyevo, she had just turned eighty-three years old.
>
> "Secret monasticism" is something that began to happen during the persecutions of the Church of the twentieth century. Having been secretly given monastic vows, monks and nuns would remain living in the world,

---

3 Archimandrite Tikhon, *Everyday Saints and Other Stories* (Dallas, TX: Pokrov Publications, 2012). I am not unaware that some of the Russian Orthodox were in collusion with the Communists and that they did horrible things (or allowed them to be done) to Greek Catholics and Roman Catholics. But let us have the fairness to acknowledge the greatness of the witness and resistance given by so many of the Orthodox, too. Anyone who reads this book will be able to see that greatness and will be inspired by it.

would wear normal secular clothes, and would work in normal secular institutions, while strictly fulfilling all their monastic vows in secret. Only a father confessor or spiritual father would know about their vows and about their new names. . . .

Everyone thought that Mother Frosya had simply once been just a novice in the former monastery. And if curious persons would ask her questions about her past, Mother Frosya would answer completely honestly that there once had been a time when she was a novice in the Monastery of Diveyevo.

She was only forced to reveal her true monastic name in the beginning of the 1990s, with the blessing of Abbess Sergia, the first appointed abbess of the resurrected Diveyevo Monastery, to which Mother Frosya moved back for her last three years before her death. But until this time everyone just called her Frosya.[4]

Mother Frosya herself describes what it was like when the Soviet soldiers came to expel them from the monastery in September of 1927 and then destroy its buildings:

One week later, before the final Evening Vespers we rang all the bells, sounding all their chimes, all of them—letting them ring for the last time. We rang and rang them, and then we said our Divine Service. Then we were scattered like little birds, scattered to the wind! Just like that—in the pouring rain. The cops came and kicked us out into the street! Lord! We were getting it from everywhere: from the people on one side, and God on the other. Oh, Queen of Heaven!

What could we do? It was impossible for us to wear our nuns' habits anymore. The authorities had forbidden it. So we had to wear secular clothes. And all icons were forbidden. They made us put up pictures of Lenin instead. None of us would agree to that! . . .

On the second day, they took our Mother Superior off to jail. And we got scattered all over. There was a bishop there secretly, and he said to us all, "They drove you out of the monastery. But we have not released you from your monastic vows."

---

4   Tikhon, *Everyday Saints*, 223–24.

Fast forward ten years:

> It was the year 1937. I and several of the other nuns were
> still living near the monastery. I was right here on Kal-
> ganovka Street. And on the other side of the street there
> were also little houses in which nuns were living . . .[5]

She talks about how the nuns were eventually rounded up and sent
to a work camp, accused of being "vagabonds":

> We were searched! They took everything from us! They
> took away our crosses! Lord forgive them! Oh, Mother of
> God . . . One policeman ripped off my neck cross, then
> threw it on the ground and trampled on it, barking at
> me: "Why are you wearing that?" You know, when they
> were taking away our crosses, the feeling I had—it was
> as if our Lord and Savior himself were standing there
> crucified, suffering and enduring it all himself! They
> took away our crosses! How could they? It was so awful!
> And then what? How could we live without our
> crosses? Well, in those days we all were set to work as
> seamstresses, using locally picked Uzbek cotton. They
> had these little forklike twigs, those cotton balls, and if
> you cut them a little bit they were like little crosses. So we
> all made ourselves little crosses. But then we went with
> our makeshift crosses into the prison bathhouse. Some
> of the women there ratted us out to the bosses: "Those
> nuns are wearing crosses again!" But they didn't bother
> taking away our little homemade crosses. There was no
> point. Take them away and we'd make new ones. . . .
> Some of our group had been in the choir. And so
> sometimes we would gather together on the top prison
> planks and we would just quietly sing the Annunciation
> hymn—"The Voice of the Archangel." Several of them
> in there knew everything by heart, the church services,
> the Akathists, so it didn't matter that they didn't let us
> have any books. Yes, they took all our holy books away.[6]

The nightmare scenario of the total destruction of monasteries
by an atheistic political regime is not yet upon us. If Mother Frosya

---

5 Tikhon, 239–40.
6 Tikhon, 241–42. The whole section on Mother Frosya (pp. 217–51) is one of
the most moving and delightful accounts of a contemporary hero of Christianity
that I have ever read.

and forty other nuns in prison could continue their religious life, all the more can it be continued in any place in the world where people are still free to associate, to pursue a common interest, and to live under the same roof.

The author of *Everyday Saints*, Archimandrite Tikhon, writes about his experience of visiting the secret nuns in the 1980s, at the tail end of Communism, and when the monastery of Diveyevo was still in ruins (it was subsequently gloriously rebuilt):

> Father Boniface was on his way to Diveyevo in order to give Communion to a few old nuns still living in the area around the monastery — some of the last few still living in our time of the thousand who once inhabited the pre-Revolutionary convent.... Father Boniface tried to dress in a way so that no one would ever suspect him to be a priest: carefully tucking away the pleats and folds of his cassock beneath his coat, and hiding away his very long beard into his thick scarf and upturned collar....
>
> In a ramshackle little hut on the outskirts of Diveyevo I saw something that I could have never imagined even in my most radiant dreams. I saw alive the Church Radiant, invincible and indefatigable, youthful and joyful in the consciousness of its God, our Shepherd and Savior.... And what's more, the most beautiful and unforgettable church service in my life took place then — not in some magnificent grand cathedral, not in some glorious ancient church hallowed with age, but in a nondescript building in the community center of Diveyevo, in Number 16, Lesnaya Street. It was not even a church at all, but an old bathhouse somehow vaguely converted into communal housing.
>
> When I first arrived with Father Boniface, I saw a dingy little room crowded by about a dozen elderly women, the youngest of whom could not have been younger than eighty, while the oldest were definitely more than 100 years old. All of them were dressed in simple old country maids' clothes and wearing peasant kerchiefs. None of them was wearing a habit or any kind of monastic or ecclesiastical clothing. Of course, these weren't nuns — just simple old ladies; that's what anyone would have thought, including me, if I had not known

that these old women were in fact some of the most courageous modern-day confessors of our faith, true heroines who had suffered tortures and decades in prisons and concentration camps for their beliefs. And yet despite all their ordeals, their spiritual loyalty and unshakable faith in God had only grown. . . .

As Father Boniface and the old women were exchanging greetings, I looked around. Icons in ancient ceremonial frames, dimly lit by flickering lamps, were hung on the walls... Meanwhile I started to prepare myself for the Vigil service. It took my breath away as the nuns started to take out of their secret hiding places and set down on the crudely put-together wooden table genuine artifacts belonging to St Seraphim himself. Here was the stole of his ecclesiastical vestment; there was his heavy iron cross on thick chains, worn for the mortification of the flesh, a leather glove, and the old-fashioned cast iron pot in which the saint had cooked his food. After the Revolution when the monastery was pillaged and destroyed, these holy relics had been passed down from sister to sister by the nuns of the Monastery of Diveyevo.

Having put on his vestments, Father Boniface gave the priest's pronouncement that begins the Vigil service. The nuns immediately perked up and began to sing. What a divine and utterly amazing choir they were!... These incredible nuns sang the entire service virtually by heart. Only very rarely did one of them glance at the thick old books, for which they needed to use not just eyeglasses but gigantic magnifying glasses with wooden handles. They had risked death or punishment saying this service in concentration camps and prisons and places of exile. They said it even now after all their sufferings, here in Diveyevo, settling into their wretched hovels on the outskirts of the town. For them it was nothing unusual, and yet for me I could scarcely understand whether I was in Heaven or on Earth.

These aged nuns were possessed of such incredible spiritual strength, such prayer, such courage, such modesty, goodness, and love, and they were full of such faith, that it was then at that wonderful service that I understood that they with their faith would triumph over everything – over our godless government despite all its power, over the faithlessness of this world, and over death itself, of which they had absolutely no fear.[7]

It goes without saying that we find similar stories in the Western tradition (think of the period of the French Revolution). I quote at length from Mother Frosya's story because it is so near to our times, because it concerns women who continued to live out their monastic life under the most atrocious circumstances and in spite of the most numerous hindrances, and because, finally, the mentality and the actions of the 'c'atholic persecutors of traditional religious life are strangely and sickly akin to those of the Communists.[8] The sooner we recognize this, the sooner we will develop a healthy realism and a gritty determination about how to proceed, abandoning nothing of tradition except—temporarily—a few of its outer trappings.

---

7   Tikhon, 218–21.
8   See Michael Hichborn, "Vatican Agency Directly Tied to Communism, Abortion, and Idolatry," *Lepanto Institute*, October 6, 2021.

27

Mother Maravillas de Jesús: Guarding the Teresian Reform[1]

I N A R E M A R K A B L E A D D R E S S F R O M 1 9 6 6, "Catholicism after the Council," Joseph Ratzinger already expresses the essential problem of the direction in which the Church was rapidly heading.[2] First, he sets the stage by pointing out the two basic opposing views:

> For some the Council has done much too little, it got bogged down at the very start and bequeathed to us nothing but a series of clever compromises, it was a victory of diplomacy and caution over the mighty wind of the Holy Spirit who wants not complicated syntheses but the simplicity of the Gospel message, and so on. For others again the Council was a scandal, a delivering up of the Church to the evil spirit of our time, which has turned its back on God with its mad preoccupation with the world and with material things. They are aghast to see the undermining of all that they held most sacred and turn away from a reform which seems only to offer a cheapened watered-down Christianity where they expected stiffer demands in regard to faith, hope and love.
>
> It is with heavy hearts and anxious misgivings that they compare this reform, which by its concessions and compromises seems to them to whittle away the great

---

1 This chapter pertains to the ongoing campaign against traditional contemplative life unleashed by Pope Francis. For more on Madre Maravillas, see Mary Cuff, "The Beauty of Austerity," *Crisis Magazine*, January 8, 2022, and Sr. Gabriela Hick, "St. Maravillas: A prophetic witness for Vatican II," *Where Peter Is*, January 13, 2022. I find Sr. Gabriela's article to be unconvincing in its attempt to fit out the saint as a precursor of the Council, for reasons that will become apparent.

2 The address was given at the Katholikentag of 1966 in Bamberg and then published in English in *The Furrow*, vol. 18, no. 1 (January 1967): 3-32. Dom Hugh Somerville Knapman, OSB, discusses the article in a blog post "Ratzinger 1966 – An Unexpected Prophet," *Dominus Mihi Adjutor*, April 14, 2014. A PDF of the address may be found at https://rb.gy/mrayi.

seriousness of following Christ and the necessity of unconditional surrender and service, with the reforms of past times, as for instance with that reform which is linked with the name of the great St Teresa.

REFORM MEANS RETURN TO FORM

With an eloquence that suggests sympathy, Ratzinger then describes the awakening and eventual mission of the great reformer Saint Teresa of Avila (1515-1582):

> Before her conversion, the convent in which she lived was a perfectly modern place in which the old-fashioned idea of the enclosure with its petty annoying restrictions had given way to more generous "modern" ideas and in which she was allowed to have visitors at any time; it was a modern convent in which the gloomy asceticism of the old rule had been replaced by a more "reasonable" manner of life, more suited to the tastes of people of the new era which was just then beginning; it was a modern convent which had an open-minded attitude to the world and all belonging to it and which permitted all kinds of friendly contacts.
>
> But one day she was touched to the quick by the Presence of Christ and her soul came face to face with the inexorable truth of the Gospel message, untrammeled by all the petty phrases of excuse and extenuation which had been used to obscure it, and then she realized that all that had gone before had been an unpardonable flight from the great mission to which she had been called and a shirking of the conversion of heart which was being asked of her, whereupon she rose up and was "converted."
>
> And what that meant was that she rejected the *aggiornamento* and created a reform which had nothing of concession in it but was a challenge to all who heard it to give themselves up entirely to Jesus Christ for the sake of an eternal reward, to divest themselves entirely of all possessions along with the Crucified Savior in order to belong fully in Him to the whole Body of Christ.

Thus, St Teresa's reform consisted precisely in *opposing* the modernity of her time, *denying* the spirit of her age, closing the door to a broader, more "humanistic," more "sensible" approach, yielding not an inch to the fashionable concessions of the day. As Martin Mosebach likes to say, "reform," when it is genuine, always means *return to form* — that is, a return to a purer, stricter, more committed way, not a loosening and relaxation:

> The monastic reforms of Cluny and Cîteaux, and of the Carmelites, and the reforms introduced by the Council of Trent, are associated with a return to a stricter order, a tightening of the reins, a return to a more radical religious practice and a restoration of a spiritual discipline that had been lost. The postconciliar liturgical reform is the first reform in the history of the Church that did not have the aim of re-establishing order, but of softening, abolishing, and relativizing it.[3]

Ratzinger draws the sharp conclusion:

> That section of the faithful of whom we are now speaking [i.e., the more traditionally-minded] asks whether the Council has not, in fact, taken the opposite direction to Saint Teresa, going away from true conversion to worldliness on the part of the Church.

ST TERESA SPEAKS FOR HERSELF

For her part, St Teresa, who never minced words, spoke very plainly of the problems of religious life in the sixteenth century and the urgency of just such a reform, a moving away from worldliness. She was particularly insistent on the value of *strict enclosure* and an *unmitigated observance* of the Rule:

> Everything connected with the religious life caused me delight; and it is a fact that sometimes, when I was spending time in sweeping floors which I had previously spent on my own indulgence and adornment, and realized that I was now free from all those things, there came to me a new joy, which amazed me, for I could not understand whence it arose.[4] . . .

---

3 Martin Mosebach, *Subversive Catholicism: Papacy, Liturgy, Church*, trans. Sebastian Condon and Graham Harrison (Brooklyn, NY: Angelico Press, 2019), 62. And: "true reform consists of putting on the bridle, of returning to a stricter order... Reform is a return to form" (ibid., 98; 100).
4 *Life*, ch. 4, trans. and ed. E. Allison Peers; text at www.ewtn.com/catholicism/library/life-of-st-teresa-of-avila-5208.

For that reason, I think it was a very bad thing for me not to be in a convent that was enclosed. The freedom which the sisters, who were good, might enjoy without becoming less so (for they were not obliged to live more strictly than they did, as they had not taken a vow of enclosure) would certainly have led me, who am wicked, down to hell, had not the Lord, through very special favors, using means and remedies which are all His own, delivered me from this peril. It seems to me, then, that it is a very great danger for women in a convent to have such freedom. For those who want to be wicked, it is not so much a remedy for their weaknesses as a step on the way to hell. . . .

Oh, what terrible harm, what terrible harm is wrought in religious (I am referring now as much to men as to women) when the religious life is not properly observed; when of the two paths that can be followed in a religious house – one leading to virtue and the observance of the Rule and the other leading away from the Rule – both are frequented almost equally! No, I am wrong: they are not frequented equally, for our sins cause the more imperfect road to be more commonly taken; being the broader, it is the more generally favored. . . .

I cannot think why we should be astonished at all the evils which exist in the Church, when those who ought to be models on which all may pattern their virtues are annulling the work wrought in the religious Orders by the spirit of the saints of old. May His Divine Majesty be pleased to find a remedy for this, as He sees needful.[5]

A TRADITIONAL CARMELITE IN MODERN TIMES

A major Carmelite figure of the twentieth century, Mother Maravillas de Jesús (1891-1974), who suffered through the Spanish Civil War and founded many Carmels in her life, was a true daughter of St Teresa of Jesus – a clear-sighted nun who resolutely guarded the reformed Carmelite way of life handed down from the sixteenth century on. Mother Maravillas strongly opposed efforts made both before and after the Second Vatican Council to deform

---

5 *Life*, ch. 7.

the Carmelites in the name of modern adaptations. In other words, exactly the problem Ratzinger described in 1966.

One of Madre Maravillas's collaborators, Sr. Magdalena de Jesús, published as an octogenarian some recollections of the saint in a book entitled *Admiración, Amor y Dolor.*[6] Chapter 13 discusses Madre Maravillas's attitude toward the Second Vatican Council, which Sr. Magdalena regards as ill-informed, suspicious, and reactionary, but which, in retrospect, we can see to have been intuitively accurate, illumined with a prophetic light.

When, for example, in 1965 the Father General Anastasio announced obligatory liturgical changes, such as the nuns making the responses at the Mass with lights on and veils drawn, the convents under Mother's guidance did not follow these stipulations. Communion under both kinds was resisted. The erection of free-standing altars facing the people was highly displeasing to Madre and was kept at bay as long as could be managed. A new translation of the psalter was brought to the nuns but was rejected. In some parlors, signs were posted that said: "No admittance to priests without cassock, religious without habit, or women in pants." The Madre clearly discerned, in the confusing and ever-growing list of changes suggested or demanded of Catholics in general and of religious in particular, a spirit of relaxation and dissipation that threatened to undermine Catholic life and religious life and, in point of fact, brought about exactly that result, as every plummeting statistic has indicated for over fifty years now.[7]

I appreciate Sr. Magdalena's honesty in noting that many official biographies of Madre Maravillas tell fibs about her "prompt and wholehearted obedience to the Council, the bishops, the liturgical reforms," etc. For this outstanding Carmelite foundress understood a thing or two about the limits of obedience; she knew that it could not be given at the cost of the primacy of the spiritual life, the integrity of the Rule, or the common good of the Church, and that the hierarchy do not enjoy a monopoly on the perception of these realities.

6　The full title is *Admiración, Amor y Dolor: Testimonio directo acerca de su vida solicitado por los Carmelos de Holanda y Alemania* (Burgos: Monte Carmelo, 1992).
7　And of course, wherever stricter religious life is practiced, new vocations begin to flow in. There are by now dozens of communities that one could point to as examples. See Kwasniewski, *Ministers of Christ*, 219-34.

"PERFECTION IS IMPERFECTIBLE"

In history, certain things do actually achieve a perfection that cannot be surpassed in the same sphere. For example, in regard to Christological dogma, the formulas of Pope Leo the Great are perfect and cannot be improved upon. In regard to Gothic architecture, the cathedral of Chartres is a superlative masterpiece; any attempt to modernize a Gothic cathedral's interior or exterior would result only in its degradation. The piano concertos of Mozart realize the highest possibilities of the genre; a rare composer may be worthy of mention alongside him, but none rivals him. (It was the musicologist Alfred Einstein who described Mozart's concerti as an achievement "beyond which no progress was possible, because perfection is imperfectible.")

The same is true with regard to the greatest work of art known to Western man: the Solemn Pontifical Mass of the classical Roman Rite, which possesses a splendor and sublimity that cascades through all of its derivatives—the *Missa solemnis*, the *Missa cantata*, the *Missa recitata*. The Roman Rite attained its providentially-guided perfection in the late Middle Ages; in response to heretical distortions of liturgy, St Pius V codified and canonized this rite in the sixteenth century, after which, with eminent good sense, the Church held fast to it with only minor additions until the unhappy experiments of the post-War period.[8] Traditionalists maintain that this rite *is* the rite of the Church of Rome, and that Catholic piety has but one responsibility, namely, to receive it and cherish it.

The same, finally, is true of the great religious orders. Each, in its own way, achieves a certain perfection in its rule of life and its unique role within the Mystical Body that cannot be improved upon and will tend to be only degraded by adaptations, relaxations, and modernizations. The Benedictine life, for example, has been fixed in all its essentials since the *Holy Rule* was written in the sixth century, and every great reform movement in monasticism has taken for its polestar renewed fidelity to the *Rule*—not only in its general lines but often in its most concrete details. Benedictine communities flourish to the degree that they adhere to the *Rule*. Renewal means rediscovering the full Divine Office and its

---

8 For a full defense of the claims made in this sentence, see Kwasniewski, *Once and Future Roman Rite*.

horarium, days and seasons of strict fasting, the manual labor, the total individual poverty, and so forth. Similarly, the cloistered Carmelite life achieved perfection in the sixteenth century under St Teresa of Avila; its strength, too, will typically be measured by adherence to that perfect form, not only in general principles but in specific details.

Some religious nuns or sisters, supportive of *Cor Orans*, will object that their communities are doing fine and are benefiting, or will benefit, from the new Vatican provisions. Although reasons for serious skepticism exist about how beneficial the provisions are for anyone, for the sake of argument let's grant that such claims may be true for some communities. It would still not follow that the provisions of *Cor Orans* are beneficial *for all*, or that they are *so* necessary and urgent that *every* house of Carmelites — or of any other branch of religious — must adopt them. A more traditional way of life in customs and liturgy, a stricter observance of the rule, has its rightful place in the Church and will *always* have a place of honor. Unity properly understood has never demanded absolute uniformity, otherwise we wouldn't have many religious orders to begin with — some active and others contemplative, some confederated and others autonomous, some making use of modern technology and others eschewing it for good reasons.

So many today talk about "freedom," but how few are willing to live lives free of ideology or to let others live freely according to their charism, conscience, and calling! *At the very least*, Christian charity together with respect for one's own heritage demands that all those who wish to live according to an order's original rule should be allowed to live it unmolested.

A CARMELITE "RESISTER" VINDICATED

Against the objections of those who accused her of defiance of ecclesiastical authority, disobedience to reforms mandated by the Holy See, and inflexible adherence to Carmelite tradition, Pope John Paul II beatified Mother Maravillas in 1998 and canonized her on his apostolic visit to Spain in 2003. Doubtless the Polish pope — a keen student of St John of the Cross[9] and one who had

---

9   See Michael Waldstein, *Glory of the Logos in the Flesh* (Ave Maria, FL: Sapientia Press, 2021), 557-93.

not been afraid to ordain clandestinely in the teeth of Paul VI's *Ostpolitik*[10]– understood, in a way many others could not, the time-tested wisdom and burning fire of charity that nourished Madre Maravillas's firmness of principle. She had resisted, to the best of her ability, the whirlwind of change that had swept through the Church during and after the Council and had reaffirmed the permanent value of St Teresa of Avila's heaven-inspired vision of enclosed Carmelite life.

Just as St Teresa was misunderstood and opposed in her time, so was Madre Maravillas in ours; and the same incomprehension and incredulity will meet us today and in every age, whenever the advocates of *aggiornamento* and the martinets of modernization confront the champions of constancy and the cherishers of continuity. At a time when her virtues are needed more than ever, Madre Maravillas is a model for her own religious family and for all who adhere to the traditional beliefs and practices of Catholicism. Ours is the resistance of love, the defiance of devotion, the tenacity of tradition.

St Maravillas de Jesús, pray for us.

---

10   See chapter 13.

APPENDIX

Letter of Michael Davies
to Bishop Donohoe

Now that Church leaders are acting as if their motto were "Back to the '70s," it is worthwhile to dust off some of the great writings from that period, such as this masterful letter penned by the premiere English-language apologist for the TLM, Michael Davies, in response to Bishop Donohoe of Fresno's vitriolic letter against the traditional Mass. After sending it to the bishop, Davies published the text in The Remnant *on March 20, 1976.*

Most Rev. Hugh A. Donohoe,
Bishop of Fresno, California,
February 23, 1976.

My Lord Bishop,

A friend who lives in your diocese has sent me a copy of your letter stating that you are prepared to declare that priests who celebrate, and the faithful who attend, the Tridentine Mass are "contumacious" and will be "excommunicated." We had begun to believe that, in the era of the "Spirit of Vatican II," no one could be excommunicated; but now we know, there is one crime in the "open Church" that will not be tolerated, at least in the Diocese of Fresno, the crime of worshipping as our forebears worshipped; the crime of using that form of Mass which Fr Fortescue, the greatest liturgical historian of my own country, tells us "goes back without essential change to the age when it first developed out of the oldest liturgy of all. It is still redolent of that liturgy of the days when Caesar ruled the world and thought he could stamp out the faith of Christ, when our fathers met before dawn to sing a hymn to Christ as God."

Clearly, my Lord, you think that you can succeed where Caesar could not.

Cranmer, too, thought he could stamp out the traditional Mass. When he replaced it with a new English Communion Service in

333

1549, the peasants of the west rose up against him and demanded the right to worship once more with the same Latin Mass that their fathers had used. I would suggest, my Lord, that if you study Cranmer's methods you could improve upon excommunication. Priests were hung from the church towers in their Mass vestments for the very act for which you now threaten to excommunicate them; humble peasants were hung in their hundreds because they assisted at the Mass which you, like Cranmer, condemn as "gravely illicit." But Cranmer could not stamp out the traditional Mass – and you think you can succeed where he failed!

With the reign of Elizabeth came the rack, the hanging, the drawing and quartering – but the reply of the faithful was always the same: "We will have the Mass!" And the Mass they would have was the one codified by Pope St Pius V in 1570, but not a new form of Mass like that promulgated in 1969, but the Mass of the Ages codified, as Pope St Pius V intended, for all eternity. No priest could ever be made to say any other form of Mass, he insisted. But now if a priest uses that Mass in the diocese of Fresno, he will be "excommunicated"!

My Lord, forgive me if I seem impertinent, but in my country we have a great devotion to our martyrs; we also know our history. When I read your letter, I could not believe that it was not written by an English bishop of the sixteenth century. "I wish you to make it a matter of conscience to discover if such a Mass is being celebrated in any hall, house, or wherever within the confines of your parish." These are your exact words.

My Lord, have you no more urgent business to employ your priests upon? Have you, for example, ordered them, as a matter of conscience, to go into their parish schools to discover whether the faith of the children, for whom you are responsible before God, is being corrupted by inadequate or even heretical textbooks? Have you ordered your priests to discover, as a matter of conscience, whether secularist-humanist sex-education programs are being used to corrupt the morals of the children in any of your parochial schools? Have you, my Lord, as a matter of conscience, ever attempted to discover whether what few liturgical laws remain are being flouted in your diocese – is Communion being given in the hand?[1] Are

---

1 Note that permission for administering Communion in the hand was not granted to the United States until June 17, 1977, about fifteen months after this letter was written.

unauthorized Eucharistic prayers being used? If you discovered such abuses would you excommunicate those involved? I wonder?

I am quite certain, my Lord, that in a spirit of ecumenism, you would not only NOT excommunicate members of your diocese who take part in Protestant services, but probably encourage them to do so. Can you see no incongruity? You must surely be aware that the Secretariat of Christian Unity issued an Ecumenical Directory in 1967. This Directory not only authorized Catholics to take part in the liturgy of the Orthodox Church on Sundays, but said that this satisfied their Sunday obligation. Yes, my Lord, to take part in the worship of schismatics fulfills our Sunday obligation, but to worship in the manner which has inspired so many saints and has been sanctified by the blood of so many martyrs – this must be punished by excommunication.

My Lord, unless your diocese is unique in the western world, the introduction of the new Mass for pastoral reasons will have been followed by a serious decline in Mass attendance. Thousands of your flock, who assisted at Mass each Sunday before, no longer do so – but they will not be excommunicated. Oh no, my Lord! Better no Mass at all than the Mass of our fathers.

And please, my Lord, do not say that you have no alternative. Do not say that you are only obeying orders. One thing which has become clear since Vatican II is that the clergy in general and the bishops in particular take the laity for fools. Not all the clergy, of course. There are some who are determined to remain true to the Faith into which they were baptized and to the Mass which they were ordained to offer. Fr Henri Bruckberger, to mention but one, has written: "Do our bishops take us for idiots? We are as familiar with the relevant documents as they are. We know that the new Mass has simply been authorized and not been made mandatory." Fr Bruckberger was Chaplain General to the French Resistance, my Lord. He has had ample experience of men who were only obeying orders. I would also remind you, my Lord, that here in England the Tridentine Mass is not absolutely prohibited. It is, of course, celebrated all over the country, in houses and halls, whether the bishops like it or not – but is also celebrated on occasions in churches and in cathedrals, with their blessing, and, I might add, with the full knowledge and consent of Pope Paul VI. What is permitted in

Britain could certainly be permitted in the United States.

My Lord, once more without wishing to be impertinent, I would ask you whether you are really clear as to what the word "pastor" really means. If you have not forgotten the Parable of the Good Shepherd, you will remember that in the east a shepherd leads his sheep; he not only leads them, but he loves them; and because he loves them he leads them to green pastures. My Lord, because some of your flock wish to take their spiritual refreshment from the pastures they have always known and loved, you threaten to cast them out from the sheepfold. My Lord, this is not the action of a good shepherd but a bad bureaucrat, a man who believes that the reason for our existence is to be made to obey regulations and that his vocation is to use any means to ensure that this is done.

My Lord, do the basic principles of moral theology no longer apply in the renewed Church? You will certainly have been taught as a seminary student that a legislator should not simply refrain from demanding something his subjects will find impossible to carry out, but that his laws should not be too difficult, too distressing or too disagreeable, and should take account of human frailty. A law can cease to bind without revocation on the part of the legislator when it is clearly harmful, impossible, or irrational. If forbidding faithful Catholics to honor God by worshipping Him in the most venerable and hallowed rite in Christendom does not meet these conditions, it would be hard to imagine anything that did. For a Catholic to contemplate disobedience to his bishop is a terrible thing, but Fr Bruckberger has reminded us of Montesquieu's dictum: "When one wants only good slaves one ends up with bad subjects!"

My Lord, as a postscript to your letter, you add a suggested petition on behalf of the Jews in Syria, a petition to be used on March 14 in the parishes of your diocese. Might I suggest a similar petition which Catholics elsewhere could use – for, after all, charity begins at home: "That there be an alleviation of the suffering experienced by the Catholics living in the Diocese of Fresno and that they may be free to worship God according to the traditions of their fathers as they desire, let us pray to the Lord."

I remain, my Lord,

Yours *in Domino*,

Michael Davies, London, England.

WORKS CITED

Hyperlinks have been provided only for those items that are somewhat difficult to find by search.

CHURCH DOCUMENTS

Benedict XVI. *Caritas in Veritate*. Encyclical Letter, June 29, 2009.

——. *Con Grande Fiducia*. Letter to Bishops Accompanying *Summorum Pontificum*, July 7, 2007.

——. *Sacramentum Caritatis*. Post-Synodal Apostolic Exhortation, February 22, 2007.

——. Saint Elizabeth of Hungary. General Audience, October 20, 2010.

——. *Summorum Pontificum*. Apostolic Letter, July 7, 2007.

Congregation for Divine Worship and the Discipline of the Sacraments. *Redemptionis Sacramentum*. Instruction, March 25, 2004.

Constance, Council of. Thirty-ninth session, October 9, 1417.

Francis. "Pope Francis responds to dubia submitted by five cardinals." *Vatican News*, October 2, 2023.

——. *Traditionis Custodes*. Apostolic Letter, July 16, 2021.

Gelasius I. *Famuli vestrae pietatis*. Letter. AD 494.

International Theological Commission. "*Sensus Fidei* in the Life of the Church." 2014.

John Paul II. *Ecclesia de Eucharistia*. Encyclical Letter, April 17, 2003.

——. *Ecclesia Dei*. Apostolic Letter, July 2, 1988.

Sacred Congregation of Rites. *Inter Oecumenici*. Instruction on Implementing Liturgical Norms, September 26, 1964.

Vatican Council I. *Dei Filius*. Dogmatic Constitution, April 24, 1870.

——. *Pastor Aeternus*. Dogmatic Constitution, July 18, 1870.

Vatican Council II. *Dei Verbum*. Dogmatic Constitution on Divine Revelation, November 18, 1965.

——. *Lumen Gentium*. Dogmatic Constitution on the Church, November 21, 1964.

——. *Sacrosanctum Concilium*. Constitution on the Sacred Liturgy. December 4, 1963.

WORKS BY THE AUTHOR

"'All That Matters at Mass is Jesus': Responding to Liturgical Heresy." *OnePeterFive*, February 16, 2022.

And Rightly So: Selected Letters and Articles of Neil McCaffrey. Edited by Peter Kwasniewski. Fort Collins, CO: Roman Catholic Books, 2019.

Are Canonizations Infallible? Revisiting a Disputed Question. Edited by Peter Kwasniewski. Waterloo, ON: Arouca Press, 2021.

"Are Traditionalists Guilty of 'Private Judgment' Over the Popes?" *OnePeterFive*, December 22, 2021.

"Between Christ the King and 'We Have No King But Caesar.'" *OnePeterFive*, October 25, 2020.

"Beyond *Summorum Pontificum*: The Work of Retrieving the Tridentine Heritage." *Rorate Caeli*, July 14, 2021.

"Can a Case Still Be Made for Reforming the Reform?" *OnePeterFive*, May 3, 2023.

"Can We Call Ourselves 'Traditional Catholics'?" *OnePeterFive*, April 12, 2023.

"Cardinal Roche (Unwittingly?) Utters the Most Ironic Statement Since the Council." *Rorate Caeli*, August 30, 2022.

"Christian Militancy in the Prayer of the Church." *OnePeterFive*, March 16, 2022.

"Contemplative Religious: The Heart of the Church and the Measure of Her Health." *OnePeterFive*, October 2, 2019.

"Discovering Tradition: A Priest's Crisis of Conscience." *OnePeterFive*, March 27, 2019.

"Enter His Courts With Praise: Liturgical Reverence for Christ the King." *New Liturgical Movement*, May 2, 2022.

"Fidelity to Liturgical Law and the Rights of the Faithful." *OnePeterFive*, March 1, 2023.

"Finding Christ in Present Sufferings Does Not Mean Embracing Abuse, Error, or Deformation." *OnePeterFive*, February 8, 2023.

"The Four Qualities of Liturgy: Validity, Licitness, Fittingness, and Authenticity." *New Liturgical Movement*, November 9, 2020.

From Benedict's Peace to Francis's War: Catholics Respond to the Motu Proprio Traditionis Custodes *on the Latin Mass*. Brooklyn, NY: Angelico Press, 2021.

"From Extemporaneity to Fixity of Form: The Grace of Liturgical Stability." *New Liturgical Movement*, October 11, 2021.

Good Music, Sacred Music, and Silence: Three Gifts of God for Liturgy and for Life. Gastonia, NC: TAN Books, 2023.

Holy Bread of Eternal Life: Restoring Eucharistic Reverence in an Age of Impiety. Manchester, NH: Sophia Institute Press, 2020.

"How Contrary Orientations Signify Contradictory Theologies." *New Liturgical Movement*, November 5, 2018.

"If your Mass is defective or abusive, find another one." *LifeSiteNews*, November 7, 2019.

Illusions of Reform: Responses to Cavadini, Healy, and Weinandy in Defense of the Traditional Mass and the Faithful Who Attend It. Edited by Peter Kwasniewski. Lincoln, NE: Os Justi Press, 2023.

"Interview with Dom Alcuin Reid on his ordination, his community, the diocese of Fréjus-Toulon, and *Desiderio Desideravi*." *Rorate Caeli*, July 15, 2022.

"The Kingship of Christ and the Anti-Kingdom of Modernity." *OnePeter-Five*, February 8, 2018.

"The 'Latin Novus Ordo' Is Not the Solution." *OnePeterFive*, August 24, 2022.

"Living Corpus Christi in a Liturgical Desert." *OnePeterFive*, June 7, 2023.

"The Many Meaningful Signs of the Cross in the Roman Canon." *Tradition & Sanity*, August 17, 2023.

"The Maronite Liturgy's Corruption under Modern Western Influence." *New Liturgical Movement*, September 27, 2021.

"Mass 'Facing the People' as Counter-Catechesis and Irreligion." *New Liturgical Movement*, August 20, 2018.

"The Mass Should Not Be a Torture Device." *New Liturgical Movement*, February 7, 2022.

"May His Kingdom Come: Catholic Social Teaching, Part VII – The Kingship of Christ, Source and Summit of the Social Order." *Catholic Family News* online, October 25, 2020.

"Men Must Be Changed by Sacred Things, and Not Sacred Things by Men." *OnePeterFive*, September 15, 2021.

Ministers of Christ: Recovering the Roles of Clergy and Laity in an Age of Confusion. Manchester, NH: Crisis Publications/Sophia Institute Press, 2021.

"Minutes from the Commission of Cardinals That Advised John Paul II to Lift Restrictions on the Old Missal." *New Liturgical Movement*, January 9, 2023.

"Newly Ordained Priests and Permission to Offer the Traditional Latin Mass." *OnePeterFive*, May 11, 2022.

Noble Beauty, Transcendent Holiness: Why the Modern Age Needs the Mass of Ages. Kettering, OH: Angelico Press, 2017.

"No Eucharistic Revival without Restoration." *Tradition & Sanity*, April 20, 2023.

"The Normativity of *Ad Orientem* Worship According to the Ordinary Form's Rubrics." *New Liturgical Movement*, November 23, 2015.

"Not Abandoning the Flock – Not Abandoning the Truth." *OnePeterFive*, July 13, 2022.

The Once and Future Roman Rite: Returning to the Latin Liturgical Tradition after Seventy Years of Exile. Gastonia, NC: TAN Books, 2022.

"'O, What a Tangled Web...': Thirty-Three Falsehoods in the CDW's *Responsa ad Dubia*." *OnePeterFive*, January 5, 2022.

"The Pope's Boundedness to Tradition as a Legislative Limit." In *Benedict's Peace to Francis's War*, 222–47.

Reclaiming Our Roman Catholic Birthright: The Genius and Timeliness of the Traditional Latin Mass. Brooklyn, NY: Angelico Press, 2020.

"Resistance is never futile: An interview with Christian Marquant, founder of Paix Liturgique." *Rorate Caeli*, December 16, 2020.

The Road from Hyperpapalism to Catholicism: Rethinking the Papacy in a Time of Ecclesial Disintegration. Volume 1: Theological Reflections on the Rock of the Church. Volume 2: Chronological Responses to an Unfolding Pontificate. Waterloo, ON: Arouca Press, 2022.

"St. Thomas on the 'Asperges' (Sprinkling Rite)." *Views from the Choir Loft*, August 7, 2014.

"Should the Feast of Christ the King Be Celebrated in October or November?" *Rorate Caeli*, October 22, 2014.

"Things That Remit Venial Sins – The Traditional Liturgy Is Full of Them." *New Liturgical Movement*, February 8, 2016.

"Thoughts of a Young Modern Traditionalist Catholic." *New Liturgical Movement*, July 3, 2023.

True Obedience in the Church: A Guide to Discernment in Challenging Times. Manchester, NH: Crisis Publications, 2021.

"Two 'Disobediences' Compared." *OnePeterFive*, January 18, 2023.

Ultramontanism and Tradition: The Role of Church Authority in the Catholic Faith. Lincoln, NE: Os Justi Press, 2024.

"The 'Unique Expression of the Roman Rite' in the Wild: New Zealand Priest Ad-libbing Eucharistic Prayer." *Rorate Caeli*, October 9, 2023.

"What's the Big Deal with the Pentecost Octave?" *The Remnant*, May 22, 2021.

"Why I Couldn't Go Back... to the Novus Ordo." *OnePeterFive*, April 14, 2021.

"Why the 'Reform of the Reform' Is Doomed." *OnePeterFive*, April 22, 2020.

"Your Local Mass Canceled? Try Meditating on the Texts of the Traditional Mass." *OnePeterFive*, March 20, 2020.

WORKS BY OTHER AUTHORS

Alcorn, Trevor. "Chicago: The Saga of a Canceled Parish." *OnePeterFive*, September 2, 2022.

Alderman, Matthew. "On the Size of Altars." *New Liturgical Movement*, October 8, 2010.

Altieri, Christopher R. "Trying to make some sense of the *responsa ad dubia.*" *Catholic World Report*, December 19, 2021.

Anonymous. *AA-1025: Memoirs of the Communist Infiltration into the Church.* Edited by Marie Carré. Gastonia, NC: TAN Books, 2013.

——. "El obispo de San Luis prohibió la presencia de mujeres en los altares." *Clarín*, November 1, 2019.

——. *The New Raccolta, or Collection of Prayers and Good Works to which the Sovereign Pontiffs Have Attached Holy Indulgences.* From the 3rd Italian edition. Philadelphia: Peter F. Cunningham & Son, 1903.

——. "Pope insists traditionalist FSSP priests must concelebrate new rite Chrism Mass: French archbishop." *LifeSiteNews*, April 26, 2022.

——. *Priest, Where Is Thy Mass? Mass, Where Is Thy Priest?* Expanded edition. Kansas City, MO: Angelus Press, 2004.

——. "Synod Forced to Acknowledge What Young People Really Want: An End to TLM Restrictions." *Rorate Caeli*, September 8, 2023.

Archbold, Matthew. "No Abp. Cordileone, These People Wish Catholics Ill." *Creative Minority Report*, November 24, 2020.

Aristotle. *Nicomachean Ethics*. Translated by Robert C. Bartlett and Susan D. Collins. Chicago: University of Chicago Press, 2011.

Babych, Art. "Ukrainian bishop fights to hold eparchy: he claims Vatican II rule does not apply." *National Catholic Reporter*, September 24, 1993.

Baresel, James. "Archbishop Roche: 'The Traditional Mass Must Go.'" *Inside the Vatican*, https://insidethevatican.com/magazine/archbishop-roche-the-traditional-mass-must-go/.

Batiffol, Pierre. *History of the Roman Breviary*. Translated by Atwell M.Y. Baylay. New York: Longmans, Green and Co., 1912.

Bellescize, Fr Luc de. "The True Meaning of Our Liturgies." *Rorate Caeli*, June 6, 2023.

Benson, Robert Hugh. *By What Authority?* Stamullen: Cenacle Press of Silverstream Priory, 2022.

Billot, Louis Cardinal. *Liberalism: A Critique of Its Basic Principles and Various Forms*. Translated by George Barry O'Toole and Thomas Storck. Waterloo, ON: Arouca Press, 2019.

Boniface [Phillip Campbell]. "The Last Gasp of Our Akhenaten." *Unam Sanctam Catholicam*, November 5, 2023.

——. "Stop Using This Word So Recklessly." *Unam Sanctam Catholicam*, August 10, 2023.

——. "The Problem of the 'Reverent Novus Ordo.'" *Unam Sanctam Catholicam*, September 10, 2020.

——. "Reform of the Reform: Liturgical Russian Roulette." *Unam Sanctam Catholicam*, December 5, 2022.

Bourne, Lisa. "Will bishops look at why millennials are fleeing the church? The answer is closer than they think." *LifeSiteNews*, June 21, 2019.

Bouyer, Louis. "The Word of God Lives in the Liturgy." In *The Liturgy and the Word of God*, 53–66. Collegeville, MN: Liturgical Press, 1959.

Buck, Roger. *Cor Iesu Sacratissimum: From Secularism and the New Age to Christendom Renewed*. Kettering, OH: Angelico Press, 2016.

Bürger, Martin. "US Archbishop forbids priests to say public Masses if they offer Communion on tongue." *LifeSiteNews*, June 2, 2020.

Burke, Raymond Leo Cardinal. "Liturgical Law in the Mission of the Church." In *Sacred Liturgy: The Source and Summit of the Life and Mission of the Church*, ed. Alcuin Reid, 389–415. San Francisco: Ignatius Press, 2014.

Calmel, Roger-Thomas, OP. "Apologia Pro St. Pius V." English translation from *The Angelus*, vol. 38, no. 1 (January-February 2015).

Casey, Paul. "Can a Catholic Ever Disobey a Pope?" *OnePeterFive*, July 17, 2020.

———. "SSPX Masses and Fulfilling the Sunday Obligation." *Catholic Family News* online, April 28, 2023.

Chalk, Casey. *The Obscurity of Scripture: Disputing* Sola Scriptura *and the Protestant Notion of Biblical Perspicuity.* Steubenville, OH: Emmaus Road Publishing, 2023.

———. "The Protestant Doctrine That Gave Us Pro-Trans Churches." *Crisis Magazine*, March 23, 2023.

Charles, Joshua, and Alec Torres. *Persecuted from Within: How the Saints Endured Crises in the Church.* Manchester, NH: Sophia Institute Press, 2023.

Charlier, Michael. "The amorphous 'Roman rite' and the authentic Roman Rite." *Rorate Caeli*, July 6, 2022.

———. "Concelebration as compromise?" *Rorate Caeli*, May 3, 2022.

———. "Obedience in Crisis." *Rorate Caeli*, May 14, 2022.

———. "Suspendiertes Lehramt zum Xten." *Motu-proprio: Summorum-Pontificum*, July 4, 2022.

Chessman, Stuart. *Faith of Our Fathers: A Brief History of Catholic Traditionalism in the United States, from* Triumph *to* Traditionis Custodes. Brooklyn, NY: Angelico Press, 2022.

———. "*Traditionis Custodes*: Dispatches from the Front." *The Society of St. Hugh of Cluny*, August 18, 2021.

Chiron, Yves. *Annibale Bugnini: Reformer of the Liturgy.* Translated by John Pepino. Brooklyn, NY: Angelico Press, 2018.

———. *Dom Gérard Calvet, 1927–2008: tourné vers le Seigneur.* Le Barroux: Éditions Sainte-Madeleine, 2018.

———. *Paul VI: The Divided Pope.* Translated by James Walther. Brooklyn, NY: Angelico Press, 2022.

Cipolla, Richard. "A Primer for a Tradition-Minded Celebration of the OF Mass." Published by Gregory DiPippo at *New Liturgical Movement*, September 14, 2017.

Clark, Stephen R.L. *Can We Believe in People?: Human Significance in an Interconnected Cosmos.* Brooklyn, NY: Angelico Press, 2020.

Clovis, Linus. "The Anti-Church Has Come. Why Faithful Catholics Should Not Be Afraid." *LifeSiteNews*, May 18, 2017.

Condon, Edward. "Does Roche's rescript dispense with Vatican II?" *The Pillar*, February 22, 2023.

Cuff, Mary. "The Beauty of Austerity." *Crisis Magazine*, January 8, 2022.

Cupich, Blase. "A Eucharistic Revival that Renews the Church." Parts I and II, March 12 and 22, 2023, www.eucharisticrevival.org/.

Cusick, Kevin. "The Death of a Parish." *Rorate Caeli*, August 4, 2022.

Davies, Michael. *The Order of Melchisedech: A Defence of the Catholic Priesthood.* Fort Collins, CO: Roman Catholic Books, 1993.

Davis, Henry. *Moral and Pastoral Theology.* Sixth edition. Volume 2: *Commandments of God and Precepts of the Church.* London/New York: Sheed and Ward, 1949.

de Lassus, Dom Dysmas. *Abuses in the Religious Life and the Path to Healing.* Manchester, NH: Sophia Institute Press, 2023.

de Mattei, Roberto. *Blessed Pius IX.* Translated John Laughland. Leominster: Gracewing, 2004.

——. *Love for the Papacy and Filial Resistance to the Pope in the History of the Church.* Brooklyn, NY: Angelico Press, 2019.

——. "The 'Ninth Crusade' of the Papal Zouaves." *The Remnant,* April 1, 2020.

Denzinger, Heinrich. *Enchiridion symbolorum definitionum et declarationum de rebus fidei et morum,* 43rd edition. Edited by Peter Hünermann, Robert Fastiggi, and Anne Englund Nash. San Francisco: Ignatius Press, 2012.

De Souza, Raymond J. "Ukrainian Cardinals Husar and Slipyj are heroes to Church community." *The Catholic Register,* June 22, 2017.

DiPippo, Gregory. "Compendium of the Reforms of the Roman Breviary, 1568–1961: Part 7.2 – The Breviary Reforms of St. Pius X (Continued)." *New Liturgical Movement,* November 3, 2009.

——. "Concelebration in the Byzantine Rite." *New Liturgical Movement,* September 6, 2014.

——. "A Few Notes on the Reform of the Readings of the Easter Vigil." *New Liturgical Movement,* May 15, 2020.

——. "The Legal Achievement of *Summorum Pontificum.*" *New Liturgical Movement,* July 5, 2017.

——. "Paul VI Did Not Exist: A 'Nostalgic' Response to George Weigel on Vatican II." *OnePeterFive,* October 24, 2022.

——. "The Revolution Is Over." *New Liturgical Movement,* August 1, 2022.

——. "What Really Happened to the Sequences?" *New Liturgical Movement,* May 5, 2022.

——. "You Are Evangelizing Through Beauty!" *New Liturgical Movement,* June 9, 2020.

Dudzik, Savannah. "We Know that God is on Our Side in This Fight." *OnePeterFive,* April 8, 2022.

Dulac, Raymond. *In Defence of the Roman Mass.* Translated by Pedar Walsh. N.p.: Te Deum Press, 2020.

Dupuis, M. Jean-Claude. "A Tribute to Father Yves Normandin (1925–2020), Hero of the Traditional Mass in Canada." *Rorate Caeli,* February 7, 2021.

Echeverria, Eduardo. "*Solum Magisterium?*" *Crisis Magazine,* September 15, 2023.

Eco, Umberto. "Ur-Fascism." *New York Review of Books,* June 22, 1995, https://theanarchistlibrary.org/library/umberto-eco-ur-fascism.

Eger, Gerhard and Zachary Thomas, trans. "'I Shall Keep Inviolate the Discipline and Ritual of the Church': The Early Mediæval Papal Oath." *Canticum Salomonis*, July 31, 2021.

Eno, Robert B. *The Rise of the Papacy. Eugene, OR: Wipf and Stock*, 2008.

Fabre, Père Jean-Dominique. *Le père Roger-Thomas Calmel, 1914–1975: un fils de saint Dominique au XXe siècle.* Suresnes: Clovis Fideliter, 2012.

Fenton, John. "What is a 'Private Mass'?" May 15, 2021, https://cum-angelis-et-archangelis.orthodoxwestblogs.com/2021/05/15/what-is-a-private-mass/.

Ferrara, Christopher A. and Thomas E. Woods, Jr. *The Great Façade: The Regime of Novelty in the Catholic Church from Vatican II to the Francis Revolution.* Kettering, OH: Angelico Press, 2015.

Feser, Edward. "Fastiggi on Capital Punishment and the Change to the Catechism." August 26 and August 30, 2023, at https://edwardfeser.blogspot.com/.

——. "Magisterium: The Teaching Authority of the Church." In *The Faith Once for All Delivered: Doctrinal Authority in Catholic Theology*, ed. Kevin L. Flannery, SJ, 149–70. Steubenville, OH: Emmaus Academic, 2023.

Fessler, Joseph. *The True and False Infallibility of the Popes.* New York: The Catholic Publication Society, 1875. https://en.wikisource.org/wiki/The_True_and_the_False_Infallibility_of_the_Popes.

Fiedrowicz, Michael. *The Traditional Mass: History, Form, and Theology of the Classical Roman Rite.* Translated by Rose Pfeifer. Brooklyn, NY: Angelico Press, 2020.

Fimister, Alan. *Iron Sceptre of the Son of Man: Romanitas as a Note of the Church.* Lincoln, NE: Os Justi Press, 2023.

Flanders, Timothy. "The Dubia of Vatican One." *OnePeterFive*, September 15, 2022.

——. "Every Bishop Must ACT NOW." *OnePeterFive*, March 10, 2023.

——. "Has the Magisterium Been Suspended?" *OnePeterFive*, August 1, 2023.

——. "The Third Pornocracy: What We Are Living Through." *OnePeterFive*, December 16, 2021.

——. "Why the Term 'Extraordinary Form' is Wrong." *The Meaning of Catholic*, August 9, 2019.

Foerster, Hans, ed. *Liber Diurnus Romanorum Pontificum.* Bern: Francke Verlag, 1958.

Foley, Michael. "A Reflection on the Fate of the Feast of Christ the King." *New Liturgical Movement*, October 21, 2020.

Francés, Antonio. "May a Bishop in Extraordinary Circumstances Ordain Another Bishop Without Papal Consent?" *OnePeterFive*, October 23, 2023.

——. "The Pope Cannot Depose Bishops Without Grave Cause." *OnePeterFive*, November 28, 2023.

——. "Pope Francis does not have the right to dismiss Bishop Strickland without cause." *LifeSiteNews*, November 23, 2023.

Gaspers, Matt. "Can the Pope Abolish the Traditional Latin Mass?" *Catholic Family News* online, March 3, 2023.

——. "Kwasniewski's *True Obedience* Provides Critically Important Insights." *Catholic Family News*, June 22, 2022.

Graham, Daniel. *Lex Orandi: Comparing the Traditional and Novus Ordo Rites of the Seven Sacraments.* N.p.: Preview Press, 2015.

Gurtner, Michael. "The Current Crisis of Faith in the Church Has Its Ground in the New Mass." *Rorate Caeli*, December 15, 2022.

Hall, Kennedy. "Little Christendom on the Prairie." *OnePeterFive*, May 9, 2023.

——. *SSPX: The Defence.* N.p.: Augustinus Press, 2023.

Hayden, Augustine, OFM.Cap. *Ireland's Loyalty to the Mass.* Manchester, NH: Sophia Institute Press, 2023.

Haynes, Michael. "Cardinal Schönborn cites death penalty revision when asked about changing Catechism on LGBT issues." *LifeSiteNews*, October 23, 2023.

Hazell, Matthew. "'All the Elements of the Roman Rite'? Mythbusting, Part II." *New Liturgical Movement*, October 1, 2021.

Heintschel, Luke. "Opinion: I'm a Catholic who prefers Latin Mass. For my family, it's about handing on tradition." *The San Diego Union-Tribune*, April 7, 2023, www.sandiegouniontribune.com/opinion/commentary/story/2023-04-07/opinion-catholic-latin-mass-san-diego-easter-tradition.

Hichborn, Michael. "Vatican Agency Directly Tied to Communism, Abortion, and Idolatry." *Lepanto Institute*, October 6, 2021.

Hick, Gabriela. "St. Maravillas: A prophetic witness for Vatican II." *Where Peter Is*, January 13, 2022.

Hickson, Maike. "Liturgical expert shows how Catholics needn't obey papal decrees that attack common good of the church." *LifeSiteNews*, March 14, 2022.

Houghton, Bryan. *Unwanted Priest: The Autobiography of a Latin Mass Exile.* Brooklyn, NY: Angelico Press, 2022.

Howard, Thomas. *Evangelical Is Not Enough: Worship of God in Liturgy and Sacrament.* San Francisco: Ignatius Press, 1988.

Hubert, D.G. *Sundays & Festivals with the Fathers of the Church: Homilies on the Gospels of the Ecclesiastical Year.* Waterloo, ON: Arouca Press, 2019.

Imbelli, Robert P. "Perinde ac Cadaver." *Commonweal*, February 21, 2008.

Jillions, John A. "'Thicket of Idols': Alexander Schmemann's Critique of Orthodoxy." *Wheel Journal* online, www.wheeljournal.com/blog/2018/7/24/john-jillions-alexander-schmemann.

John Chrysostom. *Exposition of Psalm XLI.* In *Source Readings in Music History from Classical Antiquity through the Romantic Era*, ed. Oliver Strunk, 67-70. New York: W.W. Norton & Co., 1950.

Jone, Heribert. *Moral Theology*. Translated by Fr Urban Adelman. Westminster, MD: The Newman Press, 1962.

Joy, John P. *Disputed Questions on Papal Infallibility*. Lincoln, NE: Os Justi Press, 2022.

Kilpatrick, William. "Francis, Fatima, and Garabandal." *Crisis Magazine*, September 14, 2023.

Kozinski, Thaddeus. *Modernity as Apocalypse: Sacred Nihilism and the Counterfeits of Logos*. Brooklyn, NY: Angelico Press, 2019.

Krutsinger, Alphonsus Maria. *The Story of Fr George Kathrein*. St. Marys, KS: Angelus Press, 2022.

Kwasniewski, Julian. "Do to Your Wife as You Would Have Your Bishop Do to You." *Crisis Magazine*, September 26, 2023.

———. Kwasniewski, Julian. "Eight Activities of the Renaissance Woman," *Crisis Magazine*, April 26, 2023.

———. "The Enjoyment of Persons is Man's True Happiness." *OnePeterFive*, May 12, 2023.

———. "Hilaire Belloc's List of Eight Manly Activities," *Crisis Magazine*, April 18, 2023.

———. "Money is for Coffee." *Salvo*, May 8, 2023.

———. "The Universal Call to Hobbitness." *Crisis Magazine*, December 19, 2022.

Kwitny, Jonathan. *Man of the Century: The Life and Times of Pope John Paul II*. New York: Henry Holt, 1997.

Lamont, John R.T. "Dominican Theologian Attacks Catholic Tradition" [a response to Fr Henry Donneaud, OP's critique of *True Obedience*]. *Rorate Caeli*, September 13, 15, 17, and 19, 2023.

———. "Pope Francis as Public Heretic: The Evidence Leaves No Doubt." *Rorate Caeli*, November 24, 2023.

———. "The Significance of Pope Francis for the Church." *The Society of St. Hugh of Cluny*, March 21, 2023.

———. "Tyranny and Sexual Abuse in the Catholic Church: A Jesuit Tragedy." *Catholic Family News* online, October 27, 2018.

———. "Is the Mass of Paul VI Licit?" *Dialogos Institute*, March 20, 2022. https://dialogos-institute.org/blog/wordpress/disputation-on-the-1970-missal-part-1-dr-john-lamont/.

Lang, U. Michael. "Theologies of Blessing: Origins and Characteristics of *De benedictionibus* (1984)." *Antiphon* 15.1 (2011): 27–46.

Lanzetta, Serafino M. *"Super Hanc Petram": The Pope and the Church at a Dramatic Moment in History*. Lincoln, NE: Os Justi Press, 2023.

Lawler, Philip F. *Contagious Faith: Why the Church Must Spread Hope, Not Fear, in a Pandemic*. Manchester, NH: Crisis Publications, 2021.

Libresco, Leah. *Building the Benedict Option: A Guide to Gathering Two or Three Together in His Name*. San Francisco: Ignatius Press, 2018.

Lofton, Michael. "That Time the Eastern Churches Accepted Papal Infallibility." *Catholic Answers*, June 6, 2022.

Losleben, Kevin. "Holy Water in the Time of Coronavirus: Old and New Compared." *OnePeterFive*, March 16, 2020.

Lovell, John P. "What is a Canceled Priest?" *OnePeterFive*, October 4, 2021.

Magdalena de Jesús. *Admiración, Amor y Dolor: Testimonio directo acerca de su vida solicitado por los Carmelos de Holanda y Alemania.* Burgos: Monte Carmelo, 1992.

Marcel, Gabriel. *The Mystery of Being*, vol. 2: *Faith & Reality*. Translated by René Hague. Chicago: Henry Regnery Co., 1960.

Maritain, Jacques. *On the Church of Christ*. Translated by Joseph W. Evans. Notre Dame, IN: University of Notre Dame Press, 1973.

Marquant, Christian. "Resistance is never futile: An interview with Christian Marquant, founder of Paix Liturgique." *Rorate Caeli*, December 16, 2020.

McCaffrey, Neil. *And Rightly So: Selected Letters and Articles of Neil McCaffrey*. Edited by Peter A. Kwasniewski. Fort Collins, CO: Roman Catholic Books, 2019.

McCall, Brian. "The Ordinary Mission of the SSPX – Reply to Salza." *OnePeterFive*, January 17, 2022.

McHugh, John A., and Charles J. Callan. *Moral Theology: A Complete Course Based on St. Thomas Aquinas and the Best Modern Authorities.* New York: Joseph F. Wagner, 1958.

McManus, Frederick R. *Handbook for the New Rubrics.* Baltimore: Helicon, 1960.

Mersch, Emile, SJ. *The Whole Christ: The Historical Development of the Doctrine of the Mystical Body in Scripture and Tradition.* N.p.: Ex Fontibus Company, 2018.

Miles, Brian. "Revolution in Tiara and Cope: A History of Church Infiltration." *OnePeterFive*, May 10, 2016.

Monaco, John. "Are There Limits to Papal Power?" *Catholic World Report*, October 13, 2021.

———. "The Church of the Papal Fiat." *Crisis Magazine*, January 20, 2022.

———. "Was the Sacred Liturgy made for the pope, or the pope for the Sacred Liturgy?" *Catholic World Report*, July 28, 2021.

Moreau, Theresa Marie. "Recaptured Paris Church Preserves True Mass." *Catholic Family News*, December 2005, www.theresamariemoreau. com/blog/archives/09-2017.

Mosebach, Martin. *The Heresy of Formlessness: The Roman Liturgy and Its Enemy.* Translated by Graham Harrison, revised and expanded edition. Brooklyn, NY: Angelico Press, 2018.

———. *Subversive Catholicism: Papacy, Liturgy, Church.* Translated by Sebastian Condon and Graham Harrison. Brooklyn, NY: Angelico Press, 2019.

Murray, Fr Gerald. "Guarding the Flock: A Canon Lawyer's Advice to Bishops on Latest Vatican Crackdown on Tradition." *The Remnant* online, February 15, 2022.

———. "Strickland's removal was against canon law." *Daily Compass*, November 22, 2023.

Mutsaerts, Rob. "An Evik Ukase from Pope Francis." In *From Benedict's Peace to Francis's War: Catholics Respond to the Motu Proprio* Traditionis Custodes *on the Latin Mass*, ed. Peter Kwasniewski, 132–34. Brooklyn, NY: Angelico Press, 2021.

Newman, John Henry. "Ceremonies of the Church." *Parochial and Plain Sermons*, vol. 2, no. 7.

———. *Conscience and Papacy (Letter to the Duke of Norfolk)*. Edited with an Introduction and Notes by Stanley L. Jaki. Pinckney, MI: Real View Books, 2002.

———. *Newman on Worship, Reverence, and Ritual*. Edited by Peter A. Kwasniewski. N.p.: Os Justi Press, 2019.

Normandin, Yves. *Pastor out in the Cold: The Story of Fr Normandin's Fight for the Latin Mass in Canada*. St. Marys, KS: Angelus Press, 2021.

O'Connor, James T., trans. and ed. *The Gift of Infallibility: The Official Relatio on Infallibility of Bishop Vincent Gasser at Vatican Council I*. Boston, MA: St. Paul Editions, 1986.

Oldendorf, Clemens Victor. "Who Actually Delegitimizes the *Novus Ordo Missae*?" *New Liturgical Movement*, December 30, 2021.

O'Malley, John W. *Vatican I: The Council and the Making of the Ultramontane Church*. Cambridge, MA: Belknap Press of Harvard University Press, 2018.

Ott, Ludwig. *Fundamentals of Catholic Dogma*. Translated by Patrick Lynch. Edited by James Canon Bastile. Revised by Robert Fastiggi. London: Baronius Press, 2018.

Pantin, William Abel. "Grosseteste's Relations with the Papacy and the Crown." In *Robert Grosseteste, Scholar and Bishop*, ed. D.A. Callus, 178–215. Oxford: Clarendon Press, 1955.

Pappin, Gladden J. "The Mass Is the First Necessity." *First Things* online, November 20, 2020.

Pasley, Robert. "Mater Ecclesiae's Assumption Mass." *New Liturgical Movement*, August 17, 2014.

Pelikan, Jaroslav. *Confessor Between East and West: A Portrait of Ukrainian Cardinal Josyf Slipyj*. Grand Rapids, MI: William B. Eerdmans, 1990.

Pentin, Edward. "After Outcry, Vatican Eases Restrictions on Individual Masses in St. Peter's Basilica." *National Catholic Register*, June 22, 2021.

———. "'Like a Museum': Dead Silence in St. Peter's Basilica as Suppression of Individual Masses Comes into Force." *National Catholic Register*, March 22, 2021.

Peters, Noah. "The National *Summorum Pontificum* Walking Pilgrimage." *OnePeterFive*, September 21, 2022.

Pierantoni, Claudio. "The Need for Consistency between Magisterium and Tradition: Examples from History." In *Defending the Faith against*

Present Heresies, ed. John R.T. Lamont and Claudio Pierantoni, 235-51. Waterloo, ON: Arouca Press, 2020.

Pietrzyk, Pius. "A Dominican Canonist Responds to the *Responsa ad Dubia*." February 8, 2022.

Pink, Thomas. "Is *Traditionis Custodes* Lawful?" *The Lamp*, Issue 18 (Assumption 2023): 17-25.

——. "Papal Authority and the Limits of Official Theology." *The Lamp* online, December 2, 2022.

——. "Vatican II and Crisis in the Theology of Baptism." In *Integralism and the Common Good: Selected Essays from* The Josias, vol. 2: *The Two Powers*, ed. P. Edmund Waldstein, O.Cist., 290-334. Brooklyn, NY: Angelico Press, 2021.

Psarev, Andrei. *The Limits of Non-conformity in the Byzantine Church (861-1300): A Study of Canon 15 of the First and Second Council in Constantinople (861)*. Online at www.rocorstudies.org/wp-content/uploads/2011/06/psarev_canon15_1n2council.pdf.

Rao, John C. "The City of Light and the Regime of Darkness: Historical Meditation on Current Events." *Rorate Caeli*, September 3, 2018.

——. "Louis Veuillot and Catholic 'Intransigence.'" In idem, *Catholic Christendom versus Revolutionary Disorder*, 26-53. Waterloo, ON: Arouca Press, 2023.

Ratzinger, Joseph. Address to Roman Pilgrims for the Tenth Anniversary of *Ecclesia Dei*. October 24, 1998. Translated by Ignatius Harrison, O.Cong. *Southern Orders*, March 11, 2010.

——. *Called to Communion: Understanding the Church Today*. Translated by Adrian Walker. San Francisco: Ignatius Press, 1996.

——. "Cardinale Ratzinger Lectio su teologia e Chiesa." *Cooperatores Veritatis*, April 9, 2018.

——. "Catholicism after the Council." *The Furrow*, vol. 18, no. 1 (January 1967): 3-32.

——. *God and the World*. Translated by Henry Taylor. San Francisco: Ignatius Press, 2002.

——. *Salt of the Earth*. Translated by Adrian Walker. San Francisco: Ignatius Press, 1997.

Reid, Alcuin. "Benoît XVI: liturgiquement inclassable." *Esprit de la Liturgie*, January 17, 2023.

——. "Reflections on Authority in Liturgy Today." *Catholic World Report*, July 14, 2019.

Ripperger, Chad. "Conservative vs. Traditional Catholicism." *Latin Mass Magazine*, vol. 10, no. 2 (Spring 2001): 40-46. Online at www.latinmassmagazine.com/articles/articles_2001_SP_Ripperger.html.

——. *The Limits of Papal Authority over the Liturgy*. Keenesburg, CO: Sensus Traditionis Press, 2023.

Rist, John M. *Infallibility, Integrity, and Obedience: The Papacy and the Roman Catholic Church, 1848–2023.* Cambridge, UK: James Clarke & Co., 2023.

Rivoire, Réginald-Marie. *Does "Traditionis Custodes" Pass the Juridical Rationality Test?* Lincoln, NE: Os Justi Press, 2022.

Salza, John, and Robert Siscoe. *True or False Pope? Refuting Sedevacantism and Other Modern Errors.* Winona, MN: STAS Editions, 2015.

Sammons, Eric. "The Hyperinflation of the Papacy." *Crisis Magazine,* November 8, 2023.

——. "Our Incurious Bishops." *Crisis Magazine,* May 8, 2023.

Sample, Alexander K. "The Bishop: Governor, Promoter, and Guardian of the Liturgical Life of the Diocese." In *Sacred Liturgy: The Source and Summit of the Life and Mission of the Church,* ed. Alcuin Reid, 255–71. San Francisco: Ignatius Press, 2014.

Saward, John. *World Invisible: The Catholic Doctrine of the Angels.* Brooklyn, NY: Angelico Press, 2023.

Schmitz, Matthew. "Pope Francis has followed a similar path to Pius IX." *Catholic Herald,* January 24, 2019.

Schneider, Athanasius. "Bishop Strickland's Removal is a 'Blatant Injustice.'" *LifeSiteNews,* November 11, 2023.

——. *The Catholic Mass: Steps to Restore the Centrality of God in the Liturgy.* Manchester, NH: Sophia Institute Press, 2022.

——, in conversation with Diane Montagna. *Christus Vincit: Christ's Triumph over the Darkness of the Age.* Brooklyn, NY: Angelico Press, 2019.

——. *Credo: Compendium of the Catholic Faith.* Manchester, NH: Sophia Institute Press, 2023.

——. "Eucharistic Concelebration: Theological, Historical, and Liturgical Aspects." *New Liturgical Movement,* August 11, 2021.

Shaw, Joseph, ed. *The Latin Mass and the Intellectuals: Petitions to Save the Ancient Mass from 1966 to 2007.* Waterloo, ON: Arouca Press, 2023.

——. "Obedience, Disobedience, and Rash Obedience: A Virtue in a Time of Crisis." *OnePeterFive,* May 12, 2022.

——. *Sacred and Great: A Brief Introduction to the Traditional Latin Mass.* Lincoln, NE: Os Justi Press, 2023.

Silveira, Arnaldo Xavier da. *Two Timely Issues: The New Mass and the Possibility of a Heretical Pope.* Spring Grove, PA: The Foundation for a Christian Civilization, 2022.

Sire, H.J.A. *Phoenix from the Ashes: The Making, Unmaking, and Restoration of Catholic Tradition.* Kettering, OH: Angelico Press, 2015.

Slater, Thomas. *A Manual of Moral Theology for English-Speaking Countries.* Volume 1. New York: Benziger Brothers, 1908.

Slaves of the Immaculate Heart of Mary. *The Liturgical Rosary: Meditations for Each Hour, Day & Season of the Liturgical Year.* Waterloo, ON: Arouca Press, 2023.

Sonnen, John Paul. "Book Review: *True Obedience in the Church.*" *Liturgical Arts Journal*, April 6, 2022.

Spadaro, Antonio, SJ, and Simone Sereni. "Bishop Mario Grech: An interview with the new secretary of the Synod of Bishops." *La Civiltà Cattolica*, October 23, 2020, www.laciviltacattolica.com/bishop-mario-grech-an-interview-with-the-new-secretary-of-the-synod-of-bishops/.

Stannus, Jane. "France Declares War on the Mass (Again)." *Crisis Magazine*, November 19, 2020.

Stark, Thomas Heinrich. "The Historicity of Truth: On the Premises and Foundations of Walter Kasper's Theology." In *The Faith Once for All Delivered: Doctrinal Authority in Catholic Theology*, ed. Kevin L. Flannery, SJ, 69-100. Steubenville, OH: Emmaus Academic, 2023.

Stickler, Alfons Maria. "Recollections of a Vatican II Peritus." *New Liturgical Movement*, June 29, 2022.

Storck, Thomas. "Liberalism's Three Assaults." In idem, *From Christendom to Americanism and Beyond: The Long, Jagged Trail to a Postmodern Void*, 22-33. Kettering, OH: Angelico Press, 2015.

Stridon, Jerome. "The Coetus: Trad Godfathers at Vatican II." *OnePeterFive*, December 12, 2022.

Stump, Phillip. *The Reforms of the Council of Constance (1414-1418)*. Leiden: E.J. Brill, 1994.

Taylor, Darrick. "Can We Learn Anything from the Critics of Vatican I?" *OnePeterFive*, November 13, 2023.

Teresa of Jesus. *The Life of St. Teresa of Avila*. Translated and edited by E. Allison Peers. www.ewtn.com/catholicism/library/life-of-st-teresa-of-avila-5208.

Thomas Aquinas. *Summa theologiae*. Second and revised edition, 1920. Literally translated by Fathers of the English Dominican Province. Online edition by Kevin Knight, 2007.

Tierney, Brian. *Foundations of the Conciliar Theory: The Contribution of the Medieval Canonists from Gratian to the Great Schism*. Cambridge: Cambridge University Press, 1955.

Tikhon, Archimandrite. *Everyday Saints and Other Stories*. Dallas, TX: Pokrov Publications, 2012.

Tomberg, Valentin. *The Art of the Good: On the Regeneration of Fallen Justice*. Brooklyn, NY: Angelico Press, 2021.

Tomlinson, Chris. "Traditionalism and Conservatism Thriving Among Young U.S. Catholic Priests." *European Conservative*, November 12, 2023.

Topping, Ryan N.S. *Thinking as Though God Exists: Newman on Evangelizing the "Nones."* Brooklyn, NY: Angelico Press, 2023.

Turner, Reid. "Papal Polemics and the Disparagement of Grace." *The Five Beasts*, May 17, 2023, https://thefivebeasts.wordpress.com/2023/05/17/papal-polemics-and-the-disparagement-of-grace/.

Ureta, José Antonio. "Cardinals Roche and Cantalamessa: The Mass of Paul VI Corresponds to a New Theology." *Rorate Caeli*, April 11, 2023.

——. "Why a Good Bishop Should Not Ignore but Obey His Unjust Deposition by a Pope." *OnePeterFive*, October 17, 2023.

van Slyke, Daniel G. "The Order for Blessing Water: Past and Present." *Antiphon* 8:2 (2003), 12–23.

Viganò, Carlo Maria. *A Voice in the Wilderness: Archbishop Carlo Maria Viganò on the Church, America, and the World*. Edited by Brian M. McCall. Brooklyn, NY: Angelico Press, 2021.

Vost, Kevin. *Memorize the Stoics*. Brooklyn, NY: Angelico Press, 2022.

Waldstein, Edmund. "The Primacy of the Common Good." *The Josias*, June 19, 2023.

Waldstein, Michael. *Glory of the Logos in the Flesh*. Ave Maria, FL: Sapientia Press, 2021.

Weigel, George. "The Casaroli Myth." *First Things*. September 29, 2021.

——. "The *Ostpolitik* Failed. Get Over It." *First Things* online, July 20, 2016.

——. *Witness to Hope: The Biography of John Paul II*. Revised edition. New York: Harper Perennial, 2020.

Weinandy, Thomas. "Pope Francis and Schism." *The Catholic Thing*, October 8, 2019.

White, Hilary. "Don't be afraid of the Big Bad *Traditiones Custodes*." *World of Hilarity*, January 15, 2022.

——. "A Warning to the Carmelites of Fairfield." *OnePeterFive*, October 21, 2021.

Ybarra, Erick. *The Papacy: Revisiting the Debate Between Catholics and Orthodox*. Steubenville, OH: Emmaus Road, 2022.

Zambrano, Andrea. "Seminario cerrado y sombras sobre Roma: 'El obispo se ha equivocado.'" *Brújula Cotidiana*, August 3, 2020.

Zuhlsdorf, John. "Can priests say the 'Tridentine Mass' alone, without a server?" *Fr Z's Blog*, December 30, 2016.

——. "How long does holy water stay blessed?" *Fr Z's Blog*, January 3, 2018.

——. "QUAERITUR: Is water blessed with the newer rites really holy water?" *Fr Z's Blog*, June 4, 2012.

——. "When Life Gives You Manure, Maybe It's Time for Changes." *OnePeterFive*, July 23, 2022.

INDEX OF NAMES AND DOCUMENTS

ABOUT THE AUTHOR

Peter A. Kwasniewski holds a BA in Liberal Arts from Thomas Aquinas College and an MA and PhD in Philosophy from the Catholic University of America, with a specialization in the thought of Saint Thomas Aquinas. After teaching at the International Theological Institute in Austria, he joined the founding team of Wyoming Catholic College, where he taught theology, philosophy, music, and art history and directed the choir and schola until 2018. Today, Kwasniewski is a full-time writer and lecturer known especially for his work on the liturgy and on music; his writings have been translated into over twenty languages. He regularly posts at his Substack Tradition & Sanity, and runs a publishing house, Os Justi Press. He is also a composer whose sacred choral music has been performed around the world.

VISIT HIS SITES:
www.peterkwasniewski.com
www.CantaboDomino.com
www.osjustipress.com
https://traditionsanity.substack.com/
www.soundcloud.com/drkwasniewski
www.facebook.com/ProfKwasniewski
www.youtube.com/@DrKwasniewski

Made in the USA
Coppell, TX
28 February 2024